Trying to Please

Trying to Please

A Memoir

John Julius Norwich

Axios Press
P.O. Box 118
Mount Jackson, VA 22842
888.542.9467   info@axiospress.com

Library of Congress Cataloging-in-Publication Data

Norwich, John Julius, 1929–
      Trying to please : a memoir / John Julius Norwich.
      p. cm.
      Originally published: Dorset : Dovecote Press, 2008.
      Includes bibliographical references and index.
      ISBN 978-1-60419-031-1 (hardcover : alk. paper) 1. Norwich, John Julius, 1929–
2. Authors—Great Britain—Biography. 3. Great Britain—Politics and government—
20th century—Biography. I. Title.

DA566.9.N75A3 2010

941.082092—dc22

[B]

2010006691

Contents

Chapter One

Beginnings

"POOR OLD BABY," said the nurse when, a day or two after my birth, I was bawling my lungs out. "Poor old baby, he's only trying to please." It was one of my mother's favorite reminiscences. I suspect, in a way, that I have been trying ever since.

I was a late arrival. My parents had married in the summer of 1919; a few years later, after consulting the most fashionable specialists in London, my mother had been told to give up all hope of a child. She tried everything, including prayer at Lourdes; and then, a full decade after the marriage, her prayers were granted: at 10:25 AM on Sunday, September 15, 1929, in Lady Carnarvon's nursing home in Portland Place, I was born by Caesarian section. The name Julius accordingly seemed indicated; and that too, accompanied by the rather less imaginative John, has stuck with me for the past eighty years. So there I was, the infant John Julius Cooper, standing—or, I suppose, more accurately lying—at life's threshold.[1] My mother, in majestic ignorance of the limit of three

---

[1] Cooper was—and is—always the family name. 'Norwich' is merely the title that I inherited on my father's death, he himself having been awarded it only two years before.

godparents prescribed by the Church of England, had decided on quantity as well as quality. One day, many years later, I tried to tot them all up; the total came to seventeen. Of these, one—the Aga Khan—was a Muslim who was worshipped in his own right; several were Jews, including the mega-rich banker Otto Kahn, who gave me $5,000 in shares for a christening present, all of which became worthless as a result of the Wall Street crash. Then there were several Roman Catholics, among them the writer Maurice Baring, and of course a smattering of Church of England, including Betty Cranborne (later Salisbury) and Margot Asquith, widow of the Prime Minister in the First World War. Betty proved to be the best; none of the others seemed to take their duties with very much seriousness.

My mother, already thirty-seven—she was born on Monday, August 29, 1892—was a celebrity. She was, first of all, startlingly beautiful; secondly she was a member of the aristocracy—in those days still an advantage, rather than the millstone that it so often proves today—who had been brought up in one of England's most spectacular country houses, Belvoir Castle, as the youngest daughter of the eighth Duke of Rutland. (Her adoring public would have been horrified to know that she was in fact the result of a long and passionate love affair between the Duchess and the Hon. Harry Cust, from the neighboring estate of Belton.[2]) But there was more to it than that. Ever since her presentation at Court in 1911 she had been the darling of the society and gossip columns; when she married my father—a penniless commoner of whom no one had ever heard—a body of mounted police had to be detailed to control the crowds outside.

---

2 There have long been persistent rumors that another recipient of Mr. Cust's attentions was Lady Thatcher's maternal grandmother, who is said to have been a member of the domestic staff at Belton, and that our former Prime Minister is in fact his granddaughter and my first cousin. I should love to know, but have never dared to suggest a DNA test.

Commoner he may have been, but my father's lineage was not altogether without distinction. He was in fact the great great grandson of King William IV, who had no fewer than nine illegitimate children by Mrs. Dorothy Jordan, the leading comedienne of her day. One of their countless grandchildren, Lady Agnes Hay, married James, fifth Earl of Fife—curiously enough, at the British Embassy in Paris—and had four children, the youngest of whom was named Agnes, like her mother. She grew up to be extremely attractive but also more than a little flighty, and at the age of nineteen in 1871 eloped with the young and dashing Viscount Dupplin, heir to the earldom of Kinoull. Two years later the young Lady Dupplin gave birth to a daughter, Marie, who married into the family of Field Marshal von Hindenburg and settled in Germany. (I dimly remember meeting her, an elderly and rather formidable lady in black, when I was four or five.) Marie—a romantic novelist—loved to talk about what she called "the Jordan blood," and no wonder: when she was only two years old her mother eloped for a second time, on this occasion with a young man called Herbert Flower, whom she married in 1876 as soon as Lord Dupplin had been granted a divorce—on the grounds, it need hardly be said, of his wife's adultery. The Flowers went off on a world cruise, but their idyll was to be all too short: just four years later in 1880, Herbert died at the age of twenty-seven.

Agnes was heartbroken; he was the love of her life. She herself was still only twenty-eight; her family had disowned her; she was virtually penniless; and after two elopements and a divorce not even an earl's daughter with royal connections—her brother Alexander had married the eldest daughter of the future King Edward VII—could hope to be accepted in society. But she had never lacked spirit: in the hopes of becoming a nurse, she took a menial job in one of the major London teaching hospitals, and there in

1882, it is said while she was scrubbing the floor, she caught the eye of one of the consulting surgeons, Dr. Alfred Cooper.

Now Dr. Cooper was a good deal more interesting than he sounds. Born in 1838 in Norwich to a family of lawyers, he had completed his medical studies at St. Bartholomew's in London and by the mid-1860s had built up a highly successful practice in Jermyn Street. According to the *Dictionary of National Biography*:

> Cooper, whose social qualities were linked with fine traits of character and breadth of view, gained a wide knowledge of the world, partly at courts, partly in the outpatient rooms of hospitals, and partly in the exercise of a branch of his profession which more than any other reveals the frailty of mankind.

It did indeed; that branch was, moreover, forked: piles and syphilis.[3] Within a short time my grandfather and grandmother together were said to know more about the private parts of the British aristocracy than anyone in the country. Despite this—or perhaps because of it—he quickly made his name in London society, becoming a member of all the right clubs and an ever-popular guest at dinner parties, country houses and even on grouse moors. Among his patients he numbered Edward, Prince of Wales, whom in 1874 he accompanied to St. Petersburg. From which of the above distressing complaints His Royal Highness suffered is not known; the Palace announced at the time that Dr. Cooper was treating him for a form of bronchitis—but what else could the Palace have said? In any case the two remained friends, and in 1901, when Prince Edward succeeded his mother on the

---

3 His two principal publications were *Syphilis and Pseudo-Syphilis*, 1884, and *A Practical Treatise on Disease of the Rectum*, 1887. I am proud to possess a copy of the first, lavishly illustrated in color; but I show it only to those of a strong constitution, and never after dinner.

throne and became King Edward VII, he was to award my grand-father a knighthood in his Coronation Honours.

The story goes that at some earlier point in his distinguished career Alfred Cooper had already seen Lady Agnes Duff—as she would then have been—and had immediately fallen in love with her; but knowing that he was fourteen years older and of relatively humble birth he had never cherished any hopes of mar-riage. The sight of this attractive girl on her knees on the floor seemed strangely familiar. Intrigued, he asked her name; she told him; and in 1882 they married, living happily ever after at 9 Hen-rietta Street. Somehow the whole thing seems a little too like a fairy story to be entirely credible; in any event we know that they had four daughters, one of whom died in infancy. Finally, on Friday, February 22, 1890, Lady Agnes gave birth to a son. They called him Alfred Duff, but only once—I remember him chuck-ling about it—did he ever receive a letter greeting him as "My dear Alfred." Duff he was from the start, and Duff he remained.

⁕

Dr. Cooper had done well: well enough to send his son to Eton and Oxford where, according to his biographer John Charmley, "he trailed clouds of dissipation," drinking, gambling, roistering and pursuing regiments of women, whom he wooed—on the whole successfully—not only by his charm and wit but also by bombarding them with sonnets, for which he had a quite extraordinary facility. (One of them, which he is said to have tossed off for a bet in five minutes flat on the subject of William Wordsworth's illegitimate child, now hangs, framed, in White's Club.) These were a by-product of a genuine passion for literature, in particular poetry and nineteenth-century novels in both Eng-lish and French; by the end of his life it was almost impossible to find one of these that he had not read and remembered. But at this early stage he was seriously considering a career in the Foreign Office, into which—after spells in Tours and Hanover to brush up his French and German—he was accepted in August, 1913.

Five months before, he had met my mother and fallen in love with her, as everybody did. She was enchanted by his sonnets and his superbly funny love letters—he was later to write to her: "My love for you resembles a red, red rose less closely than a nasty attack of delirium tremens"—but she had other admirers and he always had a train of other women, so neither took each other too seriously. All too soon, however, came the war; and with the war everything changed. My father, as a member of the Foreign Service, was exempt from the call-up—a fact for which I am heartily thankful, since had he not been I should not be here writing this book—but his friends were not so lucky. So much has been written of the massacre of the First World War, particularly of the young officers, that it seems superfluous to add any more: but I remember my mother telling me that by the end of 1916, with the single exception of my father, every young man she had ever danced with was dead. Much against her mother's wishes—the Duchess could not bear the thought of her favorite child washing the wounded and emptying bedpans—she became a nurse at Guy's Hospital. All the time she and my father were growing closer; only he, it seemed, could provide the strength and consolation she so desperately needed.

In June, 1916, he was invited to stay the weekend with the Prime Minister, Mr. Asquith. He wrote, characteristically, to his mother: "There was no motor to meet me at the station and no champagne. I think it's high time the PM resigned." A few months later his wish was granted. Asquith was succeeded by David Lloyd George, one of whose first actions—to relieve what was becoming a serious shortage of manpower—was to extend conscription to several of the "reserved professions," including the Foreign

Office. My father, who had been feeling increasingly embarrassed by what he saw as his enforced inactivity, confessed his feelings to my mother. On May 17, 1917, he wrote in his diary:[4]

> I explained to her that it was no nonsense about dying for my country or beating the Germans that made me glad to join, but simply the feeling I have had for so long that I am missing something, the vague regret that one feels when not invited to a ball even though it be a ball that one hardly would have hoped to enjoy.

The training was the worst part. It had been described by his friend Eddie Grant as "being stuck in a six-foot bog, trained like an Olympian athlete and buggered about like a mulatto telegraph boy," and he hated it. He used to love to tell the story about a certain evening in late July when he briefly escaped to London from his training camp at Bushey in Hertfordshire only to discover that no one he knew, male or female, was in town. For once, he felt genuinely depressed; there was nothing for it but to go to his club—the Junior Carlton in those days, rather than the beloved White's of his later years—and order the best dinner he could get, with a pint of champagne. From the library he took down a copy of *Through the Looking-Glass*, always one of his favorite books. "Then," he wrote, "as by magic my untroubled mind came back to me, and not alone, but bringing courage, joy and hope." On April 27, 1918, he left for France.

Even there, his high spirits did not desert him. "From a comfortable dugout" he reported to my mother that "the horrors of war have been much exaggerated," and offered to send her a food parcel; but he soon had reason to change his mind. At 5 AM on

---

4 A much abridged—but by no means bowdlerized—edition of *The Duff Cooper Diaries* was published by Weidenfeld and Nicolson in 2005.

August 21, he and his company went over the top in a heavy mist, and before long his platoon became separated from the rest. They reached their objective of the Arras–Albert railway line—the only platoon to do so—but immediately ran into heavy fire from a German machine gun post. He went forward to destroy it, not knowing that all the men following him had been killed, and on his arrival—still almost miraculously unscathed—shot one man and called upon the others, in what German he could still remember, to surrender. Believing themselves to be outnumbered, to his intense surprise they did; and so it happened that a callow young Second Lieutenant with practically no experience of battle managed to capture eighteen Germans single-handed. He was recommended for the Victoria Cross, but had to settle for the Distinguished Service Order which, particularly when awarded to a subaltern, was generally considered to be the next best thing.

Only two nights later his company attacked again. This time he described it as "one of the most memorable moments of my life . . . a thrilling and beautiful attack, bright, bright moonlight and we guided ourselves by a star . . . it was what the old poets said it was and the new poets say it isn't." After one more battle "the sun rose beautifully and the enemy fled in all directions including ours with their hands up, and one had a glorious Ironside feeling of Let God Arise and let His enemies be scattered. And then they came back again over the hill and one was terrified and had a ghastly feeling of God is sunk and His enemies are doing nicely." Fortunately "the battle rolled away." It was his last engagement.

On June 2, 1919, my parents were at last able to marry at St. Margaret's Westminster. They had known each other for six years, and had been seriously in love for three. Few suitors have encountered more furious opposition. To the Duchess, only the Prince of Wales would have been good enough for her beloved daughter; how could she give a thought to this penniless young man who was well known to drink too much and play too hard and to pursue—all too often successfully—any girl that came within range? He had hoped that after the news of his DSO came through they might relent; but it made no difference at all. Only dogged persistence at last wore the Rutlands down. On April 30, 1919, he wrote in his diary:

> In the evening Diana had the interview with her father. I met her afterwards at the Ritz. They have given in completely and are willing for us to be married as soon as we wish. It seems too wonderful and hard to realize. The Duke, she says, was perfect—and gave away the whole case by saying to her after the interview which only lasted about 10 minutes—"Don't go upstairs for a little, as I don't want your Mother to think I gave in at once." I felt wonderfully happy and elated.

They spent their honeymoon in Italy and were back in London at the beginning of July. My father returned to the Foreign Office, but not for long. The work bored him—much of it consisted of deciphering, a nightmare job which in those days had to be done by hand—and he could not bear his chief, Lord Curzon, who had first of all complained that he was taking too much leave and then, when proved wrong, minuted: "It is not so much his ordinary leave to which I object as his ability while performing his duties to enjoy an amount of social relaxation unclaimed by his fellow workers." Besides, Parliament beckoned. The only question was, could he afford it? With his intelligence, his gift for oratory—honed at the Oxford Union—his war record and above all the postwar dearth of eligible young men, finding a seat would not be difficult; but a life in politics would mean giving up an assured salary of £900 a year—which, though far from princely, was worth a good deal more than it is now—for a precarious existence in which a single defeat might mean the end of a career.

Then something happened to make up his mind for him—something that neither he nor my mother could ever have expected. In 1922, at the age of thirty and to the horror of her parents and their friends, my mother became a film star. She did so by playing the lead in two films for the well-known—in those early days—producer J. Stuart Blackton. Of the first of these, a seventeenth-century costume drama called *The Glorious Adventure*, I had always understood that all prints had been lost—as has certainly been the fate of her other film, *The Virgin Queen*, in which she played Queen Elizabeth I; but just a few years ago a copy turned up in the National Film Archive, and I now possess it on videotape. It is silent of course—it seems unfortunate that the very first shot should be of a uniformed trumpeter sounding a fanfare—but it proved something of a technological milestone, being shot in what was known as Prizma, an early color process which weighed rather too heavily on green and orange but undeniably added a certain style to the production.

Blackton is said to have been the first man ever to put a story on the screen; at this time, however, he still seems to have been a little uncertain about how to do so. In the first half at least, there seems to be almost as much text as action; and although the antique Gothic lettering slows one's reading considerably; the words still remain on the screen for so long as to cause serious doubts as to the standards of literacy among English picturegoers in the early twentieth century. The plot, on the other hand, is perfectly splendid—as glorious a piece of kitsch as any of us could hope for. My mother plays a rich but feckless girl who has lost all her money at the card tables and dare not face her father; then one day a friend tells her that all she needs to do is to go down to Newgate gaol, find a prisoner who is awaiting execution and marry him. By law he must then assume all her debts—which will of course be cancelled by his death. She finds a condemned highwayman—played by Victor McLaglen, a former prizefighter, who was to pursue a highly successful film career for the next thirty years—who willingly falls in with her plans. But then disaster strikes: the year is 1666, and within a few hours London is ablaze. The prisoners escape and the highwayman comes to claim his own, climbing the ivy of the great Tudor house in which our heroine lives, seizing her from her magnificent four-poster and carrying her off, struggling pitifully but vainly in his arms. Alas, an appropriate *dénouement* proved beyond the powers of Mr. Blackton: the highwayman—whom we now discover to be already married—is spotted in the street by his wife, publicly berated and hurried away. Our heroine thus escapes a fate worse than death and returns to her family. What happens to her debts is not entirely clear.

The two films, it must be said, did little for my mother's reputation in London society; but they led to something far more important. They brought her to the attention of the world-famous Austrian producer Max Reinhardt, who was seeking actresses for the two leading parts in his forthcoming new production of *The Miracle*. This free adaptation of a medieval miracle play, presented by the impresario C.B. Cochran, had had considerable success at Olympia shortly before the First World War; Reinhardt now proposed to take it to New York and to give it a completely new and far more ambitious production at the Century Theatre. If successful there, it would tour America.

For my mother this was an opportunity indeed. Full of foreboding, she and my father took the train to Salzburg—where Reinhardt lived in considerable style in the former palace of the Prince Bishops, Schloss Leopoldskron—for an audition; and to the astonishment of both of them she was offered one of the two principal parts, that of the statue of the Virgin which comes miraculously to life. She was still more gratified to hear the great man mutter aside to an aide: "*Sie könnte vielleicht auch die Nonne spielen*"—"She could perhaps also play the Nun."

———— ⚬✦⚬ ————

In the second volume of her autobiography, *Trumpets from the Steep*, my mother has already told the story of her years with *The Miracle* far more brilliantly that I could ever hope to do. The action is set in a vast medieval abbey which houses a convent of nuns. It also possesses a life size statue of the Virgin credited with miraculous properties. The plot, in brief, is that of a beautiful young nun who prays before the statue for her freedom—at which the statue comes to life. The Virgin slowly descends from her pedestal, dons the nun's habit and takes her place. The nun's venture into the outside world, however, proves disastrous: she is betrayed, corrupted and abused, and a year or two later returns to the abbey, broken in body and spirit, a dying baby in her arms. While all the other nuns are congregated at prayer, one—apparently—of their number suddenly rises from their midst, removes her habit which she returns to the girl, takes the baby—now dead—from her and slowly returns with it to the niche, where she once again becomes the statue. Reinhardt's production was a triumph, the Century Theatre was closed for six months while it was transformed into a Gothic abbey—its bells were to ring for half an hour every night before the performance—and the play opened on January 15, 1924. After a long run in New York, playing sometimes the Virgin—a part in which she had to stand motionless in the niche for some fifty minutes before slowly coming to life—and sometimes the Nun, my mother remained with the company for an extended tour of America.

It was a grueling life. Quite apart from the constant traveling—by train of course—there were the demands of the performance itself. Standing stock-still for nearly an hour while carrying a heavy wooden Christ-child was not easy and it was made still harder by the additional burden of a high baroque crown, of almost equal weight. My mother loved to tell of the dramas within the drama: of the night when she had suddenly felt faint and had known that she was going to fall—almost inevitably on one or more of the countless votive candles, stuck on sharp iron spikes, by which she was surrounded. Then there was the almost pathological jealousy of one of her costars—the exquisite Austrian dancer Tilly Losch, later Lady Carnarvon—who once, knowing that my mother had a quick change ahead of her, sewed her sleeves together; or the night when, soon after she had taken up her position in the niche, she was aware that a flea had somehow got inside her crown and was making a slow progress across her forehead. The itch was almost unbearable; fortunately, however, this was the night of the general election in England at which my father was standing for Oldham, and she repeated to herself over and over again: "The more it itches, the more votes for Duff." The thought carried her through, and my father—thanks, no doubt, to that happy insect—won his seat.

One of the many advantages of *The Miracle* from my mother's point of view was that it contained no spoken dialog. Thus, when a year or two later the cast reassembled for another long tour, this time of Central and Eastern Europe, she was once again included, performing in a long series of cities including Vienna, Salzburg, Prague, Budapest, and Dresden. This meant, inevitably, long separations from my father, but these she reluctantly accepted because of the money she was earning: money which would sustain him through the first years of his political career and which, incidentally, would continue to support her for the rest of her life.

The final tour of *The Miracle*, through the British Isles, was rather less demanding; and it provides me with one of my earliest recollections. According to my father's diary it can be dated to Saturday, February 11, 1933, so I must have been nearly three and a half. I distinctly remember being told that I was to be taken to see my mother on the stage, and that I should be sitting in a box. The picture loomed up in my mind of an immense cardboard hatbox; how, I wondered, should I be able to see anything at all in that? My next clear recollection is that of walking into the box. The play had already started, and there on the right of the stage was a figure looking suspiciously like my mother, but absolutely motionless and, in my memory, bright green. I immediately panicked, and can still hear myself shouting "Is that *real* Mummy?" Nanny shushed me and reassured me as best she could; but I did not entirely recover until the interval, when I was taken backstage to her dressing room.

That same dressing room was the setting for another story that my mother—when in suitable company—loved to tell. It concerned the Great Russian bass Feodor Chaliapin, whose appetites—all of them—were commensurate with his enormous frame. He developed a passion for her (as so many people did) and one afternoon went to a matinee of *The Miracle*. As soon as the curtain had fallen, he came bursting into my mother's dressing room to find her cleaning the makeup off her face with cold cream. He was clearly in a state of considerable excitement, to demonstrate the degree of which he seized her hand and clamped it firmly to his crotch. "Feodor, *please!*" she protested, snatching it away, "What will my dresser think? Besides, half a dozen other people will be round at any moment. You *must* behave yourself." Scarcely was she back at the makeup table when the other friends appeared, and as she introduced them she saw to her horror, "like the hand of Fatima over some

Islamic doorway," the snow-white imprint of her hand in cold cream on the great man's trousers.

Fortunately for me, Chaliapin had conceived the notion—mistakenly, as it turned out—that the way to my mother's heart might be through her son. He accordingly showered me with presents, including several of his records for me to play on my wind-up gramophone—from the age of five, *The Death of Boris* and *The Song of the Volga Boatmen* were as familiar to me as *Three Blind Mice*—and an enormous woolly dog on wheels, always known gratefully as Theodore. But my clearest recollection of him dates from when I was about six. I had gone to bed, vaguely aware that my parents were giving a dinner party downstairs, and was already asleep when my mother shook me awake. "Put on your dressing gown," she said, "and come downstairs. Chaliapin is going to sing in the garden." It was, she explained to me later, all quite unexpected. She had invited him to the party as an ordinary guest; then suddenly, at the end of dinner, he had said "Now I shall sing." He telephoned a friend, who came round at once with his balalaika. It was a warm summer evening; we all trooped into our tiny garden and the music began. Gradually heads began to appear at neighboring windows—not, as one might have expected, to protest that some people wanted to get some sleep but obviously with the realization that this tremendous voice was something very special indeed; the applause, at the end of each song, seemed to come from everywhere.

In those days we lived at 90 Gower Street, Bloomsbury—an address to which my grandmother—always known to me as Noona—who believed that human life was possible only in Mayfair or Belgravia, was never entirely reconciled. Violet, Duchess of

Rutland, was the only one of my grandparents who was still alive by the time I was born. My mother, being a love child, was her favorite of her four surviving children; and I, being my mother's sole offspring, was I believe similarly preferred among her numerous grandchildren. Born in 1856, she was already well into her eighties when I remember her. (If only I had been old enough to pump her about her past; in her youth she must have known old men who had fought at Waterloo.) She was a superb portraitist in pencil and in those days spent much of her life drawing admirable—if occasionally over-flattering—portraits of all her friends; although I occasionally stayed with her for weeks at a time I hardly ever saw her—in an armchair, in bed, even on the train—without an orange-colored HB pencil in her hand, a drawing pad on her knee and, somewhere nearby, a crust of stale bread, which she always preferred to any other kind of eraser. She made literally hundreds of drawings of me, which I didn't mind a bit; all I hated was her determination to teach me to draw too. To this day, any attempt I make looks like the work of a retarded child of six; even then I knew that my grandmother's efforts to improve me would always be in vain, and felt bitterly the humiliation of lying beside her in bed in the mornings, forever trying to copy the noses, eyes, and mouths with which she effortlessly covered the paper.

My other memory of her—more distasteful still—is being taken by her on afternoon drives. Like so many children, I was a martyr to carsickness; and, as any fellow-sufferer will confirm, one longs at such moments for two things only: to have all the windows wide open—preferably sticking one's head out of the nearest—and to reach one's destination as quickly as possible. On my uttering the usual warning, my grandmother's instant reaction was to shut any window that might have been fractionally open and to order the chauffeur to reduce speed—which seldom, in any case, rose to more than thirty miles an hour. The consequences would be almost instantaneous, but she never learned. I adored her none the less, and was I think consciously grateful for all the time she gave me—however misspent—and for her endless patience; and I was broken hearted when she died in 1937, three days before Christmas. There was, as usual, a huge family Christmas at Belvoir. I am sure all the grown-ups must have known—my mother had stayed in London to be with her—but the news was kept from the children so as not to spoil the festivities.

The Belvoir Christmas was a fixture for the first ten years of my life—until the war came—and to this day the Castle and the feast are indissolubly linked in my mind. My parents normally went up by car—my mother had a lifelong passion for driving—while Nanny and I, usually accompanied by my grandmother and her maid, would take the train (always third class) from King's Cross. I, from the age of about four, would have my head buried in a book, from which I would look up from time to time to see my grandmother drawing yet another portrait of me, all oblivious of the jolting train. Night would have fallen by the time we pulled up at Grantham station, lit in those days by gas lamps; I can still see their mantles glowing a greenish yellow through the clouds of steam from the engine as we followed the porter, pushing a barrow-load of cabin trunks (for just a week's stay) along the platform to the two Rolls-Royces waiting outside.

The next half hour was one of mounting excitement: driving through the darkened (and, in those days, quite often snow-covered) countryside—in itself a thrill for a five-year-old; watching the rabbits standing transfixed in the headlights before they scampered away; and then—most magical moment of all— catching sight of the lighted castle high above us on its hill, like something out of a fairy tale. Arriving at the great Gothic porch, we would walk down a short passage to the main entrance hall— always known as the Gun Room—in which stood an enormous

Christmas tree, cut on the estate and at least twenty feet high, surrounded by brilliantly colored parcels and set with hundreds of real candles, while a bevy of liveried footmen wandered round with sponges on long poles, making sure that there were no accidents. Then to Nanny's and my room—always the same one— with a fire blazing in the hearth; and finally to a quick supper in the nursery with half a dozen cousins and their nannies before being put reluctantly to bed. And even then the day's excitement would not quite be over: presently, as I lay waiting for sleep, I would suddenly be conscious of a most wonderful sound, soft at first but increasing in a thrilling crescendo until it seemed to fill the whole castle. It was the First Gong, sounded by an aged servitor as he hobbled along the passages, warning the guests that it was time to dress for dinner. Three-quarters of an hour later there would be the Second Gong, for dinner itself.

My uncle John—he was my mother's elder brother and the ninth Duke of Rutland—was I think moderately unusual, even in those prewar years, in insisting on white tie and tails every evening. There was a story that he had once been asked, incredulously, if he *never* wore a dinner jacket; his reply had been "only when I am dining with the Duchess alone in her room." He was a strange, austere man, of whom all his family was, I think, a little frightened. A passionate antiquarian, he had been present with his friends Lord Carnarvon and Howard Carter at the opening of Tutankhamen's tomb; he had also thoroughly studied and cataloged the vast collection of family and other papers in the castle muniment room, binding them in volumes and taking elaborate measures for their conservation. But his greatest achievement was the rescue of his second family seat, which will always be for me the most romantic house in England: Haddon Hall.

As all lovers of English country houses will know, a significant number of the loveliest and most unspoiled belong to families fortunate enough to possess two. On the first house, in which they normally live, the bulk of the family money has been spent. These houses have been altered, modernized, adapted for everyday modern living, and in all too many cases largely ruined. (Longleat, perhaps the first great Renaissance house to be built in England but with an interior almost entirely of the nineteenth century, is a case in point.) The second house, on the other hand, stands a good chance of remaining inviolate. For many years it may have been virtually uninhabited; sometimes it may have sheltered a grandmother or two, or a few maiden aunts. With any luck the roof will have been maintained in moderately good repair, and the windows will still keep out the birds and the bats. But that will be all. These are the houses which, over and over again, reveal themselves as the real wonders of unspoiled English architecture. Hardwick, Compton Wynyates and Cotehele are merely the first examples that come to mind. But the loveliest of all is Haddon, and to it my uncle devoted his life.

The house is set on a gentle hill in the Peak District of Derbyshire. The earliest part dates from Norman times, the most recent addition—the great Tudor Long Gallery—from those of the first Elizabeth. When Uncle John married Kathleen Tennant—my Aunt Kakoo[5]—in 1916 it had not been a permanent residence for some two hundred years and still had no electricity, gas or running water. He decided, nevertheless, to live there—his parents were still in occupation of Belvoir—and for the next quarter of a century until his death (in 1940, at the age of only fifty-four) he gave it what may well be the most informed and sensitive restoration ever received by any country house. Reluctantly, he installed electricity and a modicum of plumbing; for the rest, "if anyone spots anything I have done," he would say, "I have failed." One of the great

---

5 Pronounced "Karku."

beams supporting the roof of the medieval Hall—it is nowadays almost impossible to say which—is a replacement, cut from a giant oak tree on the estate; in it he later inserted a casket containing a full account of his work. The old Norman kitchen—probably the oldest in England, and still with its original chopping block—he refused to replace. Instead he built a completely new kitchen a hundred yards or more from the house, with a little underground railway to bring the food up to the Hall. Naturally it always arrived stone cold—but that, for him, was a small price to pay.

———————

In my own early childhood, however, Haddon played little part; Belvoir was the place for me. The scale of my uncle's Christmas hospitality astonishes me, even now. He would invite the entire family, including those of his four siblings, together with several more elderly relations; most of them, in those days, would bring their valets and ladies' maids. For lunch and dinner there would be twenty or more grown-ups in the dining room, with perhaps a dozen extra in the servants hall, over and above the immense staff of the Castle itself. Then there were the children, with their nannies and governesses, divided between the schoolroom and nursery—perhaps another twenty altogether. All told, there cannot have been less than fifty or sixty extra mouths to feed, most of them for more than a week, since most of the guests stayed over the New Year.

The Castle itself was enormous, and admittedly a little terrifying: I remember clearly one night when, at the age of about five, I suddenly panicked, leapt from my bed and ran, barefoot in my pajamas, a good hundred yards down the icy stone corridors to the nursery, where the nannies were still chatting round the fire. But although in fact it was built only at the beginning of the nineteenth century as a superb example of the Gothic revival, to me it looked and felt exactly like a real castle—and I loved it. First of all there was the companionship. As an only child, I had few if any close friends of my own age; at Belvoir there were fourteen cousins for a start. Because my mother was the youngest of her generation and because my parents had had to wait so long for me, these cousins were all considerably older; but I don't believe I felt seriously left out. Nor was I ever bored. There were the stables to be visited, with apples and lumps of sugar to give the horses; the kennels, spoilt only by the fact that the hounds could not be fed; the dairy, with its marvelous dairy smell and its butter churns and huge dishes of cream, where one was given glasses of warm, foaming milk straight from the cow; the sawmill, where for the first—and very nearly the last—time in my life I planed a piece of wood; and the blacksmith's forge where I was allowed to work the bellows. Best of all was the Boxing Day meet of the Belvoir Hunt—all pink coats and excited, yelping dogs and stirrup cups and ladies bolt upright and sidesaddle, with top hats and veils, their flowing black skirts descending to the heels of their riding boots.

As the day began the older children would have their breakfast upstairs, but would go down afterwards to join the grown-ups in the dining room. I can still smell the little paraffin lamps that flickered under the silver dishes of eggs, bacon, sausages, kidneys, and kippers; beyond them on the sideboard stood huge chargers bearing hams, tongues, cold chicken, and cold pheasant. On the table itself were silver toast racks—constantly replenished—plates of hot scones, innumerable marmalades and jams (all homemade in the still-room) and glass bowls in which floated discs of dark yellow butter, each stamped with the Rutland crest, a peacock in its pride. (Real peacocks wandered about on the terrace outside.) All the men—the ladies had their breakfasts upstairs in their rooms—would be in deliciously fragrant tweeds, ready for the day's shooting.

Shooting dominated Belvoir life. Uncle John was a superb shot, as were his three sons and the vast majority of his houseguests. My father too, otherwise so sedentary, was never happier than when tramping through the woods with a gun in his hand. (Later, when I was in my teens, he bought me one and used to take me out whenever the opportunity arose; but I never enjoyed it—my heart was always on the side of the birds—and he soon gave up on me.) At about ten they would all stride off, accompanied by some half a dozen golden retrievers and a small regiment of gamekeepers, and would probably not be seen again till half-past three or four, when they would return in the gathering dusk to inspect the day's bag, join the ladies who had been waiting for them all day and consume an enormous tea. Bridge and backgammon would then pleasantly fill up the hour or two until it was time to dress for dinner.

Even today, to be sure, that world is far from dead. Shooting weekends are still, I am told, a popular institution and will doubtless continue to thrive, at least until some cretinous government attempts ban the sport altogether. But what has gone (or very nearly) is the sense of amplitude—the sheer scale of that aristocratic life of three-quarters of a century ago, made possible only by the existence not just of an enormous staff but of a thriving social community numbering several hundred people, with the great house at its center. One or two may still continue, at Chatsworth for example, or perhaps Blenheim; but the combination of hereditary wealth and old tradition without which such houses cannot survive is nowadays rare indeed. In the 1930s it was not. Belvoir was in no way exceptional. There were in those days dozens—perhaps hundreds—of houses in which that sort of life went on, not all of them on quite the level I have described, but not a few on a scale more magnificent still. Nor, in the surrounding country, was there any resentment, any more than there was any servility. The house was a source not only of employment, but of pride.

Chapter Two
Childhood

ALL TOO SOON it was back to London and 90 Gower Street. This, till I was seven, was home; it is consequently the scene—with Belvoir—of most of my earliest memories. It was not, however, a bit like the Castle: just an ordinary terrace house in Bloomsbury. My parents had married on £1,100 a year—which in those days allowed them four or five servants. On the very top floor lived my mother's maid Miss Wade, the cook Mrs. Wales, and various housemaids who came and went and whose names I have therefore forgotten. The floor below belonged to Nanny and me, with the nursery looking out on to the street, the night-nursery giving on to the usual narrow strip of garden behind. Every morning after breakfast I would go downstairs and join my mother in the bed that my father had recently vacated. There she would read aloud to me: *Alice in Wonderland* and *Through the Looking-Glass*—still my favorite books—*Doctor Dolittle* and the works of a certain Hampden Gordon, a Civil Service acquaintance of my father's, about a gnome called Paradoc. Then it would be time for lessons:

addition, subtraction and multiplication—to her dying day my mother cheerfully admitted that she had never grasped the concept of division—followed by geography, which to her meant knowing the capitals of all the countries in the world. (From the age of about five I could reel off the lot.) Most important of all was reading. She started me off when I was three, with a book called *Reading Without Tears*, by the anonymous author of *Peep of Day*, published in 1861. Where I was concerned it did its job swiftly and, as promised, painlessly; I was reading easily long before my fifth birthday. Some of the exercises it contained, however, might be looked at somewhat askance by modern educationalists. Here are two of them.

> What is the mat-ter with that lit-tle boy? He has ta-ken poi-son. He saw a cup of poi-son on the shelf. He said "This seems sweet stuff." So he drank it. Why did he take it without leave? Can the doc-tor cure him? Will the poi-son des-troy him? He must die. The poi-son has destroyed him.

> Wil-li-am climb-ed up-stairs to the top of the house, and went to the gun-pow-der clos-et. He fil-led the can-is-ter. Why did he not go down-stairs quickly? It came into his foolish mind, "I will go into the nur-se-ry and fright-en my lit-tle bro-thers and sis-ters."

> It was his de-light to fright-en the chil-dren. How un-kind! He found them a-lone with-out a nurse. So he was a-ble to play tricks. He throws a lit-tle gun-pow-der in-to the fire. And what hap-pens? The flames dart out and catch the pow-der in the can-is-ter. It is blown up with a loud noise. The chil-dren are thrown down, they are in flames. The win-dows are bro-ken. The house is sha-ken.

Mr. Mor-ley rush-es up-stairs. What a sight! All his chil-dren lying on the floor burn-ing. The ser-vants help to quench the flames. They go for a cab to take the chil-dren to the hos-pit-al. The doctor says, "The chil-dren are blind, they will soon die."

These reading sessions, though frequently interrupted by the telephone, would go on every morning for an hour or more, my mother never moving from her bed. It was not that she was a congenitally late riser; she had no difficulty in getting up at five or six AM if she wanted to. It was simply that throughout her life her bed was her workstation, the place from which she most easily and efficiently operated. On it were her telephone, her address book and her diary. There, sitting cross-legged and bolt upright, she would write her letters (always in pencil so as not to get ink on the sheets), talk to her friends, discuss meals with the cook, and perform every duty that most people do at a writing table. She would get up when she had to, not before; and if she returned home in the middle of the afternoon or early evening with an hour to spare before her next engagement, back to bed she would go to resume work. Never did I see her sit at a desk, let alone relax in an armchair. Only in bed was she ever still and not even there—except when she slept at night—did the activity ever stop.

The one subject to which my mother attached immense importance but did not feel competent to teach me herself was French. Her solution for this was Mademoiselle Perrier-Gentil, an elderly and excessively thin lady who came in on Monday, Wednesday and Friday afternoons to give me an hour's tuition. Language lessons, I firmly believe, cannot start too young: only consider how well we succeed with our own, which most of us learn without effort and in which we are normally fluent (and possessed of a perfect accent) by the age of four or five. Alas, all too soon the brain loses its absorbency, and well before adulthood true bilinguality has become an unattainable dream. Starting as I did at five, I acquired fluent French by the age of six and have never lost it; and for this—as well as for introducing me to the *Fables de la Fontaine* which I have loved ever since—I have Mademoiselle Perrier-Gentil, and her alone, to thank. I only wish I had been nicer to her.

My mother's other outstanding educational success was in the field of English history. It happened that in the early 1930s there appeared a book called *Kings and Queens*, by Herbert and Eleanor Farjeon, with illustrations by their niece Rosalind Thorneycroft. On one side of each spread was a picture of every monarch from William the Conqueror on, boldly and brightly colored, many of them striking attitudes vaguely reminiscent of those early nineteenth-century theatrical prints highlighted with tinsel; on the other was a short descriptive poem. My mother bought two copies, cut out the pages and pasted them onto a large four-leaf screen, the pictures in two vertical columns of six on each leaf, the poems between the columns. This screen stood in the nursery, constantly before my eyes, and I see it still. It endowed all the monarchs with personalities of their own—they were never just names—and it ensured that I would always know the order in which they came. To this day, if someone mentions, say, Henry VI, I see him instantly: second leaf, third picture down lefthand column, in a red gown with a large white headdress, and next to him a verse beginning:

> Considering Henry the Sixth wasn't strong,
> It's very surprising he lasted so long . . .

A year or two later, the same inspired team came up with a second volume called *Heroes and Heroines*. Alas, there wasn't room for all of them on the screen, but my mother managed to add a selection; particularly clear in my mind is the picture of Julius Caesar and the second verse of his poem:

Caesar conquered Rome and Gaul,
Belgium, Germany and all;
Then, with very little fuss,
He came and saw and conquered us.

———————◦╲╱◦———————

My father, inevitably, was a remoter being than my mother; but he too took a lot of trouble over his only son. I would go into his study when I was three or four and invariably find him sitting at his desk, writing away with an old-fashioned dip pen—he never used anything else—constantly replenished from the silver inkstand which I still possess. At his side there was always a stick of sealing wax, which I loved playing with; I can smell it now, as the blob of flaming wax hit the envelope, to be instantly imprinted with the seal on his ring. Sometimes, when he was not too busy, he would get up and go to the bookcase, from which he would pull out my favorite book, an enormous folio volume full of superb nineteenth-century engravings of wild life in the jungle; at other times he would regale me with endless stories from English history, of which he had an encyclopedic knowledge. All that was usually in the morning; in the evening he would come upstairs to my bed-room to tell me how he had spent his day—in what, I now real-ize, was often a heavily edited version—and to kiss me goodnight. By then, as often as not, he would be in white tie and tails (which were worn even to go to the theater). I can still feel the scratch of the wing collar on my neck, and catch that faint whiff of his hair lotion—he would have despised aftershave—as he bent over me.

My parents had bought 90 Gower Street on their marriage. Soon afterwards, however, they acquired (with *Miracle* money) the first floor of No. 92, and a few years later that of No. 94, all of which they knocked together; thus, although basement, ground floor and the two upper floors had only two or three small rooms each, on the first floor there was a long enfilade, making it a veritable *piano nobile*. Here were my parents' bedroom, their separate bathrooms, my father's study and small library, and the drawing room with mural decorations by their beloved Rex Whistler, including—in the dazzling trompe-l'oeil for which he was already famous—a vast niche containing an enormous stone urn, slightly cracked and riveted, on which lurked a fearsome bluebottle which every morning the housemaid would try to brush away.[1]

In the same room (and also decorated by Rex) was a tiny upright piano, which fascinated me. My mother used to play it from time to time—my father was tone deaf and recognized the National Anthem only when people stood up—and when I was six I demanded piano lessons. I was lucky. Mrs. Dora Milner was a fine pianist but—far more important—a brilliant teacher. She smelt deliciously of warm biscuits and had a huge wart nestling up against her left nostril that I couldn't take my eyes off. She gave her lessons in the Wigmore Studios, next to the Wigmore Hall; and once a year she hired the Hall for an afternoon's concert given by *all* her pupils—including those who had only just begun. Thus it was shortly before my seventh birthday that I first appeared on the stage at the Wigmore Hall—dressed, for some reason, in a kilt—for a solo performance before the assembled parents. The piece I played—it was called *The Snowman*—was just sixteen bars long and involved each hand playing only one note at a time, the notes being in octaves; but I performed it faultlessly and left the stage to polite if scarcely enthusiastic applause.[2] The following

---

1 The house was, alas, demolished after the war; but the murals were saved and now decorate a small private dining room in University College, a hundred yards or so away.

2 Some fifty years later I was being interviewed on BBC radio and mentioned *The Snowman*. There happened to be a piano in the studio, and on the spur of the moment I got up and played it again—unquestionably the first and last time it was ever broadcast.

year I had graduated to Schumann's *Merry Peasant*—but played it, I seem to remember, with rather less assurance.

All my life I have loved making music. It must have been soon after beginning my piano lessons that my mother, knowing my hero worship for the late George Formby, gave me a ukulele as a Christmas present. I still remember my discovery soon afterwards of what I used to know as the three chord trick—tonic, dominant seventh, and subdominant—which provides the basic accompaniment for hundreds of simple songs; and I soon had quite a repertoire, ranging through Stephen Foster (*The Old Folks at Home, Old Black Joe, Camptown Races*) to the records of an American popular singer called Frank Crumit. These included *Abdul Abulbul Amir* (which I still joyously perform), *The Gay Caballero* (which I do not, the lyrics being nowadays liable to misunderstanding), and my own particular favorite, *The Song of the Prune:*

> Oh no matter how young a prune may be, he's always
>   full of wrinkles,
> We get wrinkles on our face, prunes get 'em every
>   place;
> Peaches and bananas have that skin you love to
>   touch,
> But no matter how young a prune may be, it don't
>   amount to much. . . .

Later I was to graduate to the guitar and build up a rather larger repertoire of harmonies and chords—which came in extremely useful when, in much later life, I reverted to the piano.

I am miserable when there is no piano around. In the years of my childhood and youth, no house seemed to be without one; nowadays, especially in London, the instrument has become a rarity, competent amateur pianists rarer still. I suppose that television is largely to blame; it may be, too, that our lives are all

so busy that people no longer have time to practice. My mother
and I were never happier than with after-dinner sing-songs; during my late teens, when we lived in Paris, they seemed to happen spontaneously, in one house or another, every week or two.
Now I seldom get one more than once a year—perhaps not even
that—though from time to time I enjoy myself hugely with my
son Jason, who shares my musical tastes and sings our favorite
songs with immense gusto to my accompaniment. This is not
to suggest that I have ever been more than a very mediocre per-
former myself. Apart from anything else I have always, try as I
may, been hopeless at sight-reading. All I can fall back on is harmony, which has in turn given me a certain ability to play by
ear. Largely because of this, I no longer even attempt the classics, confining myself instead to George Gershwin, Cole Porter, Jerome Kern and their contemporaries, whose music I have
always loved.

———————◦❦◦———————

For at least a year before my first visit to Mrs. Milner I had
attended a kindergarten ("Miss Betty's") in the middle of
Regent's Park—though the far more valuable lessons in bed with
my mother continued in the holidays and at weekends. With my
seventh birthday I was considered old enough to start a proper
education and was accordingly dispatched to Egerton House, a
London preparatory school in the northwest corner of Dorset
Square. Strangely enough, the incident of my first day there that
made the deepest impression on me occurred not at school, but
when I returned home that evening. My mother naturally wanted
to know how it had gone.

"Oh, all right," I said, with a child's usual reluctance to commit
itself.

"Now come on," she retorted, "that's not nearly good enough. You can't just say 'all right' like that—you must tell me all about it. To begin with, did you make any new friends?"

"Yes," I said, "or at least I think so. There's a very nice boy called James Davis." Then I thought for a moment, and added "He's a Jew though."

This, I protest, was not ill meant. I was seven years old and had absolutely no idea what a Jew was. I said what I did only because I had heard a boy laughingly say, "Oh, Davis is a Jew, you know" and I was simply echoing his words more or less as I had heard them. But my mother gave me no chance to explain. The next thing I remember was a stinging slap across the face: "And what's wrong with the Jews, pray? Never, *ever* let me hear you say that sort of thing again."

Of course, she never did. But the story sticks in my mind not just because of the slap. It is also an indication of the anti-Semitism that prevailed, I think, in virtually all English schools before the war; and if it existed in the schools it must also have existed among the families from which the boys came. I was to witness several more cases of it while I was at Egerton House; there were even to be a handful—though mercifully far fewer—at Eton. I should love to think that it was now dead throughout England— but I fear we may still have to wait another generation or two.

Egerton House was not, I think, a very good school; but neither was it a very bad one. Most of the instruction was pretty unimaginative—though probably no more so than in most others—with countless hours devoted to Kennedy's *Shorter Latin Primer* (invariably altered to *Shortbread Eating Primer*) and Caesar's Gallic Wars. The French teaching was appalling—it was the responsibility of a large lady called Miss Watson, who pronounced the first day of the week exactly as if it were an island off the coast of Devon. I fell in love, on the other hand, with another, much younger teacher called Miss Hardwick, who taught "Nature Studies" and who told me—I am ready to swear, I can hear her now—that the eyes of a potato were poison. (I believed this till I was sixty-five.) Every morning at eleven, rain or shine, we all walked in a brisk crocodile to Regent's Park, whistling in unison *Marching through Georgia, Men of Harlech* or *The British Grenadiers*—never anything else—and returned to a perfectly filthy lunch: the shepherd's pie—now one of my favorite dishes—I remember as having apparently been boiled instead of baked, and retaining most of the water. Of the blancmange that followed I would rather not speak. On two afternoons a week we then boarded a private double-decker bus and were driven to a large field near Hampton Court for cricket or football, stopping on the way back to buy penny buns with icing on the top. Cricket I quite enjoyed; football I loathed, though nowadays on television I find that it has a certain appeal.

The summer holidays and most summer weekends, we spent at Bognor, in West Sussex. Since in fact we lived about four miles away, beyond the little village of Aldwick, why we always called it "Bognor" is something of a mystery. The word is, to say the least, unmelodious, the town architecturally undistinguished. King George V had recuperated from a grave illness there a year or two before I was born, and in gratitude had suffixed the word *Regis*; but even Bognor Regis was never considered a top-drawer resort like Brighton or Bournemouth or Eastbourne, and its prestige had not been increased by the popular legend that when, during her husband's last illness, Queen Mary had said consolingly "Cheer up my dear, in no time we shall have you back at Bognor again," His Majesty had murmured the words "bugger Bognor," turned his face to the wall, and expired. Our house, however, was a little gem of white pebble-dash in vaguely Georgian Gothic, utterly unassuming and extremely pretty. It was approached by a short drive, curving so sharply that visitors did not see the building itself until they were perhaps thirty yards away. On the far side was a medium sized garden on two levels, separated by a hedge of rosemary; beyond it was a wicket gate which led straight out on to the shingle of the beach.

Comfortable, on the other hand, it was not. It had no central heating of any kind. Its six bedrooms boasted two bathrooms between them, the second being distinctly primitive; my parents, in the master bedroom, were as far as it was possible to be from both. The water was gently warmed by a minute coal boiler, always referred to as "the donkey," which if continually stoked produced about two tepid five-inch-deep baths an hour. Both double bedrooms were of reasonable size, but two of the singles were little more than *wagon-lits*. (One day my mother received a telegram from an old friend, reading "Delighted accept invitation weekend as long as don't get room at top of stairs.") I look back with astonishment at the house party my parents always had for Goodwood Week, when the house was full of members of the smartest racing set, most of whom in those days would bring their valets and personal maids with them as a matter of course. The latter were accommodated in a local bed-and-breakfast, where they were probably a good deal more comfortable than their employers; but it is strange indeed in our modern age to think of gentlemen who would expect to have their evening clothes laid out for them every night and ladies whose dresses were ironed before each wearing, cheerfully trudging down a chilly corridor in their dressing gowns and waiting outside the bathroom until another of their number emerged, only to find that he or she had taken all the hot water. The queues after breakfast— there were only two loos—must have been even more embarrassing; but nobody ever seemed to mind, or even to notice.

It seems extraordinary that in a house as primitive as ours—at least by today's standards—we should have had such a copious domestic staff. Every weekend the whole lot would come down by train from London. Apart from Miss Wade, who had a room of her own at the end of the upper floor, there was Mrs. Wales the cook, Holbrook the butler (doubling at Bognor as my father's valet) and at least three continually changing maids, two of whom slept in a room next to the kitchen while another—the kitchen maid—shared Mrs. Wales's room in the Lodge (of which more in a moment). Both these bedrooms had old-fashioned washstands, with basin and jug—nothing more; but once again, at least as far as I was aware, there were no complaints. It was probably no worse than the poor girls had been used to at home, and here at least they were by the sea—which, I remember, several of them had never seen before.

West House had clearly not been designed by an architect. No room ever seemed to lead directly into another; the ground floor in particular was a warren of winding passages which must have taken up almost half its total area. Apart from the pitch-dark kitchen (in which, as I remember, the refrigerator was powered by gas) and servants' hall—these high sounding names suggest a size and distinction which the house was far from possessing—it boasted only two reception rooms: a pretty dining room looking out on to a little side lawn by the drive, and the sitting room, which was minute, able to accommodate no more than five or six with a squash. Before my birth, however, my father had added a study for himself, leading straight out of the sitting room and, like it, looking out on to the garden. In it were a desk, a glass fronted bookcase, a table, and a sofa; the floor was covered with rush matting. All inner walls, upstairs and down, were whitewashed.

By the front gate, perhaps two hundred yards from the house, was the Lodge, also vaguely Gothic, tiny, single-storied and with a generous verandah on two sides. It had six rooms, one of them a bathroom, with a little kitchen at the back. Two of the rooms were kept for guests and normally used only when the house was full; one, with two big iron bedsteads, belonged to Mrs. Wales and one of the maids; the other two were the day nursery and night nursery, occupied by Nanny and me. My days and weeks as a child at Bognor were deliriously happy. I would wake in the morning to the noise of the wheelbarrow crunching the gravel outside the bedroom window as Mr. Broome, the gardener, wheeled it to his work; after breakfast I would go over to "the House" to see my mother for the usual reading or lessons in her bed. Then she would either take me into Bognor to buy lunch or Nanny and I would head for the beach.

The best part of going into Bognor was the drive. It was the antithesis of driving with my grandmother. My mother had a succession of extremely dashing cream convertibles which—unless it was actually pouring with rain—she always drove with the hood down. This was ideal for me since, apart from anything else, it kept the carsickness at bay. If I wanted more air still, she encouraged me to sit on the top of the seat with my feet where my bottom should have been, my head sticking up a foot or two above the windscreen. (Today she would be stopped by the first policeman and told that children must travel in the back securely strapped in and probably facing backwards—and I can just imagine the ensuing outburst. Thank God she lived and died before the coming of Health and Safety and the nanny state.) Our favorite—sometimes our only—stop was a blue-jerseyed old salt on the sea front called Billy Welfare, from whom she bought lobsters, crabs, and prawns that he had caught only an hour or two before. Then we would head for home. As we swung through our gate she would probably drop me off at the Lodge for my "dinner" and then, with much revving of engine (because she knew it amused me) and more crunching of gravel she would shoot off round the bend in the drive to deliver her purchases proudly to Mrs. Wales.

On those shopping days the beach would have to wait till afternoon. At high tide the sea would come right up to the shingle; a few hours later one might have a hundred yards or more of sand to negotiate—sand that got wetter and soggier the further one advanced—before reaching the water. In early childhood I would wear a series of "swimming costumes" (as they were always called) knitted by Nanny, with shoulder straps and a band of contrasting color round the middle; only when around seven did I graduate to pants. Nanny, it need hardly be said, never did more than paddle, her skirts tucked up into the enormous elastic bloomers she always wore; but I would splash about in ecstasy until forcibly brought in, teeth chattering and covered with gooseflesh, loudly protesting that I wasn't cold at all ("No, Nanny, it's *b-b-boiling!*") and that I could easily have stayed in for hours.

———◎◆◎———

After a short afternoon rest it was back to the House, where my parents and their weekend guests would be still sitting round the dining table after lunch (always outdoors, when weather permitted). There must, I suppose, have been political colleagues of my father's, but I remember very few of them: Winston and Clemmie Churchill (occasionally, but not often), Bobbety and Betty Cranborne (later Salisbury), Brendan Bracken and one or two others. Of them all, I remember Brendan best. His hair, which contrived to be both fuzzy and carrot-colored, his strange, clipped voice and his curious secretiveness all fascinated me. Of course I had no idea in those days of the widespread rumor that he was the son of Winston Churchill—a theory which, having known the Churchill family moderately well nearly all my life, I don't accept for a second—but his parentage was in any case a mystery. My mother would tell me of how he had spent his childhood on a sheep station in Australia, then come to England and paid his own way through public school. He was mysterious in other ways too. He would arrive at breakfast in his dressing gown, bath towel over his shoulder, apparently straight from the beach, saying "Oh, the sea was wonderful this morning"—but no one ever saw him actually entering the water, or even in a bathing suit. My mother maintained that there were only two possible explanations: either he couldn't swim and was bitterly ashamed of the fact, or he had a tail. We never discovered which.

Far clearer in my memory than the politicians—I think they must have come much more often—were the writers. One who seemed to be always there in my early childhood (until he was incapacitated by Parkinson's) was another godparent, Maurice Baring, always known in our family as Mumble, who did not-very-good conjuring tricks which I loved and, at the end of lunch, would balance a full glass of port on the top of his egg-bald head. He spoke six or seven languages fluently, and knew the litera-ture of all of them. Not many people read his novels nowadays, excellent though they are; but his book of memoirs *The Puppet Show of Memory* is a joy—especially the stories of prerevolution-ary Russia—and his polyglot anthology *Have You Anything to Declare?* is for me the best ever compiled. Another regular was Alfred ("A.E.W.") Mason, with his ever-present monocle, blazer, white ducks, two-tone co-respondent shoes, and infectious, cack-ling laugh. His novels, *The Four Feathers, Fire Over England,* and many others—all of which he wrote in tiny notebooks like pocket diaries in microscopic handwriting—are also now largely forgotten but were hugely popular in their day; *The Four Feath-ers* was filmed four times. He once offered to buy me a present—"anything you like"; why on earth did I choose a dartboard?

Often, too, there was H.G. Wells, with his last long-term mistress Baroness Moura Budberg, a glorious Russian with a formidable list of previous conquests which included (during the Revolution) Sir Robert Bruce Lockhart and (after it) Maxim Gorky, who she maintained had actually died in her arms on Capri. "H.G."—nobody called him anything else—was to my child's eye immensely unprepossessing: about five foot high and with a curiously high-pitched, squeaky voice. I remember once being included in a party that went off to the annual Bognor Bank Holiday fair. H.G. was refused a hideous woolly rabbit that he wrongly thought he had won, lost his temper, and screamed "This is a swindle!" over and over again. My mother once asked Moura to what she attributed his phenomenal success with women. "My darrrrling," she replied in her musical-comedy Russian accent, "his bryeath smyells of honey."

Most fun of all was Hilaire Belloc—"Hilary" to his friends. Broad and burly, with a huge close-cropped head, he always wore a black suit with stiff wing collar and black tie in memory of the wife he had lost many years before. His manner, on the other hand, was anything but funereal. He would arrive, having driven himself from his home near Horsham, in a beat-up old Standard car. Once—I must have been about ten—I tried to help him off with his cloak, and almost collapsed under its weight. It seemed to have pockets everywhere—and every pocket contained its flask. There was one of brandy, one of whisky, one of port—the man was a walking wine cellar. And how he held the table: most lunches and dinners ended up with his singing ancient and raucous French songs in his cracked old voice, sometimes little more than a stage whisper. *Si la Garonne avait voulu* was one of them, *elle serait allée jusqu' en Espagne;* or *Chevaliers de la table ronde, goûtons voir si le vin est bon.* Sometimes, too, he would recite his own poems—*Do you remember an inn, Miranda* was a particular favorite. (The BBC has a wonderful recording of this; I wish they would broadcast it more often.) Yet another speciality of his was to describe any of the decisive battles of the world. Every object on the table would be commandeered and made to represent a wooded hill, a line of archers, a regiment of cavalry or a gun emplacement. His account of the chosen battle, once he got into his stride, was electrifying: you could hear the thudding arrows, smell the cordite, and see the smoke rising from the burning villages. My father—no mean historian himself—used to maintain that there was only one drawback to the Belloc descriptions: they bore not the slightest resemblance to what had actually occurred. But it hardly seemed to matter.

Sooner or later on these occasions I had to perform myself. Both my parents—but my mother in particular—had a passion for recitation. At no moment during my childhood was I ever given free pocket money; invariably it had to be earned, and it was earned by learning poetry. A poem once learnt must then be recited to my parents or, preferably, to a group of their friends; and it had to be word perfect. A single hesitation, the very suggestion of an "er" or "um," was enough to disqualify. If, however, I got through to the end without mishap I was rewarded with sixpence or—if the poem was long or difficult enough—a shilling. The poems themselves varied; favorites in my very early years were those from my *Kings and Queens* screen. I still remember a good many of them today. I have quoted a couple already, but can't resist adding a third. The poem on William the Conqueror began:

> William the First was the first of our Kings,
> Not counting Ethelreds, Egberts, and things;
> And he had himself crowned and anointed and blest
> In ten sixty—I needn't tell you the rest.

I never cease to bless my mother for that screen; and I bless her, too, for the enforced recitations. What it was like for the unfortunate guests who were obliged to listen to this insufferable child droning on and on I dread to think; but for me the gains were immense. First of all—since anything memorized at a sufficiently tender age is so deeply embedded in the brain that it can never be entirely forgotten—I still retain in my head an enormous amount of poetry, by no means all of it childish; secondly, I have always been able to memorize quickly and, on the whole, painlessly— even though nowadays, without superhuman efforts, the piece is forgotten again in a week; finally I seem to be immune from stage fright, which means in its turn that public speaking and lecturing have never held any terrors.

And now for Nanny. Alice Ayto—a curious name whose origin is unknown to me—was born in 1895 and was consequently three years younger than my mother. She came from Grantham, and she and I always used to go and call on her parents there during our Christmas at Belvoir. (Several times I actually went to stay; the house in Harlaxton Road was lit by gas and the only loo was in the garden at the back.) She was the archetypal English nanny, now virtually extinct. She invariably wore a nanny uniform—a white blouse, grey coat and skirt, and, outdoors, a grey felt hat like a bowler. Probably less than five feet high, she had bright red hair and a rather good singing voice. She was paid £60 a year, with half a day off a week and an annual fortnight's holiday which she hardly ever took, and spent every other waking hour looking after me. Until I was seven she was the fulcrum of my life: far more important to me, and more dearly loved, than either of my parents.

There was nothing odd about this. Nannies in those days saw far more of their charges than parents did, and it was only natural that the first bonding should take place with them. My mother was, by the standards of her class and her time, extremely conscientious. She loved me, loved being with me, and spent as much time with me as she possibly could. At least once a week when we were in London she would take me out for an afternoon in her car—to the zoo, to Madame Tussaud's, to the British Museum, or the National Gallery. Sometimes, if we saw a fire engine racing to an emergency, we chased it—she never had any trouble keeping up—and watched the fire; I remember one or two spectacular ones.

"Other people's babies, that's my life; Always a mother, never a wife." Those words of (I think) A.P. Herbert sum up the basic tragedy of the old-style nanny: the only satisfactory relationships she ever had ended in separation. Her charges grew up, received the sort of education that she could never hope to have, and, all too soon, no longer needed her; affection might remain, but the close bonds of the early years would inevitably have been shattered. Already by the time I was six, my mother felt it was time to break Nanny's domination and to win me for her own. So it was that, at the beginning of September, 1936, she announced her intention of taking me for a fortnight to Aix-les-Bains in France. This for me was a huge excitement; the bad news—and it had to be broken very gently—was that Nanny would not be coming too. Instead, my mother had engaged a young French girl called Simone Laurent, whose specialty was *la culture physique* and who spoke not a word of English. Since my French, thanks to Mademoiselle Perrier-Gentil, was as fluent—and a lot more grammatical—than my mother's, the idea was that the three of us should speak only French during our stay. Nanny, it need hardly be said, did not take this well. For her it was the beginning of the end, and she knew it. Normally the most even-tempered of women, she sulked on the day of our departure to the point where my mother felt obliged to write her a stiff reprimand from the train. But for my part I hardly noticed. I was going *abroad* for the first time—and, Nanny or no Nanny, I was more excited than I had ever been in my life.

We traveled, as people did in those days, by train from Victoria to Dover, then crossed the Channel to Calais and finally took another train to the Gare du Nord. We went third class. Till the end of her life, when traveling without my father, my mother always took the cheapest tickets and stayed in the cheapest hotels; on this occasion, however, uncertain of my sea legs, she had booked on the boat not a cabin—that would have been going too far—but a curtained alcove in which I could lie flat. In fact though we rolled a good deal, the crossing took little more than an hour and I don't remember suffering much—certainly not as much as I did every time I got into a car. I was far too intoxicated by the sea, and the ship, and then the garlicky French porters in their blue *blousons* carrying our bags through the Customs and on to the waiting train. It was dark when we got to Paris— and there was the Eiffel Tower looking just as I had imagined it, and the policemen with their white *képis* and their little white batons, and I grew more excited than ever. We went by taxi to the hotel where my parents always stayed, the Berkeley on the Avenue Matignon. It was the first hotel I had ever been to; but even this, I knew, was not the end of the adventure. In just three hours we were off again—this time on a sleeper, to Aix-les-Bains. I have one recollection only of the Gare de Lyon: that of a huge Englishman, fat, florid, and extremely cross, bellowing at a cringing Wagon-Lit attendant: "*Nong, nong, nong—je pay Cooks, Cooks pay voo!*"

I was fascinated by the sleeper: the little furry ladder up to the top bunk (which my mother so generously allowed me to have), the net into which one put one's clothes, the blue nightlight, and—why do I remember it so clearly?—the small circular pad with a hook above it, on which to hang one's pocket watch. I doubt whether I got much sleep as we rattled through the night—I was enjoying it all too much—but it was an adventure in itself to have to get up at 5:30 AM and see, for I believe the first time in my life, the pale grey streaks of dawn in the eastern sky. We finished off the night at the Hotel Splendide—where Simone Laurent joined us at breakfast time—but the next morning my mother found an unpretentious little *pension*, into which we moved for the next fortnight. She must, I think, have hired a car, because every morning at 8 she drove herself to the baths—Aix-les-Bains, as its name implies, was a working spa—to take the "cure." After breakfast we would go to the artificial *plage* on the shore of the Lac du Bourget, where we would swim and play ping-pong and do gymnastic exercises with Simone, who had the rippling biceps of a prizefighter; then, following an *al fresco* lunch, we would drive off to a neighboring town like Annecy or to some local beauty spot—except on the afternoon of September 15, when I celebrated my seventh birthday with a party for the handful of children, French and English, who were our fellow guests. I was happy; I was enchanted with abroad; I loved my mother more and more; but I made no effort to conceal the fact that I still pined for Nanny.

———⊙∤⊙———

That same year, 1936, was the Year of the Three Kings. George V had died on January 20, the name of Bognor possibly on his dying lips, and the new King, Edward VIII, was already—though the fact was not yet generally known—deeply embroiled with Mrs. Wallis Simpson. The story is too well known to stand repeating here; suffice it to say that for the next eleven months the crisis steadily worsened. My parents had known the Prince of Wales—as he then was—moderately well; but they were never close friends, and were genuinely surprised when that summer the King invited them on the *Nahlin*, the yacht he had chartered for a Mediterranean cruise. His precise reasons are obscure, but may well have been based on the fact that he believed that my father was the one member of the Cabinet whom he could enlist as an ally. In this he was mistaken. My father, realizing that his mind was made up, did not waste any time trying to dissuade him; he simply counseled a year's postponement—a year in which he would be crowned and would then travel, perhaps to India for a Durbar or on a tour of the Empire, and might with any luck change his mind or even fall for someone else. But the King would have none of it. He could not possibly go through with his Coronation, he said, without first making his intentions known to his subjects. As my father wrote in his memoirs, "I could not argue against such scruples, but could only respect them."

That summer was the summer of my seventh birthday and my arrival at Egerton House. By that time, as I remember, the Crisis—it was always known as the Crisis—seemed to be the only topic of conversation, even among the boys. My mother had somehow acquired a record of a Caribbean calypso on the subject, which I learnt by heart and endlessly sang. (Why can I not remember it now, when I can instantly recall practically every other song of the time? "That Edward should fall for a Yankee girl" is the only somewhat uninspired line that remains in my mind.) Grown-ups were speculating on the Fall of the Monarchy, the same phrase that our history books used to describe the French Revolution, and I had horrible visions of the poor King going to the guillotine in Trafalgar Square. And then, just before Christmas, it was suddenly all over and George VI and Queen Elizabeth and the two little Princesses appeared on the balcony of Buckingham Palace. My mother and I were there in the crowd, cheering.

Of course, it was the best thing that could possibly have happened. King Edward VIII would have been a disaster. In October, 1937, less than a year after the abdication, the Windsors visited

Germany, the Duke calling on Hitler at Berchtesgaden and expressing his fervent admiration for everything he saw. Had he remained on the throne, and had England been invaded three years later—as we all expected—there seems little doubt that he would have been reinstated as Hitler's puppet.[3] It was a narrow escape indeed, and we owe it in considerable measure to the Duchess. Poor woman, she was always reviled in England; she may have been a pretty good nightmare, but if she had never appeared on the scene I hate to think what might have happened to the country. (Perhaps she might be the answer to the empty plinth in Trafalgar Square.)

My parents and I often saw the Windsors in Paris during the 1950s. Every time we did so I thanked heaven yet again for the abdication. He seemed to me almost unbearably sad, and bored out of his mind. He never bothered to conceal the fact that he hated living in France; his French was execrable, and he made no attempt to improve it. Even in English, apart from golf and gardening he had lamentably few topics of conversation. The Duchess, on the other hand, was a good deal more fun, quite witty, and with a penchant for rather good wisecracks. (She is said to have said to him at the height of the crisis, "You must understand, darling, that you can't abdicate and eat it.") Late one night, on a nightclub banquette, she told me the whole story from beginning to end. I sat there transfixed, conscious that I was actually hearing it at first hand and determined to remember every word the following morning. As it turned out I remembered absolutely nothing, but I don't suppose it mattered; it was all in her memoirs anyway.

---

3 This theory was largely confirmed by German official archives discovered by John Wheeler-Bennett at the end of the war.

———◦✧◦———

At the end of May, 1937, Stanley Baldwin resigned as Prime Minister, to be succeeded by Neville Chamberlain. My father—who was at the time Secretary of State for War—had never got on with Chamberlain and had confidently expected to find himself on the shelf; instead, to his immense surprise, he received what was technically a promotion—to the post of First Lord of the Admiralty—effectively Secretary of the Navy. It was a job he loved; and for me it possessed two inestimable perks. First, it involved our moving to what was, after Gower Street, immensely grand accommodation at Admiralty House at the northern end of Whitehall. This was built by Thomas Ripley in the 1720s with a tall—if absurdly narrow—classical portico; the back of it looked out on to Horse Guards Parade. My mother reacted to the move, as always, with her own characteristic brand of enthusiasm, mobilizing her old friend Philip Sassoon, then Minister of Works, to emphasize the naval aspect with busts of Nelson and what she called generically "Trafalgar trophies," and asking Rex Whistler to liven up her and my father's bed—her control center and thus always for her the most important item of furniture in any house. The result was a huge canopy rising to the high ceiling, surmounted by a crown of dolphins. My nursery—I was seven when we moved in—was even provided with a large fish tank full of tiny sea horses, which we fed on sandhoppers and water fleas, purchased weekly from a local pet shop. They were the wonder and admiration of all my school friends, whom I was twice able to invite to watch the annual ceremony of Trooping the Colour; from my nursery window we had a far better view than many of the top ministerial and VIP seats below.

An even more exciting perk was the Admiralty yacht *Enchantress*, a luxuriously converted thousand-ton sloop which was at the permanent disposal of the First Lord for visiting the various fleets for which he was responsible. Better still, it had accommodation for a number of guests; and there was no official objection to my father's inviting his friends to join him so long as he paid for them out of his own pocket. During his tenure of office there were four cruises, of which I went on two. The first began at Holyhead, which enabled us to stay a couple of nights before embarkation at Plas Newydd, the lovely James Wyatt house owned by my uncle Charlie Anglesey—he was married to my mother's eldest sister Marjorie—looking out across the Menai Strait to the mountains of Snowdonia. In the long dining room Rex Whistler was then working on what is generally accepted as his masterpiece, a vast mural—painted on the largest canvas in England—depicting a lovely Italianate town climbing up the foothills of a wild and romantic mountain range, with a peaceful port below. On the stone quayside, a trident with a few strands of seaweed attached leans up against an urn, and wet footprints lead into the town: Neptune has clearly gone to a nearby pub for a drink. This sets the tone for a thousand other tiny details—quirkish and often extremely funny—including a group of earnest tourists being turned away from a church which is all too obviously *chiuso*, and a self-portrait of Rex himself as a gardener, sweeping up the dead leaves in a side colonnade. He was at the time madly in love with my cousin Caroline, and since finishing the picture would have deprived him of a reason to keep coming to the house, he was always careful not to do so.

We all loved Rex; and we gasped with admiration and wonder as he drew, endlessly and at lightning speed, on any scrap of paper that came to hand. He specialized in monsters and ogres, often shoveling huge forkfuls of struggling people into their cavernous mouths—just the sort of picture children most enjoy. Once, when I was very young, he painted a ghastly wound all over my leg to frighten Nanny; but as I went up to her laughing instead of crying the joke fell rather flat. He would write us rebus letters, and paint us fascinating water colors that you turned upside down and the subject changed: Cinderella turned into the Fairy Godmother, Robin Hood into Sherlock Holmes. Everything he did was fun; every line was instinct with humor. Alas, he was to be killed in Normandy in 1944, a short while after D-day. He was thirty-nine. My cousin Henry Anglesey—who still lives at Plas Newydd, although it now belongs to the National Trust and is open to the public—has arranged an enchanting little permanent exhibition there of Rex's work: the perfect introduction to that glorious mural.

But we must get back to the *Enchantress*. That first cruise, it must be said, proved rather less than a complete success. Its chief objective was to visit the Home Fleet at Invergordon on the Cromarty Firth, some miles north of Inverness—a journey which involved sailing up the west coast of Scotland, along the north and down the east, finishing at Rosyth on the Firth of Forth. Everything was fine until we got to the Hebrides, where we called on another sister of my mother's: my aunt Letty Benson, who with her husband Guy took a house every year on South Uist; but after that the trouble began. Those nightmare channels that separate the islands from the mainland, the Little Minch and the North Minch, proved every bit as mean as they sounded and for two days we braved a hideous gale. I remember little except the noise of repeated crashes as one item of furniture after another came adrift of its moorings, and the inside of the washbasin in my cabin (Armitage Shanks) as I stared into it waiting to be sick yet again. The rounding of Cape Wrath at the northwest corner of Scotland was very little better, and we were all of us physical wrecks by the time we reached Invergordon on my eighth birthday.

Most children love their birthdays; I always hated mine, dreading them for weeks beforehand. Christmas was fine, because it was the same for everybody and I was just one of the crowd; but my birthday set me apart from the rest and plunged me into agonies of shyness. I had already sworn my parents to secrecy over this one; but somehow the news got around and there was a special tea party with a huge birthday cake and *Happy Birthday to You* and I nearly died of embarrassment. I still hadn't altogether recovered when we left the ship the following day and went to stay the night with the Roseberys at Dalmeny nearby. That night, as I waited for sleep, I suddenly had a presentiment of imminent death. I felt perfectly well; I simply knew that the next breath was to be my last. It turned out not to be, of course; but my first sea cruise had obviously affected me more than I realized at the time. Oddly enough, it also made me determined—I can't think why— in due course to join the Navy.

My other cruise, the following year, was little more than a weekend trip to the Isles of Scilly. It has left me with a vague recollection of the great subtropical garden on Tresco, but of very little else. More memorable—though still largely forgotten— were the five more foreign holidays with my mother, before the Second World War put a stop to such jaunts. The three winter ones were for learning to ski. Neither my mother nor I had ever been on skis until, in January, 1937, she carried me off to Sestriere. We had taken the night train and woke up, excitingly, amid deep snow at the Italian border. The first thing I saw on the station platform was a vast inscription bearing the words MUSSOLINI HA SEMPRE RAGIONE. I asked my mother what it meant. "Mussolini is always right" she replied. It chanced that a few days before she had been telling me about papal infallibility; what happened, I wanted to know, if the Pope and Mussolini disagreed? "It just shows," she said, "how idiotic fascism can be."

Of the two summer holidays, the first was again at Aix, the second—in 1938—at Geneva, where my mother was, I now believe, pursuing a light-hearted love affair with a fascinating and extremely high-powered Swiss diplomat, Carl Burckhardt, then at the League of Nations. The world was in crisis, war was threatening, and a good many of her political and diplomatic friends were attending sessions of the League, which was working flat out. It was there, one evening, that she borrowed—heaven knows how—the lovely Villa Diodati where Byron had stayed. She lit the entire building with candles and invited perhaps fifty or sixty to dinner. Among those present was a rising light in the British Foreign Service, an unusually tall young man called Roger Makins, who had a passion for dancing. This was the time of the two hugely popular "novelty" dances, the Lambeth Walk and the Palais Glide; and some weeks previously my mother had enrolled for lessons in both from a Miss Gem Mouflet ("beginners soon at ease") who advertised daily in the Personal Column of *The Times*. That evening she passed on her newly acquired knowledge to him. Little did either of them know that, some forty years later, I should marry his daughter.

———◦♦◦———

The Geneva holiday was in mid-September, 1938, soon after my parents had returned from their last cruise on the *Enchantress*, which took them to the Baltic. (I can date it precisely because I was stung by a wasp on the 15th, my ninth birthday, during a picnic in a rowing boat that we had taken out on the lake.) A week later we were back in England to share what many people were to consider my father's finest hour: his resignation from Neville Chamberlain's government in protest against the Munich agreement. At the end of August Nazi troops had begun to mass along Germany's frontier with Czechoslovakia. Neville Chamberlain and his Foreign Secretary Lord Halifax were prepared to see the destruction of what Chamberlain famously described as "a faraway country," and "people of whom we know nothing"; my father took a stronger line. He wanted us to make it absolutely clear to Hitler that if he marched into Czechoslovakia the result would be war. At first, he wrote, our alternatives seemed to him to be 1) peace with dishonor; 2) war. But then Chamberlain made two flights to Germany to see Hitler; and when he returned from the second meeting—which took place in Munich—having accepted virtually all Hitler's demands, my father saw that there was now a third possibility staring us in the face: war with dishonor. He could bear it no longer, and on October 1, sent in his letter of resignation.[4]

As a child of eight, my first memory of it all was that of a Niagara of letters, with three or four temporary secretaries sitting at a long table sorting them into piles and typing answers. There must have been a good many accusing my poor father of being a warmonger—the last thing he could ever have been; but the vast majority had written to express their agreement, and to those he wrote a stock reply: "Thank you very much for your letter of sympathy and support." It was now that I discovered a remarkable talent for forging his signature, and signed a good many of the letters myself. (I have often wondered whether he knew; I don't think I ever confessed.) My second memory is of the sad packing up of everything, for of course we could no longer stay at Admiralty House. My grandmother had left us No. 34 Chapel Street, just off Belgrave Square. For my father it had the advantage of a huge library running down all one side of the garden, so it was here that we moved. (Gower Street, I imagine, had been sold.)

---

4 The above is, of course, a gross oversimplification. Readers wanting to know more are referred to my father's autobiography *Old Men Forget*, to his recently published Diary, or to John Charmley's biography.

Despite Munich—or perhaps even because of it—the war clouds were now gathering fast. Early the following September we were at Bognor, and my mother and I were making our usual morning visit to buy lobsters and prawns from Billy Welfare. We were walking along the promenade and suddenly heard a car radio—a rarity in those days—coming from a parked open convertible. Was it the voice of the Prime Minister (". . . and consequently, we are at war with Germany") or a just a BBC announcement? I have no idea; but I have the clearest possible memory of my mother turning to me and saying, "The world is never going to be the same again" before walking silently back to our own car. As she drove home I could see that she was crying—and no wonder. It is impossible for our generation—let alone the young—to imagine what war meant to those born in the last twenty years of the nineteenth century. For my mother and father and their contemporaries we were facing another holocaust, which threatened to be as bad—or even worse, if such a thing were possible—as that which they had lived through only a quarter of a century before. Now, she felt, it was going to happen all over again; and this time, if it lasted long enough, her own son might well be one of the casualties.

Chapter Three
America and Eton

BACK IN LONDON a few days later, I watched the trenches (never to be used, thank God) being dug in Hyde Park and was fitted for my gas mask. Then, in the third week of September—school terms always seemed to begin on or very near my birthday—my schoolmates and I boarded a train at Marylebone station to take us to Westbury Manor, near Brackley in Northamptonshire, to which my panic-stricken day school had transferred itself for the duration of hostilities. The house was already a boarding school—small, and I think not particularly distinguished—which I have always suspected that the sudden arrival of another fifty-odd boys had saved from collapse. For the first time I left my own bed to sleep in a dormitory, finding to my surprise that I rather enjoyed the experience;[1] otherwise life

---

1 My father used delightedly to tell of how he had once met my godmother Margot Asquith (widow of the former Prime Minister) in the street when she had just returned from taking her son Anthony—always known as 'Puffin' and later to be the celebrated film director—to boarding school for the first time. "Can you imagine, Duff," she said in indignation, "they've put eleven other boys into Puffin's room."

seemed to go on very much as normal. Rationing, as I remember, was just about the only indication of emergency during those early days of the war—"the phoney war," as we were later to call it—and few of my school friends seemed any more conscious than I was that there was anything radically wrong. As usual, the family spent Christmas at Belvoir—and a particularly Christmassy Christmas it was, because that first wartime winter was the coldest for many years. The fields were white, the hedges covered, the trees bowed under their load; we skated on the frozen reservoir, our blades cutting thin black tracks through the virgin powder snow.

In the late autumn of 1939 my father, out of a job since his resignation, embarked on an extensive coast-to-coast lecture tour of America, in an attempt to fight the danger of isolationism which, thanks in large measure to the efforts of Colonel Charles A. Lindbergh, was assuming dangerous proportions. He and my mother were away until early March. Then, as spring turned to summer, the war took a new turn. In quick succession Hitler invaded Holland, Belgium and—smashing the much-vaunted Maginot Line like matchwood—France. There was talk of an imminent invasion of England. To confuse the expected German parachutists,[2] all signposts were removed, all names of railway stations obliterated. The boys of Westbury Manor began to realize that the war might prove quite exciting after all.

---

2 These parachutists, it was rumored, might well be disguised as nuns. In any case they would speak fluent and unaccented English, and many tests were devised by which to establish their true identity. Knowledge of nursery rhymes was one; but perhaps the most ingenious—reported to me many years later by Kingsley Amis—was to recite to any suspect the following limerick:

> A young engine-driver named Hunt,
> When he took out his engine to shunt,
> Met a runaway truck
> And by shouting out "Duck!"
> Saved the life of the fellow in front.

If the suspect failed to smile he was unquestionably German.

Soon after the summer term began, it became clear to a good many of us that the innocent young schoolmaster who had just arrived to teach us English was a German spy. We took turns to keep a watch on him, and it was one evening when two of us were shadowing him to what was clearly either a secret rendezvous or the hiding place of his short wave transmitter that I suddenly felt hideously sick and threw up in the bushes. I returned to the house, where I was found to be running a high temperature; and on the following day measles was diagnosed. Of the next fort-night I remember scarcely anything. The fall of France and the evacuation of the British army from Dunkirk made little impact; I preferred to listen over and over again to my favorite gramo-phone record, *The Flies Crawl up the Window*, sung (I think) by Jack Hulbert. Then one Sunday, when I was on my feet again but still shaky and I think technically in quarantine, my mother appeared and took me out to lunch at a Buckingham hotel.

From the moment we sat down I could see that she was wor-ried; at one moment I thought she was going to cry. Then, when they brought the stewed apple and custard—the younger gen-eration will never believe just how disgusting English restaurant food could be until well after the war—she told me that I was to be evacuated to America, and that I should be leaving in three days. Nanny, she was at pains to emphasize, would be with me. I would go to boarding school in Canada, where the educational system was closer to our own and would therefore give me a bet-ter chance of passing my Common Entrance exams in two years time; during the holidays I would stay with her friends Bill and Dorothy Paley—he was the founder-president of the Columbia Broadcasting System—on Long Island.

My reaction was far from what she had expected. She had expected me to burst into uncontrollable tears, fling my arms round her neck, and say that I wanted to stay with her for ever;

but no—for me, America was simply the most thrilling place in the world. It meant New York and skyscrapers, and cowboys and Indians, and grizzly bears and hot dogs, and Hollywood, where I should at last meet my hero Errol Flynn. (My mother had actually sat next to him during the lecture tour a few months before and pronounced him a nightmare, but I refused to believe her.[3]) I couldn't wait to be off. The next afternoon I was put on the train to London—a little nervous on my first unaccompanied journey by railway—and two nights later Nanny and I left Chapel Street on the first stage of our adventure (far more frightening for her than it was for me), first to Holyhead and then by the night ferry to Dublin. There, early the following morning, we were met by someone from the American Embassy and taken to have breakfast with the Ambassador, David Gray, an old friend of my parents. We were then bundled into another car and driven straight across Ireland—with the occasional stop for me to be sick—to Galway, where the SS *Washington* awaited us, a vast Stars and Stripes painted all over its hull in order to leave the German U-boats in no doubt of its neutrality.

My father meanwhile was having a distinctly rough passage of his own, Winston Churchill—who in May, 1940 had succeeded Neville Chamberlain as Prime Minister—having appointed him to a new post which he had just invented, that of Minister of Information. The press had been horrified: here, they assumed, was an attempt to muzzle them, if not to impose actual censorship. Led, ironically enough, by my godfather Lord Beaverbrook, they had launched a vitriolic campaign against the Ministry in general and my father in particular; and the news that he was sending his son to safety in America provided them with just the additional ammunition they wanted. Left to himself, my father

---

3 I think it was David Niven who said: "You always know where you are with Errol; he always lets you down."

would never have considered the idea for a second, but my mother was adamant. Was it not true, she argued, that the American Ambassador Joseph Kennedy was organizing the evacuation of hundreds of English children on American ships? All the signs were that London would, over the next few months, be bombed to smithereens; alternatively, Hitler might at any moment invade. Would my father ever forgive himself if his only son were killed, or even taken hostage to ensure his own good behavior? Besides, they had anyway intended to send me for a year to a school in Switzerland before I went to Eton. Switzerland was now obviously out of the question, and so if I now remained in England it would be *because* of the bombing, which was obviously ridiculous. Logic, it will be seen, was never my mother's strongest suit; but despite an indignant question or two in the House my father allowed himself to be persuaded and the resultant storm finally blew itself out.

———⊙†⊙———

SS *Washington* was the largest thing I had ever seen, far too long to tie up alongside anywhere in Galway harbor.[4] As we chugged out to it in the tender it seemed to occupy the entire sky. In prewar days it had been the pride of the United States Line; now it had been adapted as a transport, with the result that the amenities I was particularly looking forward to—the swimming pool, gymnasium, and cinema—were all full of beds. No matter: the excitement far outweighed such minor disappointments, and the five days of the crossing passed rapidly and uneventfully. Suddenly one morning there was the Statue of Liberty, there were the

---

4 Boarding it a few years before, the comedienne Beatrice Lillie was heard to enquire: "How soon does this place get to New York?"

skyscrapers soaring up out of the summer mist—and there on the dockside was my guardian Dr. Rudolf Kommer, ready and waiting.

Dr. Kommer was my mother's oldest friend in America—older and closer than the Paleys, who were little more than acquaintances. He was a curious and slightly mysterious figure. When I remember him he must have been in his middle fifties, and rather like one of the less sinister creations of Eric Ambler; he breathed Central Europe from every pore. Even his nationality was problematical. He had been born of moderately prosperous Jewish parents in the city of Czernovitz, then part of the Austro-Hungarian Empire; at the Treaty of Versailles it had been handed over to Romania, its name changed to Cernauti; it is now part of the Ukraine. His native language was German, but he seemed to speak most of the languages of Europe with equal fluency; apart from a heavy accent his English was perfect. He was round as a football, was exquisitely dressed with an invariable bow tie, smelt overpoweringly of some obscure Central European unguent and chain-smoked Turkish cigarettes, seldom removing the current one from his mouth.

The mystery, to which his friend the American journalist Alexander Woollcott once devoted an entire article, was encapsulated in its title: *Where does Dr. Kommer get his money?* He seemed to live on a fairly lavish scale, inhabiting a suite at the now-defunct Ambassador Hotel on Park Avenue and giving small but select luncheon parties several times a week at the Colony restaurant, where he had his own table; but there were no obvious means of support and he seemed to have all the free time in the world. My mother had first known him in the earliest days of *The Miracle*, when he had been a sort of secretary to Max Reinhardt; he, like so many others, had fallen in love with her, but with him it was always a platonic love—the kind that she—and, I feel quite sure, he—almost invariably preferred. After the days of *The Miracle* were over they continued as close friends, corresponding regularly; when in England Kaetchen (the little cat)—as he was always called—was a regular visitor to Gower Street and to Bognor, and on at least one occasion he joined us on a summer holiday in France. He was kind, generous, amusing, thoughtful, and utterly reliable, and it was he whom my mother unhesitatingly chose to be my guardian during my indefinite stay in America. She could not have made a better choice. He assumed complete responsibility for me, meeting me and seeing me off at stations, taking me out to lunch and the cinema, providing for my every want, all with unfailing good humor and charm. My mother wrote to him, in a letter I carried with me:

July 2, 1940

Here is my child and here is Nanny armed with £25, and now they belong to you for the duration. He shall go to some Canadian school. Establish him in Long Island with the hospitable Paleys until the term starts and overlay them with my gratitude. Never have I put more in your dear gesticulating hands, never have I taken your order "Use me" more literally.

If we are killed you will know best what to do for his good. If a miracle ends this war victoriously for us, then what a glorious jaunt he will have had! If a miracle subjugates and occupies this land beneath Hitler and we are in prison or Duff is fled to Ottawa with King and Council, he might, if here, become a hostage to force Duff's hand or mine. It is for this reason, not because of bombs, that he leaves. You'll be glad to hear that my spirit is unexpectedly high, but of course I am very unhappy. Perhaps this citadel island will have fallen before this reaches you and all will be over. If it is, you know that I am certain no one ever had a better friend than I had in you and no one loved you better.

A week later she wrote again:

July 10

Please, Kaetchen, do not let my little boy get spoiled by riches; buses not taxis, drug stores not restaurants, and not too many cinemas. He is a very good child and will give no trouble, I am confident. If you see him in any way fresh with Americans or if he is not perfectly mannered, reprove him with all your might. Do not let him be loaded with presents; keep your own hands from your pockets. Nanny will buy him clothes cheaply— from Bloomingdale's please, not at Saks. You must be tolerant of my idiosyncrasies and conform to them. I feel very strongly that it must never be said that English children are living on charity, so I would like my suggested money arrangements done almost legally [sic] immediately. Who would have thought you were to be a father so soon? I like Doll Iris's[5] influence on John Julius, so ask her to see a lot of him. Keep me in his mind a bit and teach him to admire Duff. Tutor him hard in American history and current events (war and peace). I'd like him to be braver than most and not to be taught "Safety first."

There, too, were the reporters. In normal times they met every arriving passenger ship as a matter of course; there would always

---

5 Iris Tree—known as "The Doll"—was one of the three daughters of the actor Sir Herbert Beerbohm Tree. My mother had grown-up with the Tree children; later Iris had toured America with her in *The Miracle*. In the '30s she had been part of the entourage of Krishnamurti in Ojai Valley, California.

be a celebrity or two on board, only too ready to be interviewed. Now they had a new and different story: that of the pathetic, frightened little refugees arriving from war-ravaged Europe, seeking the protection of Big Brother America. Word of the parliamentary battering my father had suffered as a result of my departure had reached New York before me, and I was instantly surrounded. Did I miss my parents? What were my father's last words to me? Did I think it right that I should be in America when so many of my friends and contemporaries were obliged to stay behind? Was England going to win the war? Heaven knows how I answered most of these questions; the only reply I remember is that to the last, simply because it was splashed across the page above a photograph of me seated on my suitcase and registering a wistfulness I was far from feeling. "I am convinced that she most assuredly will" were the words attributed to me. They accurately reflected my opinion such as it was, but I cannot believe that I actually uttered them.

———⊙⁊⊙———

We had a quick wash and brush-up at the Ambassador, but no chance to have a proper look at New York. That was promised for later; now we were off again, to the house that was to be my home for the next twenty months—Kiluna Farm, Manhasset, Long Island. It was what I later came to recognize as the quintessential New England house—white painted clapboard, green shutters, tall columned portico—but also very grand, with a whole nursery wing tacked on to one end and, in its spacious grounds, a saltwater swimming pool and a magnificent indoor tennis court. The copious staff was headed by an English butler, Mr. May, and from the moment of our arrival it was plain that we were going to be very comfortable indeed.

Bill and Dorothy Paley were perfect hosts. They had two small, adopted children, Jeffrey a toddler, Hilary a baby in arms, whose nanny—clad always in white sharkskin—was changed on principle once every three months to prevent bonding. (Dorothy's somewhat advanced ideas on child psychology were later to cause painful problems where my own Nanny was concerned.) Eating as we did in the nursery, we children—we were joined a few weeks after my arrival by Serena and Nell Dunn[6]—did not see too much of them on a daily basis: Bill, at thirty-eight already the leading figure in New York broadcasting, would leave early in the morning for his office, and Dorothy too led her own busy life. But they took us to the New York World's Fair and for a fortnight that first summer to Mount Desert Island in Maine; and Long Island's top tennis professional, Joe Farrell, arrived to give me an hour's lesson every morning on the indoor court. Thanks to him I became a moderately good player, good enough to enter—though never to win—local junior tournaments. Alas, I peaked at the age of eleven; in sixty-seven years you can go a long way downhill.

To this luxurious and pampered life the Preparatory School of Upper Canada College, Toronto, came as an abrupt and salutary contrast. In those days it meant an overnight train journey from New York; one slept in curtained couchettes ranged along each side of the central corridor of the carriage—a scene well known to admirers of *Some Like it Hot*. For the first of the twelve journeys I was to make, Nanny came with me; subsequently I traveled by myself, looking forward to it—or at least to the return trip—for weeks beforehand as the adventure it always was. Even that first time, I don't think I was particularly nervous. After a year at Westbury I was well accustomed to boarding schools; and though Canadian boys were always said to be much tougher than we British were, I was much reassured

---

6 Serena was later to marry Jacob Rothschild; Nell became a highly successful author and playwright (*Poor Cow, Steaming,* etc.).

by the news that there would be some fifty others from England in the same situation as myself; and of all these, the most intelligent, interesting and unpredictable was Milo Cripps.

I had known Milo slightly since toddlerhood; his parents and mine having long been friends. His father, Fred Cripps, was the brother of the austere socialist Sir Stafford Cripps, at that time Ambassador to Moscow and future Chancellor of the Exchequer, but was as unlike him as it was possible to be: a man who preferred socializing to socialism, a hard-drinking pillar of White's Club, lover of the Turf, and general man-about-town. Milo combined the tastes and character of his father with the intelligence and culture of his uncle. He was quite astonishingly precocious. Even at the age of eleven he seemed to have read everything worth reading; names like Schopenhauer and Thomas Aquinas rolled effortlessly off his tongue. His forceful personality made him a natural leader; and he hit the Upper Canada College Prep School with much the same force as that with which the young Harold Acton had hit Oxford some twenty years before. When all the young toughs around him talked ice hockey, he set himself up as an ardent champion of ring-a-ring-a-roses, and somehow got them all to join in. He also developed an extraordinary walk with his hands hanging limp-wristed in front of his chest, rather like a rabbit. This affectation too was widely adopted, and drove the masters—who, not surprisingly, had never seen anything remotely like it before—raving wild, not least because they had no idea how to deal with it.

Milo's baleful influence apart, Upper Canada College was agreeable enough. In those days Toronto had the reputation of being the most boring city in the British Empire, which was saying a good deal;[7] every English visitor who came to see me—there weren't many, but they did almost unbelievably include Sir Thomas

---

7 I would remind the reader that I am speaking of some sixty-five years ago. It is a very different place today.

Beecham with his passionate patron Emerald, Lady Cunard—complained bitterly about the impossibility of buying a drink except in a brown paper bag from a government store, and then having no way of drinking it except out of a tooth glass in the hotel bedroom. But my eleven-year-old lips were still unpolluted by hard liquor, and since—except to visit the dentist—we were anyway never allowed outside the school gates, such inconveniences meant little to me. Unlike Westbury Manor, the school staged regular evening parties—a big one for Halloween (which I had never heard of; in those days it was virtually unknown in England) and an only slightly more restrained one for St. Patrick's Day, when there was always green ice cream; but the feature that delighted me most was the total absence of football. Instead, the neighboring field was deliberately flooded to make ice hockey rinks—if memory serves, no less than eleven of them. I loved hockey—the "ice" went without saying—as much as I hated football, though I never remotely distinguished myself. For the rest, the atmosphere at Upper Canada was much the same as that of an English prep school. Naturally we all looked forward enormously to the holidays—which for me were always heralded by that thrilling night on the train—but we were certainly not unhappy.

The holiday weeks on Long Island, enjoyable as they were, were also fairly uneventful. During my second summer I went up to join my friend Milo, who was staying with Mr. and Mrs. James Forrestal—he was at that time Secretary of the Navy—in their house near Poughkeepsie in upstate New York. One afternoon there was great excitement: President Roosevelt came to tea. He arrived entirely alone, having driven over from his house at neighboring Hyde Park, at the wheel of his own car—specially adapted for his disability with all the controls hand-operated. I saw him only behind the wheel, as he was leaving; greatly daring, I asked him for his autograph, but he smilingly refused. "The office won't let me," he said. The following day, a Sunday, we went to the local church. Just before the service started, the congregation suddenly rose to its feet—and there he was again, with Mrs. Roosevelt this time, struggling on his crutches with agonizing slowness along the nave, supported by half a dozen men fussing round him. No one had told me how crippled he was, and I don't believe that 99% of the Americans of his day had the slightest suspicion of it.

I always longed to see more of America—the Wild West, the Deep South, and most of all Hollywood—but it never happened. In the summer of 1941 there was no Maine; my life revolved around the Long Island tennis court and above all the swimming pool, where I learnt to dive and to swim impressively long distances under water; of the winters I have little recollection, apart from the blistering cold. Once a week, on what was nominally her day off, Nanny and I would take the train to New York: on arrival we would normally call in on Kaetchen at the Ambassador, and he would quite often take me to lunch at the Colony with a few of his friends—usually theater people or writers, with a sprinkling of New York high society. If not, I would go with Nanny to a cafeteria (I was particularly fond of the automat) and then, as likely as not, to Radio City Music Hall; there you could see not only two full-length feature films but also an hour-long performance on the stage, featuring that greatest of all chorus lines, the world-famous Rockettes, and one of the big bands—Glenn Miller, Benny Goodman, Tommy Dorsey and the rest—which were then in their heyday, and of which I could never have enough.

I remember one, and only one, wave of homesickness. It came towards the end of my time in America, when for some reason or other I was looking at a large map of England. It was the place names that did it: names like Nottingham and Worcester and Macclesfield, which had no special significance—I had never been to any of them—but which suddenly induced an almost

Proustian pang. It was acute while it lasted, but it didn't last long. Had I known at the time how soon I should be on my way home, it would probably never have happened at all.

———— ❧ ————

During the first two and a half years of the war, my parents had a very much more exciting time than I did. First there had been the American lecture tour, then the Ministry of Information. In this, as my father would have been the first to admit, he had not been a signal success. The reasons are long and complicated, and have no real place in this story;[8] suffice it to say that when in July, 1941, the Prime Minister asked him to undertake a special mission to Singapore he accepted with alacrity. As always—and despite strict Whitehall instructions—my mother insisted on going with him. On the first leg of their journey they took a flying boat known as the *Yankee Clipper* to New York and stayed a few days with the Paleys. I was naturally overjoyed to see them for the first time in over a year, though I remember being horrified by what seemed to me their grotesquely exaggerated English accents. (They presumably felt much the same about my American one, but we were all too polite to mention it.) A day or two after their arrival my mother took me on a day's visit to Washington. It was my first journey by air and I distinctly remember palpitating excitement—though she later maintained that I showed no interest of any kind and read comics throughout. We lunched, I think, at the British Embassy, visited the Lincoln Memorial, and went on a tour of the FBI, where I practiced killing people with a machine gun and had my fingerprints taken. We flew back to New York in time for dinner.

---

8 The fullest account is to be found in John Charmley's biography. After my father's departure Churchill offered the job to Brendan Bracken with the warning that it was "worse than manning a bomb-disposal unit."

My father's brief was to report on the general condition of the British Empire in the Far East in view of the obvious threat from Japan, with whom war was becoming increasingly likely. He did not take long to form an opinion:

> The civil population appears to have been asleep in a comfortable dream, that the Japanese will not dare to attack and have been lulled into a sense of false security by misleading reports of their impregnable fortress from the effete and ineffective Military Intelligence.

The Commander-in-Chief, Far East, Air Chief Marshal Sir Robert Brooke-Popham, was "damned near gaga" and "quite out of business from dinner time onwards." He went on to point out that the machinery of government would have to be drastically revised, "having undergone no important change since the days of Queen Victoria." But alas, it was too late. On December 7, less than three months after his arrival in Singapore, the Japanese bombed Pearl Harbor: a day or two later the *Prince of Wales* and the *Repulse* were both laying at the bottom of the ocean. My parents left on January 13, arriving at the military airfield during an air raid, during which, as my father later wrote, they were hustled into an air raid shelter made entirely of glass. It seemed somehow an appropriate end to the mission.

They arrived back in England in mid-February, having flown around the world—a rare accomplishment in 1942. Then, back safely at Bognor with my father now temporarily unemployed, they decided that they wanted me back in England. The dreaded invasion had never happened; the blitz was over; and, as my mother pointed out, it would be embarrassing for me in later life if I had to admit that I had spent nearly all the war years in the safety of America. Besides, I was now twelve and a half and my father was determined that—provided only that I could pass my Common

Entrance exam—I should go to Eton in the autumn. But there was a war on, and nonessential passages across the Atlantic were hard to arrange. Fortunately my father had his naval contacts—he had after all been First Lord—and consulted the former Captain of the *Enchantress*, Peter Frend. He could have made no more fortunate approach. The Captain told him that in a few weeks time he himself would be bringing a cruiser from America to England, and would be delighted to have me on board.

I was back at Upper Canada College, just at the beginning of the summer term, when I was summoned after breakfast by Mr. Chick—would any housemaster at an English school be so named?—Carson, the Senior Housemaster. Such summonses usually spelt trouble, and I knocked at the door full of trepidation; it was an immense relief to see, as I walked into the room, that he was smiling from ear to ear. "Get your things packed up, Cooper," he said, "you're going back to England." "But how, Sir?" I asked him. He had no idea. That was all he had been told. His job was simply to get me on to the night train to New York. I should doubtless learn more in due course.

At Grand Central station the next morning, Kaetchen was waiting. He knew very little more: only that he was to put me on the train that afternoon for Norfolk, Virginia, where I should board the ship that was to carry me home. On arrival at Norfolk I was to report to some office—the name of which had been carefully written on a piece of paper—where I should be given further instructions. It was my first experience of the wartime secrecy in which all troop movements were shrouded; my excitement was growing by the hour. Early the next morning I boarded the cruiser—HMS *Phoebe*—and was taken straight to see Captain Frend, whom I remembered well from three years before. He welcomed me warmly and told me that I should have a companion on the journey, another returning evacuee called Jake Pleydell-Bouverie. We should be expected to pull our weight on board, act jointly as a midshipman of the watch, and keep a full log of all that occurred. The Atlantic was full of German U-boats and we were traveling alone, without a convoy, which meant life jackets day and night.

Our crossing—which involved a zigzag route dictated by suspected U-boat locations—took sixteen days, of which I remember surprisingly little. We were given our meals separately, neither with the Captain (who was usually on the bridge anyway) nor in the Wardroom, nor on the mess deck; for the rest, we had the run of the ship, of which on our first day at sea we had been given a comprehensive tour from engine rooms to gun turrets. We learned the full sailor's repertoire of four-letter words; we watched torpedo and some spectacular depth charge practice; we did seemingly endless lifeboat drill—which might easily have proved extremely useful. And yet, for some reason, the thought of enemy action scarcely entered my mind—a fact which I attribute less to courage than to a lamentable lack of imagination. The weather was kind to us, and there were no repetitions of those dreadful days four years before on the *Enchantress*. And so, in the first days of May, 1942, we landed at Plymouth and I took the train to Bognor, where my parents were waiting on the platform.

It was an ecstatic reunion—particularly for my mother, who had confidently expected never to see me again. Our only misgivings concerned poor Nanny; no women were allowed on warships, and she had had to stay on in Long Island. Relations between her and Dorothy Paley had been deteriorating for some time, since she represented everything that Dorothy most disapproved of where the upbringing of children was concerned. For my mother, too, this had been a problem. On the one hand, there was her gratitude to Dorothy for giving me refuge; on the other, loyalty to Nanny for devoting to us twelve years of her life. In the circumstances, Nanny could not possibly be sacked—her wages were being paid, through Kaetchen, by my mother—but some months previously she had been shunted on to Dorothy's secretary, who lived with her husband and two small children in a separate house at the end of the drive. It must have been a considerable relief: once again she had a proper job to do—for, as we both knew, I had no need of her any longer and had it not been for the war she would probably have left us two years before—and the atmosphere at Kiluna Farm was becoming intolerable for her. True, for my last few months there we did not see as much of each other as we had done; but I still loved her dearly, and she loved me, and we had continued to go to New York together on her days off.

Now that I was home again, all we could do was to keep in close touch and arrange for her repatriation as soon as we could. She was back, I believe, well before the end of the war—though I'm ashamed to say I can't remember how she returned—and settled back into the little house where she had always lived with her parents in the suburbs of Grantham. There she devoted the rest of her life to looking after them—they must have been well into their eighties—with the same devotion that she had showed towards the young. Occasionally in later years I used to go and stay the weekend. The house had an outside loo at the back and when I first knew it was still lit by gas, with candles upstairs; we lived in the kitchen, the front drawing room being used only when we had company. After the parents died she lived there alone—by this time she was pretty old herself—and the weekends stopped; but I still used to drop in fairly regularly for a cup of tea until, in the mid-1970s, she died.

————⊙⌖⊙————

O n her return to England early in 1942 my mother had settled back at Bognor, where she had flung herself enthusiastically into farming. In the phoney war before the lecture tour, she had worked on the top floor of the Army & Navy Stores, making camouflage nets; but now she had decided that the cultivation of our pathetically few acres—about four—while raising the maximum number of animals would be a more worthwhile contribution to the war effort. She had no knowledge of agriculture or husbandry but she learnt fast, relying on innumerable handouts from the Ministry of Food and the advice of her devoted friend and admirer Conrad Russell: a tall, slow moving, slow speaking man with a thatch of thick white hair—"the Gothic Farmer" she used to call him—who had run his own smallholding in Somerset for a quarter of a century and had practical experience of everything she needed to know. A bachelor who had loved her for ten years but who was, like her, perfectly content that the relationship should remain platonic, he would come down for two or three nights a week and give advice on the growing of cabbages or kale, on milking and cheese making, on the proper composition of poultry-meal or pig-swill.

She always claimed that this was the happiest time of her life. In the last volume of her autobiography, *Trumpets from the Steep*, she wrote:

> Making the cheese was the greatest of the new miracles.... A cow can inundate a small family with milk, and from one widowed cow's cruse came twenty pounds of cheese a week, a pound or two of butter, plentiful sweet milk for our refugees and ourselves, and enough whey to fatten potential porkers. I loved my cow as the Russian peasant (I suppose) did before her cow was communal. She represented to me life, riches, sweetness, and

warmth. Dressed as Babushka, I would go, lantern in hand, through the half-light of spring with the birds' first chorus to enliven me from bleary sleep, straightening up under my inevitable yoke that suspended the milk pail and another pail of dairy cubes. The flickering oil lamp I would light and hang on a hook in the dark shed while this beneficent beast welcomed me with her soft moo that ejected breath like a dragon's. I would find her ointments and washing cloths, and there I would sit for twenty minutes or so, my cheek deep in her furry flank, her sweet smelling warmth enveloping me in content. . . . At last I would stagger back under my yoke to the dairy [it must have been a good three hundred yards] and pour the rich foaming gallons into their appointed tub, skim yesterday's yield, put the kettles on, and start miracle making.

There would be a cheese made every other day, Cheddar normally alternating with Pont-l'Evêque. She had no helper except Conrad on his visits and her old maid Miss Wade, who concerned herself exclusively with the chickens.

My father—if he was there, since he was now Chancellor of the Duchy of Lancaster and was spending four or five nights a week in London—would meanwhile be working on his life of King David; he took little or no interest in the farming operations. In the evenings, he and my mother and Conrad—if *he* was there—would read aloud or do *The Times* crossword, which played an important part in all our lives. Spending so much of his time alone, Conrad was quite astonishingly erudite and well read, as well as being a self-made Latin scholar; I have never known anyone with such an inexhaustible fund of useless but fascinating information. I remember my father once mentioning some obscure character from the early nineteenth century;

"Oh yes," said Conrad, "his grandfather was harness maker to George III."

This, then, was the atmosphere in which I spent my twelfth summer, the summer of 1942. It was a very different Bognor from the one I remembered from before the war. There was no sea bathing. Along the heavily mined beach three rows of tank traps stretched in both directions as far as the eye could see. They were made of what appeared to be triangular scaffolding, about ten feet high; the theory was, I think, that when the German army landed its tanks would crush them, and would then themselves be destroyed by the steel tubes as they collapsed. Fortunately, they were never put to the test. Every morning I helped my mother on her smallholding—milking the cow, sometimes turning the cheeses, feeding the ducks and geese, always accompanying her on her morning drive into Bognor—the cream convertible had long since been replaced by a tiny Austin Seven—picking up edible rubbish from a dozen different locations and bringing them back on a little trailer to be boiled into pig swill.

The afternoons were devoted to study. The all important Common Entrance was looming, and my mother found me a crammer, a certain Mr. Neville C. May, who lived in a pretty but villainously dark little cottage in the close of Chichester cathedral. Every afternoon, gas mask slung over shoulder—nobody really feared gas bombs any more, but the law required it and somehow it made me feel safer—I took the bus the seven-odd miles to Chichester, where this rather seedy but perfectly pleasant retired schoolmaster took me through the syllabus while his radio blared *Music While You Work* from the next-door room. What and how much he taught me I have no idea—except in geometry, where he seemed to show a little touch of genius. The subject fascinated me as it never had before: Suddenly I saw the beauty of mathematics, the inevitability, the iciness of the logic. Now, sixty-odd years later, it is all forgotten; but I still promise myself that one day, in my very old age, I shall take it up again and try to recapture something of the excitement and pleasure it gave me then.

There was one subject that Mr. May could not teach: the composition of Latin verse. It seems astonishing today to think that this was a requirement for eleven-year-olds before going to Eton, but so it was. Fortunately I suppose, Mr. May's next-door neighbor in the close was an elderly clergyman qualified—up to a point—to instruct me, and to him I went. He taught me at least the rudiments of the subject; far clearer in my memory, however, is the fact that he was the only adult male who ever made what might be described as a pass at me. On the other hand it might not; but I was struck by the frequency of his enquiries as to whether I wanted, as he rather charmingly described it, "to retire." On one occasion I said that I did; and was not a little surprised when he entered his extremely small loo with me, undid his fly, and simultaneously peed into the same pan. That was all— no touching, no further conversation on the subject—but I must have been a bit shaken or I would not remember it now. On all subsequent lessons there was the same invitation, which I always politely declined. He would look a little disappointed, but never insisted further.

My visits to Chichester must anyway have paid off, because I passed my Common Entrance and on September 17, 1942—two days after my thirteenth birthday—I took the train to Slough (no petrol for unnecessary motoring in those wartime days) and entered Mr. Herbert's house, the Hopgarden, at Eton.

I was, I think, quite frightened—more so than I had been when going to Upper Canada College. There I had my friend Milo; at

Eton I knew no one, and despite my father's enormous enthusiasm for it I felt daunted by the school's very age and reputation. Would I be popular? I certainly longed to be, but I had no self-confidence and was far from certain whether anyone would like me at all. It must have been a good four months since I had seen or spoken to anyone my own age. I had no desire to distinguish myself. My best course, I decided, would be to try and be exactly like everybody else, one of the herd; then at least I couldn't go far wrong. Meanwhile I would concentrate on making just one real friend.

I had been kitted out a few weeks before: short black cutaway jacket—known as a bumfreezer—on which was overlaid a two-inch starched collar, black waistcoat and grey striped trousers. This costume was to be exchanged, after one reached the critical height of five foot four inches, for a black tail coat and a normal size of collar, beneath which were tucked the ends of a tiny bow tie of white cotton. And of course a top hat. Before the war this last had been obligatory whenever a boy left his house; with the coming of wartime austerity top hats were required only for journeys beyond the parish church, halfway down the High Street. One never ceases to wonder at the measures our country took to beat the Germans.

Eton proved tough, uncomfortable, and unforgiving; but it did provide its boys with one inestimable advantage. From the outset—unlike poor Puffin—we each had our own room. It might be—indeed, in the early stages of one's Eton life, it was—little more than a *wagon-lit*, but it was our own personal property and refuge. For reasons of space the bed, hinged at its head, would during the daytime be swung up against the wall, its foot almost touching the ceiling, and covered discreetly by a curtain; for the rest there was a washstand with basin, one of those padded chests called ottomans and a "burry," which had three drawers at the bottom, a hinged panel that opened up to make a desk in the middle, and at the top a glass-fronted cupboard in which we kept our books. All these arrangements except the washstand will probably be familiar to young Etonians today; but they now have central heating. We had tiny fireplaces in which alternate rooms were allowed an infinitesimally small coal fire on alternate nights. On the off-nights one was expected to move in for the evening with one's next-door neighbor, but as he had only a single chair and a single working space those two hours or so of nightly homework were difficult indeed. Double-glazing in those days was unheard of; and the cold of those damp, remorseless Thames Valley winters—though I am sure not comparable to that suffered by those who were simultaneously enduring the siege of Leningrad—was such that at one point my closest friend, Martin Jacomb, had both arms simultaneously in slings to preserve his chilblained hands.

When the late Lord Harlech—he who was our Ambassador in Washington in the days of his old friend Jack Kennedy—was at Eton between the wars, one of the boys committed suicide. The same evening his housemaster summoned the whole house together after prayers and asked if anyone could suggest any reason for the tragedy. The young Ormsby-Gore (as he then was) slowly raised his hand and asked: "Could it have been the food, Sir?" Many years later he confirmed the story to me, and assured me that he had intended his words as a serious suggestion. Knowing as I did our own wartime provender, I can only say that it would never have occurred to me that they were anything else. Not all this was the fault of the authorities. They had rationing to contend with, together with all the horrors of powdered egg, powdered milk, Spam, margarine, and several other concoctions now mercifully forgotten. We each had our one-pound jar of jam at breakfast, which had to last us a month. The only consolation was tea, which we took in groups of three or four in our rooms and which, with any luck, was supplemented by such few delicacies we were still able to find in the shops or—better still—in food parcels from home. Thanks to the Bognor farm I nearly always had a supply of eggs; and if the top of the jam was occasionally found to be covered in green fur or if the butter, devoid of preservatives and denied the comfort of a refrigerator, tended to go off a little during the summer months—well, it was a small price to pay.

Then there was the fagging. "Lower boys"—you remained a lower boy until you got into Fifth Form, usually about eighteen months after your arrival—were fags, each being allotted an individual fagmaster who was at least three-quarters of the way up the school. Your duties included cooking eggs for his tea, tidying his room, and laying and lighting his fire during the winter. The jobs were not particularly onerous; but all fags had also to be permanently on the alert for the shout, by any one of the half-dozen members of "Library," of the single word "Boy!" They then had to run at full tilt to the source of the shout; the last to arrive had to do what was required, often to take a message to another boy in another house which might be two or three minutes walk away. Fags were however spared any serious housework; this was the task of the "boys' maids"—elderly women especially selected for their hideousness of aspect in order not to arouse impure thoughts—who woke us in the morning, made the beds and cleaned the rooms. Looking back on it, I am rather surprised: why were we not called by a bell and required to look after ourselves?

I suppose because we simply had no time. Our first lesson of the day—"early school" as it was called—began at 7:30 AM (There was hot but watery cocoa and buns at 7:15 AM for those not in too much of a rush, but most of us preferred another five or ten minutes in bed.) The classrooms might be as much as five minutes run from the boarding houses, to which at 8:20 AM we would return for breakfast. Exactly an hour later the whole school would be congregated in one of the two chapels—College Chapel or

Lower Chapel according to one's seniority—for twenty minutes of hymns, psalms and prayers. Then lessons again, with one twenty-minute break, till lunch (always referred to as Boys' Dinner). After lunch, the dreaded "games."

I hated games, particularly during the autumn half. (Terms at Eton were always called halves, doubtless because there were three of them to a year.) I hated the longish walk to the playing fields in football boots, then taking off one's coat and sweater in the bitter cold ("Just run harder, Cooper, you'll soon warm up."); most of all I hated spending the next hour and a half playing Eton's own particularly unpleasant form of football, "the Field Game," running hopelessly backwards and forwards up and down after the ball, which I seldom touched unless—as occasionally happened—it hit me by mistake. To this day the smell of mud instantly recalls those nightmare afternoons. On Tuesdays and Thursdays, which were half holidays, the torment continued even longer. After Christmas, though, things improved, since instead of football we were allowed to play fives. This admirable game—not unlike squash, but using the gloved hand rather than a racket—should be far better known and more generally played than it is. The court, unlike that of squash, has no wall behind the players; instead, there is a curiously shaped projection from the left-hand side—in fact modeled on the banister of the outside stairway of College Chapel where the game was invented—off which the ball bounces at wild and unexpected angles. I was never very good at it but, apart from tennis, it is the only outdoor game that I have ever really loved.

During the summer half you could choose to be a dry-bob, which meant that you played cricket, or a wet-bob, which meant that you rowed on the river. I plumped for rowing—which had the considerable advantage, it seemed to me, of being the only sport that could be pursued sitting down. Apart from the blisters that almost immediately arose on hands and bottom, I found it mildly enjoyable; although a minimum distance had to be covered each week, it was usually possible to pull in under an overhanging tree and read a book for an hour or two. The only misery was racing. I think I did it only twice, each time coming in last by quite a long way, but with heart pounding, lungs bursting and a certainty—almost a hope—that I should very soon be dead. One of the things I most disliked about Eton was its fixation on sport; there must have been forty or fifty different colored caps awarded to those who excelled even moderately in whatever game they might play. I was one of the relatively few who managed to move my way up the school for four years without winning one of them.

Evenings were devoted either to homework or to one of the innumerable societies in which the school abounded: Literary, Musical, Debating, Archaeological, and many others. (The Archaeological Society should really have been called the Art Society; but at Eton art, if not actually a dirty word, was at least a questionable one.) Supper was at 8:15 PM; prayers at 8:50 PM Between supper and prayers there might or might not be a beating. No aspect of school life in those distant days strikes more horror in the modern breast than the thought of corporal punishment; I can only say that to me and my contemporaries it seemed perfectly normal. Up to six strokes of a springy cane can hurt a lot at the time, but the whole thing was over in twenty or thirty seconds and was followed a few minutes later by a rather agreeable warm feeling in the affected area. It elicited a good deal of sympathy from one's friends, and it certainly seemed to most of us infinitely preferable to the possible alternatives—usually staying in all afternoon copying out one of Virgil's *Georgics*. What in retrospect seems wrong is that beatings were administered by the Captain of the House, entirely at his own discretion and without consultation with the housemaster. In my very first half there was at least one beating on most evenings, our House Captain—as I later discovered—having a distinctly sadistic streak. Knowing no better, I assumed that this was the norm and bore no grudge when I copped it twice myself for what seemed rather mild misdemeanors: the first for repeatedly forgetting to hang my emergency air raid clothes on the hook outside my door, the second for not playing football "keenly" enough. But the sadist left that Christmas, and I was quite surprised to find that under his successors there were perhaps only one or two such incidents a half—sometimes fewer still.

I have noticed over the years that mention of fags and fagging tends to raise a few eyebrows among my American friends; so perhaps it may be worthwhile to put on record that at Eton—where the system has by now long been abolished—the words carried no questionable connotation. This is not to say, of course, that homosexuality did not exist. There is a celebrated verse, which I suspect once again of being by A.P. Herbert (no relation of my housemaster), in which the name in the penultimate line could be replaced by any number of others:

> Long and extensive researches
> By Morgan and Huxley and Ball
> Have conclusively proved that the hedgehog
> Can never be buggered at all;
> But further extensive researches
> Have incontrovertibly shown
> That comparative safety at Eton
> Is enjoyed by the hedgehog alone.

Some years ago, when the House of Lords was discussing whether to decriminalize homosexuality, Field Marshal Lord Montgomery of Alamein confidently assured Their Lordships that nothing "of that sort" had ever occurred in any unit for which he was responsible. For a moment there was silence; this was followed by one of the most remarkable noises I have ever heard, as some thousand Peers of the Realm simultaneously bared their teeth and sucked the air in through them. On the other hand the lines quoted above are—at least where Eton in the 1940s was concerned—a wild exaggeration. At the Hopgarden I am fairly confident that actual buggery was virtually non-existent. There was inevitably a certain amount of moderately innocent fiddling and fondling: when some fifty or sixty normal teenage boys, all desperately trying to cope with puberty, maddened and bewildered by that first terrifying surge of testosterone, are closeted together for three months at a stretch with absolutely no female company, how could there possibly not be? It seems to me astonishing that the school authorities appeared to have no understanding of this, not only threatening as they did with instant expulsion any boy found in a remotely compromising situation, but saddling many of them with an almost intolerable burden of guilt by telling them that even if a little mild masturbation did not—as some believed—make your ears fall off or cause a long, black hair to grow out your left palm, it certainly put you straight on the road to hell.

Nowadays, I am told, to have been educated at Eton is a positive disadvantage; universities and employers alike are biased against old Etonians even before they see them. As a result I notice that many of the younger ones actually try to conceal their background: whereas Harrovians and Wykehamists have no difficulty in saying "when I was at Harrow" or "when I was at Winchester," Etonians tend to say "when I was at school." Any sort of snobbery is bad enough; inverted snobbery is surely the worst of all. Good schools must by definition turn out better pupils than bad ones, and Eton remains a splendid one—better indeed by far than it was in my day; to discriminate against it seems to me to be little short of grotesque. It is a measure of how much the world has changed in the last half-century that proud Etonians and closet homosexuals have been replaced by proud homosexuals and closet Etonians.

Chapter Four

The Embassy

EVEN MY MOTHER balked at staying at Bognor through the winter. There was no suggestion of central heating, the walls ran with damp and our tiny boiler could not begin to cope. The cow and pigs would be sold at Barnham market, the other livestock meeting whatever fate seemed appropriate; and the Coopers would move to a suite of three rooms at the Dorchester Hotel, in one of which I would continue my attempts, not altogether unsuccessful, to teach myself Russian. One or two Christmases back I had prevailed upon a generous godparent—I can't remember which—to give me a Linguaphone course in the language, which I was pursuing with fascination. In our second decade of life we have not yet lost that wonderful faculty of absorption which in our first makes the learning of our native tongue so remarkably effortless, and I mopped up the first dozen lessons with such ease that even today I can recite most of them by heart. By the beginning of our third decade, alas, the faculty is lost. Some time in the 1970s I decided to learn Modern Greek by the same method, and though the language is far easier the words somehow refused to stick. Apart from the stock formulas of politeness the only Greek sentence that still comes tripping off my tongue is one which, in lesson four, is uttered at a dinner party by one of the lady guests when her food is set before her. "It has a beautiful appearance," she remarks, "and I do not doubt but that its taste will be equally delicious." I use it constantly in Greek restaurants; the waiters fall about laughing and I usually get an ouzo on the house.

In a suite above us at the Dorchester, summer and winter alike, lived Emerald, Lady Cunard, who has already made one rather surprising appearance in this book. Tiny and delicate, she was already well into her seventies. She can never have been beautiful, but certainly never stopped trying: bright yellow hair, thick makeup which was rather sticky when you kissed her; the effect was one of a very small tropical parrot. She was the widow of Sir Bache—pronounced Beach—Cunard, a son of the founder of the shipping line. In the twenties and thirties, when living in a huge mansion in Belgrave Square, she had been London's most prominent hostess, and in spite of wartime austerity she continued to entertain as lavishly as circumstances allowed. She had always looked on me as a sort of honorary godson—hence her visit to Upper Canada College—and whenever she invited my parents to her luncheon or dinner parties she always made a point of inviting me too. Though almost unbelievably well read—she never forgot a name or a plot—she may not have been a dazzling talker herself; but she was a superb manager of conversation which, with never more than eight people gathered round a small table, she invariably kept general, almost imperceptibly drawing out each guest in turn. The guests themselves were chosen with little regard for age or suitability: when she introduced them to each other she always added a one sentence description which got them talking to each other: "This is Stuart Preston—he is an American sergeant and he knows everything there is to know about Henry James." Just occasionally she went too far: "John Julius dear, tell us your views about love" was something of a challenge to a fourteen-year-old. But at that age one is always grateful to grown-ups who show an interest and take trouble: she was kind, generous, and treated me as an equal; and whatever shyness I may once have had she could almost instantly dispel. She also took me to my very first symphony concert—conducted, it need hardly be said, by Sir Thomas Beecham himself.

At the beginning of 1944, with the outcome of the war no longer in doubt, my father had been sent to Algiers, there to be Winston Churchill's personal representative to General de Gaulle until the liberation of Paris, on the understanding that he would then be our first postwar ambassador to France. So it was that halfway through my time at Eton, my family life suffered a sea change—and what it changed into was something rich and strange indeed. Paris was liberated at the end of August, my father was officially given the post of Ambassador that had been promised him, and early in September he and my mother moved into the British Embassy. He had never really enjoyed life in Algiers— unlike my mother, who had loved it—largely because he was always having to keep the peace between Winston Churchill and General de Gaulle. This ungrateful task—which had actually put no small strain on his thirty-year friendship with Churchill—was obviously by no means over; but the Paris Embassy made up for everything. My mother viewed the prospect with some alarm, but he was happy and that was enough for her. As for me, my principal emotion was, as I remember, wild excitement; I should be going over for the Christmas holidays—one of the first English civilians, and certainly one of the youngest, to set foot in the French capital after the German occupation.

———◦┬◦———

The summer of 1944 was a steady climax of excitement. At the beginning of June was D-Day, when the Allies landed in Normandy. There was not an Eton room without a huge wall map, on which we marked—with shadings and tiny flags—the lines of the British and American advance. During the holidays I had hoped to join my parents in Algiers, but not surprisingly this proved impossible; I went first for a week or two to stay with my Aunt Letty Benson at Compton Bassett in Wiltshire, and then on to my other Aunt Marjorie Anglesey at Plas Newydd. It was there that the real excitement began, with the news of the sudden allied breakthrough and the landings on the south coast of France. Every day brought news of huge advances; then, at the end of August, came the liberation of Paris. My parents returned hot-foot from Algiers, and around the middle of September, escorted by a squadron of RAF fighters, flew off to take up residence in the British Embassy.

In fact, they could not do so quite as soon as they had expected. The Embassy's diplomatic status had been respected throughout the German occupation, and proved to be bursting with the possessions of British residents in Paris and elsewhere in the country who had piled them into the building four years previously for safekeeping. It was a good fortnight before the hundreds of cabin trunks, skis, tennis rackets, and birdcages could be cleared and somehow returned to their owners. In the interim my parents lived in the Bristol Hotel, almost directly opposite the Embassy across the Faubourg St. Honoré. On their very first evening they found themselves going down in the lift with Mr. and Mrs. P.G. Wodehouse.

Here was embarrassment indeed. The Wodehouses, virtually alone among British residents in France, had made no effort to leave the country in 1940 and had consequently spent the war in Nazi Germany, as guests of Hitler's government. During their time in Berlin, Wodehouse had at German instigation made a series of broadcasts to America. These were not overtly political—he had absolutely no interest in or understanding of politics, which was why he and his wife had not returned to England like everyone else—but they suggested that the Nazis were really perfectly decent chaps, and that the whole war was really unnecessary and rather ridiculous. As such they played straight into the hands of the isolationist camp, undoing much of the good work that my father had hoped to do on his lecture tour. When he went in 1940 to the Ministry of Information he had overruled the BBC—something that would have been impossible in peacetime—and ordered them to withdraw their objection to a swinging attack on Wodehouse by one of the most vitriolic of British journalists, William Connor ("Cassandra") of the *Daily Mirror*. The Wodehouses were never convicted, and—though they spent the rest of their lives in America—were over the years tacitly forgiven; but in 1944, with the war still raging, they were generally considered little better than traitors. There could certainly be no question of them living in the same hotel as the British Ambassador. They were accordingly shifted to another one, equally commodious; who actually paid their bills I never discovered.

Within a day or two of my parents' departure for Paris I returned to Eton, thinking only of their promise that I should join them for the Christmas holidays. But in those days going to France was easier said than done. The war was still on, all air transport was in the hands of the RAF and, as Christmas approached, the weather grew progressively and predictably nastier. My father had returned to London a short time before our intended departure, and he and I were due to fly back to Paris together; but now for four days we shared a small room in the Dorchester Hotel. It was a boring and frustrating time, but there were two high points: we went to see Laurence Olivier's film of *Henry V,* and on the third day my father took me to lunch at 10 Downing Street with Winston Churchill.

I had met the great man several times as a child, when he and his wife Clemmie came down to Bognor; but in those days he was merely a politician in the wilderness; now, having brought us to the point of victory as Prime Minister, he was the hero of the world. The other two guests were Lord Salisbury and—rather surprisingly—the Bishop of Winchester, who was apparently a possible candidate for Canterbury and had come, as it were, on approval. The Prime Minister was dressed in his "siren suit"— which might have been known as battledress had it not been made of black velvet—and, to my surprise and delight, did not ignore me as I had expected but asked me a great many questions about my life, my school, even my thoughts on the war. I did not show up well. This was the time of the flying bombs; and at one moment, fearing a concentration of too many boys in one place, the Eton authorities had decided to cancel the daily services in Chapel. The Prime Minister asked whether the boys minded: I replied that they were only too pleased—Chapel was generally considered a pretty good bore, and there was a general feeling that a single Sunday service was more than enough. This proved a most unfortunate mistake. His face clouded over. "In my view," he said sternly, "they should be angry that the pattern of their lives should be upset by these dastardly contrivances. If necessary they should make a peaceful demonstration and *demand* that the services be restored." My father stepped in with a spirited defense. Boys, he pointed out, would be boys; they could hardly be expected to see things in such a light. But the Prime Minister continued to frown, shaking his head sadly from side to side, before the conversation fortunately turned to other matters. I was surprised indeed when, just as we left, he took me aside, fumbled in his pocket and smilingly drew two pound notes from his wallet.

A pound was a lot of money then, perhaps twenty or thirty times what it is now; few people had ever tipped me more than one. I was, I felt, forgiven.

Finally the weather cleared, and just two days before Christmas we bumped down at Le Bourget—to the inexpressible relief of my mother, who was waiting for us at the airfield (in those days it could hardly have been described as an airport) convinced, as she always was, that we had both been killed. I still remember the drive into Paris through the deserted streets, passing the great landmarks that I dimly remembered from childhood visits—six years is a long time when one is growing up—and finally swinging in through the great *porte-cochère* on the Faubourg St. Honoré, crunching across the gravel and drawing up in front of the British Embassy.

———— ⊙╬⊙ ————

Its splendor filled me with awe. The former home of Napoleon's sister Pauline Borghese, and bought by the Duke of Wellington soon after Waterloo, it was far and away the grandest and most beautiful house we had ever lived in. At the far end of the superb enfilade of drawing rooms on the first floor was Pauline's bedroom, with hangings of crimson silk. Her *retour d'Egypte* bed, with ancient Egyptian figures and sphinxes carved at each corner, was still there. It was perhaps a little short and narrow by modern standards, but my mother wasn't going to pass up an opportunity like that: she and my father were to sleep happily in it for the next three years. My own accommodation was a good deal more modest: a couple of simply furnished rooms on the mezzanine floor. But it suited me to perfection.

I have several clear memories of that first Christmas holiday in Paris. First there was the perishing cold; it was the most savage winter the city had experienced for fifty years, and the British

Embassy was one of the few buildings that had any heating. We were also among the still fewer that could provide limitless gin and whisky, obtained at tax-free, privileged, NAAFI[1] prices—around sixpence a bottle. From the start, my mother instituted free-for-all drinks parties in the *salon vert* every night at 6:30 PM, open to all friends, French and English alike, who cared to drop in. Of the English, the first—he had arrived in Paris, I think, even before my parents—was their old friend Victor Rothschild. A Cambridge scientist now in uniform, he had already won the George Medal for his bravery in defusing antipersonnel bombs; what he was doing in Paris I never quite knew. When he first arrived he was billeted at the YWCA, which made my father weep with laughter ("Since you're neither Y, W, nor C . . ."). He then moved briefly into the Embassy, but before long managed to take over the Rothschild family house in the Avenue de Marigny, together with his friend the philosopher Stuart Hampshire and his secretary Tess Mayor, whom he soon afterwards married. I shall always be grateful to Victor for taking me under his wing; it was he, I shall always remember, who gave me my first jazz piano lessons—I later had more from a black professional who came twice a week to the Embassy—and bore me off to my first Paris nightclub, the Bal Tabarin, whose topless showgirls roused me to a fever-pitch of excitement.

In those very early days, entertaining constituted something of a problem: it was not always easy to know who had been a hero of the Resistance, who a died-in-the-wool collaborationist. More than once a lunch or dinner guest would glance round the room on his arrival and murmur to my mother that he was sorry but he could not possibly sit at the same table as Monsieur so-and-so, whose shady dealings with the Germans were common knowledge. Eventually

---

1 The Navy, Army, and Air Force Institute, which provided additional food and drink for members of the armed forces.

my parents resorted to submitting every guest list to their friend Gaston Palewski, at the time *chef de cabinet* to General de Gaulle; with his help they succeeded in filtering out most of the undesirables, though even then there were the occasional embarrassments.

An example of the many dubious wartime reputations was that of the great Maurice Chevalier—the subject of one of my clearest recollections of that extraordinary month. The war was still on, and the Supreme Headquarters of the Allied Expeditionary Force—SHAEF—was at Versailles, which was consequently teeming with British and American servicemen. Another universal acronym at the time was that of ENSA, an organization which existed to entertain the troops; and at Christmas 1944 ENSA had sent out, to Marie-Antoinette's exquisite little theater at Versailles, a rather second-rate production of *The Merry Widow*— starring, as I remember, that long forgotten husband-and-wife team Cyril Richard and Madge Elliott. One evening just after Christmas my parents and I went to see it, were invited backstage in the interval to meet the cast, and were astonished to see a tall man with a protruding lower lip, wearing an immaculate dinner jacket and, rather more surprisingly, a straw boater. It could have been no one else but Chevalier. His record during the occupation had not been above suspicion; on the other hand there had been no formal accusation and what, after all, did one have to do to be a collaborationist? It was said that he had sung for the Germans; but if one or two members of the *Wehrmacht* came into your nightclub you couldn't very well stop the orchestra and refuse to perform to them: to do so would have been a very short cut to a concentration camp. The last act of *The Merry Widow* is set in Maxim's; there is therefore the possibility of bringing on anyone or anything as part of the cabaret, and we were told that Chevalier had asked to come on, unadvertised, unannounced and unpaid, for his first performance since the Liberation, to see how he would be received. And so, during that last act, the Master of Ceremonies suddenly bellowed "Your own, your very own, Maurice Chevalier!" And on he came.

His reception was muted. The audience, consisting almost entirely of men and women in khaki, was taken by surprise. Had they not heard that he had collaborated? On the other hand if he had, would he be with them now? They applauded, but by no means uproariously. Chevalier must have felt the tenseness; anyway, he started off—and within five minutes the entire audience was eating out of his hand. They cheered and cheered; and when after three or four songs he bowed, waved his boater, and walked off, they refused to let him go. Back he came for one encore, and then another, and then another. Instead of the ten minutes that had been foreseen he was there for a good forty; and when he finished there seemed little point in continuing with the adventures of Prince Danilo. It was my first experience of star quality—and never to this day have I seen that quality more spectacularly demonstrated.

Those Paris days—from that time onwards I returned every holiday—were, I now recognize, an extraordinary experience; stolid, unimaginative child that I was, I seem to have taken them very much for granted. I wandered around that palatial house, occasionally taking Russian lessons but spending much of my time strumming on the piano in the *salon vert* in a desultory sort of way, never getting very much better. My mother spent hours a day with me, taking me to the Louvre and the Musée de Cluny to see the tapestries of the Lady and the Unicorn—since she had a thing about unicorns—and a rather dotty little waxwork museum along the Grands Boulevards called the Musée Grévin for which she also had a particular affection; but I remember no particular excitement. I don't think I was actually bored, but I tended to take things as they came. Why did I not buy myself a really good guidebook and get to know Paris properly? Or go back to serious piano lessons? Five years later, older and a little more mature, I should have. But it was then that I had the time, and the opportunity; and—to my lasting shame and regret—I wasted them both.

The trouble was that I was just a bit too young: still an awkward adolescent, superficially sophisticated perhaps for my age, but at bottom a rather slow developer without any real understanding or appreciation of what was going on around me. There, for example, almost every evening, were all the great and famous of the French artistic and literary world—writers like Jean Cocteau, designers like Christian Bérard, actors like Louis Jouvet, assembling nightly in the *salon vert* where I would call them by their first names and mix them dry martinis or massive whisky-and-sodas; but although my French was fluent enough, neither my conversational powers nor my understanding were up to the challenge. Had I been eighteen instead of fifteen, I should have got a thousand times more out of it all and, I like to think, acquitted myself rather better.

Nevertheless, my memories of those evening parties are many and varied. There was Colette, barefoot and with her great fuzzy halo of hair, being carried bodily in by a large elderly gentleman and holding court from a sofa; there were those two arch villains Molotov and Vyshinsky—for the Paris Foreign Ministers Conference began in 1945—together with the Soviet Ambassador Mr. Bogomolov, whom my mother asked if he could arrange for me to go and stay with a family in Moscow or Leningrad for a few months to improve my Russian. He replied tonelessly: "*Chez nous ce n'est pas la coutume.*"[2] I remember too another Russian

---

2 "With us it is not the custom."

diplomat finishing his drink and then, to my mother's astonishment, crunching up his glass and swallowing it. This elicited a furious diatribe from his wife, to which he made a spirited reply. When my mother asked him what she had said he confessed that she had reproached him for his bad manners; he had defended himself on the grounds that she frequently did it herself, to which she had merely said that was beside the point—she didn't like *him* doing it. Then there was Isaiah Berlin, later to be my Oxford tutor, not only the most brilliant but also the funniest man I had ever met, refusing a very small drink on the grounds that it would induce "complete stupefaction." Best of all I remember an evening when Christian Bérard—always known as Bébé—painter, designer, and book illustrator, gloriously unkempt, with hair to his shoulders and a bushy brown beard full of cigarette ash (twenty years later it would hardly have been noticed, but the style was rare indeed in the 1940s), turned up with his pet pug under his arm. Soon after his arrival he put it on the floor, where it instantly deposited a formidable turd. Bébé, horrified, unhesitatingly—and to the immense admiration, it must be said, of all around him—picked it up and put it in his pocket. My mother always said that it was the best example of good manners she had ever seen.

Perhaps the most memorable of all our visitors in those days were Prince and Princess Felix Youssoupoff. Some thirty years previously he had murdered Rasputin; but in those days he had been still in his twenties, so even now he was scarcely more than middle-aged. The Princess, niece of the last Tsar, was immensely imperial in manner; he was a degree more relaxed, though it was generally agreed that there was a sinister side. His hair was dyed very black—it may even have been a wig—and there were rumors, as far as I know unsubstantiated, of necrophilia. My mother had known him when he first came to London before the First World

War and had become unofficially engaged to her eldest sister Marjorie. She remembered him as dazzlingly good-looking and intensely romantic, wearing exotic Russian clothes and singing incomprehensible Russian gypsy songs to the guitar. Dreaming doubtless of balls in the Yousoupoff Palace at St. Petersburg, evening visits to the gypsies, and journeys through the birch forests in sleigh or troika, she encouraged the match all she could; in the circumstances, we can only be grateful that it did not materialize.

Then came the Rasputin affair; the Yousoupoffs fled St. Petersburg (or Petrograd, as it was by then called) on the night of the murder and settled in Paris. They had brought out some money and a good many jewels, but by the thirties they were in serious financial trouble. The windfall came just in time. Metro-Goldwyn-Mayer made a film about the affair, in the course of which they implied that the Prince had lured Rasputin to the Palace with the promise of his wife—virtually the only lady of the court with whom the rascal monk had not slept. In fact, it is far from certain that Yousoupoff did not do precisely that; he sued none the less for criminal libel, claiming that the suggestion was an insult both to his wife and to himself, and won substantial damages. The case was heard in London, and my mother was in the court for each of the three days it lasted. She often told me how extraordinary it was to sit in an English court of law and listen to a self-confessed murderer giving a detailed account of a hideous and peculiarly messy crime—not from the dock but the witness box, where he was immune from prosecution.

We all looked forward to the investitures, when my father had to award decorations—usually the King's Medal for Courage—to the heroes and heroines of the Resistance. Even now my eyes fill with tears when I think of them. Most were humble men and women from the remotest areas of France, quite often simple peasants who had never before been to Paris. Some had sheltered escaped British prisoners for weeks until they could be provided with false documentation and taken across the border into neutral Spain; others had regularly slipped out under cover of darkness to light a landing strip for the tiny little aircraft that flew from England to drop weapons, radio equipment, and occasionally undercover agents; yet others had planted bombs under railway viaducts or blown up Nazi staff cars. All, in doing so, had risked their lives. Some had been arrested and tortured by the Gestapo, but had refused to talk and on release had instantly resumed their old activities. And they were not, for the most part, stalwart young men; far more often they were middle-aged, even elderly women, who worked on the land or helped in their husband's garage or served in the village shop. Eric Duncannon, my father's secretary, would read their citations, his voice choking with emotion; then a small, frightened figure would step forward and my father would pin on the medal, tears pouring down his cheeks. These were, he used to say, the most moving moments of his life.

We were by no means always in Paris. An ambassador's duties take him all over the country, and my father always tried to arrange his provincial tours to coincide with my holidays. But my very first expedition was with my mother alone. She had been made *marraine*—"godmother"—to a French regiment, the *Premiers Chasseurs d'Afrique;* and early in January, 1945—while the war was still on—she arranged to go with me to visit them at the front. I wore my uniform of the school training corps—khaki battledress with "Eton College" on the shoulders—and off we drove to Strasbourg, where a French army car took us to the headquarters of the Supreme Commander of the French Sector, General de Lattre de Tassigny. Here lunch was waiting, during which the General questioned me closely about my school life, showing particular interest in the fagging system. I described it as best I could, finishing up with a brief description of what happened when someone shouted

"Boy!" The General, much intrigued, announced his intention of instituting a similar system at the headquarters; several of the junior officers at the table visibly paled.

After lunch my mother and I, almost asphyxiated by our host's copious ministrations of eau de cologne, joined him in his car for his daily tour of the front—and the front it really was: shells bursting, buildings burning, and once even a group of German prisoners emerging from a house with their arms above their heads. Every half hour or so, we would stop while maps were unfolded and senior officers made their reports. Occasionally, too, we would pass a military lorry which would be flagged down—there was no mistaking the General's enormous car, with four stars to front and back and the hooter blaring—so that he could gently reprimand the driver for careless driving, which usually meant failing to get out of the way quickly enough. His attitude was more fatherly than anything else: the terrified soldiers were always addressed as *tu* and frequently as *mon petit*.

That drive—which took us to every part of the French Sector—lasted for nearly twelve hours. Shortly before the end, a sudden blaze of light appeared ahead of us, and I heard the General chuckle to himself. We turned a corner—and there, a hundred yards ahead of us, was the Rhine, floodlit as I am sure it had never been before and spanned by a bridge recently completed by French army engineers. We got out of the car and de Lattre invited my mother to baptize the *fanion*; she naturally accepted. Her only anxiety lay in the fact that she had no idea what a *fanion* was; but before she could betray her ignorance—presumably with "bring the little lad along" or words to that effect—a long lance was thrust in her hand, bearing at the end a triangular pennant. This she obediently dipped into the rushing water below. As she did so a military band played a fanfare followed by both national anthems, after which the delighted General led us back to the car.

We eventually returned at 2 AM to the headquarters, where dinner had been waiting for some four hours. The staff, pale before, were now ashen. Not only were they dying of hunger; they had expected us well before midnight, the General had not thought to tell them of our delay, and they had been convinced that we were all dead. The forest through which we had driven was known to be full of Germans still at liberty and an ambush, we were told, would have been perfectly possible. My mother and I were by this time longing for bed; but our host, showing no sign of fatigue, insisted that we tuck into an enormous four-course dinner before letting us go.

De Lattre had become a friend—though I'm not sure that I ever saw him again. General de Gaulle was, it need hardly be said, a friend to no one. Greatness he undoubtedly possessed, but few great men have ever been more impossible to deal with. My mother remembered one ghastly dinner in Algiers when she found herself sitting next to him. She prided herself on being able to crack the hardest of conversational nuts, but now she realized that she had met her match. By the pudding, in sheer despair, she had embarked on the wildlife of Australia—an unfortunate choice of subject, since her French vocabulary hardly ran to it: "*Et puis, mon général, il y a les* wallabys, *et aussi les* wombats. *Ah, ils sont si amusants, les* wombats. . . ."

The General (mournfully, with a deep sigh): "*Il paraît qu'il y a aussi les kangarous.*"

Winston Churchill made no secret of his detestation. There was one occasion while she and my father were in Algiers when the Prime Minister had suffered a very slight stroke and had gone to Marrakesh to recuperate. De Gaulle had suddenly announced his intention of flying down to pay him a formal visit, and it was my father who had to break the news. The first reaction was categorical refusal.

"No Duffy, I shall not see him."

"Winston, I'm sorry but I'm afraid you must. You know how prickly he is. If you refuse to see him he'll take it as a mortal insult. It need only be for ten minutes."

"I told you Duffy, I shall not see him. I am here to recover my health. Ten minutes with that man will bring about a serious relapse."

"Winston, I beg you. I know what he's like, and so do you. He'll take it as an insult, he'll never forgive you, and he'll just be more of a nightmare than ever. To both of us. So please, Winston, please...."

(Long and pregnant pause.) "All right then. Just for you, Duffy, I will. But it will be for five minutes only." (Another, still longer pause; then, threateningly:) "And I shall wear my Chinese dressing gown."

My only meeting with de Gaulle occurred in very different circumstances, on the second anniversary of D-Day in June, 1946. I had recently learnt to drive and the occasion marked my first long journey alone—to Arromanches on the coast of Normandy, where a service had been held on the beaches in the morning, attended by de Gaulle, my parents, and assorted French dignitaries. After the ceremony, a buffet lunch had been laid on in a local hotel. I drove up that morning from Paris, got lost, missed the ceremony, and arrived at the lunch at around two o'clock—to find that it was virtually over; people were sitting around on sofas and armchairs with plates and glasses lying around, almost all of them empty. On one of the sofas was General de Gaulle, to whom for the first time my father introduced me. I still remember my astonishment as he rose to his feet—all six foot six of him—to shake my hand. It had never occurred to me that so distinguished a figure would get up to greet a sixteen-year-old boy; but he did, and I have never forgotten it.

During our extremely brief conversation I had noticed at his side an almost untouched plate of delicious looking apple pie. Having had no lunch and feeling ravenous, I pointed it out to my mother and whispered: "Is that the General's? And if so do you think he's going to eat it?" "You'd better ask him," she replied; and so, greatly daring, I did. The General politely confirmed that it was indeed his, that he had no intention of eating it and was delighted that I should; unfortunately, he added, he had spilt rather a lot of cigarette ash on it. I said that it would be an honor for me to eat his cigarette ash—an appalling piece of over-the-top flattery which even now I blush to recall; but it seemed to go down rather well. The apple pie certainly did.

My very next holiday—at Easter, just a month before the end of the war in Europe—was to me even more exciting: my mother took me for a week to Algiers. She told me that it was because she wanted me to see the place she had loved so much when she and my father were there the previous year, a statement which I am sure was true as far as it went; but her paramount reason—which, such was my innocence, occurred to me only long afterwards— was to see Bloggs Baldwin, son of the former Prime Minister, who was in the RAF and had been stationed there for some time. He had always been a family friend—indeed, we now know that he had leapt to my defense in 1932 when I was three years old[3]—and some time in 1944 they had, I now realize, begun a lighthearted affair. Such things—second nature to my father—were rare occurrences in my mother's life; sex was never as important to her

---

3 Only a few years ago the present Lord Baldwin of Bewdley, while going through some family papers with the intention of selling them, came upon a written wager between his father and Evelyn Waugh which he kindly allowed me to buy. It now hangs in our loo, and reads as follows: "October 18, 1932: A WAGER: Boaz [early nickname of Waugh] bets that when John Julius Cooper reaches the age of 25 (twenty-five) he will be voted to be a shit by a committee of competent judges. This will be in the year 1954. The wager is for £5 only, provided that A.W. Baldwin is unmarried; in which case the stakes are £1."

as were admiration and affection, and neither of them would ever have allowed their relationship to get out of hand; Bloggs's marriage was as safe as her own. But—although it was many years before I was to put two and two together—I could already sense her happiness, and her excitement.

That week in Algiers was my first encounter with the Muslim world. We flew from Marseille, arriving at Maison Blanche airfield quite late at night, and were driven into the city in an open jeep; it was one of the most exhilarating experiences of my life. From that very first moment, I was entranced by the snow-white buildings in the moonlight, the mosques and minarets, the calls to prayer, the mysterious Arabic writing everywhere, the noise and bustle of the innumerable market stalls which seemed to stay open all night, the smell of spices, and a thousand other things less immediately identifiable. Nowadays it would simply have reminded me of the lower reaches of the Edgware Road; then, so far as I was concerned, it was a Hollywood film come to life: one expected to bump into Humphrey Bogart, or Peter Lorre, or the gargantuan Sidney Greenstreet, around every corner.

We stayed that first night in the Aletti Hotel, but the next morning discovered that the exotic Moorish house where my parents had spent most of the previous year was untenanted, so the three of us moved in. I must have been distinctly *de trop*, though I was never allowed to feel it; on the other hand Bloggs had his work to do and could not be with us all the time—a fact which enabled my mother and me to spend an unforgettable night in a little town on the very edge of the desert called Bou-Saada. There, in the Transatlantic Hotel, we watched as the local girls, not so much topless as stark naked, danced for our delight—an entertainment which I found strangely disconcerting; and there too, the following morning, we called on Miss Fitzsimmons.

Miss Fitzsimmons was one of that curious breed of elderly English female eccentric—I suspect more common then than now—who settled in some far-flung corner of the world and lived there, alone and for the most part completely happy, for half a century. When my mother had been in Bou-Saada the previous summer she had been walking round the town, which was composed largely of mud huts, and had suddenly come upon one whose front door bore a wooden plaque on which was carved, in large Gothic letters, the single word FITZSIMMONS. Intrigued, she had knocked at the door. Miss Fitzsimmons had answered it herself, welcomed my mother as a long-lost friend and told her the story of her life; and now, at my mother's urging, she told it again for my benefit. She had come to Bou-Saada for a holiday when still in her twenties, and had fallen in love with Ben, whom she described as a near genius but who had not advanced beyond the post of camel keeper at the Transatlantic. She and Ben had shacked up together; he had taken her to meet his tribe in the deep Sahara, where she had fallen seriously ill but had been cured by some appalling local technique—which she described in the most lurid detail but which I have now, perhaps fortunately, forgotten. After many happy years Ben had died—he had been considerably older—and she had remained in Bou-Saada ever since. We asked her what she did with herself nowadays; "Oh," she said, "I make myself useful."

———⚬⟊⚬———

The next major excitement was the Nuremberg Trials. They had started in November, 1945—six months after the end of the war—and were held before a panel of eight judges, two British, two American, two French, and two Russian. In those early postwar days normal travel was still by train, and at the end of the Christmas recess the two British judges, Sir Geoffrey Lawrence (who presided over the whole thing) and Sir Norman Birkett,[4] passed through Paris on their way back to Nuremberg. With Sir Norman were his wife and son Michael, who was almost exactly my age; and to my excitement and delight they invited me to accompany them and stay a few days to watch the proceedings. That night we took the *wagon-lit*, arriving the next day in the frozen remains of Nuremberg, virtually flattened by Allied bombing. At nine o'clock on the following morning I took my seat in the Visitors' Gallery of the Palace of Justice—which had somehow remained standing—and excitedly adjusted my headphones: this was my first experience of simultaneous translation and I was determined to make the most of it.

And there they were below us, perhaps twenty yards away: apart from Hitler, Goebbels, and Himmler—who had committed suicide—all the other principal Nazi leaders whose names we had spoken with loathing throughout the war were arraigned before us in the dock, eleven of them in the front row, ten in the row behind. There in front of me was Goering, next to him Rudolf Hess, then Ribbentrop; further on were Admiral Doenitz, Ernst Kaltenbrunner—principally responsible for carrying out the "Final Solution," as the Holocaust was known—and the Jew baiter Julius Streicher; and they were only the beginning. Illuminated by harsh fluorescent light, they looked totally impassive, but at the same time drawn and haggard; I couldn't take my eyes off them. I noticed too that while they listened attentively on their earphones to all that was going on they never addressed a word to each other. Just before they walked out of the courtroom at lunchtime I had taken up a position by the door: as they walked past me I could have touched them. The three days I sat in the court room were not as exciting as many had been, but I

---

4 Later respectively Lord Oaksey and Lord Birkett.

was never bored for an instant. I felt that I was watching history, and whenever things threatened to get tedious there was always the simultaneous translation to play with. My hosts the Birketts were enchanting: she Swedish, he with an astonishing knowledge and love of English literature, his talk constantly punctuated by quotations, sometimes long enough as almost to qualify as recitations in their own right. As for Michael, after perhaps thirty years during which we never once saw each other he is now one of my dearest friends. (So, oddly enough, is the son of the other English judge, Geoffrey Lawrence, who as John Oaksey has ridden in eleven Grand Nationals—coming second in one of them—and was for many years Racing Correspondent of the *Daily Telegraph* and presenter of racing on Channel Four television. He too was at Nuremberg; but not, alas, at the same time as I was.)

When the time came for me to leave, a kind member of Sir Norman's staff, Gavin Cliff-Hodges, drove me across the mountains to St. Anton, where my mother was staying with her old Algiers friend Minou Béthouart, now married to the general commanding the French army in Austria. After a few days skiing, she took me on a sightseeing visit to Vienna, of which I have only one clear memory: a Sunday morning symphony concert which was the most electrifying I had ever heard. The young conductor, our program told us, was a certain Herbert von Karajan; we both made a note to remember the name if we ever heard it again.

The worst moment for my parents in all those Embassy days came in June, 1945, when Winston Churchill was defeated in the general election and the Labour party was returned to power. My father had never been a career diplomat; a Conservative politician, he had found himself Ambassador only because Churchill had thought him the right man to deal with his *bête noire,* de Gaulle. Now that the Conservatives were out, it seemed more than likely that the Cooper family would very soon be out too.

That we were not was due entirely to the new Foreign Secretary, Ernest Bevin. Rough-hewn—my mother maintained that he looked like a bit of Stonehenge—he had left school at eleven and was the warmest and most delightful of men. My parents loved and admired him, and he loved them in return. His affection for my mother was such that, one evening when she was showing him to his room she found herself seized in a huge bear hug and asked for "one sweet hour." Poor Ernie never had his hour; but soon afterwards, when the Foreign Ministers Conference opened in Paris and he was spending a night or two a week at the Embassy, she certainly gave him a wonderful time. There was one memorable summer evening after dinner when she packed him into her open car and drove him up to Montmartre for a drink in the Place du Tertre. He enjoyed every moment of it; the people around of course recognized him and cheered "*Eh, voilà Ernie! Bravo, Ernie!*" and he enjoyed that too. Could anyone imagine doing that with Gordon Brown?

Most evenings when he was staying with us ended up round the piano. My tone-deaf father was always trying to drag him away to discuss the conference; but Ernie, once settled in, would not be shifted. He knew all the old music hall songs by heart; my mother knew a good many of them; I, fortunately, was able to vamp adequate accompaniments; and away we went. *Daisy, The Old Kent Road, Down at the Old Bull and Bush, My Old Man said Follow the Van*—his repertoire was endless. Occasionally I would relinquish my seat at the piano to the Defense Secretary, A.V. Alexander. He too played by ear, in many respects far better than I did; but having been brought up a strict Methodist, he played everything like a hymn, in four part harmony—often with hilarious results. One evening, I remember, when the sing-song ended, we discovered that Ernie's detective had fallen sound asleep in the best armchair; when we woke him, he was copiously sick on the carpet. Ernie looked at him and smiled indulgently. "Poor chap," was all he said, "he must have had a bit too much."

————— ◦⊱◦ —————

But the brightest of all the stars that shone in the Embassy firmament was Louise de Vilmorin. The Vilmorins were—and, for all I know, still are—France's leading seedsmen, their name well known to all those, farmers and gardeners alike, who cultivate the soil. Louise, when she first came into our lives, must have been around forty. She had had two husbands: with the first, an American rather surprisingly named Leigh Hunt, she had lived, equally surprisingly, in Las Vegas—in the early thirties an inconsequential desert village very unlike it is today. There had followed a passionate affair with the dashing young author/aviator Antoine de Saint-Exupéry, after which she had married a Hungarian, Count Palffy, on whose vast estates she was living in September, 1939. Hungary soon came in on the German side; thus, for almost the entire duration of the war, she had remained in enemy territory. This did not at first improve her social standing when she returned to Paris after the Liberation; but to remain with your husband when the going got tough could not be considered a crime. In any case, not having been in France during the German occupation, she could hardly be accused of having collaborated.

I loved her from the start. I loved her gaiety, her superb sense of humor, and her ability to hold a dining table spellbound: she was the best and funniest *raconteuse* I have ever heard. But I also loved her for the immense trouble she took over me. Most of my parents' smart friends were pleasant enough, but didn't normally go out of their way—why should they?—to have long conversations with a sixteen-year-old boy. Louise on the other hand would talk to me for hours, grown-up to grown-up; sometimes, when my parents had some official engagement, she and I would have a *tête-à-tête* lunch together, when she would tell me about her life or ask me about mine. Afterwards she would teach me the wonderful old French songs of which she had an inexhaustible repertoire, and how to accompany myself on the guitar—a major step forward from the ukulele that I had strummed from the age of six. It seemed to me perfectly natural that she should have virtually moved into the Embassy, in which she made one of the top floor bedrooms for all practical purposes her own. I must have been one of the last people in my parents' circle to realize that she and my father were carrying on a passionate affair.

Did my mother know? Of course she did. And did she worry? Not in the least. "So common to mind," she used to say. She was well aware that she had a serially unfaithful husband; on the other hand, she was equally certain that she would always be the first in his affections. "They were the flowers," she said to me years later, "but I was the tree." She loved Louise as much as any of us— Paris gossips even hinted, quite unjustifiably, at a lesbian relationship—and was totally at ease in her company. Often they would drive off together, my mother at the wheel, to the *Marché aux Puces* (the Flea Market), or to some curious corner of Paris that Louise thought would amuse her. On at least one occasion the three of us went on a week's motoring holiday together, leaving my father behind. When finally his ardor cooled and he found a new attachment, it was on my mother's shoulder that Louise sobbed her heart out; and after he died and she had taken up first with Orson Welles and later with André Malraux, whenever she came to London it was with my mother that she would stay.

At this point we rather surprisingly fast-forward to the summer of 2006 and to the unlikely location of Port Erin, Isle of Man. Port Erin is the scene of an annual arts festival, at which— for I think the third time—I had been invited to lecture. I was accommodated most comfortably in the Ocean Castle Hotel, in a beautiful room overlooking the bay. Its en suite bathroom was papered in a rather unattractive color of old parchment, with a grayish design of which I took no particular notice—until I started brushing my teeth before bed. I then realized to my utter astonishment, that the grayish design was in fact an alternation of two four-line poems by Louise in her own exquisite and very distinctive handwriting which I knew almost as well as my own. The next morning I went to see the proprietor, who happened to be French. "Are you aware," I asked him, "that my bathroom is papered with the poems of my father's penultimate mistress, Louise de Vilmorin?" He shook his head. The paper had been there longer than he had. So who put it there, and why? I should dearly love to know.

Some months after our arrival at the Embassy, my mother found a country house. Never in her life had she ever been able to resist an open drive gate; she would swing in, take a brief look at the house then turn round and swing out again. If accosted by the owner, she had a regular routine: "Is this Mrs. Fordyce's house? No? Oh I'm so sorry" and off she would go. (Only once did this formula get her into trouble, when she received the reply "I *am* Mrs. Fordyce.") It chanced that in just this way, one afternoon in 1945, she found a perfectly beautiful small eighteenth-century house, with a garden running down to the artificial lake that extends eastward from the Château de Chantilly. There was no sign of life, so she rang the bell. The door was opened by an American soldier, who told her that the house belonged to Bill Bullitt, the prewar American Ambassador to Paris. Bullitt happened to be still in France, attached to SHAEF at Versailles, so my mother rang him up. He told her that he in fact leased the house before the war from the Institut de France, but that he had no intention of returning to it. The transfer was soon arranged: and the Château de Saint-Firmin was to be ours, first as a weekend retreat and then as a permanent home, for the next fifteen years.

Meanwhile my Eton life was approaching its end. Being quite good at exams I had mildly distinguished myself academically, but as a sportsman was generally known to be hopeless. I could have stayed on another year and become a member of Sixth Form, but there seemed little point: although the war was over, young men were still obliged to do compulsory National Service, and I knew that at any time after my eighteenth birthday in September 1947, I could expect to be called up. My father was a great believer in what is nowadays called a gap year—though the term was then unknown—and at Christmas 1946 I left.

I had never been unhappy at Eton; though the winter cold remained intense and the plumbing still left much to be desired, as we moved gradually up the school we were allotted larger and more comfortable rooms. Also, as far as we were concerned, having to fag was a thing of the past; we were fagmasters now, with fags of our own. Besides, I had many friends, both inside my house and in the rest of the school—although I see only two or three of them nowadays. Another advantage was that after taking School Certificate—the forerunner of GCE—we were allowed to specialize: I dropped the hated Latin and the mildly enjoyable Greek (both of which I now desperately regret) and mathematics and science (which I don't), and concentrated on modern languages: French and German principally, with Russian as an "extra study." A short essay in each language had to be delivered once a week, the German one in the old German handwriting which even then was rapidly growing obsolete. I find, rather to my surprise, that unlike most Germans I can still write it today.

On the other hand, Eton still seemed in many ways curiously old fashioned. It had no theater, no swimming pool; the little backwater of the Thames, Cuckoo Weir, in which we occasionally immersed ourselves, was said to have dysentery in every drop and would almost certainly be condemned by any modern health authority. Although there was an active Musical Society, music— with one or two exceptions—was poorly and inefficiently taught. It was a struggle to get more than half an hour's tuition a week, and no time was allowed for practice. (One of my several hopeless piano teachers made a practice of trying to twist off my right ear while I played to him; come to think of it, I suppose this too was a pass—though oddly enough it never occurred to me at the time.) Drawing was considered much more important, and was brilliantly taught by Wilfrid Blunt—though with me, alas, he was no more successful than my grandmother had been. At one moment I turned despairingly to pottery, but every time I inserted my thumb in the top of my neat castle of clay I pushed it too far and out it came at the bottom. Several times I sought to be excused these unnecessary humiliations and to use the spare time for piano practice, but always in vain.

Perhaps it was as a result of all this that I never loved Eton in the way that my father had loved it or as many of my friends did. I was never bullied; I was never unhappy; perhaps indeed—largely because I never questioned its values—I was more impressed by it at the time than I was afterwards. The fact remains that when I left in December, 1946, I did so without a pang of regret. In January, 1947, with some excitement and not a little trepidation, I embarked on the penultimate stage of my formal education and enrolled at the University of Strasbourg.

Chapter Five
Strasbourg and the Navy

ONCE I HAD decided to go to a French university, Strasbourg had been the obvious choice. Alsace—of which it is the capital—had been part of France before the Franco-Prussian War; after 1870 it had been annexed by Germany, and then in 1919 had been returned to France. Virtually every educated citizen was consequently fluent in both French and German, and most of them had German names; the local dialect, Alsatian, sounded like German spoken by a Welshman and was very much closer to German than it was to French. Here, it seemed, was the perfect place in which to polish up my second foreign language; and the fact that the University boasted what was almost certainly the best Russian faculty in the country gave me high hopes for progress in my third. Peter Storrs—nephew of the still celebrated orientalist Sir Ronald—was at that time Director of the official British Reading Room, and my father asked him to find a suitable local family prepared to accept me as a lodger. His choice fell on Monsieur and Madame Paul Schmidt; it could hardly have been a better one.

The Schmidts were both in their early thirties. Paul was a lawyer, a rising light of the Strasbourg bar; his wife Betty was attractive, possessed of considerable charm as well as a wonderful figure, and an excellent tennis player. Both were highly intelligent and well read; neither spoke a word of English. They had two little boys— they must have been about five and three—and an extremely hostile Airedale called Carlo who lived on the first floor landing and terrified me, growling threateningly every time I passed. I had a charming room at the top of the house and shared the single bathroom with all four Schmidts. Every morning, after breakfast with a bowl of steaming coffee and *Les Dernières Nouvelles d'Alsace*, I would walk down Rue Herder (we lived at No. 27) to the Place Golbéry where I took the tram to the University, coming back for lunch—which, in approved Alsatian fashion, was invariably followed by a glass of schnapps—and sometimes (but not always) returning there in the afternoon. In my spare time I took lessons on the piano accordion, visited Peter Storrs and other friends (including an enchanting family called Schoen, whose younger daughter Francine I rather fancied), and played furious games of ping-pong in the local café with Betty Schmidt.

It was after one of these sessions, just as we were leaving the café and were between its two sets of double doors that I suddenly found myself seized by Betty and kissed as I had never been kissed before. Totally inexperienced and still fairly insecure, I felt nothing but embarrassment: a reaction that must have been somewhat disappointing to Betty on each of the many subsequent occasions on which the same thing occurred—more than once, before Paul's return from work, on the living room sofa. She was not, I think, in love with me—how could she have been?—but she probably liked the idea of giving me some practical knowledge of the facts of life, and perhaps even making an end of my seventeen-year-old virginity. Alas, she failed: that same old embarrassment held me back, as did certain qualms of conscience; it seemed a strange way of repaying my host's hospitality.

In later years I have often regretted this cowardice—which, more than anything else, is what it really was. Even had I been ready, Betty might never have allowed me much beyond first base; and even if she had, there would have been plenty of time for those qualms. When I think back, I realize that Paul was probably perfectly aware of the situation, of which he showed absolutely no sign of disapproval. If his wife had succeeded in devirginizing me she would probably have told him all about it; and he, quite possibly, would have reacted to the news more with amusement than with indignation. Besides, we are often told that a sympathetic older woman at the right moment can provide the best possible initiation into the mysteries of sex; and I have little doubt that a gentle lesson or two from Betty Schmidt would not only have done me a power of good at the time but would also have spared me several awkward situations in the years to come. Too bad: I had my opportunity and I passed it by: there's no more to be said.

Anyway, Betty never seemed to mind my unsatisfactory responses (though she never gave up trying) and we remained firm friends, going to the theater and concerts—one with Yehudi Menuhin and his dazzling teacher Georges Enesco—playing tennis when the weather grew warmer, and of course keeping up the ping-pong. The Schmidts also led an active social life and made me a part of all their innumerable dinner parties. There were several particularly enjoyable evenings in May during the asparagus season, when a dozen of us would pack into three or four little Citroens and drive off to the nearby village of Hoerdt—*capitale de l'asperge*—for dinner. This would consist exclusively of vast platefuls of asparagus: not our slender green stems but the fat white ones, turning a pale green at the tip and consumed with industrial quantities both of mayonnaise and of that glorious

Alsatian wine—Sylvaner, Traminer, or Riesling—which contrives to be fruity without being remotely sweet. The evenings would always end with singing. There was a special asparagus song fraught with *double-entendre*, the verses of which were largely unprintable but were each followed by the chorus:

> *Asperge, asperge divine,*
> *Pour nous tu n'as que des appâts;*
> *Nos roses ont des épines,*
> *Asperge, tu n'en a pas.*[1]

Not for the first or last time, I had reason to be grateful to Louise de Vilmorin. Thanks to her I had any number of French songs of my own to contribute, which were always applauded to the echo and did much to make me feel one of the gang. It would be after midnight by the time we drove home. Fortunately the dread breathalyzer was still unknown; had it existed, we should none of us have stood a chance.

I left Strasbourg in the summer of 1947, and Betty and I soon lost contact: it was fifty-five years before I heard from her again. Then, in December, 2002, she telephoned me—having presumably discovered my whereabouts from somebody in the European Parliament. She sounded bright as a button, telling me that she was then a widow of eighty-six and that she had been for three consecutive years women's veteran (i.e. over sixty) tennis champion of France. She still played three times a week. For some months we were back in regular communication. I sent her a French translation of the above paragraphs—pointing out that she emerges from the story a

---

1 I fear it loses something in translation:
> Asparagus, divine asparagus,
> For us you have nothing but charm;
> Our roses may have thorns,
> Asparagus, you have none.

good deal more creditably than I do—and she unhesitatingly gave me permission to publish them. Then one day, on the telephone, she told me that she was recovering from pneumonia, after which there was silence. Letters and telephone calls went alike unanswered. She has at last gone, I fear, to the great tennis court in the sky.

My life at the University was rather less rewarding than my life with the Schmidts. The mere six months of my stay allowed no possibility of my taking any degree, nor was there any real tutorial system to keep me up to the mark: I don't remember writing a single essay in either French or German. The Russian faculty struck me as a good deal better, largely because there were surprisingly few students; but its head, Professor Boris Unbegaun—whom I was to encounter later at Oxford—was principally interested in Old Church Slavonic and the morphology of the Russian noun in the twelfth and thirteenth centuries; there was thus little opportunity of improving my conversation. Much the same was true of my German. Just about everyone in Strasbourg could speak it, but after five years of Nazi rule—during which the use of French had been forbidden—hardly anybody would: the notices in all the trams reading *C'est chic de parler français* were unnecessary. Again and again with the Schmidts and their friends I would try to switch into German; they would play along with me for a sentence or two, but switch back at the earliest possible moment into French again. (Among themselves they always spoke Alsatian, but they were far too well mannered to do so in my presence.) And so, although Strasbourg was enormous fun socially, academically it was a flop.

———⟨⟩———

The university term came to an end in June, and I returned to Paris. I was due for call-up any day after my eighteenth birthday in September, so in August my parents took me off to their favorite hotel in the world. It was a small fifteenth-century building, rising from the very edge of Lake Garda, at the tip of a little promontory called San Vigilio; before the war they had gone there every summer. The proprietor was a ruffianly old Irishman called Walsh—known to everyone as Leonardo. He drank like a fish and was frequently plastered, occasionally even abusive; but he was a memorable character and a superb cook, and we loved him. There were only about eight rooms, all fairly primitive; none had a bathroom (which didn't matter much as there was very little hot water anyway) and the beds were hard as rocks. But the view from the front rooms was ravishing. There was a tiny little harbor to one side where the fishing boats would tie up in the early morning, so that one would wake to find the window completely blocked by a huge orange sail; there was no sound, as my mother once wrote to a friend, "but the sound of peace, and a girl rinsing her hair." Breakfast, lunch and dinner would all be served on a little terrace, also looking out across the lake, with a tiny fifteenth-century chapel closing it off on the far side. The table cloths were virginally white, the silver shone; the food consisted largely of fish taken straight out of the lake. Service was provided partly by Leonardo himself, partly by two elderly chambermaids in rustling black bombazine, one of whom possessed the largest bottom I have ever seen on a human being.

Having driven down from Paris, we had my mother's convertible at the door; and one morning she said "Why don't we go to Venice for the day?" She and my father knew the city well from prewar days, when eight people could rent a floor of a palazzo for £100 a month, with gondolier. It was only two hours away along the *autostrada*, so we made an early start and were there soon after ten. It was my first visit of well over two hundred, and from the moment of our arrival I was hooked. We took a gondola from the car park in the Piazzale Roma down the Grand Canal—in those days gondolas were a tenth of the price that they are today and were normally used, as they always had been, as taxis—and it seemed to me then that I had never seen anything so beautiful. I have had no reason since to change my opinion. The Piazza hit me like a bombshell. That afternoon my mother had an appointment to go and see an old friend. "Right," said my father to me, "now I'll show you Venice." The first thing to understand about the city, he explained, was that however beautiful the individual churches and palaces might be, the greatest miracle of all was the *ensemble*: Venice itself, seen as a single, unique work of art. We would therefore spend the next two hours walking through it, during which time we would enter two buildings only: at the beginning, St. Mark's; at the end, Harry's Bar.

And then, after meeting up with my mother on the Piazza and a farewell drink at Florian, we took the gondola back to the car park. It was dusk, and the lights were coming on in the palaces along the Grand Canal. I imagined all the lucky people living in them, and the innumerable parties that were soon to start, and I felt a lump in my throat. Never do I remember leaving any city with a more aching feeling of regret. Little did I know how important a part, twenty-five years later, Venice was going to play in my life.

———❦———

My National Service, meanwhile, was looming nearer and nearer. On the whole I think I quite looked forward to it, though with certain misgivings. At least I was not going into the Army—a prospect which would have filled me with gloom. I had done my stint in the Eton College Junior Training Corps, and remembered all too clearly those appalling Field Days, many of them spent crawling on my stomach through Windsor Great Park on dank November afternoons; the thought of 365 of these every

year was more than I could bear. I had therefore put myself down
for the Navy—and had, to my delight, been accepted. The Navy
did not at first seem particularly eager to have me: I had to kick my
heels for six months rather than the expected three. But finally the
call-up papers arrived; and on the last day of 1947—ten days or so
after the farewell ball given by my parents at the Embassy—I presented myself at HMS *Royal Arthur*, Corsham, Wiltshire.

Every naval conscript did his basic training at *Royal Arthur*,
which, like all shore bases, pretended that it was a ship. The very
first command that I received—from the Petty Officer in charge
of admissions—was to put my suitcase down on the deck, and
we went on from there. My class (number 701, I still remember)
was about thirty strong. It included one old school friend, Miles
Huntington-Whiteley; for the rest, my new *oppos*—naval slang
for friends—were a pretty mixed bunch, from every class and
background. One or two were highly educated, others barely lit-
erate. All were friendly. There were no jokes about posh accents
or famous parents, although I soon acquired "Duff" as a nickname; and the close proximity in which we lived—two or four in
each of the cubicles which led off a central passage running the
length of the concrete hut, with communal washing facilities in
a separate building—meant that we made friends fast. My sole
disappointment was that, as a short-term National Serviceman,
the seamanship branch was closed to me; it required a considerably longer period of training, which for conscripts like me were,
from the Navy's point of view, simply not worth the candle. At
that moment there were vacancies in three branches only: those
of writer, stoker and cook. I had little hesitation in choosing to be
a writer; writers were either secretaries or kept the ships' ledgers (I
very much hoped for the former) and an office was obviously a far
more congenial place to work than an engine room or galley. Of
course I should rather have been a seaman—apart from anything

else I should have worn a proper sailor's uniform with bell-bottoms instead of a dreary navy blue jacket and trousers, black tie and peaked cap—but I was soon to discover that the writer's job, however unromantic, had immense advantages when one joined a real ship.

I remember little—perhaps mercifully little—of my days at Corsham. Parade ground drill—"square bashing"—took up a good deal of it; as good sailors we learnt to tie all those knots, but as a writer I was never to use one of them and I had forgotten them all within a month or two. For the rest we attended classes, taken by Petty Officers and Chief Petty Officers who told us about the Navy and its ways. But our time was not exclusively given to training. There were, inevitably, countless general jobs to be done: I remember the early hours of one particular morning, well before dawn, when we were given the job of bummarees, heaving huge carcasses of beef around on our shoulders. There was also an endless amount of cleaning, kit inspection and—rather more surprisingly—painting. The old sailors' joke, "if it moves, salute it; if it doesn't move, paint it white" sometimes seemed almost like a serious admonition. Life was pretty boring on the whole; I cannot imagine how we managed to fill our days. In the evenings we went to the cinema in Corsham, or to one of the several pubs favored by the Navy. Once or twice—though I tended not to advertise the fact—I was invited by old Lord Methuen to dinner at Corsham Court. Sadly for me, I was not in those days particularly interested in pictures: the Corsham collection is famous. But the food was a considerable improvement on that provided by His Majesty, and the company a good deal more stimulating. Almost always there was a ravishingly beautiful, languid girl lying on a sofa. I took her to be a sort of resident invalid, and fell a little in love with her; it came as quite a shock, perhaps thirty years later, when I read that she had married Sir Kenneth Clark.

Back in the camp, there was one perennial question which haunted us all: was our tea, or was it not, being spiked with bromides? Most of us, I think, seemed to feel a distinct decrease in our youthful libidos—a surprising phenomenon among eighteen-year-olds—but was it true, or were we just imagining it? I certainly took the possibility seriously enough to report our suspicions to my parents. My father—who had certainly never suffered a similar experience—shrugged it off, possibly reflecting that in the circumstances it might be just as well; but my mother was outraged. Did she—as she threatened to do, and I would certainly not have put it past her—write to the First Lord of the Admiralty, or even to the Prime Minister? They would surely have denied it—and probably rightly: it seems nowadays hard to believe. And yet, from time to time, I still find myself wondering.

One spring morning we all dispersed—the writers, sick bay orderlies, cooks, and officers stewards among us being sent to do six months specialized "Supply and Secretariat" training in another one of those innumerable shore establishments. This time it was HMS *Ceres*, Wetherby, Yorkshire. Here we learnt how to run a Captain's Office, how to draft our ship's official correspondence, how to keep a file on every member of the ship's company, and—a nightmare to me—how to keep the books. This was a task of almost unbelievable complication—pouring over enormous ledgers, noting whether a given man was receiving his daily tot of rum or being paid threepence in compensation, deducting the amounts regularly sent direct to his family, adding increments and bonuses, subtracting fines and other penalty payments (usually for drunkenness), working out the sum due to him at the end of the week—at only six shillings a day for an Able Seaman it was never more than a pound or two—and finally preparing the precise amounts of cash which were to be formally placed on (never in) his cap on pay day. How incredibly antiquated it all seems now, when presumably one small computer handles the whole thing—but then the Navy *was* antiquated: to take but one example, the penalty for returning drunk from shore was imprisonment in the cells picking oakum, just as it had been in Nelson's time.

On the secretarial side I was taught how to lay out letters so that they looked reasonably elegant—generous margins, one space after commas, two spaces after semicolons, colons, and full stops. Alas there was no touch typing—a skill which, had I acquired it, would have made a vast difference to my future life. The problem, it seemed, was the same as I had already encountered over the seamanship branch: time was too short. I should have less than two years to serve before being demobilized, and such an investment of time and money was simply not worthwhile. None the less, Wetherby proved a good deal more enjoyable than Corsham. The spring soon came, and by early summer the sun seemed to be always shining. With our own money—I don't remember, but probably less than a tenner—we bought ourselves "tiddly suits," made-to-measure uniforms made of black doeskin which were certainly a lot smarter and better fitting than the regular Navy issue—in which we had plenty of spare time to go to York, Leeds, and Fountains Abbey. My mother's oldest friend, Irene Forbes Adam, lived with her husband Colin only a mile or two away and encouraged me to drop in whenever I liked; other neighbors, the Lane Foxes—whose cousins were also destined to play a significant part in my later years—were equally welcoming. Camp life continued to be spartan to say the least, but to my surprise I soon found that I was enjoying myself. I also became the resident pianist of the *Ceres* dance band, the quality of which varied with the constant arrivals and departures but which always provided the music for the officers' weekly Saturday night dance. I continued to play until my own departure when, in June or early July, I passed out as a fully fledged Writer.

But what was going to happen next? One thing was certain: I should go first to my home base at Chatham (HMS *Pembroke* this time), where I would kick my heels until the Navy found something for me to do. I longed, naturally, to be posted to a proper sea-going ship, or at least to some naval base abroad—Malta perhaps, or Trincomalee, or Hong Kong—but as a National Service man I suspected a year at Scapa Flow to be a good deal more likely. Meanwhile I took a room in a sailors' hostel—it cost a shilling a night, but at least it gave me a touch of privacy—and it was there, just a week or two later, that I received a posting better than anything I could have dreamt of: to join HMS *Cleopatra*, a light cruiser at present refitting in Portsmouth in preparation for joining the projected Home Fleet cruise to the Caribbean in the autumn.

———— ⊙¦⊙ ————

The next morning I was on the train. I still remember the journey with kitbag and hammock, and the mounting excitement: Guildford, Haslemere, Havant, Petersfield, Fratton,[2] and finally Portsmouth Harbour. Through the docks I walked, past the *Victory*—and there, in a dry dock just beyond, was the ship that was to be my home for the next twelve months. "Yes," they said, "you'll be working in the Captain's Office." This was welcome news—I had dreaded those ledgers—but it was only a few hours later that I discovered just how lucky I was. The first action of any experienced sailor on joining a new ship is to look for a quiet and private place to sling his hammock—ships are so overcrowded that he is allowed to do so practically anywhere.

---

2 I was soon to learn—from my mother—that the naval slang for *coitus interruptus* is "getting out at Fratton."

The communal mess-deck could be misery: a hundred or more men packed together with barely a foot between them, all chain-smoking. At sea it could be even worse, because there was absolutely no ventilation; the portholes were just a few inches above the waterline and could be opened only in the deadest calm. The Captain, it need hardly be said, never went near his Office, having his own commodious apartment on the deck above; there was thus nothing to stop me sleeping in my place of work, sharing it with only one other fellow writer, Frank Sutcliffe, who was hoping to become a professional organist and who didn't smoke either. Here, I realized, was luxury indeed.

Secretary to the Captain's Secretary, I beavered away—opening letters, registering them, answering them, and filing them—all the time dreaming of that glorious day at the end of September when we should sail, southwest across the Atlantic, to those islands in the sun of which I had always dreamed. And then suddenly, in the middle of August, I opened a letter and saw to my horror that it contained my own name. Even as I read it, it chilled me to the heart. I was to be transferred to HMS *Vanguard*, the battleship that was to carry King George VI and Queen Elizabeth to Australia and New Zealand some time in the following year. I read the letter over and over as the horror sunk in. It was the work, I had absolutely no doubt, of my mother. She could never resist pulling strings; hearing of the royal arrangements she would have joyfully got to work, telephoning friendly admirals—perhaps even the First Lord himself—and cajoling them to get her little boy on board somehow. I would not have expected her to consult me first, since she knew perfectly well that I should have told her not to interfere; and this was the result. A royal cruise might be all very well; but there would be several more months of drudgery through a long winter before its departure and I was unlikely to get anything like such a nice job. It was clear, too, that the discipline would be mercilessly strict, and that we should constantly have to look our best. (As we had to do all our own laundry—including the daily washing and ironing of our white tropical uniforms—this was a serious consideration.) But my strongest emotion was sheer disappointment. I had set my heart on this Caribbean trip, working for it, planning for it, looking forward to it as much as I had ever looked forward to anything in my life. And now, just a week or two before we were due to leave, it was being snatched away.

For the first and last time in my naval career I applied to see the Captain. It was like applying to see God: in the Navy one's Captain was an infinitely remote, all-powerful being whom even I, who worked in his office, seldom clapped eyes on and whose name the most insubordinate of the ship's company mentioned with bated breath. But I was desperate. Tremblingly and on the verge of tears, I knocked at his door and advanced, the letter in my hand. Was there, I asked him, any way in which this order could be countermanded? Captain Peter Reid was a dear man— the nephew, as I later discovered, of my godfather Maurice Baring, but it would have been unthinkable to have mentioned such a thing—and, I suspect, immediately understood the situation. He smiled, and promised to see what he could do. After a few days of almost unbearable suspense he sent for me: I was reprieved.

That winter the King was found to be seriously ill, and his journey to the Antipodes was called off; had I accepted my fate without protest I should have missed that cruise as well.

———— ❦ ————

Some time during that summer of 1948—it must have been only a few weeks before we sailed for the Caribbean—I had a short spell of leave and went to stay with some friends in Norfolk. On my last day there—it was a Sunday—the telephone rang while we were having breakfast. It was my mother, who had just been offered two tickets for *Così fan tutte* that same afternoon at Glyndebourne. Could I be there by four-thirty? Having never been to Glyndebourne, I was enormously excited. I was returning to London anyway that evening; this simply meant taking a rather earlier train. Of course I could, I said, and hung up.

It all proved rather more difficult than I had expected. After three years, England had still not recovered from the war. The timetable revealed one very slow Sunday train, leaving in an hour from a station fifteen miles away. Fortunately it was late, or I should never have caught it; and it was a good deal later still when it finally crawled into Liverpool Street. A mood of relative serenity during the early stages of the journey had long since given way to one of panic. There was only one possible connection to be made. Had I arrived on time, I should have had over an hour to get from Liverpool Street to Victoria; I now had exactly twenty-five minutes. Mercifully it was a Sunday, the City streets were a lot emptier than they are now and there was a waiting taxi. I offered the driver double fare if he made it. He looked doubtful, but his response was magnificent. We hurtled across London and arrived at Victoria with a minute to spare. There was no time to buy a ticket, only to hurl my suitcase and myself into the last, rapidly accelerating carriage and to fall, half dead but happy, into an empty seat.

We were among green fields before I recovered sufficiently to size up my fellow travelers. There were two ladies bedecked, as I remember, in yards of mauve chiffon, looking like large flustered moths. Only at the ankles did the chiffon stop, giving place to intricate systems of gold and silver strapping. Their escorts wore stiff collars, winged like archangels; one of them sported one of those square, single-breasted black evening waistcoats now found only on the older and seedier waiters in French provincial cafés.

Suddenly I became conscious of an almost tangible atmosphere of disapproval. I was an outsider, an intruder. I had forced myself upon their company and in doing so had cheapened both myself and them. Sartorially, I was letting down the side.

A terrible thought struck me. I was only eighteen and had spent most of the past three years abroad; but had I not heard somewhere that at Glyndebourne evening dress was *de rigueur*? Perhaps without it I should be refused admittance, bringing disgrace upon my mother and rendering pointless this whole ghastly journey. With relief, I remembered that my dinner jacket was in my suitcase. (People changed for dinner a good deal more often in those days than they do now.) I would brave the disapproval a little longer; then I would betake myself and suitcase along the corridor and emerge on Lewes platform metamorphosed.

Twenty minutes before our scheduled arrival time I was locked safely in the loo, stripped to my underpants and struggling into a white shirt, when suddenly the train stopped. I could see nothing through the frosted glass, but I heard, all too clearly, a voice of genteel doom: "Brighton, this is Brighton. The special Glyndebourne train leaves for Lewes in five minutes from platform six. Brighton, this is Brighton. . . ."

I felt like Job, or Titus Andronicus. When would this fearful slumber have an end? No one had told me that we had to change trains. Speed, by now, was a good deal more important than elegance, even than decency. Still, I could hardly race across Brighton station in my underwear. Shirt, trousers, and shoes seemed the best compromise. Stuffing everything else huggermugger into the suitcase, I fled down the platform—remembering only at the barrier that I had no ticket. There was no time to explain; neither, however, was there any need to. The ticket collector, after one incredulous look, knew instinctively that his duty was to see me either on to the Glyndebourne train or into the nearest

police station. He took—I gratefully record it—the correct decision. Leaving his barrier unattended, he seized the suitcase and
hustled me to platform six. A colleague held out his hand for my
ticket, but was imperiously waved aside. The train was already
grunting into motion. Doors were banging, flags waving. This, I
realized, was not only a nightmare; it was a recurring nightmare.
I had done all this before; the only difference was that this time
I was half naked. It is not easy to jump into a moving train with
one hand clutching a suitcase and the other holding up one's
trousers, but I made it.

The last stage of the journey threatened to be the worst. This
time there was no empty seat, just eight more passengers, obviously all from the same stable as the other lot, all looking like something out of a cartoon by H.M. Bateman—shocked, horrified and
personally affronted. I could think only of escape—down the
corridor again. But this time there was no corridor. I was trapped,
and at bay. With what little power of speech remained, I tried to
explain the situation; and then the miracle happened. They all
started to laugh. Better still, they helped. A gentleman took my
suitcase and held it open on his knees. A lady raised aloft a tiny
mirror while I tied my tie. Somebody else held me steady in the
lurching train while I put on my socks. By the time we reached
Lewes I was, I think, relatively presentable. I thanked them all,
but not nearly enough.

It had been raining in Norfolk, but at Glyndebourne the sun
was blazing down, and my recent passage through hell sharpened
my appreciation of paradise. All that I had ever heard about the
place suddenly came together, in focus for the first time. Members of the orchestra were playing croquet. Bottles of champagne
were being cooled in the lake. In a distant dressing room, a tenor
was warming up with an arpeggio or two. Even the mauve chiffon and the wing collars had lost their terrors for me; they looked

no longer formidable, but festive. With mounting excitement, we left the golden afternoon outside and trooped into the theater. Fritz Busch raised his baton and one magic spell was succeeded by another. The young Sena Jurinac gave what I still feel must have been the performance of her life. It was my first *Così*, and for me it has never been surpassed.

At the end of September we left our dry dock in Portsmouth and headed—with perhaps two dozen or more other ships of the Home Fleet—for the wide ocean. The crossing took us just over a fortnight, owing to various exercises on the way; during the second week when the weather had grown warmer, the entire fleet would stop for an hour in midafternoon, so that all the ships' companies could swim over the side; it was strange, but curiously invigorating, to know that one was immersed in water two thousand miles away from land and perhaps five miles deep. Aboard *Cleopatra* we had only one serious mishap, when one of our Leading Signalmen dived straight into the middle of a Portuguese man-of-war. After a week or two in the sick bay he recovered, but I can still hear the scream.

San Fernando, Trinidad, was our first port of call. After a radiantly beautiful dawn—most of us were up early to greet our first landfall—the weather clouded over, much to my disappointment and surprise. I had never before been to the tropics, where I had somehow always imagined that the sun shone all day, every day. In the afternoon we went ashore, wearing our white tropical uniforms for the first time, carrying in our pockets the two statutory condoms without which no man was allowed to leave the ship—and were instantly overwhelmed by the local hospitality. That day and for the rest of the cruise, it seemed that in the entire

Caribbean there was not one institution, one club, one family even, that did not open its doors to the English sailors. The only problem was the rum. From the moment we landed it was poured down our throats—sometimes in the form of planter's punch, sometimes mixed with Coca-Cola,[3] sometimes neat in a tumbler, but always in industrial quantities. For those who preferred not to be privately entertained, downtown San Fernando—where the Navy's arrival was a cause for celebration for any number of reasons—provided a particularly lethal variety at about a penny a tot, and the local girls charged very little more.

Now *Cleopatra*—and, I suppose, a good many of the other ships—carried a considerable number of Boy Seamen of perhaps sixteen or seventeen, most of whom had never been abroad before and had little experience of serious drinking. (The Navy's traditional daily tot of rum was limited to twenty-one-year-olds and over). And after more than two weeks at sea their elders and betters hardly set them a shining example. By eleven o'clock the last liberty boats returning to the ships were loaded with senseless sailors and awash with vomit. Those of us who could still stand were mobilized to search the uniforms of the unconscious for the paybook which each man had to carry, identify him, and somehow get him back to his ship—as unpleasant a task as I have ever had to tackle, which went on for most of the night. On the following morning the worst cases were formally disciplined, though with precisely what punishment I cannot now remember; there were certainly nowhere near enough cells—or, probably, oakum—to go round. Fortunately, no subsequent evening involved a repetition

---

3 At that time the island's favorite calypso ran:

> When Yankee come to Trinidad,
> The local population is glad,
> Trinidad girls are very nice,
> Think Yankee dollar is paradise;
> Singing rum and Coca-Cola. . . .

of the experience. There were always a few drunks returning from shore—one or two of them, I suspect, had never returned to a ship sober in their lives—but most of us had learnt our lesson.

From Trinidad we sailed to Tobago, and thence to St. Vincent, St. Lucia and Montserrat, with a few days in Bermuda on our way home. I loved every minute of it, the more so since as a writer I was not obliged to work watches. Those who did—the vast majority—were allowed ashore only every other day, port watch one day, starboard the next. I and my half-dozen or so similarly privileged fellows—who were allowed basically to do our work in our own time—could get off whenever it was done, and since I was normally able to do all mine by lunchtime, the afternoons and evenings were usually my own. The only fly in the otherwise immaculate ointment was that white uniform. Since we were always subjected to inspection before going ashore, it had to be washed and ironed virtually every day; and this usually involved the best part of two hours. Laying it out on the washroom floor and scrubbing, then drying it as best I could (the sun helped, but the Navy is somewhat sensitive about allowing its ships to be draped with washing) and finally ironing it on the office desk.

It was a wrench to leave what had seemed to me to be a succession of island paradises and to butt our way back through increasingly angry seas to Portsmouth; but Christmas was on the way, and it had already been announced that early in the new year—1949—we should be heading for Gibraltar. Gibraltar, however, was nowhere near such fun. I felt that for the Rock—admittedly half a century ago—a couple of hours would have been about right; we were there for six remorseless weeks. During that unconscionable time we were allowed just three visits to Spain; for the rest, we would walk up and down the main (indeed almost the only) street until we were intimately acquainted with every item in every shop window, eventually finding our way to one or the other of the two pubs which catered exclusively to the Navy. Each of these featured what might optimistically be described as a cabaret, provided by two aging ladies in the regulation frilly, spotty dresses like very old lampshades, who every hour or so performed a traditional flamenco. These two—one of them, I remember, was known to all as Sweaty Betty—had each entertained generation after generation of sailors but had somehow managed to keep their castanets clicking; their performances were invariably greeted with rapturous and wholly undeserved applause.

Not surprisingly, a visit to Spain—always with two or three of us together, since complicated Anglo-Spanish regulations forbade us to go on our own—was always an excitement. On two occasions we got no further than the nearest town, only just across the frontier, of La Linea. It was there that I saw my first bullfight. I approached the ring with trepidation, uncertain whether the experience might not be more than I could bear; to my surprise I found myself fascinated. Far from being cruel, the ceremony—there is no other word for it—seemed to me astonishingly humane. Of course the bull is killed, but so are hundreds of thousands of others every day; the question is how it meets its death. Almost all are herded—often panic-stricken—into a slaughterhouse. How infinitely more agreeable, I thought, if one were a bull, to be pampered throughout one's youth and finally to be allowed to star in a magnificent drama, feeling only anger—a far more pleasurable emotion than terror—fighting a small group of much smaller and weaker people on whom one has a sporting chance of inflicting hideous wounds, and probably convinced of one's ultimate victory until the last couple of minutes. All those other bulls should be so lucky.

My other experience in La Linea was somewhat less edifying—when a friend and I were inveigled into one of the town's innumerable houses of ill fame. I had never been to one before and was, I think, more relieved than anything else when the staff all proved to be three times our age, constituting little or no temptation. We eventually settled rather weakly for what was known as an "exhibition," which was provided by two elderly ladies and a large banana. Our condoms were returned unused.

The last jaunt from Gibraltar was an unexpected bonus: a day trip in a submarine across the straits to Tangier. Disappointingly, we didn't submerge; and even on the surface the view from a submarine—which has no portholes—is, to say the least, limited. The journey therefore had little enough to recommend it apart from its destination. I was scooped up by our old family friend David Herbert, the dearly loved black sheep of the Pembroke family, aptly dubbed "queen of Tangier," taken off to Dean's Bar—much frequented by the numerous Anglo-American gay colony—and then to a luncheon party in his house, which made no concession to Moorish taste and seemed virtually indistinguishable from the one he had formerly lived in at Wilton. The return journey to Gibraltar, when most of my fellow passengers—including the ship's padre, who was by then wearing a fez—were all in fairly bad shape, represented a striking but possibly salutary contrast to the super sophistication of what had gone before.

—◦•◦—

It seemed that we were hardly back in England before we went off again on the last of my three cruises. This time our destination was Scandinavia. The first stop was not, alas, Copenhagen but Esbjerg, a not terribly exciting city on the west coast of Jutland, about as far away from the capital as it was possible for a Danish town to be. But I had two friends, the writer Kelvin Lindemann and his wife Tot, who lived near Copenhagen and whom I had promised to visit if I could; and on the third and last day of our stay my oppo, Dental Sick Bay Attendant Tony Griffiths, and I decided to take the train across the whole country—the journey included two sea ferries—to the capital. We knew that we should have only a few hours there, but there would be time to have dinner with the Lindemanns before returning, and anyway the dubious pleasures of Esbjerg had been exhausted and there was nothing else to do. Kelvin was his country's leading novelist, first introduced to me as "the Danish Somerset Maugham." He was there to meet us at the station, and to tell us delightedly all the plans he had made for the evening; and when we broke it to him that we had to leave in some four hours time his face fell. "You can't," he said. But then he suddenly brightened. "Don't worry; I'll get on to an old friend who happens to be head of the Danish Navy. He'll telephone your Captain, who won't be able to say no. Leave it to me."

We left it to him. I had, I remember, considerable misgivings; departure days were always busy in the Captain's Office. But no was clearly not going to be taken for an answer, and sure enough the Admiral telephoned back a few minutes later with the news that our leave had been extended until an hour before we sailed the following afternoon. It was midsummer; the days were long and the sun was still high in the sky when we arrived at Tivoli, a vast amusement park frequented by all classes and conditions of Dane, in which bands play, switchbacks clatter, jugglers juggle, and various other little performances go on under the trees. Several of Copenhagen's top restaurants have branches there during the summer months. Neither London nor Paris can provide anything quite like it; perhaps the Prater in Vienna comes nearest. One of the first things that struck me was the fact that everyone was clearly having a wonderful time, slapping each other on the back and frequently shaking with laughter. A few, I suppose, were mildly drunk, but only in the nicest possible way. The prototype of the melancholy Dane was nowhere to be seen.

The Lindemanns gave us a glorious evening—perhaps the happiest of my naval career—before driving us back to their lovely modern house at Fredensborg for the night; and around midmorning we boarded the train again. But when we returned, oh dear: it was naturally assumed that we had deliberately manipulated the whole thing, the Captain's Secretary—my boss—had been up half the night doing the work I should have done, and he (and everybody else) was exhausted and understandably furious. I had, it was pointed out, put my Captain in an impossible position; this was a goodwill visit and he could hardly have refused a personal request from so exalted a source. I explained that we had never asked the admiral to act as he did, and somewhat to my surprise got off with a reprimand.

Our next stop was Kristiansand, near the southern tip of Norway. Here an experience awaited me more traumatic, even, than that I had suffered at Esbjerg. On our first evening there, the ship was open to visitors: any members of the local citizenry who liked to come on board were welcome to do so. Suddenly and surprisingly, I found myself talking to one of those ravishing, ash blond girls which seem to be a Scandinavian specialty—and fell for her. She, I thought, seemed not entirely indifferent to me, and I invited her out to dinner the following evening. I explained that I had very little money, and could not hope to give her the sort of dinner that she deserved and to which she was presumably accustomed; she laughed that one off, and said that the weather—which was warm and cloudless—was far too wonderful for sitting in restaurants: why didn't we just get a few sandwiches and go for a lovely walk in the woods? She would be on the quayside at seven o'clock.

By this time my heart was beating fit to burst. All that night and the next day I thought of the joys that awaited me, scarcely daring to speculate on how the evening would end. I imagined us lying down in the grass by one of the lakes she had told me about; then perhaps a tentative kiss, to which she would passionately respond; and then what? Might it, could it mean a final—and certainly not to be regretted—farewell to my long preserved virginity? The working day seemed endless, until finally I put the cover back on the typewriter, changed into my tiddly suit and, at about a quarter to seven, went down the gangplank to await our rendezvous.

And she never turned up. I waited for two hours on the quay, growing first worried, then anxious, and finally despairing. Finally, around nine, I accepted the fact that she had no intention of coming, that the evening I had so longed for would remain a dream, that dreary old virginity must be put back in the cupboard. I can remember few more excruciating disappointments.

That summer marked the end of my naval career. It had not been distinguished—indeed, it had no chance to be—but it had taken me to several places I had never seen before (or, for that matter, since). Life on the lower deck, moreover, had been an education in itself. Not only had it done me the world of good; looking back, I was surprised how much I had enjoyed it. I had, of course, been ridiculously lucky—there was no question about that: many national servicemen had remained cooped up in Chatham, Portsmouth or Devonport until they had been demobilized. But there it was: the Navy had been good to me. I was hugely grateful to it, and I still am.

Chapter Six

Oxford, Marriage, and the Foreign Office

M Y MANY PRECONCEPTIONS about Oxford University certainly did not include life in a prefabricated hut in an outer quadrangle; but postwar Oxford was bursting at the seams as innumerable demobilized majors and wing commanders returned to complete their education, and—at least for New College—there was no alternative. My old school friend (and almost exact contemporary) Philip Ziegler was allocated proper, old-fashioned accommodation in the long range of buildings that runs parallel to Holywell Street. I consoled myself with the thought that he was obliged to share three rooms with a colleague, while I had a refuge, however humble, of my own. Both of us, on the other hand, were doomed to a walk of a hundred yards or more in our dressing gowns—often, in that winter of 1949–1950, through deep snow—every time we wanted a bath. Did we mind? Not, I think, very much. At last we were virtually independent, able to do as we liked. Oxford we were all determined, was going to be fun.

There was, of course, a modicum of supervision; and my first priority on the day after my arrival was to call on my Moral Tutor—whose responsibility proved fortunately to be not at all what his title suggested. Morals had nothing to do with it. His job was simply to keep an eye on how I was getting on, to give advice when sought, and generally to be a friend when I needed one; and I had been delighted to learn that he was to be the great Isaiah Berlin himself. By now Isaiah already enjoyed a formidable reputation on both sides of the Atlantic; his name was normally spoken only in the most reverential of whispers. I, on the other hand, had seen quite a lot of him in Embassy days and knew just how unfrightening he really was. No one could possibly doubt the power of his intellect or deny the coruscation of his talk, but he was also a wonderful listener, with the enviable ability to bring out the best in whomever he was with. He could dazzle a dinner table with his brilliance, and two minutes later—since he was a superb raconteur—make his hearers laugh till they cried. He also happened to be a very nice man.

All this I knew from experience; but although Isaiah was, when you knew him, the least intimidating of men, many people were daunted by the prospect of meeting him for the first time. Among them was another moral pupil of his, my old Eton chum Anthony Blond. Never in the sixty-odd years that I knew him did Anthony strike me as a shrinking violet; but on our first evening at New College he confessed to me that he too had to call on the great man the following morning, and was terrified. I of course assured him that he had nothing whatever to worry about; in any case, I suggested, since our appointments were at 9 AM and 9:15 AM respectively, why should we not go together so that I could introduce him? He jumped at the idea, and promptly at nine the next morning we knocked on Isaiah's door. No answer. We knocked again, once again without result; then we very gingerly opened the door into his study. It was empty, but there was another door on the far side of the room, from beyond which I thought I heard a noise, so I knocked on this as well. The answer this time was a loud grunt, followed by that unmistakable clipped bass voice calling "Come in." In we went, and found to our horror Isaiah tucked tightly up in bed, face to the wall. "What is it?" he mumbled. I explained that we had appointments to see him, and that we had decided to come together. "My time was actually nine fifteen," said Anthony: "I'm Blond."

He turned and faced us for the first time, his eye lighting on Anthony's jet black hair and swarthy complexion. "Palpably untrue" was all he said; then he turned back to the wall and went to sleep again. Our two interviews were over.

Oxford should be fun, and so it was; but for me it was perhaps not quite as much fun as it might have been, because at the very outset I made a fatal mistake: I decided to read modern languages. My father had done his utmost to dissuade me. The only successful way to learn a language, he maintained, was by total immersion: to go off to the appropriate country, stay with a local family and saturate oneself in it all day, every day, from morning to night. As for literature, to study it academically was to turn what should be pleasure into drudgery. Briefly, I allowed myself to be persuaded and put my name down for PPE—politics, philosophy, and economics—but after a fortnight I could bear it no longer. I changed schools, for the rest of my Oxford life devoting all too many of my waking hours to French and Russian; and by the time I realized how right my father had been it was too late to change back again. (I am surprised, in retrospect, that I did not unhesitatingly plump for history, the writing of which has been my principal occupation since my mid-thirties. Perhaps the knowledge that I should be required to study the Pandects of Justinian in Latin may have had something to do with it.)

Three years later when I left, my spoken French—always pretty fluent and further polished up in Paris and Strasbourg—was not appreciably better than it had been when I started; and though I could read Russian without too much difficulty, conversationally I could still barely get off the ground. What Oxford did do for me—though I have only myself to blame—was to ruin two of the greatest literatures of the world. After three years of force-feeding (I remember having to read three Dostoyevsky novels in a week) I had enough of them. I have hardly read a single French or Russian novel since. The one exception—if you can call him a novelist— was Rabelais, to whom Oxford introduced me and whose sheer fantasy and ebullience enchanted me and still does; but Rabelais is an exception to every rule.

Extracurricular life was enjoyable enough. The prefab didn't last long: after a term or two I was moved into a funny little rickety cottage in the back quad, opposite the Library, where I had two rooms of my own which I loved and which were far better for entertaining friends and—a growing passion—making and listening to music. The year 1950 saw the introduction of the vinyl Long-Playing Record—which had a far greater impact than the later tape cassette or the CD, freeing one as it did from the drudgery of changing those heavy, fragile 78 rpm records every three or four minutes, endlessly sharpening or renewing the needles. The twelve inch classical LPs were expensive—thirty-nine shillings and sixpence each—which meant that one treasured them, playing them again and again. It was at Oxford more than anywhere else that I got to know the classical repertoire; but I never ventured very far outside it. Isaiah once confessed to me that he drew the line at a 1900 birth date; to composers born before then he was delighted to listen, those born afterwards bored him to death. I am prepared to make an exception for Benjamin Britten—who was born in 1913—but I otherwise feel much the same. For years I tried, spending countless hours at concerts of modern music and a small fortune on records, always hoping that the curtain would lift; but it never did, and on my fiftieth birthday I decided to give up. After all, there was far more music of the seventeenth to nineteenth centuries that I could hope to enjoy in my lifetime; why waste any more time and money on that of the twentieth? It was one of the most sensible resolutions I have ever made.

But there was other music too, which I made myself. By our Embassy days I had graduated from my mother's ukulele to the Spanish guitar, as well as becoming moderately efficient on the piano; and thanks to Louise de Vilmorin and innumerable visits to the *Lapin Agile* in Montmartre—my favorite of all the Paris *chansonniers*—I had by this time built up a repertory of well over a hundred songs, sentimental and comic, in French and English. My vocal performances had not been much sought after in the Navy, where I had no guitar and where the mess-deck pianos had suffered too much regular abuse to be playable; but at Oxford I seemed to come into my own and sang to small audiences—not all particularly enthusiastic, but audiences none the less—once or twice a week. For a brief period I may have rented a piano, but with uprights you have to perform with your back to your listeners, and there was no room, either in my rooms or in my bank balance, for a grand; so I transferred my hero-worship from George Formby and Frank Crumit to Burl Ives, the guitar came into its own and for many years I hardly moved without it.

For the rest, I was far less adventurous than I should have been. Never greatly interested in politics, I steered clear of the Union; nor, though I loved the theater and always suspected that I might possess a certain thespian talent, did I ever involve myself with the OUDS. (Everyone was still talking about Ken Tynan, who had taken Oxford by storm but had unfortunately left the term before I arrived.) Altogether, the truth is that I did not get anything like as much out of my three university years as I should have. Pressure of work was one reason. Although it mostly consisted of reading novels, French and Russian novels tend to be inordinately long, and I have always been a lamentably slow reader. But that is no real excuse. I was highly social and made or consolidated a number of lasting friendships; but I failed absolutely—just as I had at Eton, at Strasbourg, and in the Navy—to distinguish myself.

———⊶⊷———

I did, on the other hand, fall in love. Among my mother's greatest friends in Paris was Paul-Louis Weiller. He had been an air ace in the First World War, after which he had gone into industry, and by the 1950s he was among the richest men in France. I once asked him how many houses he owned. He turned my question aside—he was the least self-centered man in the world and never talked about himself—but some of his other friends and I later tried to make a list: the total came to sixteen, but it was almost certainly not complete. One of these houses was a large villa, near Le Lavandou in the South of France, called La Reine Jeanne; and here he gave house parties every August. It was a wonderful house, set among pines immediately overlooking the sea, with an enormous terrace in front and, in the center, an enclosed courtyard smelling of verbena in which we would sit down, perhaps twenty or more, to dinner in the evening. Lunch was in a little natural ravine on the beach below. There was a high powered motor boat for waterskiing (Paul-Louis, already well into his sixties, was a champion, able when going fast enough to kick off his skis and skim along the water, sometimes backwards, on the soles of his feet) and a larger one for going off to one of the restaurants on the islands of Porquerolles, Port Cros, or the Ile du Levant, the last of which possessed the added attraction of being a nudist colony. I remember seeing my father in the village shoe shop, being fitted with a new pair of espadrilles by a ravishing girl wearing nothing but what my mother later described as a piece of toast. He clearly enjoyed it, but his face went a very curious color.

Since our host was an assiduous and unashamed headhunter there were always a couple of film stars among the guests, together with assorted writers and politicians. I remember, among many others over the years, Charlie Chaplin and his enormous family, Joan Fontaine, Merle Oberon, Aldous Huxley, and the Richard Nixons before he became President. A regular visitor was the pianist Jacques Février, who could be relied upon to play Chopin (or anything else) before or after dinner; and because Paul-Louis was Paul-Louis, there was always any number of fantastically pretty girls.

Most of these were starlets or models, but among those at La Reine Jeanne in August, 1950, were the three lovely daughters of Sir Bede and Lady Clifford. Sir Bede had been a colonial Governor, first of the Bahamas, then of Mauritius, and finally of Trinidad and Tobago. (Once, in a tabloid newspaper, he had been described as "the monocled tyrant of Trinidad," and his delighted daughters had never allowed him to forget it.) But although he did indeed sport a monocle, his normal manner was anything but tyrannical. He was a passionate do-it-yourselfer—the girls maintained that he even did his own dentistry—and a bit of a wag, whose penchant for telling mildly off-color jokes occasionally embarrassed his friends but greatly endeared him to me. So, indeed, did his passion for dry martinis, which he made of pile-driving strength. Whenever the family traveled, he would always stop the car at exactly 12:30 PM, unpack the gin, vermouth, and ice thermos from the boot and consume two whoppers by the side of the road, dispensing further overflowing tumblers to his passengers. Six hours later, the ceremony would be repeated. How he would have coped with the age of the breathalyzer I should rather not think. Anyway, I took to him from the start. His wife had been born Alice Gundry in Cleveland, Ohio, wore alarming quantities of mascara and—though she seldom read a book—was kindness personified. Their three daughters had been born in little over four years: when I first met them that summer, Anne was twenty-one, Pandora nineteen, and Atalanta seventeen. I too was twenty-one and I fell—hook, line and sinker—for Anne.

She was tall and very slim, with long fair hair and a lovely pure singing voice, and was already a gifted painter. At the age of sixteen she had been commissioned to paint the murals at Butlin's holiday camp in the Bahamas, and she had had no shortage of commissions since; later she was to provide a whole series of trompe-l'oeil panels for Dot and Antony Head's house in Wiltshire, and a vast over-mantel trophy for the Douglas Fairbankses. We had an idyllic fortnight, of swimming, waterskiing, singing to guitars after dinner, cruising to the islands, and—for two of us at least—enjoying all the exhilaration and excitement of first love. But then, some three or four days before we were all due to leave, Anne told me that she didn't feel that she could carry on. Bewildered and miserable, I confided in—of all people—Merle Oberon, a fellow guest whose unaffected and utterly unstarlike thoughtfulness and warmth had endeared her to us all. She was as sympathetic as I knew she would be, and promised me that she would talk to Anne, find out (as I had never been able to do) why she wanted to break it off and try to persuade her to change her mind. Heaven knows how she did it, but she was totally successful. A year later Anne and I were engaged to be married.

B y now Venice was once again playing a part in my life, though not yet a very large one. Soon after my father left the Embassy at the end of 1947, his old friend Alexander Korda had asked him to be the official representative of the British Film Producers Association at the annual Venice Film Festival. My father confessed that he had hardly ever even taken a photograph, but Alex was unconcerned. The job would be simply to show the flag, to preside at the occasional reception or dinner, and naturally to attend all the prestige showings of new British films. In return he and my mother would be accommodated, as guests of the BFPA, at the Gritti Palace Hotel for the duration of the Festival, and would of course be provided with their own personal gondola. Since the Festival fortunately fell during the University vacation, I was able to go along too.

Those were the days in which I began to get to know Venice. My father took his duties very seriously, forever heading off—often quite early in the morning—to the huge and hideous theater on the Lido to see some obscure Bulgarian documentary. My mother and I were rather less conscientious. Every morning at nine our gondolier would appear at the hotel for his instructions, and an hour or so later off we would go. Looking back on it today, the luxury seems almost inconceivable; but in the forties and early fifties many Venetians still had their own private gondolas, and a good number of foreign visitors would hire one by the week. Some would even employ two gondoliers, rowing fore and aft, normally dressed in white, with brocade sashes at the waist. Evenings were spent either watching a film or entertaining distinguished people to dinner.

Of all our guests, the most distinguished of all were Winston and Clementine Churchill. They regularly came to Venice for a fortnight in September, staying at the Excelsior on the Lido; and as Winston had a passion for the cinema the five of us frequently went together. He would immerse himself totally in the film, keeping up a running commentary to himself throughout. On one occasion I heard him muttering, "Oh jealousy, jealousy—the most barren of all vices." On another, during a film about the life of wandering Irish tinkers, there were repeated murmurs of "poor people, oh poor people" and, once, "poor horse." Sometimes the Churchills would come to dinner with us at the Gritti. There was one agonizing evening when Clemmie whispered to my mother as they arrived, "I'm sorry Diana, but Winston's in a very black mood"—and indeed he was, scowling furiously across the table, answering all my mother's ever more frantic attempts at conversation with an angry grunt. His depression spread over the party like a leaden pall; before long we were all reduced to an embarrassed silence. Then, quite suddenly, he turned to my mother and said, "I shall be much better when I have had another glass of your excellent champagne." Five minutes later the fog had lifted and he was singing old music hall songs, one of which ended "This is what comes of a night at the Metropole, Look what it's done for me." I have been trying to find the words ever since.

In early September, 1951, the Venice Film Festival passed almost unnoticed, being hopelessly upstaged by what has gone down in history as one of the grandest and most glamorous fancy dress balls ever staged in Venice—which has had more than its fair share of them. It was given by a certain Charles de Bestegui, a cosmopolitan dilettante of Mexican origin, with exquisite taste and all the money in the world to indulge it, in the Palazzo Labia which he owned. Though not directly on the Grand Canal—it is actually a hundred yards or so away on that of Cannaregio— the Labia is as sumptuous a palace as can be found anywhere in that city of palaces, with a huge central hall entirely painted by

Tiepolo with frescoes depicting the story of Antony and Cleopatra. Proceedings, the invitations informed us, were to begin with a grand *entrée*, the principal guests in their magnificent costumes entering the hall one after the other with their retinues. My mother was invited by our host to play Tiepolo's *settecento* idea of Cleopatra, looking more like Madame de Pompadour than the Egyptian queen, the minor problem of one naked breast being solved by a thin layer of gauze with a silver snail-shell (in fact one of her favorite earrings) fastened at the strategic spot. I seem to remember with particular clarity the dress designer Jacques Fath, kitted up in a blaze of glory as the *Roi Soleil*; but by far the most opulent performance was that of another Latin American billionaire, the Chilean Arturo Lopez, who entered as the Emperor of China, borne on a litter by a train of attendant slaves. Anne—whom our host had very generously allowed me to bring, since tickets were the hottest property in international café society—and I were more modestly cast as members of a group of strolling players from the *commedia dell'arte*.

Of the ball itself I have regrettably few recollections; a greater impression, oddly enough, was made by the popular party outside. There had been immense quantities of advance publicity, not only in Italy but all over western Europe; the gossip columnists had never had it so good, and for weeks the Venetians had been talking about little else. The Communist Party, inevitably, had been outraged, and had done their best to whip up popular feeling; but they had had remarkably little success. It was not for nothing that Venice had for well over a century been the pleasure capital of the civilized world, and most of the city's population had flocked into the adjoining *campo* to see what they could of the fun. These too had been liberally catered for; orchestras played, acrobats flung themselves in all directions, the wine flowed in rivers. All this succeeded, of course, in taking the wind out of the protesters' sails; but I honestly do not believe that this was its principal purpose. Bestegui genuinely wanted the people of Venice, as well as his invited guests, to enjoy his great evening; and he made perfectly sure that they did. It may well be, indeed, that the outdoor festivities proved more enjoyable than those within; the palace, being lit entirely by candles, soon grew insufferably hot. By 1 AM at any rate, a good many of the privileged had emerged on to the square: the image of the Begum Aga Khan, rocking with laughter in the arms of a particularly dishy gondolier, will remain in my memory forever.

In those days Venice was still unpolluted by mass tourism, with most visitors still coming and going by train. You strolled down to the Piazza at noon for a drink, largely to see who had arrived on the previous day; instead of the five or ten thousand people you would find there today there might be a couple of hundred, of whom you might recognize a dozen or more. Then at one o'clock or thereabouts you would take a motorboat to the Lido for a beach lunch, sometimes at Harry's Bar (which in those days had a branch there) sometimes in somebody's cabin, where it would as likely as not be served by a couple of flunkeys in white jackets and gloves. I loathed the Lido and loathe it still: to this day I never set foot there if I can possibly avoid it. Sand I have always thought to be a vile substance at the best of times, and the actual bathing must be the worst in Europe—the water unpleasantly yellowish and frustratingly shallow: fifty yards offshore it still reaches to only just above the knee. Besides, the Lido has *cars*, which any sensible person comes to Venice to escape. For me it was always a huge relief, after those lunches, to get back to the city again.

Meanwhile I still had two years to go at Oxford. For my last, 1951–1952, I moved out of New College and into digs just round the corner in Holywell Street, run by a certain Mrs. Hall. My fellow lodgers were to remain friends for life: Johnny Lawrence (later Oaksey), Miles Jebb (later Gladwyn) and—alas no longer with us—Raymond Bonham Carter, father of the lovely Helena.

We were fond of Mrs. Hall, though we teased her mercilessly, but were a good deal less enamored of her French bulldog, one of the ugliest and smelliest beasts I have ever encountered. By now I was—after a fashion—mobile, having bought for £75 my first car, a 1922 Bean. Hardly anybody now remembers Beans; it was, I suspect, not only because of their ridiculous name that they went out of production at an early stage of motoring history. Mine, though it boasted a rudimentary self-starter, almost always had to be cranked by hand—not a pleasant job in pouring rain. But rain, together with cold, revealed other, more serious defects. The car had a retractable hood but no windows, a windscreen but no wipers. The screen was composed of two separate panes of glass of which the upper could be raised outwards on a hinge, creating a narrow gap through which the driver could peer while the rain beat mercilessly on to his face. The only positive attribute was a splendid hooter, activated by a sharp squeeze on a rubber bulb, which gave us all intense satisfaction. With this perfectly dreadful machine my poor Anne would show superhuman patience, frequently arriving at parties windswept and blue with cold.

It was soon after I settled into Mrs. Hall's that I received a letter from my father. He told me that he had been offered a viscountcy. All things being equal, he wrote, he would quite like to accept. By now he had more or less given up politics in favor of literature, but he would like nevertheless to feel able to go to the House of

Lords and make a speech whenever he felt like it. On the other hand a peerage—which could not in those days be renounced—would be a considerable disadvantage to me if I ever wanted to pursue a political career, and he would not dream of spoiling my chances. I wrote back at once to reassure him. I had no political bent whatever and absolutely no intention of going anywhere near the House of Commons. I sent him my congratulations and told him to go ahead.

There was much discussion that Christmas over what name he would choose. One Lord Cooper already existed, and we all agreed anyway that place names were not only more traditional but also a good deal more elegant. The only trouble was that there were only two locations in England with which my father had been closely associated, London and Bognor Regis; and neither of these—though for very different reasons—seemed entirely suitable. He finally picked on Norwich. He himself had been born in London, but his father, grandfather, and just about all his paternal antecedents had been Norwich men. It was a beautiful and historic city whose name he would be proud to bear. The decision taken, he wrote at once to the mayor to seek his approval. For several months there was no answer of any kind—though he shortly afterwards heard from the local Conservative Association, who warmly welcomed the idea. Meanwhile the government wheels had started to turn. Then, just a week or two before the publication of the honors list, there came a letter from the mayor—the successor, I believe, of the one to whom my father had originally written. Much as Norwich appreciated the honor, he wrote, it had a long radical record and had always discouraged the use of its name in connection with public honors. He would be grateful therefore if my father would think again. The city, he added, possessed several delightful wards and suburbs that might be thought appropriate, and would surely raise no objection if he applied to them.

My father could only write and say that had the mayor replied to his letter three months before he would naturally have reconsidered; in the circumstances he was very sorry but it was too late: nothing could now be done. So Lord Norwich he became, and there was I fear a certain amount of ill feeling in the city and in Norfolk as a result. One evening several years after my father's death I remember being approached by Lord Mancroft. His father had actually been Mayor of Norwich and had also wanted to take the title; but he had been stopped in time and had to accept the name of one of the city's wards. (St. Peter Mancroft is the most magnificent of all Norwich's many medieval churches, second only in splendor to the Cathedral itself.) Clearly he had been an infinitely more deserving case than my father, and I felt extremely embarrassed about it. I only hope that successive mayors of the city do not still breathe curses when they read my name.

The only person who minded my father's change of name was my mother. She was pleased by the honor—in her opinion he could never be honored enough—but she refused absolutely to call herself Lady Norwich. She had been Lady Diana for over half a century, she argued, and she had no intention of changing now. She continued to sign herself "Diana Cooper" until the day she died.

I have little recollection of my last year at Oxford. That it was pleasant enough I have no doubt, but it was in no way memorable. I seem to have spent most of my waking hours sitting in an armchair reading French and Russian novels, knowing full well that I wasn't enjoying them as I should be and always keeping my right forefinger at the page on which the current chapter ended. At last, and usually late at night, I would sit down to write my weekly essay on Lermontov or Lamartine, Turgenev or Flaubert. Then one day in June, 1952, we put on our white bow ties, dark suits, gowns, and mortarboards and headed for the Examination Schools, where for the best part of a week we were put through our paces. Knowing that I was not first-class material, I had set my sights on a goodish second—which, as it turned out, was precisely what I got.

The fact must be faced: I had been no more of a success at Oxford than at Eton. Perfectly happy, perhaps, in both; but in both equally undistinguished. At the first, it had not been altogether my fault—I was simply not good enough at games. I could probably have made Sixth Form if I had stayed, but there frankly didn't seem to be much point: I had had the best Eton could offer me, and it was time to move on. At Oxford, on the other hand, the fault was my own. I had first chosen the wrong subject; and I had then let that subject dominate my life, spending far too many hours a day with all those novels instead of getting out into the University, joining the Union or the OUDS, or seizing on any of the countless other opportunities it offered. I had fun—sometimes tremendous fun—at the time; but when I look back on it, at the chances I had and at the use I made of them, I can't help feeling just a little bit of a wimp.

Some months before, I had applied to join the Foreign Service. I had never been particularly tempted by diplomacy as such, but I loved foreign travel and in those far-off days when civil aviation was still in its early stages it seemed as good a way as any to see the world. Neither of my parents was enthusiastic either. My father had admittedly ended his career as Ambassador in Paris, but he had never been a career diplomat: he owed the Embassy only to the fortunes of war and to Winston Churchill's desire to have a good stout buffer between himself and the detested de Gaulle. He would have infinitely preferred to see me a successful businessman, and even began making enquiries about the possibility of my entering Harvard Business School before I stopped him. To this day I have no understanding of even the basic principles of economics, I do not know the meaning of the bank rate (no, please don't explain) and I should have been a disaster. My mother wanted me to be a journalist or to go into television, which was then still in its infancy but for which she astutely predicted a future. Both of these ideas had a certain attraction for me too; but the Foreign Office remained my first choice. Besides, several of my friends had applied at the same time, largely because— so long as one left the university with a creditable degree—there was no special examination to cram for.

This was replaced, however, by a rather terrifying interview. I was shown into a large room somewhere in Burlington Gardens and found myself confronted by a panel of a dozen distinguished elderly gentlemen. One only did I know: Ashley Clarke, who had been Minister in Paris under my father and was soon to be appointed Ambassador in Rome. They asked me a number of questions about why I wanted to join the Foreign Service, which I answered as best I could. Then one of them said, "Suppose you were posted to somewhere very remote, perhaps with no other diplomatic colleagues; how would you keep yourself occupied in your spare time?" I replied that I loved music and that I was sure that would keep me going. "Ah," he said, "do you play any instruments?" "Yes," I said, "the piano and the guitar." Suddenly there was consternation; they all started muttering to each other. (Rock groups, I should explain, had not in those days been invented; guitars, if seen at all, were almost invariably of the Spanish variety.) I was conscious of having put a foot disastrously wrong, and was still wondering how when I saw Ashley lean forward and say in a reassuring manner: "He said the guitar." There was a corporate sigh of relief and the interview went on. Some time later when I next saw Ashley I asked him what had happened. "Only a little misunderstanding," he said. "They thought you said the harp."

Before I knew my Oxford results I received a letter informing me that, given only that I obtained a first or second-class degree, I had been accepted into the Foreign Service. Soon afterwards came the news of my second. My feelings, as I remember, were less of exhilaration than of relief. I still had no burning desire to be a diplomat; on the other hand the days of indecision were over. I had a job, and indeed a career; and although my salary would be far from princely—for my first year's work I was to receive £450—I had a few hundred of my own and at least I would know where the next meal was coming from: an important consideration for one who was soon to have a wife, and perhaps children, to support.

As our wedding day approached in the summer of 1952, Anne and I were conscious of a problem. The Cliffords were Roman Catholics, one of the oldest recusant families in the country. Anne's parents for their part never went to church except for weddings or funerals; but the head of the family, Sir Bede's elder brother Lord Clifford of Chudleigh, seemed to have come straight out of one of the more improbable novels of Evelyn Waugh or Graham Greene. (When his daughter had married a Protestant, I was told, she was never again permitted to sleep under the family roof. On their occasional visits she and her husband would eat with her parents, but as their relationship was in her father's eyes openly adulterous they always had to return at night to the local pub.) One day Sir Bede took me aside and told me how much he loved his brother and how distressed he would be if our marriage were to provoke a split in the family. He knew he was asking a lot, but would I therefore please accept whatever was required of me with regard to the wedding arrangements?

Naturally I agreed. I loved his daughter and wanted to marry her; it seemed a small enough price to pay; though myself rather half-heartedly C of E, I certainly had no bias against Roman

Catholicism. I reassured him that I was perfectly ready to do whatever was asked. Little did I know what that would entail. First of all I was presented with a statement, written entirely in Latin, beginning "*Ego, Johannes Julius Cooper, apud. . . .*" with, at the bottom of the page, a footnote in English reading "Insert full postal address." In this I undertook to accept Catholic instruction, to marry in a Catholic church according to the full Roman rite and to bring up all our children as Catholics. All this I was more than happy to do—though as it turned out I never got the instruction—and I signed without hesitation. Then it was Anne's turn. She was given a form, similarly in Latin, to fill in stating exactly why she wanted to marry me. There were, as I remember, seven possible reasons: true love was not one of them. She could marry me for my money; she could marry me to avoid a scandal; she could marry me because I obviously represented the last chance she would ever get (*necessitas*); but she could not marry me for love. The local priest, Father Gordon Albion—he had a press cutting from some racing newspaper pinned to his office wall, bearing the headline FATHER ALBION—SECOND IN THE NOVICE CHASES—strongly advised her to go for *spes conversionis*, "hope of conversion," which he described as "always popular," so that was what she did—though I am glad to record that throughout our married life she was to make not the slightest effort to bring me to the light.

Having both toed the line as required, we turned to the marriage service itself. I suggested that we might begin with "The Spacious Firmament on High," and then . . . but Father Albion cut us short. "I'm afraid we can't allow any music," he said. Nor, as it later emerged, would they allow any flowers; and it soon became clear that, although the Roman Catholic Church had reluctantly accepted the possibility of a mixed marriage, it was determined to make the actual service as unpleasant as it possibly could. It was at this moment that Anne put her foot down. "I'm sorry, Father," she said, "but in that case I think we'll go to Caxton Hall." The effect of this threat—Caxton Hall being the main London Registry Office where civil marriages were performed—was better than either of us could have expected. Instantly resistance crumbled away. When the great day came—it was Tuesday, August 5, 1952—we seriously overworked the organist, and the little Catholic church at the gates of Sutton Place in Surrey (my new parents-in-law lived a few hundred yards down the road) was awash with flowers.

It is only fair to point out that this occurred well before the Second Vatican Council, when Pope John XXIII put an end to all such ridiculousness. Several of the changes he made—such as the use of the vernacular language in the Mass, and the requirement that the priest should in future face the congregation rather than the altar—have, I personally believe, proved disastrous. They have demystified the Faith and taken away much of its former magic, with catastrophic results to congregations all over the world. But at least those contemplating a mixed marriage will find themselves navigating a path a good deal less stony than ours.

San Vigilio was the perfect place for a honeymoon. When I was last there in the late 1960s Leonardo Walsh was dead, and without his firmly controlling hand the place had become a nightmare of water skis and screaming children, with the crystal clear lake water covered by a scum of *ambre solaire*; but in 1952 it was as peaceful as it had ever been, smoothing away—as honeymoons should—all the stresses and strains of the wedding itself and preparing us for the equally harrowing first experience of married life and a professional job, to say nothing of house hunting. We had no accommodation waiting for us when we returned to London, but moved into sepulchrally gloomy lodgings in Wigmore Street while we looked for something better. The singer Olga Lynn— known universally as Oggie—was a lifelong friend of my mother's whom I had known and loved since early childhood. She had a small flat in Chesham Place which she told us she would be leaving in about a year; we could then take over the lease at an annual rent of £600. It was rather more than we could afford, and we hesitated for a long time; but it was bright and spacious and only fifteen minutes walk from the Foreign Office (mostly across St. James's Park) and the temptation finally proved too great to resist. For the interim, we rented No. 30 Beauchamp Place, just round the corner from Harrods.

Beauchamp Place is essentially a shopping street. The ground floor and basement of every house is either a shop or a restaurant, most of them fairly smart; this means that the three floors above are normally arranged in a topsy-turvy sort of way, with their living rooms and bedrooms where you would expect to find them but the kitchens and dining rooms at the very top. By the time we moved in towards the end of 1952 Anne was pregnant and was, alas, having a pretty rough time of it, with morning sickness and—more often than not—evening sickness as well, lasting not just the first three months but all through the nine. In the evenings, therefore, she tended to go to bed, and I would go up to the kitchen to make her cups of tea and boil an egg or two for us both. As time went on, however, I began to dread those journeys upstairs more and more.

I have never been remotely psychic. In December, 1945, with three or four Eton friends, I had gone to the ruins of Borley Rectory, which had been described by Harry Price—at the time the country's leading ghost hunter—as "the most haunted house in England." We had spent all of one bitterly cold night in the summerhouse, where Mr. Price (whom I had previously called on at the Reform Club) had assured us that strange phenomena were constantly occurring, but we had been disappointed.[1] At much the same time, one evening at Eton, my friend Christopher Bonn and I decided to try out a *planchette* which he had recently bought. This time the results were more dramatic: the board started moving under our hands, its mover describing herself—in infantile but perfectly clear handwriting—as Mary Bonn, Christopher's grandmother, who had died "a century tonight." That was all: there was, as I remember, no other message. When we put the lights on again, Christopher informed me that neither of his grandmothers was called Mary; but I could see that he was trembling. I was certain that he had not been manipulating the board, at least consciously; nor, I knew, had I. The mystery remains unexplained.

And now, in the upstairs kitchen of 30 Beauchamp Place, I would feel, for no apparent reason, far more fear than I ever experienced at Borley Rectory or in Christopher's room at Eton. I saw nothing; I heard nothing. But, night after night up there by myself, I would be unable to stop shivering, conscious as I was that I was in the presence of something unknown, but unquestionably evil. It was a sensation that I had never had before and have never had, thank God, since; but even as I write these words over half a century later, I can feel the hair rising up on the back of my neck.

The following summer was that of the Coronation, and accommodation in central London for the deluge of foreign visitors was

---

1 I saw Mr. Price for a debriefing after our visit and—not wanting to let him down altogether—described a tiny incident to which in other circumstances we should none of us have given a second thought. I was horrified a year or so later to see in his latest volume, *The End of Borley Rectory*, an account of this incident, attributed to me and inflated out of all proportion. Suddenly I realized what a ghastly old charlatan he was.

in short supply; we accordingly let Beauchamp Place to Paul-Louis Weiller for what seemed to us the almost sinful sum of £90 a week, while I commuted daily from the house of my parents-in-law near Guildford. Paul-Louis typically invited far more of his friends than the house could possibly hold, to the point at which one of them was put up on a camp bed in the dining room. He too saw nothing and he heard nothing; but the next day he returned to France, after what he later described as the most terrifying night of his life.

My work in the Foreign Office was fairly humdrum. I was allotted to the Northern Department, which despite its name catered not only for the whole of Scandinavia but also for what was in those days the Soviet Union and its five satellites: Poland, Czechoslovakia, Hungary, Romania, and Bulgaria. Although the war had been over for seven years there were still any amount of postwar claims to be settled, one of the most important of which had been lodged by a Dutch organization with the irresistible name of the Bank vor Handel in Scheepfahrt. I was also responsible at the lowest level for the satellites, opening all the mail that arrived from our two Embassies and three Legations,[2] dealing with as many as I could and referring the rest to my superiors. It seems to me now that the very words at the head of the letters— "British Embassy, Prague" or "British Legation, Bucharest" made my heart beat faster; brought up as I had been on the novels of Eric Ambler and many others of the same ilk, Central Europe and the Balkans exercised a strange fascination. I longed to be there and awaited my first foreign posting with growing impatience.

Meanwhile our daughter Artemis was born in the Middlesex Hospital, on the stroke of midnight between April 22 and 23, 1953. I found myself in the unusual position of being able to choose either of these dates for her birthday; the 23rd being St. George's

---

2 Hungary, Romania and Bulgaria have all long ago been upgraded to Embassy rank.

Day and the official birthday of the Queen, I plumped for the 22nd, which seemed to involve less competition. We chose her name partly because of my mother—the Greek Artemis being the counterpart of the Roman Diana—and partly because of the tendency of the Clifford family to choose names from Greek mythology. When the time came for her christening, the Catholic church inevitably protested: how could it be expected to baptize a child with the name of a pagan goddess? By this time there could be no invoking of Caxton Hall, so we capitulated. She was eventually baptized Alicia (after her maternal grandmother) Clare (after her godmother, Lady Clifford) Opportune—because, as I discovered to my inexpressible delight, April 22 was St. Opportune's Day. But Artemis she has remained to everyone. Her parents have never regretted the name; nor, I hope and believe, has she.

After a couple of years dealing with Eastern Europe, I was allotted Scandinavia instead. This seemed to me somewhat less romantic, but I soon discovered that there was one important exception—Iceland. It was just as well, because within a short time I found this smallest and most obscure of the Scandinavian countries taking up more of my time than all the other four put together. The reason was what was officially described as the Icelandic Fishing Dispute, but was more generally known as the Cod War. Iceland, whose entire economy was based on the superb fishing around her coasts, had unilaterally declared a vast increase in what she considered to be her territorial waters, declaring a limit of twelve miles out from her shores—a figure she later increased to two hundred; we, on the other hand, who had to protect our own fisheries, stoutly maintained the internationally accepted three. There were further complications too: were the boundaries of these waters to follow every indentation of coastline, or were they to be measured from imaginary lines drawn from the tip of one cape or peninsula to the next? One look at a map of Iceland will show that the adoption of this second alternative would add thousands of square miles of protected water on the northern and western coasts.

While working on all these problems—and many another equally ticklish—I grew more and more fascinated with all I read about the country itself. Its people, I discovered, was the only one in the western world among whom the vast majority had no surnames; they consequently had to make do with patronymics—Svensson, or Olafsdottir—which by their very nature changed with every generation. Their capital, Reykjavik, which was roughly the size of Salisbury, boasted a university, museums of history and of art, a symphony orchestra, opera and ballet, a national library, and more good bookshops for its size than any other in the world, more books being read per head per year in Iceland than anywhere else. Virtually every Icelander wrote poetry. One of their innumerable writers, Halldor Laxness, had won the Nobel Prize for Literature. Best of all, there was no television on Thursdays, or throughout the month of August. To Iceland, I resolved, I must one day go.

———⊙✠⊙———

In the last days of 1953, just after Christmas, my parents left by sea for Jamaica, where they had been invited to spend a couple of weeks with their friend Perry Brownlow. The SS *Colombie* was to sail from Southampton. I had meant to see them off from the station, but idiotically went to Paddington instead of Waterloo and missed them. Long afterwards, my mother told me that my father had been strangely upset by my nonappearance. She and I could both see that he was ailing; but only he knew how ill he was.

At around teatime on New Year's Day 1954, I was working at my desk in the Foreign Office when the telephone rang. I can still hear the crackles on the ship's telephone line, and the familiar but almost inaudible voice behind them: "My darling, it's the worst." I knew exactly what she must mean, but played for time. "What do you mean, the worst?" "I mean the worst—Papa's dead." The hemorrhage had apparently started the day before; realizing that one of his passengers was seriously ill, the Captain had turned back towards Vigo on the northwest coast of Spain, but it was too late. My father was six weeks short of his sixty-fourth birthday. Fortunately he had lived just long enough to see the publication of his autobiography, *Old Men Forget*, which he had ended with the words:

> Autumn has always been my favorite season, and evening has been for me the pleasantest time of day. I love the sunlight but cannot fear the coming of the dark.

By the time he wrote this he knew all too well what was coming: cirrhosis of the liver was a killer. All his life, as he had cheerfully admitted in the same book,

> I have consistently drunk more than most people would say was good for me. Nor do I regret it. Wine has been to me a firm friend and a wise counselor. Often . . . wine has shown me matters in their true perspective and has, as though by the touch of a magic wand, reduced great disasters to small inconveniences. Wine has lit up for me the pages of literature, and revealed in life romance lurking in the commonplace. Wine has made me bold but not foolish; has induced me to say silly things but not to do them. Under its influence words have often come too easily which had better not have been spoken, and letters have been written which had better not have been sent. But if such small indiscretions standing in the debit column

of wine's account were added up, they would amount
to nothing in comparison with the vast accumulation
on the credit side.

Alas, if he had stuck to wine, all would have been well; but
there were also dry martinis before lunch and dinner, port and
brandy afterwards, a whisky-and-soda or two before bed. This is
not to say that he was in any degree an alcoholic: I only once saw
him seriously the worse for drink, and that was after an intimate
dinner for six at the Soviet Embassy in Paris. After the thirty-
fourth toast he had lost count; he had been seriously ill for a fortnight, and never touched vodka again. But diplomatic life, the
endless lunches and dinners in which the French did their gastronomic best to impress him—our own Embassy not doing too
badly either—eventually proved too much, and his liver simply
packed it in. For the last two years of his life he had drunk nothing but Vichy water and ginger ale, but it was no use: the damage
had been done.

So there was my poor distraught mother, about to be put
ashore in a small Spanish seaport, speaking not a word of the language, with the body of an adored husband. Could I, she asked
through the crackles, charter a small plane and come and collect
her, and him? Meanwhile she would find a local undertaker to do
all that was necessary. Vaguely, I remembered hearing of a small
private firm called Olley airlines; I telephoned them; they said
that they could certainly do the job and would start off at once.
The only trouble was that they could not take me with them—on
the return journey, with my mother and a heavy Spanish coffin,
there would simply not be room. I pleaded, but in vain.

The next few days are a blank. Strangely, I have no memory of
my mother's return to England, which is perhaps just as well. My
next clear recollection is of the funeral. My cousin Charles Rutland had willingly given permission for the body to be buried at

Belvoir. It was a bitterly cold January day, and the road up the steep hill to the Mausoleum and family cemetery was covered with ice. The huge and heavy hearse had a good deal of difficulty on the slope; most of us preferred to walk. Lunch was provided at the Castle for everybody—we must have been about a hundred in all, for nobody had had more friends—after which forty or fifty of us took the train back to London. Fortunately it had a large bar car. The wake has always struck me as being an admirable idea: after the stiffness and solemnity of a funeral service it encourages the pendulum to swing the other way: people relax, and even—I use the words advisedly—enjoy themselves. I remember thinking how happy my father would have been to see all his friends together there—he had always loved trains—laughing and drinking and from time to time reminiscing about him and all the fun he had been.

I had loved him dearly and missed him desperately, but I suspect that I never quite got over the slight shyness that I used to feel in his company. It was, I think, based on my feelings of inferiority. He seemed so much more intelligent than I was, so much more erudite, so much more a man of the world. My own chief interest was music, which—to his often expressed regret—he was quite unable to share. Somehow—though he himself would have denied it vehemently—I always felt that I was a bit of a disappointment to him. The sad thing is that if he had lived another ten or fifteen years we would have grown together. Our common love of history would have been a great bond, and I like to think that he would have enjoyed my books, to say nothing of my Christmas Crackers (of which more later). But there: as I have already said, I was a slow developer. He died before I was ready for him.

My mother did not attend the funeral. Six months before, when Evelyn Waugh had taken her to task for not going to Hilaire Belloc's, she had replied:

> You see I don't go to funerals. . . . I went to my fa-
> ther's funeral only to hold my mother—I did not go
> to hers. Public ones I grace, i.e. King, Generals de La-
> tre [sic], or Leclerc by official duty—but not the buri-
> als of those I love, therefore not yours if I survive you
> which I hope is unlikely.

> I shall not go to Duff's if he dies first. . . . The idea jars
> upon me—exhibition of grief—the society duty side
> does not, in my heart, *fit*.

For some time she could not face returning to Chantilly and to the sad and desperately lonely existence that she now saw stretching out before her. By this time Anne and I had moved into the Chesham Place flat and were able to take her in for a few weeks until she felt stronger. It was a difficult time for all three of us; and Artemis, not yet a year old, was still unable to give her the immense love and support that was later to mean so much to her. But she struggled through, and with the help of many devoted friends—not least of whom were my father's two last great loves, Louise de Vilmorin and Susan Mary Patten (who was later to marry Joe Alsop)—gradually managed to rebuild her life. Having been married to my father for thirty-five years, she was to survive him for thirty-two.

That summer she, Anne, and I went to Greece to stay with Paddy and Joan Rayner (whom he was later to marry), who had rented the painter Niko Ghika's lovely house on Hydra. We took a ship down the Dalmatian coast, through the Gulf of Corinth and the Corinth Canal to Athens, where we stayed a couple of nights at the Embassy with my mother's old friends Charles and Catherine Peake. For Anne and me, it was our first time in Yugoslavia or Greece, and our obvious excitement seemed to act on my mother like a tonic. Athens in those days was a charming little city, basking in that astonishingly clear Greek light for which it was then famous, still mercifully free of the tourists and nightmare pollution of today. For three nights a month over the full moon—which we were lucky enough to hit—the Acropolis was open till midnight; we would go up around ten after a jolly dinner in Plaka and, more often than not, have the whole place to ourselves apart from a solitary watchman. Wandering among the moonlit columns of the Parthenon, while feeling a cool midnight breeze caressing my face, seemed to me then something suspiciously like Paradise.

Paddy and Joan were, unlike the Peakes, relatively new friends of my mother. Anne and I, indeed, had met them only once or twice—though we were fully aware, as everyone was, that Paddy had fought with the Cretan resistance during the war, in the course of which he and a few colleagues had kidnapped the general in supreme command of all the German forces on the island, had hidden him for some weeks in a cave, and at last had successfully shipped him off as a prisoner to Cairo.[3] We were thus acquaintances rather than friends—but not for long. After those days on Hydra I was a changed man. Apart from my father, Paddy was one of the two people—we shall come to the other one later—who have had a permanent influence on my life. It wasn't just his glorious ebullience, the quickness of his mind, his encyclopedic knowledge, and the sheer fun that he created all around him; it was also the fact that in those ten days he opened up to me the whole world of the Eastern Mediterranean, which I have often felt to be my spiritual home. I owe him more than he will ever know.

---

3 One of those involved, W. Stanley Moss, subsequently told the story in a book, *Ill Met by Moonlight*. This was subsequently made into a film, in which Paddy was played by Dirk Bogarde.

In my sorrow at my father's death, I think it was a good twenty-four hours before I realized that I had become a Lord. I had been John Julius Cooper for the same number of years, and I'm not sure how I initially reacted to the change. "The Viscount Norwich" sounded faintly ridiculous when applied to me—I had never really got used to it with my father—still, renunciations of peerages were in those days unheard of and there was nothing I could do about it. But people started calling me "My Lord" or even "Your Lordship"—titles which I very seldom hear nowadays—and I soon discovered to my astonishment that in the London of the 1950s being a peer was rather like being black: some people were nicer to you and some people were nastier to you, but relatively few people were exactly the same. There was also an all-too-popular misconception that lords were richer than commoners: it was easier to get a table in a restaurant, but when the bill came it had to be examined with rather greater care. A curious mystique hung about the peerage, partly I suppose because it was still associated with aristocracy; but my father was the son of a Norwich doctor, and a year or two later with the introduction of life peerages the association was to become more tenuous still. Yet somehow the mystique still seems to survive: years later in the sixties on a television program, my dear friend Benny Green was reminiscing about his East End childhood, and I remarked on how thrilled and proud his parents must be to see him almost nightly on the box. "Don't you believe it," he said, "The only thing that impresses them is that I'm sharing the program with a Lord."

In the late summer of 1954, after some two years in Northern Department, I began to feel that my longed-for foreign posting could not be much further delayed. I had put my name down for Moscow; indeed I had been more or less promised it, and had gone so far as to buy myself a new umbrella with my name and the words "British Embassy Moscow," engraved on it in Russian. But I had reckoned without my mother. Ever since my father's death she had been determined that I should be posted to Paris. It would be a perfect arrangement, she argued; Anne and I could spend every weekend at Chantilly, where Artemis would rapidly become bilingual and we could invite all our Parisian friends. I told her again and again that there was absolutely no chance; that it was the last post I should have wanted, since with a high-profile mother, herself an ex-Ambassadress, living and entertaining at Chantilly, it could not fail to have caused appalling embarrassment all round. Ambassadors did not encourage junior members of their staff to have famous mothers and country houses within easy reach of their Embassies, and I for one didn't blame them. Our own Embassy days were still far too recent, and she—whether she meant to or not—would inevitably steal much of the present Ambassadress's fire. The situation would be intolerable for the Ambassador—and, incidentally, for me. But these were not the sort of arguments to weigh with her; she wanted me in Paris. It will already be clear from this narrative that my mother had only to see a string to be compelled to pull it, with almost invariably disastrous results; and now once again she got to work. Naturally she said nothing to me, knowing full well that I should have stopped her; instead she telephoned Anthony Eden, then Foreign Secretary, and asked him to change my posting. She was newly widowed, and she needed me; why therefore could he not have me sent to Paris?

I can only assume that Eden replied—rightly—that this would be impossible, but that he would try and arrange for me to go somewhere nearer to Paris than Moscow was. And so he did. My Moscow posting, to which I was hugely looking forward, was cancelled; instead, I was informed that I was to be Third Secretary at the British Embassy, Belgrade. It was a huge disappointment to me, and also to my mother. Once again her attempt at string pulling had backfired, and I lost no time in telling her so. In fact, I pointed out, I should now be less accessible in Belgrade than I would have in Moscow, which at least had a civil airport with regular services to Paris. Belgrade then had no airport at all. The only contact with the outside world was by road or rail. But the die was cast: and for the three months before our departure I found myself taking thrice-weekly lessons in Serbo-Croat.

Gradually I came to accept my fate. I devoured the two volumes of *Black Lamb, Grey Falcon* by Rebecca West, written in the 1930s but still—as it remains today—by far the best book ever written about the former Yugoslavia. To my surprise, I also greatly enjoyed my Serbian lessons. My teacher, a Mr. Grozdic, was by far the best language teacher I had ever had; Serbo-Croat is closely related to Russian, in which I had a degree; and by the time of our departure the following January I was, if not fluent, at least able to get by. Meanwhile an apologetic letter had arrived from the Embassy informing us that we should have no house to move into at once, and that we should be put up in a hotel until somewhere suitable could be found—which, they added ominously, might well take a considerable time.

Here was a problem. Artemis was not yet two years old; we could not keep her indefinitely in one small room of a Serbian hotel. Was Anne to leave her, or to leave me? Fortunately, my dear mother solved more problems than she created. We took her over with her Nanny—this was the last generation of the old-fashioned, grey-bowler-hatted kind—to Chantilly, where they were welcomed with open arms. Naturally we loathed leaving her; but she was in super safe hands, and the moment we reached Belgrade we knew we had made the right decision.

Yugoslav roads were, we were told, execrable, and garages few; I had therefore bought a long-wheelbase Land Rover with a four- wheel drive, and had had it fitted with an auxiliary petrol tank. It was far from beautiful, but it certainly gave one confidence. Into it Anne and I packed virtually all our worldly goods and, early one morning in January, 1955, set off for a new life in the Balkans.

Chapter Seven
Belgrade

I**T WAS A** long drive, and we took our time. We stopped for a day and a night in Venice, then drove on to Ljubljana, capital of Slovenia, which was still in those days one of the six constituent republics of Tito's Yugoslavia. There we stayed at the Slon Hotel—"The Elephant"—where I produced the brand new passport with which the Foreign Office had recently issued me. "The Right Honorable John Julius Cooper," it read, "The Viscount Norwich." The reception clerk looked it up and down, frowning; never had he read a name like this. At last he gave up, shrugged, and put me down as "Mr. Right"—something that I have always longed to be, but have never managed before or since. Up we went to our room: a minute or two later Anne shouted to me from the bathroom. "It's very odd, but I can't find the plug for the basin." A month later we would have accepted this as par for the course, knowing that east of Vienna no basins had plugs; but in those days we were still innocents abroad. "Oh dear," I said, "but it's all right—I'll go down and get another from reception." I was still only halfway down the stairs—there was, so far as I can remember, no lift—when she shouted down to me: "Don't worry—the water doesn't run out anyway." Our first lesson had been learnt: East was East and West was West. When in the Balkans never travel without a rubber squash ball—they fit all sizes of basin— and a plumber's mate. They make all the difference.

The next evening, after a gentle drive through fabulously beautiful country, we reached Zagreb. Croatia, like Slovenia, had been for centuries a province of Austro-Hungary, where the imperial nobility had maintained their country villas and vast hunting estates; and in the mid-1950s Zagreb, its capital, still gave the impression of a delightful Central European provincial city. The language on the shop signs might look strange; yet Zagreb seemed, to our inexperienced eyes, Austrian through and through. That evening we saw *The Marriage of Figaro* in its enchanting opera house: all red and gold baroque as opera houses ought to be, with frescoed ceiling and golden caryatids holding up the dress circle. The work was competently and sensitively sung in German, and the whole thing was exactly what one would have expected from a small but cultivated city of the Habsburg Empire.

We set off early the next morning: we had a long journey ahead of us. It is some 250 miles from Zagreb to Belgrade; the relatively new motorway ran straight as a die from one city to the other but with only a single lane in each direction, and there were countless horse-drawn peasant carts to be negotiated. It was as boring a drive as could be imagined, across a dead flat plain, and yet, when we reached Serbia, we found ourselves in a different world. There, on the river Sava—whose confluence with the Danube is dominated by the city of Belgrade—was the suburb of Zemun, until the end of the First World War the gateway to the Ottoman Empire. It should have looked romantic; it did not. All we could see were the skeletons of vast high-rise tower blocks of dark grey concrete, begun a year or two before and then abandoned. "Tito's Folly" they were always called.

It was a depressing introduction, in the twilight of a January afternoon, to the city which was to be our home for the next two and a half years; and as we drove into Belgrade itself our spirits did not appreciably rise. The contrast with Zagreb could hardly have been greater. Zagreb was, in its essence, Western Europe; Belgrade was the Balkans. Zagreb had been Austro-Hungarian; Belgrade had been Ottoman. Zagreb could boast moderately distinguished architecture; Belgrade had a few turn-of-the-century public buildings in a vaguely *beaux-arts* style, but that was about all. There were virtually no cars, except a few official ones; scarcely any shops except for basic provisions, and most of these were little more than stalls. The sight of a herd of pigs being driven down the main street was not uncommon. Even such things as safety pins were unprocurable. Much of the traffic was still horse-drawn, driven mostly by peasants dressed in rough brown homespun, wearing vaguely conical hats of the same material. Frequently too, one saw Albanians, who were looked upon even by the peasants as second-class citizens and given only the most menial jobs. They too were immediately recognizable by their surprisingly elaborate dress. Their homespun was white rather than brown, lavishly ornamented with strips of black braid; their trousers, similarly adorned, were cut so low at their hips as apparently to make nonsense of the law of gravity; on their heads were little round skull-caps of white felt.

And here was another lesson: my first experience of the great gulf which lay between the Habsburg Empire and the Ottoman. It used to be said in Eastern Europe that "the grass never grows where the Turk trod." This was not strictly accurate: the Sultan may have been Turkish, but the government and administration of the Ottoman Empire was for the most part Christian—composed of Greeks, Syrians, Lebanese, Armenians, Copts and the rest of that astonishing racial mix which made up what used to be called the Levant. But in another way it was all too true. Those countries which were unlucky enough, in the fourteenth and fifteenth centuries, to fall under Ottoman rule—Serbia, Greece, Romania, Bulgaria—had all enjoyed thriving, flourishing civilizations during the middle ages. Read their history: not only was Byzantium in its later centuries entirely Greek, but both Serbia and Bulgaria possessed magnificent medieval empires. Visit their churches, with walls superbly frescoed from floor to ceiling. Hear their epic poetry: every self-respecting Serbian peasant, as I was shortly to learn, could recite long passages of the old epic ballads—more often than not about the great Tsar Lazar, who for all his greatness lost the battle of Kosovo in 1389, which spelt the end of an independent Serbia until less than two hundred years ago.

Then came the Ottoman conquest; and it was as if the subject lands had been given a mild dose of chloroform and put in a state of suspended animation. From that moment on, nobody wrote a great book, nobody erected a beautiful building, nobody painted a picture or composed a symphony. The Renaissance, together with all the culture of the seventeenth and eighteenth centuries, passed by unnoticed. It was only at the beginning of the nineteenth, when the movement for independence began, that with an immediacy that was almost touching—the sudden flowering of the desert after rain—the artists and craftsmen appeared once more. But alas, they were by now some five hundred years behind their colleagues in the West; and much that they had lost was already beyond recall.[1]

As for the sheer drabness of Belgrade, one of the principal reasons was, I decided, that since the years of Ottoman rule Serbia had never had a rich aristocracy, or even much of an educated upper class; in prewar days there had been the royal family and

---

1 I am fully aware that this paragraph may be contested—especially perhaps in Romania, which was kept by the Ottomans on a rather looser rein; but I still believe it to be fundamentally true.

the peasantry, with relatively little in between. This accounted for the lack of any noble architecture; there was no Place des Vosges, no Grand Canal, not even a Belgrave Square.

But such names had a melancholy ring when we thought of our own homeless state; our problem was to find any sort of lodging at all. Since the British Embassy was increasing its staff, mine was a new appointment. I had no predecessor, no one into whose house we could immediately step; and Belgrade was, it seemed, full to bursting. We had been warned of this before leaving London, but the problem proved far worse than we had imagined. For almost six months we were deprived of our little daughter—though we went back to see her whenever we could— and forced to live in one small room in the Excelsior Hotel. This made the Slon in Ljubljana look like a palace; it had a wardrobe the size of a sentry box for both of us and—as always—a distinctly dodgy bathroom. The service in the restaurant was such that no meal took less than two hours. (Fortunately, such was the pace of diplomatic social life in Belgrade that we did not have to endure hotel dinners too often.) Twice, when other members of the Embassy staff went on leave, we moved into their house for a fortnight or so; then it was back to the Excelsior again. Not, heaven knows, that we were being choosy, for we should willingly have taken anything; but during this time we were not shown one single house or flat, and our heavy luggage—enough to last us for the next three years—which had followed us by rail to Belgrade remained piled high in the stairwell of the Chancery, where it reached almost to the first floor.

The good news was that we were sent off as often as possible— out of pity, as much as anything else—on tour; and that made up for a lot. We had a Consul-General in Zagreb and Consuls in Sarajevo and Skopje, but the Embassy staff had done very little traveling round the country and most of the provincial population had never seen an Englishman. We would sleep in local hotels, which were not very much worse than the Excelsior—a few were rather better—eat in the local restaurants (all of which smelt asphyxiatingly of *sljivovica*, the plum brandy that is the Yugoslav national hooch), call on the local mayors with friendly greetings, visit the occasional school, and drive and drive until we knew the country far better than most Yugoslavs. Soon my Serbian was fluent, which helped a lot; what helped even more was our Land Rover, with its four-wheel drive and its reserve petrol tank. Petrol was always a problem. There were no filling stations, only occasional petrol dumps somewhere on the outskirts of the major towns. We had a list of their addresses, all impossible to find; so almost as soon as our first tank was empty and we had switched over to the second, the hunt would begin.

The other problem was the roads themselves. Most of them, being unsurfaced, were a cloud of dust in summer, a sea of mud after rain; time after time the four-wheel drive got us out of tight spots—though more than once, when there was a small river to be forded, even that failed and we had to suffer the ignominy of being pulled out by teams of horses provided by the local peasantry. The peasants could always be trusted in an emergency. To them, a car on the road was like a ship at sea; to have withheld help would have been unthinkable. It was the same with the lorry drivers. There were not many—one could easily travel for an hour or more without seeing anything other than a few peasant carts—but they believed firmly in the fellowship of the road. Whenever we had a puncture—which, with the tracks invariably covered with nails from old horseshoes, was often—every driver would stop without being hailed, and not only insist on helping to change the wheel but pull out a pocket vulcanizing kit and repair the inner tube on the spot.

We loved those tours. The hotels, such as they were, could be pretty awful; the food often constituted a serious challenge. But the scenery—particularly in the south—was spectacular, and the lovely unspoilt villages were made more colorful still by the costumes. In those days virtually all the country people normally wore their local dress, which varied dramatically from place to place. In northern Croatia the girls wore long many-pleated snow-white skirts almost to the ground, which seemed to remain spotless however deep the mud; in Bosnia—still largely Muslim—the usual dress for the women—who were never veiled—took the form of brightly patterned baggy Turkish trousers; in Macedonia their clothes were the most extraordinary of all, with black skirts and heavily braided jackets studded with gold coins. But all too soon we would have to return to Belgrade. Anne, who is really happy only when she is painting, found a spare room at the top of the Chancery building in which she could set up an easel; I sat at my desk writing reports on our tours, dealing with correspondence, drafting dispatches for my seniors to amend and improve, reading and summarizing the newspapers and generally doing any odd jobs that came my way.

The work was, on the whole, quite enjoyable; but what made it infinitely more so was my boss, Sir Frank Roberts. Not much over five feet tall, he was a fireball of energy. He had the gift, moreover, of persuading every member of his staff that he or she was doing the most important job at the most important time in the most important of missions. The quickness of his mind, the breadth of his knowledge in every field, the range of his interests, never failed to astonish me. I grew to love both him and his wife Cella, a Lebanese of much the same height as her husband, always astringent, sometimes acidulous, but with a wonderful sense of humor and a warm and generous heart that, hard as she tried, she could never quite conceal.

Winter became summer, we were still homeless and were agonized that Artemis was growing up without us; but one day there arrived a music impresario by the name of Gerry Severn. (His name was, I imagine, an anglicization, since he spoke excellent Serbian and was clearly of Central European stock.) His purpose was to put authentic performances of the great Russian operas on to the still relatively new vinyl long-playing records. Ideally, he would have gone straight to the Bolshoi; knowing, however, that any such arrangement would have been an impossibility in cold war Moscow, he had come to Belgrade. At this time the Yugoslav National Opera, though hopeless at Mozart and the Italians, produced Slav operas outstandingly well. They had in particular a splendid Chaliapin-like bass in a certain Miroslav Čangalović, and a magnificent contralto called Melanie Bugarinović—I am mildly surprised at the speed and certainty with which their names (and many others) flow back into my mind—and a deal was quickly struck for recordings of *Boris Godunov, Prince Igor,* and *Khovanshchina.* This meant that Gerry was to make frequent visits to Belgrade over the next few months, and since I was a sort of unofficial cultural attaché at the Embassy we became friends. He knew all about our housing problems and one evening brought wonderful news: an architect of his acquaintance had a spacious second-floor flat in his house which he would be delighted to rent to us.

The building was on a corner of a street named Strahinića Bana, between the National Theatre in the main square and the Danube. The flat was surprisingly spacious and full of character, and we loved it the moment we saw it. From the moment we moved in, our life in Belgrade was changed. At last Artemis, now two and a half, could join us; the crates were delivered from the Chancery stairwell; the books and gramophone records were unpacked; our clothes were properly hung up and stowed away. Finally we had a home. Things were looking up. For the rest of our lives we shall remember Gerry Severn with gratitude.

———◦†◦———

Yugoslavia in 1955 bore all the outward signs of Communism. There, covering the façades of the public buildings, were the standard twenty-foot-high portraits of Marx and Lenin (though—rather pointedly—not of Stalin, with whom Tito had courageously broken in 1948 and who had died just two years before our arrival). Other walls were adorned with those slogans so beloved of governments behind the Iron Curtain: slogans like "Long Live the Five Percent Increase in Medium Light Industry" that seemed to make every Communist heart beat faster. But it was Communism with a difference; the Curtain itself was gone. In 1948 Tito had established his own personal régime, which although it paid lip service to Communist principles was certainly a good deal more flexible. For one thing, Yugoslavs no longer lived in fear; they readily accepted invitations to foreign embassies or private houses and, when they could, never hesitated to invite one back. This is not to say that there was no secret police: once every six weeks or so our cook would come to me to say that she had been summoned to the UDBA—read KGB—to report on who had come to our house; together we would concoct a perfectly innocuous list, which was apparently never questioned. Nor were there any restrictions on tourism or on travel round the country. (Our Land Rover was, I believe, once briefly followed in Macedonia; but the Macedonians saw very few foreigners and could be forgiven for being a little sensitive.)

Public life seemed to revolve around state visits. Hardly a week went by without the welcoming of some Third-World President,

Marshal, or Generalissimo, who would be met by Tito and driven with him in an open car to Belgrade's nearest approximation to a palace, where his accommodation had been arranged. I remember in particular Nehru, Gamal Abdul Nasser, and President Sukarno of Indonesia; but all faded into insignificance on that memorable day in 1956 when Nikita Khrushchev and Nikolai Bulganin arrived, cap in hand, in an effort to repair the breach of eight years before. For Tito, this was the ultimate triumph, a virtual admission by the Soviet Union that he had won the moral victory. There had always been a right-wing faction in the country, which would have welcomed the return of the monarchy even though it could obviously not say so openly; on the other hand even a good many royalists looked on the Marshal with considerable respect—even a grudging admiration. Unlike the other Communist leaders of eastern Europe, all of whom had spent the Second World War safely tucked up in Moscow, he had been fighting in the field at the head of his Partisans. He was the only native Croat who was not in some degree resented by the Serbs: he, and he alone, stood above inter-republican rivalries. He had had the courage to break with the detested Soviet Union in 1948; now, less than a decade later, he had brought it to heel. Feeling as they did about the Russians, even the most reactionary of Yugoslavs had to admit that their leader was a great man.

Despite its shortcomings, we gradually grew to love Belgrade. Short on beauty, it was long on the atmosphere of the old Balkans. By far its most interesting monument was Kalemegdan, the ancient Turkish fortress dominating the confluence of the two great rivers, by this time containing a small park. It faced due west across the great, flat, dusty plain, and there Anne and I would go in the evenings to watch the most breathtaking sunsets we had ever encountered. The problem was what to do at weekends. An hour's drive to the north of the city was a range of wooded hills

known as the Fruška Gora, not unlike the Chilterns; it was pleasant enough for country walks and summer picnics, but hardly
exciting. Apart from that, and from Smederevo, a romantic
ruined Turkish castle on the Danube, possible excursions were
few. To the adventurous sightseer, Yugoslavia could be an endless
joy; but all its star attractions—the mountains of Slovenia, the
Dalmatian Coast, the painted monasteries and churches of the
South—were, in the 1950s, a good two days away. A week's leave
could provide the holiday of a lifetime; on the average weekend,
however, time could lie heavy on the hands.

Almost every evening there was a dinner party, almost invariably at the house of a member of the *Corps Diplomatique*. Few
gatherings are more boring than the average diplomatic dinner
party, since almost all the guests are there because they have to be
asked, rather than for any special social qualities; and the gloom
induced by the discovery that for the second time in a week one
is going to sit next to the speechless and perfectly hideous wife
of the Uruguayan Counselor cannot easily be described. Thank
God for the guitar and those old English and French songs, more
recently supplemented by a good number of American. I never
had anything approaching a voice—which, in a small drawing
room, is probably just as well—but I could accompany myself
competently enough and, I like to think, came to the rescue on
many a sticky evening.

One of the things that we most enjoyed in our diplomatic
life were the sendoffs. Every few weeks some old friend would
be posted elsewhere and seen off at the station. Thanks to the
absence of an airport, the only link with western Europe—apart,
of course, from the road—was the Orient Express, always the
most romantic train in the world. Fortunately it left for Paris
shortly before midnight; so we would all leave our dinner parties
and—more often than not in black ties and long dresses—turn

up at the station at eleven-thirty to say our farewells and wish *bon voyage* to those departing. Sometimes, for someone really popular who had been there a long time, there might be up to fifty people, several of whom would have brought bottles of champagne with them. The sounds, the steam, the smells of the great train added immeasurably to the atmosphere; some of our most enjoyable parties in Belgrade were held on the station platform.

Others were with our Yugoslav friends. Belgrade being the capital of Serbia, they were virtually all Serbs; and though the odious Slobodan Milošević and his gang have seriously blotted the Serbian copybook in recent years, there were many whom we dearly loved. Few, admittedly, had the means, or very often the space, to entertain; when they did they specialized in a celebration known as a *slava*, held not on their birthdays but on the days dedicated to the saints after whom they were named. During these celebrations special cakes were baked and, it need hardly be said, vast quantities of *sljivovica* consumed. Since many Serbs share relatively few Christian names, this meant that one might attend three or four *slavas* in a single evening, with disastrous effects on one's general well-being the following morning. All Slavs know how to celebrate, and the Serbs are no exception. They would sing old Serbian songs, many of them of haunting beauty; they would join hands and form rings to dance their traditional dance, the *kolo*, to strange, unresolved, gypsy-like melodies almost always in a minor key and often ending plaintively on the supertonic; sometimes there would be recitations and even storytelling.

We also became involved with the student life at the University. Anne and her friend Rosamund Ferguson—daughter of our Naval Attaché—being both of them painters, signed on with the Arts Faculty and assiduously attended life classes. I remember one broiling summer day when we packed about twenty of their fellow students into various cars and drove them up into the

Fruška Gora for a huge picnic. Public transport being still fairly rudimentary in those days, many of them—even those born and bred in the city—had never been there before; the sun blazed down, the *sljivovica* came out in quantities bordering on the industrial, and the party was a huge success.

In the summer of 1955 Stavros Nearchos lent my mother a beautiful *caique*, which took us on a memorable cruise through the Aegean. With us were Paddy and Joan, and our friends from Paris days, Frank and Kitty Giles. We started in Piraeus, then dipped gently through the Cyclades and Sporades—visiting the grave of Rupert Brooke on Skiros—to the Dodecanese. On Santorini we called in at a taverna where a party of some kind was in progress—and, judging by the state of many of the guests, had been for some hours. This was the time when the Cyprus crisis was at its height, the Greeks calling vociferously for *Enosis*, or its union of the island with Greece. Suddenly one of the party guests, having heard us speaking English, struggled to his feet and launched into a passionate diatribe against the British, ending with a still more impassioned rendition of the Greek national anthem which was instantly taken up by his companions—but which, not altogether surprisingly, we failed to recognize.

Except Paddy. "Quick," he said, "stand up!" We all rose hurriedly to our feet, and he joined lustily in the singing. To our accusers this was something of a setback; but worse was to come when they, as they thought, finished the anthem and sat down while Paddy, still standing to attention, started on the second verse, followed by the third. Of these verses he alone knew the words, and he eventually sat down to loud cheering. Several people came up to our table afterwards to apologize for their friend—who, they said, would never have shown such deplorable manners had he been sober.

During the cruise Paddy talked fascinatingly about things Byzantine—of which I knew almost nothing—and recommended a book which, he said, would provide a first-rate introduction to the subject: *The Byzantine Achievement*, by Robert Byron. This book, it hardly seems too much to say, changed my life. It is very much a young man's book, written as it was when the author was still in his early twenties; but it filled me with a fascination for Byzantium and the whole Byzantine world which I have never lost. From that moment I read everything I could find on the subject, and determined to go to Istanbul at the first opportunity.

That opportunity came just a year later, in July, 1956. We thought the Land Rover could probably make it from Belgrade in two days, and arranged to spend the night with a colleague at our Legation in Sofia. In Bulgaria as in Yugoslavia, the roads were empty apart from peasant carts and the occasional lorry; carts meant horses, horses meant horseshoes, horseshoes meant nails—and nails meant punctures. We had about six of them in a single gruelingly hot day, and were saved again and again by the Good Samaritan lorry drivers. They never failed to stop; out would come that pocket vulcanizing outfit—a little fuse would be lit with their cigarette and the heat would seal the patch to the tube—and in ten minutes or so we were on our way again. Never would they take money, or even closed cartons of cigarettes; all they would accept was one that had already been opened, and a few packs removed. Tins of Nescafé were also welcomed, but again only if they were less than full. We in our turn adopted the general practice of never refusing anyone a lift.

But that evening, when we were only fifty miles or so from Sofia, there was a rather more serious incident. Suddenly and without warning, a large cow leaped out of a ditch immediately in front of the car. Anne, who was driving, swerved and jammed on the brakes, but there was nothing to be done; a hideous bump was followed by a sickening crunch, and then the sound of pathetic mooing from under the car. Gingerly we reversed, dreading the sight we were about to see; but to our astonishment the animal struggled to its feet and hobbled away—admittedly holding one foreleg rather awkwardly out in front of it—into a nearby field. Still shaken, we looked around in the hopes of seeing somebody to whom we could report what had happened. There was no one anywhere in sight, so we drove on.

Ever since we had crossed the border into Bulgaria we had been speculating on whether or not we were being followed. In the Soviet bloc foreign cars normally were, especially if they had diplomatic license plates; and several times already we had tried the old trick of stopping immediately after a sharp bend and seeing if anyone drove up. All such tests, however, had proved negative. The only thing to do, we decided, was to leave a full statement with the Legation when we got there—which we duly did. The next morning we were on the road again, and that evening (after one or two more punctures) we reached the Turkish border at Edirne, the ancient city of Adrianople. Even without the police and customs post we could hardly have missed it—for there, just to the left of the road, was one of the most astonishing buildings of the world: a vast mosque, far larger than any I had ever seen, its four pencil-slim minarets soaring up into the sky. I knew by this time a little about Byzantine architecture but nothing about Islamic, and was taken completely by surprise; only later was I to discover that this was the famous Selimiye, generally held to be the masterpiece of Sinan, the greatest of Ottoman architects, who had built it in the 1570s for Sultan Selim II. There was, alas, no time to visit it; darkness was falling fast and we still had several hours drive ahead of us. It was to

be forty-seven years before I saw it again, still more magnificent
than I had remembered.

---◦✦◦---

In the early hours of the following morning we finally drove
into Istanbul, pulled up, exhausted, in the car park of the
recently opened Hilton Hotel, checked in and fell into bed. Only
when we woke did we draw the curtains—and gaze down, for the
first time, at the Bosphorus. Of all the great waterways I know,
only the Grand Harbor in Malta and, perhaps, the Chao Phraya
in Bangkok seen from the Oriental Hotel can hold a candle to it.
Nowadays it is spanned by three huge bridges; in the 1950s these
were still unbuilt; consequently there were far more ferryboats
even than one sees today, milling around in all directions like
ants, while the constant parade of infinitely larger vessels—tank-
ers, cruise ships, naval destroyers—glided nonchalantly among
them on their way to and from the Black Sea. One could sit for
hours on the balcony in the summer sunshine, just watching—
and one still can. Half a century later and after heaven knows how
many subsequent visits, I find the magic as powerful as ever.

Over the next week we explored every corner of Istanbul. After
Venice, it is my favorite city; unlike Venice, however—which just
lies there looking beautiful and saying "take me, take me"—Istanbul has to be worked on, and that work was a good deal harder then
than it is now. The whole city was desperately down at heel. There
were practically no tourists, and the great monuments tended to be
open for only a few hours a week; one had to sit down and work out
a careful timetable in advance if one wanted to see them all. In St.
Sophia, access to the upper gallery (and therefore to the greatest of
the mosaics) was forbidden. Sometimes, as for St. Eirene, appointments had to be made; sometimes—at Küçük Ayasofya mosque,

for example, formerly the sixth-century Justinianic church of St. Bacchus and St. Sergius—one of the little boys forever playing around it had to be bribed with bonbons to go and find the key. The glorious early fourteenth-century mosaics at Kariye Cami were still under restoration; only a few were visible. Restaurants too were a problem. Pandeli's over the Spice Bazaar was usually the best bet (and, with its turquoise-tiled walls, wonderfully rich in local color) but like most of its kind was open only for lunch; for dinner there was the Regence, kept by two old white Russian ladies of villainous appearance, or, more often than not—since their cooking spelt gastronomic crucifixion—back to the hotel.

Istanbul today is, it need hardly be said, transformed. The Golden Horn is no longer little better than an open sewer, into which all the neighboring butchers used to throw their offal; no longer do the tanneries at the southern end of the Land Walls render the air almost unbreatheable. Whereas in the old days there was little alternative to the huge plasticated international hotels across the Golden Horn in Pera, there are now countless smaller and infinitely more agreeable establishments within a stone's throw of St. Sophia; delicious Turkish restaurants abound. Most important of all, the monuments are—with relatively few exceptions—open from soon after dawn to sunset, and infinitely better displayed than they used to be. A (literally) shining example is what is to me, together with the *Deesis* mosaic in St. Sophia, the greatest single work of art in the city: the so-called Alexander Sarcophagus in the Archaeological Museum, just below St. Eirene. Though roughly of the time of Alexander the Great, it is not his; it was actually made for a minor kinglet in what is now Lebanon, and was discovered, buried in the sand at Sidon, only in the 1880s. Thanks to this burial, the carving is as crisp as if it were done yesterday; even some of the original color has remained. The artist's name is of course unknown, but he was unquestionably a genius.

Never before or since have the excitement, the dynamism, the sheer passion of battle and hunt been better expressed by means of hammer and chisel. Beside the soaring splendor of the Alexander Sarcophagus, the Elgin Marbles hardly get off the ground.

We returned through Sofia to find that no more had been heard about that luckless cow; it was more than six months later that the Legation wrote to me in Belgrade enclosing an exhaustive account of the incident, correct in every detail and signed by three independent witnesses. Our tail had been cleverer than we thought. I also received a bill for eighty pounds. It seemed a bit steep: eighty pounds was a lot of money in those days. But I paid up. I knew I should want one day to return and had no intention, if I were ever to do so, of ending up in a Bulgarian jail.

———— ❧ ————

By this time my mother had largely recovered from my father's death. She continued to live at Chantilly—nothing would move her while she thought there was the slightest chance of my being posted to Paris—but to keep herself occupied she was once again traveling a good deal. Of course she came to see us in Belgrade, but more often than not her destination was Rome. Her lifelong friend Venetia Stanley—in her youth she had been the recipient of daily love letters from the Prime Minister Mr. Asquith—had married Asquith's Secretary of State for India, Edwin Montagu, and had one daughter, Judy. Venetia was now dead; Judy had married the American art historian Milton Gendel and the two were living in an enchanting apartment on the Tiber Island—which became for my mother in the late 1950s a home away from home. Also in the city was another close friend Jenny Nicholson, daughter of Robert Graves, married to *The Times* representative in Rome, Patrick Crosse; Patrick's deputy

Nigel Ryan; and, by a wonderful stroke of good fortune, Iris Tree.[2] Her blindingly yellow hair was cut short with a fringe; she was funny, poetical, unexpected, and one of the few true bohemians I have known.

Anne and I used to go to Rome too, as often as we could; but in the spring of 1956 I left her in Belgrade with Artemis, while I joined my mother in Rome for something rather special: an audience with Pope Pius XII. The former British Minister to the Holy See, Sir Darcy Osborne, had somehow managed to arrange it, and an enormous invitation had arrived covered with triple crowns and crossed keys and reading:

Sua Santità
ricevrà
Lady Diana Cooper
e
Il Figlio[3]

I feared that if the Holy Father were indeed expecting to receive the Second Person of the Trinity he might be in for something of a disappointment; none the less I put on my best blue suit, my mother a long dress with black lace sleeves and a mantilla, and off we sped to the Vatican. We had been carefully briefed in advance of the form the interview would take. It would last, we were told, about ten minutes, and would consist basically of small talk; any theological speculation was firmly discouraged. At the end we should produce some small religious article and ask the Pope to bless it. Finally His Holiness would enquire how many children I had of each sex, and would give me a rosary for each—black for a boy, white for a girl.

---

2 See Chapter Three, page 60, footnote 5.

3 His Holiness/will receive/Lady Diana Cooper/and/The Son.

The religious article created something of a problem. All my mother had was a very pretty little cross made up of six circular glass panels. Inside each panel were two locks of hair, plaited together: in the center, the hair of my ancestors King William IV and Mrs. Jordan,[4] around it in the other sections, that of their children. It was—indeed it is, I have it before me as I write—a fascinating piece, but not perhaps entirely appropriate for the present occasion. But it was all there was; it would have to do. "Please," my mother implored me, "*please* don't let me start explaining it all to the Pope. I shall be so nervous, I know I'm going to if you don't stop me." "I'll do my best," I said.

Much of the old Vatican ceremonial has been done away with, alas, in the past half century; but in the days of Pope Pius it was still going full blast. We were led through a whole series of splendid rooms, each of which seemed to be inhabited by people of a different century: from a nineteenth-century one full of elderly gentlemen in frock coats we would pass directly into what appeared to be the main reception room at Elsinore, with men looking exactly like Hamlet in black doublet and hose and clinking swords; then into a room full of Swiss Guards in their red, blue, and yellow Michelangelo uniforms. All the time the tension seemed to mount: the whole process was theatrical in the extreme. Finally we were halted in a smaller room, occupied only by a purple-robed gentleman whom I took to be at least a bishop, who told us to wait while he went next door; somehow it was clear that next door was the papal audience chamber. The bishop disappeared, leaving the door ever so slightly ajar. Peeping through a tiny crack, I could just see a vast expanse of purple silk spread across the floor: he had prostrated himself before his master. A moment later he had scrambled to

---

4 See Chapter One, page 3.

his feet, returned to us, and opened wide the door; and we entered into the Holy Presence.

My first reaction was of how tall he was. We all knew the famous face, with the thin-rimmed spectacles over the huge aquiline nose; but here was a man who, from his snow-white skullcap to his scarlet slippers, seemed to me to measure a good six foot two or three. He stood while we made our reverences, then indicated two gilded armchairs and settled behind a totally empty Louis Seize writing table. There followed a long silence. The conversation, we had been assured, would be in English, in which the Holy Father was naturally fluent; this proved, however, to be something of an exaggeration. My mother and I had to make the going, the Pope reacting favorably or unfavorably as required: the favorable reaction was "very fine, very fine," the unfavorable "very difficult, very difficult." (On several occasions he seemed uncertain as to which was the more appropriate, though when I mentioned Yugoslavia his face clouded and there was a slight change of emphasis: "*Very* difficult.") At last he rose to his feet; did we have, by any chance, any little object we would like him to bless? My mother fished out her little cross, and before I could stop her launched off into its history. I nudged hard, but it was too late. The Pope clearly understood something, but not much. "Very difficult, very difficult," he murmured, but blessed it without demur.

The bit about the children went like clockwork. I told him that I had a single daughter—our son Jason was not yet thought of— and a white rosary was immediately handed by a chamberlain to the Pope, who blessed it and delivered it to me. I was rather hoping that he might repeat the mistake he was said to have made among a party of American congressmen when, instead of asking "boy or girl?" he murmured "black or white?"; but no such luck.

And so the even tenor of our life went on until the autumn of 1956, when two things occurred: the singularly ill-advised reaction on the part of Britain, France, and Israel to Gamal Abdul Nasser's seizure of the Suez Canal and, almost simultaneously, the invasion of Hungary by Soviet tanks. The news reached us at Lake Ochrid in Macedonia; we drove lickety-split back to Belgrade, where we found the Embassy in a state of near panic: Tito and Nasser were, at least diplomatically speaking, close colleagues who saw themselves as leaders of the "Bandung" powers, or what we should now call the Third World. The Anglo-French action over Suez was, as far as they were concerned, unprovoked aggression. Not only had two apparently friendly countries betrayed their friendship, which was bad enough; they had done it on the backs of the Israelis, which was far, far worse. This was an offense that would not easily be forgiven. Again and again we tried to divert Yugoslav attention away from the distant Canal to the atrocities that the Russians were perpetrating on their very doorstep, but they scarcely seemed interested. They hated the Russians certainly, but they hated their Hungarian neighbors too—there were nasty wartime stories about several hundred Serbian families having been made to stand in the middle of the frozen Danube while the Hungarians machine-gunned the ice—and felt little sympathy for their present sufferings. As for the Israelis, they were the worst of the lot; no friend of Israel could be a friend of theirs. We all worked hard over the next year to minimize the damage, but where the Canal was concerned most of us secretly shared their views and we had little success. Suez had been a disaster, and dealt a blow to British prestige across the world from which it would take a long time to recover.

During our last spring in Belgrade, the Ambassador asked me to accompany him on a ten-day tour of South Serbia, Kosovo, Bosnia and the Dalmatian coast. The two of us, it appeared, would be traveling alone in the brand new Embassy Rolls-Royce. There had been much argument with the Foreign Office about the Rolls-Royce. The Embassy had been upgraded to the level which was deemed to deserve such grandeur, but Frank Roberts had protested: the roads of Yugoslavia, he argued, were not meant for Rolls-Royces and the car would be ruined in no time. Characteristically, the Foreign Office refused to listen: Belgrade was a Rolls-Royce post, Belgrade should therefore have a Rolls-Royce. Branko, the Embassy chauffeur, was sent off to Coventry for a two-week training course, and returned with a smart-suited, old-school-tied young man from the Company to hand over the car with due formality. A subsidiary purpose of our projected tour would be to put it through its paces.

And so, early one spring morning in 1957, off we set—Frank and I in the back—I call him Frank now for simplicity's sake, but in those days he was Sir—and Branko alone in front. We had been driving about an hour on a perfectly good metalled road when suddenly something went "*ping*," and what appeared to be a piece of somebody's braces shot across the car and hit the glass just behind the driver's seat. Momentarily we were baffled; later we discovered that it was the elasticated band that governed the movement of the armrest between us. Half an hour later we rounded a sharp bend and Branko put his hand on the horn; alas, when he took it off again the horn continued to sound until, a good five minutes later, he stopped the car, disappeared under the bonnet and managed to break the connection.

Our journey continued for the next week or so with—apart from the occasional inevitable puncture—no further untoward incident. I soon overcame my initial shyness, and boss and underling got on splendidly together. I particularly enjoyed showing Frank the two loveliest painted monasteries in South Serbia, Peć and Dečani. By this time, after two or three previous visits, I knew them moderately well; he had never seen them before and was as fascinated as I knew he would be. In Peć we stayed the night in the monastery at the invitation of the Abbot, an immense figure with a beard like Tolstoy and a character like Falstaff. For dinner he gave us a whole roast goose, washed down with vast quantities of rough red wine and several other concoctions of formidable potency which he claimed to have distilled himself. By the middle of the evening I had a nasty suspicion that my standards of interpretation were deteriorating fast, but British honor was at stake and we both somehow kept going. At last the Ambassador was shown to the only guest room; I was given a couple of blankets and settled down by what was left of the fire.

I awoke the next morning with the worst hangover I have ever had, and found myself seriously wondering whether I was in a fit state to continue our journey. Two nasty surprises awaited me. First, the Ambassador—who had poured just as much alcohol as I had into a far smaller frame—bounced into the room smiling, pink faced and raring to go. Second, breakfast. This turned out to be the remains of the goose we had the night before, now stone cold and covered with congealed grease. I still don't know which was harder: to force a mouthful down my throat or to keep it there afterwards. There then followed another nightmare hour, this time in the church. We had visited it the previous evening, but the Abbot was afraid that we had missed one or two of his favorite frescoes and was determined that we should see them in the morning light. Unfortunately most of them seemed to be on the ceiling, and every time I put my head back to look at them they started, very slowly and deliberately, to revolve. Meanwhile the interpretation had to go on. Seldom have I felt more desperate. At last we said our goodbyes and climbed into the Rolls, embarking on a twisty, unmetalled mountain road which was the last thing I needed, the Ambassador keeping up a stream of happy conversation as we went. I eventually recovered, but only just.

The last excitement before we left Belgrade was the arrival of the Stratford Memorial Theatre with their production of *Titus Andronicus*. It had been directed by Peter Brook, who was there in person together with as star-studded a cast as could be imagined, headed by Laurence Olivier and Vivien Leigh and with Anthony Quayle playing Aaron the Moor. I knew the Oliviers moderately well: they were old friends of my parents and had stayed several times at the Paris Embassy. Already it was clear that the marriage was under strain. He seemed exhausted, obviously saving every ounce of energy for the next performance; she—whom we later knew to be seriously manic-depressive—was in a manic phase, overanimated, overexcited, game for anything, refusing absolutely to go to bed. None the less, the visit was an enormous success. Though one of the obscurest and, frankly, the least distinguished of Shakespeare's plays, *Titus* was given the sort of production of which only Peter Brook was capable and was cheered to the echo. Even the challenge of Shakespeare's stage direction in the middle of the second act, *Enter Lavinia, her hands cut off and her tongue cut out, and ravished*, was triumphantly met, Miss Leigh even then somehow contriving to look not so much ravished as ravishing.

After they had left it was time for us too to go. It is generally believed in the Foreign Office that to ask for a particular posting is a virtual guarantee that one will be sent somewhere else; I can only say that this is—or was—simply not true. I had always longed to go to Lebanon, and had duly made my formal request. I always wondered whether Cella Roberts, a Lebanese herself, intervened in some way; in any case the posting came through.

Anne and I were overjoyed. She took Artemis back to my mother in Paris and then came back at once to Belgrade. A week later, in August, 1957, we took the train to Genoa, where we spent a happy day with David Balfour, the only British Consul-General in history to have had a former life as an Orthodox monk. "If there's only time to see one thing in Genoa," he said, "the cemetery it has to be." How right he was. Within it is a whole gallery of tableaux in stone: nineteenth-century gentlemen on their deathbeds, grieving widows and children gathered round, every hook and every button, every stitch of every sock immaculately carved. Perhaps the most memorable representation of all is that of an old lady who sold peanuts on a street corner. She saved up all her life for her monument, and she got it: there she is with a huge pile of her wares, each peanut an individual work of art.

That evening we took ship for Beirut.

Chapter Eight

Beirut

SELDOM IN MY life have I been more excited at the prospect of a journey. I had never been to the Middle East, never even to the Muslim world except for that week in Algiers twelve years before. But I had heard tell of Beirut. It was, everybody said, a terrestrial paradise of almost perpetual sunshine with a warm, benevolent sea; the place where East met West and Christianity met Islam; a land where at certain times of the year you could ski in the morning and swim in the Mediterranean that same afternoon; a country both beautiful and exotic which, thanks to the French mandate throughout the interwar years, was famous for its sophistication and, in particular, its superb cuisine. It promised, in short, to be a considerable contrast to Tito's Belgrade.

In the 1950s—and for all I know still today—members of the Foreign Service traveling for the first time to a new post normally came by land or sea, rather than by air. They were bringing with them all the household goods that they would be needing for the next two or three years, and quite possibly their car as well; in such circumstances flying was clearly out of the question. Anne and I settled Artemis once again at Chantilly with my mother, then sailed on the SS *Esperia*, an Italian ship of the Adriatica Line. The journey took a week. Our first port of call was Naples; and I had asked Raffaellina Guidotti, wife of the Italian Ambassador in Belgrade (and later in London) who was herself a Neapolitan, to recommend a place to visit that would be off the beaten track, somewhere generally unknown where we should never otherwise go. Unhesitatingly, she had recommended the convent of S. Gregorio Armeno. We found it at last, tucked away in a rabbit warren of tiny streets in the old city, and knocked on the door.

It was opened to us by a middle-aged nun in a long black habit with a three-inch scarlet stripe running down the front. This was already dramatic enough; but she then led us into a magnificent sunlit garden with a mass of baroque statuary, in which—in a scene somehow reminiscent of the opening chorus of a Rossini opera—a dozen other nuns, similarly clad, were teetering on high ladders picking oranges. We were enchanted, and gladly accepted when the first nun offered to show us the church and treasure. Only when we reached the sacristy did she tell us of the local miracle. This, she explained, was the liquefaction of the blood of St. Patricia. We knew of course of S. Januarius—S. Gennaro—whose blood annually liquefies in Naples Cathedral; but we had heard nothing of Patricia, who turned out to be an early Christian saint—daughter, the nun erroneously informed us, of Constantine the Great—who had died in the odor of sanctity and whose body had remained for centuries uncorrupted. One day, she continued, an irresponsible pilgrim had pulled out one of her teeth to keep as a relic; this had resulted in an instant gush of blood, which he had collected in a glass phial that he fortunately chanced to have about his person. Would we, she asked, be interested in seeing the miracle?

Yes, we said, of course we would. Without further ado she opened a cabinet and withdrew an elaborate reliquary containing a glass phial about the size of a tennis ball, within which was a thick coating of a dark and unpleasant looking substance mildly suggestive of very old chocolate. Cradling it between her hands, she began to tilt it from side to side, first to the left, then to the right, then back to the left again. This went on for two or three minutes, after which we saw that the contents of the phial had suddenly acquired a surface, and that surface, as she continued to sway the reliquary, was remaining horizontal. Unquestionably, what had been a solid was now a liquid. She finally pointed out several framed certificates hanging on the wall nearby, in which a number of distinguished university professors testified that they had witnessed the miracle, and that there was no scientific explanation, physical or chemical, that could possibly account for it. Duly impressed, we thanked her, made a small contribution to the convent's upkeep and took our leave.

None of the other stops on our journey eastward yielded anything quite so improbable; none the less, the Adriatica Line could hardly have chosen them better. In Syracuse we were taken to the quarries and shown that extraordinary rock formation known as Dionysus's Ear, thanks to which the King was able to hear the conversation of those working in the caves below; in Athens we climbed up to the Parthenon; and in Alexandria, having admired Pompey's Pillar, we were entertained by the gully-gully men, performing their traditional magic with day-old chicks as props. And so at last we steamed early one morning into Beirut, which was to be our home for the next two and a half years.

———— ◦◦ ————

Nothing more unlike our arrival in Belgrade on that grim January afternoon two and a half years before could possibly have been imagined. The sky was cloudless, and was to remain so for the next four months; the shops were overflowing with every sort of luxury; the swimming was superb, and whenever the heat became oppressive one could drive for perhaps forty minutes up the mountain and find oneself at 2,000 feet. Best of all was our accommodation; in a few days we had found ourselves the most enchanting house I have ever lived in. It stood high on a hill looking down over Beirut. Its plumbing and cooking arrangements were fairly rudimentary—though our man-of-all-work Mohammed never once complained—but otherwise it was a Venetian palazzo in miniature, with a long central living room running from the little garden at the back to the vast terrace at the front and, at each end, tall windows crowned with flowing tracery. And that was only the beginning. From the terrace the view took one's breath away. To the left was the cobalt blue Mediterranean; below us the white, clustered town; and to the right the Lebanon range, dominated by the twin peaked Mt. Sannine, snowcapped even in midsummer. As soon as we could arrange it Anne's sister Pandora brought Artemis out to join us, wearing the largest and blackest pair of sunglasses I had ever seen.

Oh how we loved that house. In those days Beirut was the Clapham Junction of the world's air routes—it was still about seven hours from London—and English friends and acquaintances were perpetually passing through on their way to India or the Far East. We made a point of giving a terrace dinner party on the night of every full moon, putting our foreign guests facing the mountain and watching their faces as, promptly at ten minutes past nine, an immense, luminous grapefruit appeared from behind Sannine and climbed slowly up into the eastern sky.

The political structure of Lebanon was, I think, unique. The country was said to be divided more or less equally between Christians and Muslims—in fact it wasn't, owing to the far higher Muslim birth rate, but the fiction was still maintained because it suited everybody and made for a quiet life. Among the Christians there were the local Maronites (the majority), the Greeks, and the Armenians, the last two subdivided again into the Orthodox and the Uniates—who, while following the Eastern rite, accepted the supremacy of the Pope in Rome. The Muslims themselves were split into Sunni and Shia; and finally there were the Druses, who were said to be an offshoot of Islam but who remained a mystery. It was always maintained that whenever a Druse was asked about his religion he was obliged to lie; the result was that no non-Druse could ever be sure that he knew anything about them at all.

Of all these communities, the Druses were by far the most colorful. In my day their political leader was a certain Kemal Jumblatt. He exemplified that rarest of political combinations, the doctrinaire socialist who was also a feudal chieftain, with a private army of perhaps 5,000 followers at his command. During the troubles of 1958 he was to lead them in open warfare against the government, while remaining Minister of Education. This alone would have been remarkable enough; but Jumblatt went further. He somehow found additional time for oriental mysticism, spending two or three months a year at the feet of a guru in south India. When at home he lived in a wonderful old house in the south called Moukhtara, which had a river flowing straight through the middle of it and in which, on my first visit, I was delighted to find a number of heavily armed Druse tribesmen, sound asleep on Louis Quinze sofas with their boots on.

This curious religious complexion of their country enabled the Lebanese to dispense altogether with political parties. Instead they used their various religions, each of which was carefully given its due. Thus the President of the Republic was invariably a Maronite, since there were more Maronites than anyone else. Then, to compensate, the Prime Minister had always to be a Sunni Muslim, and so on. Every government and every parliament was obliged to number eleven or multiples of eleven, so that every religion received its fair share of power. On the whole—until the summer of 1958—they all got on extremely well together; but at the time of my arrival they were more than usually united: the Suez affair had occurred less than two years before, and even the most instinctively pro-British of our Arab friends (the Lebanese Christians, it must be remembered, considered themselves Arabs just as much as the Muslims did) still bore a furious resentment against the British and French—particularly for their alliance with the hated Israel.

Sooner or later everything seemed to come back to Israel. No wonder that within a day or two of my arrival the Counselor at the Embassy, Ian Scott, gave me a word of advice. "For God's sake," he said, "don't talk about Palestine. Don't even try to argue. This is matter of deep, gut emotion; logic has nothing to do with it. Talking Palestine in this country is the quickest way to lose your friends. Just avoid it, that's all." Every day thereafter I realized once again how right he was.

⎯⎯⎯◦⌀◦⎯⎯⎯

Lebanon was to teach us another lesson too: a lesson in humility. In Belgrade we had, on the whole, been a good deal richer than our Yugoslav friends; in Beirut we were a lot poorer—frankly on the receiving end. Night after night we would take in a couple of cocktail parties before going off to some glorious candlelit garden for a buffet dinner. They were not caviar/foie gras dinners; the food was usually Arab, but with an additional French touch of sophistication. Wine flowed, both French and Lebanese—which, particularly the red, was excellent. The bad news was that you were asked at eight and never sat down before ten or later. This meant that if you had been standing and drinking since six-thirty—which you probably had—you were already longing to get the weight off your feet; you were also rapidly becoming speechless. The good news was that there was no hanging round afterwards: the moment you had downed your Turkish coffee—always, in the Lebanon, with a delicious added drop of orange flower water—you said your goodbyes and left.

My biggest failure was with Arabic. My early fascination with languages still continued, and—wrongly as I was all too soon to discover—I considered myself a pretty good linguist. My French had been fluent since I was six, I had a goodish working knowledge of German and Italian, and a degree from Oxford in Russian; more recently, I had been an interpreter in Serbo-Croat. Why should Arabic hold any terrors? I managed to get permission for an initial ten days of intensive tuition at MECAS—the Middle East Center for Arab Studies—which was run by the Foreign Office in the village of Shemlan, forty minutes or so up the mountain. This was intended primarily for professional Arabists who were to spend most of their active life in the Middle East. The full course lasted some eighteen months, but I felt that those ten days would be enough to give me a push-off, after which two or three hours' study a week would do the rest.

How wrong I was. Now for the first time I came face to face with a seriously difficult language—a language whose words, roots, and sentence structure were totally unlike anything I had come across before; whose plural nouns were apparently unrelated to their singulars; whose cursive, right-to-left script not only reduced many letters to one or two dots above or below their neighbors, but normally left out all the short vowels, so that effectively you had to know what a word was before you could read it. After a few months, still barely able to ask for the butter, I gave up. I consoled myself as best I could with the reflection that most of my Lebanese friends were themselves far happier in English or French, some of them indeed speaking Arabic not very much better than I could myself; still, it had been a salutary lesson. I have never considered myself a linguist since.

There seemed a chance, however, that Artemis might be one. She was now four years old, so we sent her (in defiance of my pre-nuptial vow) to an admirable kindergarten run by the *Collège Protestant des Jeunes Filles*—moving after a year to the college itself and so laying the foundations of the near perfect French she speaks today. I remember enjoying myself hugely teaching her to read—with, it need hardly be said, the same *Reading Without Tears* that, for all its questionable attitudes, had served me so well nearly a quarter of a century before.

Another joy of Beirut was its position. Less than half an hour's drive would bring one to Byblos, one of the oldest and most fascinating archaeological sites in the world, which was in the care of two elderly French archaeologists, man and wife. They loved showing people round, but it was fatal to do the tour with both of them together, since every single remark made by one was contradicted by the other. One of their innumerable points of disagreement was on the earliest inhabitants of the site, and in particular the shape of their skulls: were they brachycephalic—short-headed—or dolichocephalic—long-headed? This led one day to the following unforgettable exchange:

> He: *Ils étaient sûrement brachycépales, parce que . . .*
> She: *Non chéri, je t'assure, ils étaient dolichocéphales.*
> He: *Enfin, c'était les brachycéphales qui se sont dolichocéphalisés, quoi?*[1]

Even more rewarding than Byblos was Baalbek. This was nearly two hours drive from Beirut, but what a beautiful drive it was.

---

[1] He: They were certainly brachycephalic, because. . . .
She: No my dear, I assure you, they were dolichocephalic.
He: Well then, they were brachycephalics who dolichocephalized themselves, weren't they?

One climbed out of the city on the Damascus road, crossed the Lebanon range and turned left into the broad plain of the Bekaa, which ran due north between the Lebanon and the Anti-Lebanon through tawny hills that glowed purple in the sunset, until one saw a mile or two ahead the six giant columns that were all that remained of the Temple of Jupiter. Beside it was the Temple of Bacchus, roofless but in a far better state of preservation, with its glorious stone carvings still largely intact. These two buildings together, constituting what is unquestionably the most majestic Roman monument in the Middle East, drew us back to them again and again. Every summer they were the scene of a major artistic festival: we had the New York Philharmonic in the Temple of Jupiter, while the Temple of Bacchus saw a truly memorable performance of *Antony and Cleopatra* by the Old Vic.

To the south of Beirut, the ancient city of Tyre was barred to us by virtue of its position, only a mile or two from the Israeli frontier. Sidon, on the other hand, with its warren of covered souks and its lovely Crusader castle standing out just off shore, was always a favorite. Journeys there were often combined with a visit to the little mountain village of Djoun, where the grave of the celebrated Lady Hester Stanhope—niece of William Pitt, who had settled in the Lebanon in 1814 and remained there, growing ever more eccentric, for the last twenty-five years of her life—provided a perfect place for a picnic. Sometimes we would press on further to the Château de Beaufort, another ruined castle of the Crusaders standing on a great bluff high above the Litani River. All these places were exquisitely beautiful and still utterly unspoilt; and there was of course always the additional bonus that for a good six months of the year we could plan our journeys long in advance, in the certain knowledge that there would not be a cloud in the sky.

———— ❧❦ ————

Syria, like Tyre, was out of bounds. At the time of our arrival diplomatic relations with the country—broken off at the time of Suez—had not yet been restored and the frontier was closed to us. The frustration of knowing that Damascus was only two-hour drive over the mountain and being unable to get there was almost more than we could bear. A short flight, however, would bring us directly to Amman and Jerusalem; and by a marvelous stroke of good luck the Ambassador in Amman, Charles Johnston, and his Georgian wife Natasha regularly invited us for the weekend. The British Embassy was in those days within the grounds of the Royal Palace; and on many a Saturday the young King Hussein—then still in his early twenties, recently out of Harrow and obviously rather lonely—would ring up and invite himself to dinner. Charles would hastily telephone round his diplomatic staff to see if any of their daughters were available; if not, one of the prettier secretaries would be called in. On these occasions the guest of honor liked to finish off the evening dancing to what we still called the gramophone. The drawing room carpet would be rolled back; records were carefully selected, the pianist Charlie Kunz being a particular favorite; and off we went round the floor. One thing only differentiated these evenings from other similar occasions: the fact that for some reason the King—otherwise the most modest and unassuming of men—could not ask a lady to dance. She had to ask him. Anne felt, I remember, a bit diffident about this at first ("May I have the honor, Your Majesty?" "Charmed, I'm sure") but soon got used to it.

After we had been about three months in the Lebanon, in autumn 1957, my mother came to stay. She was—as I knew she would be—enchanted by it all. I wangled a few days leave and we took her down to Amman, where as usual the King came to dinner; and she started talking to him about Petra, where none of us had ever been. Instantly he put a palace car at our disposal, with uniformed driver; and at six the following morning off we went—my mother, Anne, and I—on what was then a twelve-hour journey to a flea-pit hotel in the little town of Ma'an, where we spent the night. Early the following morning we reached the police post at Wadi Musa, where we hired horses; and by sunrise we were riding into the city.

Nowadays Petra is part of the tourist beat; among my friends I know hardly anyone who has not been there at least once; on my last visit in 1999 I was astonished (and horrified) to see—though fortunately a safe distance away—what appeared to be a fair-sized town, with a blaze of neon-lit hotels and restaurants. It was very different half a century ago. In Petra itself there was a tented camp, run by the Philadelphia Hotel in Amman; you brought your food down with you, and it was cooked whenever you asked for it. You could have a tent if you wanted one, but most visitors wisely chose one of the countless small tombs hewn out of the rock—some of which were furnished with iron bedsteads and very primitive washstands—looking out on to the central valley of what everybody insisted on calling "the rose-red city."[2] ("A Tomb with a View" was a rather obvious joke, perhaps, but we thought it funny at the time.) I remember the exhilaration of our first early morning ride through the *Siq*—that extraordinary narrow cleft in the rock that leads into Petra itself. Now at last, I felt, I was no longer a tourist; I was a traveler, right up there with Burckhardt and Doughty, with T.E. Lawrence and Freya Stark. I continued to feel it until, all unsuspectingly, I opened the camp's

---

2 "A rose-red city, half as old as time," by the little-known poet Dean Burgon, must be one of the most hackneyed lines in English poetry. Charles Johnston, a far better poet than Burgon ever was, came a lot closer with his two-line poem *Air Travel in Arabia*:

We passed through Petra in a wink;
It looked like Eaton Square, but pink.

visitors' book, which went back to well before the war—and was brought rapidly down to earth. There before me on the page were the unmistakable signatures: Chips Channon . . . Loelia Westminster . . . Elsa Maxwell. . . . Suddenly I was a tourist again.

From Petra we drove back—still in the Palace car—via the Dead Sea (in which we dutifully swam, and very unpleasant it was) and Mount Nebo (from which Moses first set eyes on the Promised Land) to Jerusalem. I was greatly struck by the contrast between the extraordinary beauty of the old city—which, I felt, Jesus Christ would immediately have recognized—and the hideousness of the modern churches. Why is it, I found myself wondering for the hundredth time, that after the splendor of their medieval architecture, modern ecclesiastical authorities have such excruciating artistic taste? In all Jerusalem there were only three really great religious buildings: the Crusader church of St. Anne, that glorious flight of steps that leads down to the Chapel of the Virgin, and of course the Church of the Holy Sepulchre itself. Even this last is far from beautiful in the accepted sense of the word:[3] but its age, its darkness and its mystery give it a magic of its own. We lunched with Katy Antonius—widow of the great George Antonius, author of the seminal work on Arab nationalism, *The Arab Awakening*—and had drinks at the American Colony Hotel (by far the loveliest in Jerusalem) with the legendary Mrs. Vester, who had owned it and lived in it for half a century and loved nothing more than telling you the story of her surprisingly adventurous life. She lent me her 400-page autobiography to take to bed that night, and I was astonished to find in it not a single statement or anecdote that I had not heard from her own lips a few hours before. The following day we drove back through Jericho and the Jordan Valley to Amman.

---

3 And even less so now, since the Greek Orthodox have seen fit to disfigure it with a huge and perfectly hideous modern mosaic just inside the entrance.

Most of my spare time that autumn was taken up with rehearsals of an amateur production of Gilbert and Sullivan's *Iolanthe*, in which I had been cast in the leading—though not, I hasten to emphasize, the title—role. It was performed by the Beirut Orpheus choir and directed by the choir's founder, a musical Palestinian named Afif Boulos, who for some months had been giving me rather unsuccessful singing lessons. Most of the cast were compatriots of his: vast numbers of Palestinians had emigrated to Beirut after 1948 and many, having attended English boarding schools in Jerusalem and elsewhere, were almost more English than the English themselves, speaking the language perfectly, often without a trace of accent. The opera is essentially a dialog between a band of fairies and the House of Lords. The male characters are nearly all peers, all of them wearing their scarlet robes and coronets throughout the performance; the only exceptions are Private Willis, the sentry (who finally marries the Fairy Queen), and Strephon, the son of the fairy Iolanthe by a mortal. I was thus the only genuine peer in the cast, singing one of the only two nonpeer roles.[4] We did five performances, the fourth of which was attended by a somewhat mystified Camille Chamoun, President of the Republic; but I cannot think that I was very good, if only because Sullivan always saw his heroes as tenors and most of the music lay far too high for my almost entirely untrained voice. (On the other hand, my delivery of the line "I'm only half a fairy" regularly brought the house down.)

One person only, I think, was seriously worried by my performance: Artemis, now four, who displayed great concern at my obvious affection for Phyllis, the Arcadian shepherdess, in fact a pretty Palestinian soprano. She seemed strangely uneasy, and it

4 The late Lord Stanley of Alderley notched up another possible first: he claimed to be the only peer to have sung in *Iolanthe* wearing his own robes.

was some days afterwards that she finally plucked up the courage to ask Anne: "When is Phyllis coming to live with us?"

———————⟡———————

Looking back on my Beirut life, I see it as being somewhat gallicly divided into three parts: before the *événements*, after the *événements,* and the *événements* themselves—the key word being the almost universal euphemism used by the smarter Lebanese to describe the extremely disagreeable sequence of events that took place throughout the long summer of 1958, during which President Chamoun was blockaded in his palace and the streets resounded with almost continuous gunfire. All this, I should emphasize, was as nothing compared with the all-out civil war of the 1970s, when the city was effectively destroyed; but it seemed quite bad enough at the time.

The trouble began around Easter. We had gone to France for a fortnight to stay with my mother at Chantilly and, we hoped, to visit the Brussels World's Fair. One day, just before our departure on the second part of the program, I received a telegram from the Embassy: "Please return at once stop sorry to cut short your leave but we need you here stop." Back we went, to find the whole atmosphere in Beirut transformed: in little more than a week it had become a city of sandbags, police posts, checkpoints, road blocks, and all the paraphernalia of civil unrest. A curfew was imposed: those not possessed of a special permit had to be back in their houses by eight o'clock in the evening. Memories of wartime England flooded back; the principal difference was that the enemy, instead of being across the sea, was in our midst.

This book is emphatically not a work of history, and is consequently no place for a detailed analysis of the Lebanese political situation. Suffice it to say that in those distant days—less

My parents' wedding—
St. Margaret's, Westminster, June 2, 1919.

With Nanny, Alice Ayto,
age seven weeks.

With my father at Bognor
Regis in about 1932; a time
when suits and ties were still
de rigueur in the country.

My parents outside Admiralty
House, October 3, 1938, the day
of my father's resignation as
First Lord of the Admiralty.

With my parents on
Long Island, July 1941.

With Dr. Rudolf Kommer and
Nanny, New York, 1940.

Lunch in Soho before going
off to Eton for the first time,
September 1942.

West House, Aldwick, Bognor Regis, by Rex Whistler.

The Drawing Room at Aldwick, 1942.

Mother milking
during the war at
Aldwick, 1942 or 1943,
photographed by
Cecil Beaton.

My mother on Pauline Borghese's *retour d'Egypte* bed, complete
with ancient Egyptian figures and sphinxes carved at each corner, at
the British Embassy in Paris, 1946, photographed by Cecil Beaton.

Doing basic training at H.M.S. Royal Arthur, Corsham, Wiltshire. I am on the left.

Château de Saint-Firmin, Chantilly. My mother leased it as a weekend retreat in 1945. It was to be her permanent home for the next fifteen years.

With Anne at La Reine Jeanne, 1951.

Anne's and my wedding, August 5, 1952. Pandora (left) and
Atalanta Clifford and Pandora's daughter, Annabel Jones (now
Astor, and David Cameron's mother-in-law).

Honeymoon at San Vigilio, Lake Garda.

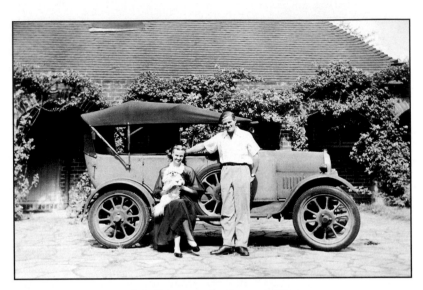

My first car, the Bean, 1952.

Serenading my mother, Chantilly, 1952.

Anne and Artemis, 1954.

At Delos during the cruise of the
Eros round the Greek Islands
in 1954.

Paddy Leigh Fermor in
Cretan costume.

With Freya Stark and my
mother at Ain Anoub, Lebanon,
September 1954.

Our Land Rover on the main
road between Belgrade
and Athens.

Villagers at Vladimirovac,
near the Romanian border, 1956

Village celebrations at Alibunar on the Romanian border.

Sarajevo in 1955.

Anne at Strahinica Bana 75, Belgrade.

Belgrade, May 1957. Dressed in the
official uniform of Third Secretary
for the presentation of credentials
by Sir John Nicholls.

Picnic at Smederevo with the Oliviers. Alan Webb,
Jenny Lambert, Frank Thring, John Lambert,
Vivien, Larry and Anne, June 1957.

With my mother and Anne, Jerash, Jordan, March 1958.

The view from our Beirut terrace, 1957. Visible on the right are
the twin peaks of Mt. Sannine, snow-capped even in summer.

Our Christmas card from Beirut, 1957.

Quartet from Rigoletto, British Embassy staff party, Beirut, 1959.
Donald Reeves, Patrick Wright, myself and Raja Hannush.

My mother and Anne,
Temple of Horus,
Edfu, Egypt,
February 1960.

Anne painting in the giant olive
groves of Calabria, 1961.

Monks on Mount Athos, photographed during my visit with Reresby Sitwell and Costa Achillopoulos in June 1964. Our visit to this remote peninsula in northern Greece was to become the subject of my first book, published in 1966.

The monastery of Dionysiou, Mount Athos, founded in 1375 and built on an outcrop of sheer rock overlooking the sea.

The Coronation of Pope Paul VI, June 30, 1963.
The Duke of Norfolk is on the Pope's right, Sir Peter Scarlett, British Minister to the Holy See, on his left.

Venice, May 1972, a Venice in Peril Tour. On the left is J. G. Links, author of the wonderful *Venice for Pleasure*, while to the right his wife Mary is hidden behind Carla Thorneycroft. Their daughter Amanda Pallant is beside me in the center.

The foothills of the Tibesti mountains in the Sahara, 1966.

A break from filming *The Gates of Asia* at Nemrut Dag, Turkey, July 1973.

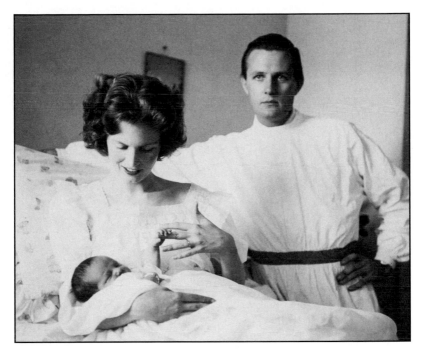

First photograph of Jason;
Hospital of American University of Beirut, October 1959.

Cecil Beaton with
Jason and Artemis,
Chantilly, 1960.

Jason 1963.

Ricki Huston and Paddy Leigh Fermor at Bruern Abbey, 1961.

Allegra age 15
on the set of
Escape to Victory,
Budapest,
Hungary,
summer 1980.

Blomfield Road, the living room.

The budding author.

A snowbound Blomfield Road in the winter of 1963–64.

Diana's 80th birthday with Jason at Prielau, Zell-am-See, Austria, 1972, photographed by Cecil Beaton.

Artemis, November 1970.

Jason and Raimund von Hofmannsthal at Prielau 1974.

Filming beside the statue of Abraham Lincoln
in Hingham, Massachusetts 1975.

Filming with Ken
Shepheard in Venice,
March 1981.

Celebrating *Round
Britain Quiz* with
Irene Thomas and
Sir Ian Trethowan,
Director General
of the BBC. On the
left is the producer
Trevor Hill; on the
right his assistant
Audrey Robins.

Mollie in India, 1984.

Safari breakfast.

Debating at the Folio Society, with
Victoria Glendenning on my right.

With Artemis, Adam, Antony, Allegra, Rafa, Jason, Mollie, and Nella in the garden at Blomfield Road, 2005.

Allegra and Cisco at Rafa's christening on the Rio Grande near Taos, New Mexico, 2003.

Jason Cooper. Architect, 2008.

Nella and Rafa, 2006.

than two years after Suez—the Egyptian President Gamal Abdul
Nasser was at the height of his power and popularity throughout
the Arab World, where his formidable propaganda machine had
whipped up left-wing, largely Muslim opinion against the West,
and particularly against the Christian and openly pro-western
Chamoun. From the start, therefore, the rebellion—for such it
was—was as confessional as it was political; but so delicate was
the balance between Christian and Muslim in the country that
this was never openly admitted. Indeed, there was at first a widespread belief that matters would quickly be resolved, and that
after a week or two everything would be back to normal.

Soon, however, it became all too clear not only that the reb-
els were digging themselves in but that the contagion was rapidly
spreading across the Middle East. In Syria, Jordan, and particularly in Iraq, the tension rose; soon afterwards the American Sixth
Fleet appeared off the Lebanese coast. In the western embassies
there was much discussion of whether wives and families should
be evacuated. Probably rightly as it turned out, the order was
never given; and to some extent at least daytime life continued
in much the same old way. We could still have our Saturday or
Sunday picnics, as long as we chose safe areas to have them in;
we could still go down to the beach and swim. But the curfew
meant that social life was very largely at an end; instead of going
out to dinner parties people read books, and lunchtime conversation grew steadily more intellectual as a result. And even those
lunchtimes could be disrupted. On one occasion the American
journalist Joe Alsop, passing through Beirut, had invited me to
lunch at the Saint-Georges Hotel; just before I left my desk Artemis's school telephoned to say that fighting had broken out in the
south of the city and that the school bus, unable to get up to our
house, was dropping her off with me at the Embassy. Clearly there
was nothing for it but to bring her to lunch too. Joe looked a little

startled when I walked into the restaurant hand in hand with a five-year-old child, but he rose magnificently to the occasion and gave her one of the largest ice creams I have ever seen.

The crisis came on that dreadful July day when the Baghdad mob rose up and murdered both the twenty-two-year-old King and his pro-western Prime Minister, Nuri es-Said. The Sixth Fleet, having spent some weeks just visible on the horizon, moved in at last. It was typical of the strange unreality of everything that half Beirut went down to watch the landings—and very enjoyable they proved to be. The troops jumped from the landing craft into the shallow water and splashed ashore, just as they had been trained to do. The next step was instantly to set up their machine guns on the sand; what the rulebook had never explained was how to handle the situation if people came up to sell them Coca-Cola or—still more disconcerting—if large numbers of beautiful girls in bikinis were sunning themselves on the beach at the time. "Scuse me, ma'am," they would say, picking their way over the prostrate half-naked bodies. The girls smiled back, but few of them bothered to move.

The presence of several thousand US troops in the city gave us all a certain amount of confidence; but it did not noticeably change the situation, which continued much as before. Indeed there were days when it seemed to be worse than ever. Anne and I were conscious, too, of occupying a fairly exposed position. Our house was not in Ras Beirut, the western end of the city where most of the foreign residents lived. The barricades that divided us from the most militant quarter of all, the almost exclusively Muslim area known as the Basta, were only a hundred yards or so from our house; more alarming still, the Presidential Palace was even nearer, almost immediately below us. Not a day passed when it did not come sporadically under fire; we seldom dared to go out on our lovely terrace, or at least to linger there too long. One suffocatingly hot evening in early

August, Freya Stark arrived to stay the night—only Freya would, or *could*, have turned up at such a time—and, flinging open the terrace windows, strolled nonchalantly out to admire the view. Almost immediately a furious fusillade rang out. "Come back, Freya!" I yelled, "you'll get yourself killed!" She turned and smiled. "Oh I don't think so," she said, "I can always recognize *feu de joie*; they shoot because they're happy—you can hear that they are only celebrating."

Towards the end of August came my Brush With Death. One evening Anne and I drove back from a drinks party to our house. It must have been around half-past eight, well after the curfew, but that did not worry me: I was due later that night to go to the airport to pick up the Queen's Messenger and had consequently been provided with a diplomatic pass. Now our house, ravishing as it was, stood on the crest of the hill that had become the border between the two warring factions in the city. The entrance was at the back, so that you had to drive halfway around it before reaching a flight of steps, leading to a narrow open passage at the far end of which was our front door. Just below, almost immediately under our bedroom window, was one of the city's countless police posts, where after curfew all cars were stopped and checked. The police were notoriously nervous, and tended to get trigger happy if they felt threatened; Anne was always going on at me for driving too fast near them. On this particular evening, I am ashamed to report, we had a row about it and when we were still perhaps some two or three hundred yards from the house she—for the first and last time in our married life—insisted that I stop the car and let her out. She felt safer, she said, walking the rest of the way. Most stupidly and reprehensibly, I agreed.

Already feeling pretty guilty, I drove up to our police post. There was no actual road block, merely a little shelter made of sandbags from which, whenever he heard a car coming, a soldier would normally emerge and spread out his arms. On this particular occasion I stopped as usual, but no soldier appeared. I waited perhaps half a minute, until there dawned on me what seemed at the time a satisfactory explanation. I knew that the shelter was airless and quite suffocatingly hot; I also knew that the soldier on duty often used to go and sit on a nearby rooftop to get a little breeze. I was driving an Isetta—a tiny German bubble car—which was the only one in Beirut; I was thus immediately identifiable and well known to the majority of the soldiers who manned the post. What, I asked myself, could be more natural? I had been seen, and I had been identified; why should the poor man bother to come down from his nice cool perch to look at my papers, which he doubtless already knew by heart? And so, after what seemed a decent interval, I drove on.

A second or two later there came a deafening report and my windscreen shattered. My first thought for some reason was a bomb, of which we had had an increasing number in recent weeks; my next, a local sniper. At all events I jumped out of the car and took refuge behind the outer wall of our house. It was only then that I looked down at my formerly white shirt, which looked like Nelson's at Greenwich—drenched and dripping with blood. But where was it all coming from? Feeling absolutely no pain anywhere, I did a quick check: arms, legs, stomach, all OK; twice one are two, twice two are four—yes, brain's all right. It was only after one or two other quick checks that I pushed back the hair that had fallen over my eyes and found that my left hand, spotless a second before, was now scarlet and rather sticky: the image of Nelson was instantly supplanted by that of Macbeth. The wound was clearly somewhere in my head; but before I could examine further I found myself surrounded by perhaps a dozen hysterical people: our neighbors, hearing the shot and ignoring the curfew, were pouring out of their houses, shouting, crying, offering me handkerchiefs, bandages, brandy, their sisters, heaven knows what. Realizing by now that I must look like something out of a horror film I quietened them down as best I could and said that I had only one thing to ask: that one of them should be kind enough to go thirty yards or so down the hill and tell my approaching wife that I had had an accident, but that despite my appearance I was in fact unhurt.

Anne, meanwhile, was just coming round the bend when a white United Nations van pulled up beside her to ask what she was doing out after curfew. She explained, and asked them to give her a lift the rest of the way to the house, which they were happy to do. At that moment she heard a shot; but shots were a permanent background to Beirut life at that time and she thought nothing of it. Then she saw the Isetta. At this point I shall let her take up the story as she remembers it:

> I can still see the scene now. Like some bigger version of Goya's *Third of May*. The headlights illuminated the small crowd around the car, and reflected through the splintered glass of the back window. It seemed to take me years to walk to it, expecting to see your slumped body inside as I'd seen no silhouette of a driver. Instead someone—you—in the middle of the excited gesticulating crowd was waving his arms above his head. Like the poor wretch in Goya's painting who is about to be shot. Only your shirt wasn't white. It was red, with blood streaming from your head wound. You were refusing to be taken off to one of the hospitals without my knowing where you had gone and which one it was. The UN van then drove us both to the American Hospital.

When we arrived they cleaned me up and examined the wound. It seemed that a number of small slivers of metal—either bits of bullet shaved off as it entered the car or bits of car shaved off by the bullet—had hit me just above my left ear. The largest of them had even tunneled two inches under the skin before re-emerging. Miraculously, the skull was unbroken, possibly even untouched.

"I suppose another eighth of an inch to the right would have done me in," I remember saying to the doctor as he bound up my head in a vast white turban.

"An eighth of an inch—oh, I hardly think so," he replied, "though of course you might have been a vegetable for the rest of your life. Now a *quarter* of an inch—well, that would have been a very different story. . . ."

Then a policeman arrived. I explained as well as I could what had happened, still assuming that a sniper had been responsible.

"Aha," said the policeman, "where is your car?" I told him it was where I had left it, by my house. "Right," he said, "just as soon as the doctor has finished with you, go back to your house, fetch the car, and bring it back here so that it can be photographed."

I found it difficult to believe my still-singing ears. There was a sniper up there somewhere, who had already taken one potshot at me that night. The UN jeep had offered to take me back, so my return home would probably be safe enough; but that, I felt, would be enough for one evening. If anyone honestly thought that I was going to brave the sniper twice more, once when I went to fetch the car and once when I returned yet again, they had another think coming. Moreover, what was the point of taking the photograph anywhere other than where the incident occurred?

I explained that I should be leaving the hospital in five minutes; why did not the photographer accompany me home and do the job *in situ*? That way it might at least be possible to work out where my assailant had stood.

"Oh no," said the policeman, "we couldn't possibly do that."

"Why not?" I asked.

"Well," he said, "things seem to be rather dangerous up that way."

A quarter of an hour later I was back at the house, to find a visibly trembling Lebanese army lieutenant waiting for me. He wished to make a formal apology. The bullet had been most stupidly fired by one of his own men, from the police post, on the grounds that I hadn't stopped. I assured him that on this particular evening nobody had asked me to stop, but that I had done so anyway; it was only after a reasonable wait that I had driven on, on the assumption that I had been recognized. The lieutenant explained that it was the poor man's first night at the post; of course all his colleagues knew me well, it was most unfortunate that he had had to be the one on duty. At any rate he was deeply sorry for what he had done and was anxious to make his own personal apologies. I protested that no apologies were necessary; the incident had been very largely my fault, no real harm had been done and, quite frankly, I had enough excitement for one evening and was rather keen to go to bed. No, the lieutenant insisted, the soldier *must* apologize. All right, I said, if he must he must; but would he please come right away and be very quick about it. Alas, he said, that was out of the question. At present he could not desert his post, but he would call at the earliest possible moment— immediately he came off duty at 6 AM the following morning.

And so he did. He arrived on the dot of six. Mohammed let him in, gave him a cup of coffee and only then knocked on our bedroom door. The soldier was thus already waiting in our living room; and the fact that this unfortunately separated me from the loo made me even keener to get rid of him. The poor boy was quaking with fear; still luxuriantly turbaned, I graciously accepted his stammered apologies, told him that he was only doing his duty, congratulated him on his marksmanship, grasped him warmly by the hand, and showed him out of the door.

The incident was over, apart from one thing: I had somehow to get in touch with my mother before she read of the incident—its gravity almost certainly grossly exaggerated—in the papers. She was, I knew, in Athens, and at nine o'clock that morning I called the Hotel Grande Bretagne. International telephoning half a century ago was not what it is today; it took me ages to get through at all, and when I did the line was atrocious. As it happened, however, she was in the entrance hall, a few yards from the telephone operator. When she came on the line I—terrified lest we should be cut off—immediately yelled: "Don't worry, I'm all right!" but she couldn't hear. I repeated, still louder. "*What?*" she screamed back. Then I made my big mistake. "I've been shot," I bellowed, "but I'm ..." That was the only bit she heard. "You've been shot?" And then to the telephonist at the hotel: "*Mademoiselle, mademoiselle, aidez-moi! Mon fils a été fusillé!*"[5] The line went dead. A telegram had to do the rest.

———————— ❦ ————————

As summer turned to autumn the situation seemed to get worse and worse; and at last the moment came when we were ordered to leave our beloved house for somewhere less exposed. We did so, and made reluctant arrangements for Anne to take Artemis home. But then, from one day to the next, the whole gloomy picture changed. We never quite understood why: one reason was that the fighting had suddenly become openly confessional, Christian against Muslim, and there were stories that people had been shot for no other reason than their religion. Both sides realized that to allow this to happen would destroy Lebanon and everything it stood for, and both hastily retreated. A truce was quickly patched up and, surprisingly, held.

———————————

5 "Mademoiselle, help me! My son has been shot ..."

The parties and picnics started up again, and within a week or two life was peaceful and as enjoyable as it had been before the troubles. In one way, indeed, it was better: Syria—which was then precariously linked with Egypt to form what was known as the United Arab Republic—decided to resume diplomatic relations, opening the frontier to British diplomats. The long frustration was over. At last we could drive the two hours to Damascus and on to Amman, or make expeditions to Aleppo, Homs, Hama, Palmyra—the horizon seemed boundless.

That autumn our new Ambassador arrived. His predecessor, Sir George Middleton, had left in the spring; throughout that dreadful summer the Embassy had been in the more than capable hands of the *chargé d'affaires*, Ian Scott. Our new boss, Sir Moore Crosthwaite, was a joy. A shamelessly camp bachelor, he was formidably intelligent, with exquisite French and a wicked sense of humor. The Lebanese, though finding his name impossible to pronounce, immediately took him to their hearts, particularly after the first large and lavish dinner party he attended. It was in a huge marble palace in the quartier Sursock—the smartest district in Beirut—and its principal reception room was furnished at its center with a small ornamental pool, of which the surface was covered in rose petals. As Moore left the buffet table, carrying in each hand a plate piled high with Arabic delicacies, he walked straight in. A moment later there he was in his dinner jacket, sitting on the edge of the pool with his feet in the water, the two plates still in his hands, not one crumb having fallen off either of them to the floor. The company was spellbound. "*Ah, vous avez vu Sir Moore, comme il a gardé son sang-froid et n'a rien laissé tomber? Mais vraiment, quel style. . . .*"[6]

---

6 "Did you see Sir Moore, how he kept his *sang-froid* and didn't drop anything? There's style for you. . . ."

The following summer the Baalbek Festival featured a visit by the Ballet Rambert. It was not the most successful of evenings. Baalbek stands some 2,000 feet above sea level and occasionally the nights, even in summer, can be bitterly cold. The Rambert hit one of the coldest. The spectators huddled in thick woolen Arab robes bought hurriedly in the interval from the local tourist shop; the dancers, we were later told, spent every moment they were offstage massaging each other's legs in desperate attempts to maintain their circulation. The *prima ballerina* moreover, Lucette Aldous, was struggling with a nasty attack of flu. Moore sat in the front row shivering, almost invisible under a heavy blanket. "Isn't it terrible," I said to him, "Miss Aldous has a temperature of 102." "Lucky girl," he muttered.

The ingrained tradition of all Beirutis, of whatever class or station in life, was to take to the hills in the summer to escape the heat. "Estivating," it was called—as opposed to hibernating. Smart Lebanese would express horror if you confessed—as we had happily done in 1957 and 1958—that you were remaining in town. *"Comment?"* they would cry aghast, *"Comment, vous n'es-tivez pas à la montagne?"*[7] In the summer of 1959, however, we followed their example. The American University of Beirut was lucky enough to have as its Professor of English Literature a mem-orably wonderful Englishman called Christopher Scaife, who had spent most of his life in the Arab world, first in Egypt and more recently in Lebanon. Christopher had a house—known, after a former English owner, as Dar Worsley—near a village called Ain Anoub; he was returning to England for a couple of months and asked us to look after it for him. Anne was once again expecting, and was keen on having as quiet a life as possible, so we agreed with delight.

---

7 "What, you're not spending the summer up the mountain?"

It was a sort of idyll: a rambling old building, dating probably from the middle of the nineteenth century, set on a wooded hillside at some 1,500 feet, with a breathtaking view over the sea. Life there was simple in the extreme—no electricity, only rudimentary running water, hard iron bedsteads, a single loo in the garden—but it was cool and beautiful, and—particularly after the previous summer—magically peaceful. There was a resident staff of two, who brought in wonderful hissing oil lamps as the light began to fail, and—best of all—Christopher's superb library. It filled two whole rooms, the books stacked in dozens of freestanding metal bookcases. All English literature was there, ancient and modern.

I would drive down into the city at six in the morning, have a quick swim and be at the office at seven. We would then work uninterruptedly till two, when the Embassy closed for the day. Back up the mountain, and after a late lunch followed by a short siesta we would be ready for whatever Beirut social life had in store for us. Better still were the evenings where we could stay at home, sitting on the terrace in the warm, still night, reading.

My mother came to stay and pronounced herself happier than she had been at any time since my father's death. Another regular guest, both at Ain Anoub and in Beirut, was Freya Stark. Whenever she came we would give a little dinner party for her. People would arrive in a state of wild excitement at the thought of meeting this most intrepid of travelers, winner of the Gold Medal of the Royal Geographical Society while still in her twenties, who had crossed vast tracts of unknown territory in the Middle East and Central Asia, mapping much of it for the first time. They would expect a tall, spare, weather-beaten woman, her hands heavily calloused after years of pitching tents and tightening the girths of camels, and would be gratifyingly astonished to see this short, dumpy figure with an extraordinary coiffure like a whirlpool, dressed stylishly if a shade overimaginatively and dripping with jewelry, her little stubby fingers heavy with huge rings. Knowing her as I did, I doubt whether she had ever pitched a tent or harnessed a camel in her life. As her books make clear, she always traveled *en princesse*, attended by a small regiment of guides and dragomen. When they arrived at a suitable camping site she would immediately retire to a comfortable spot nearby and start writing her diary or one of her exquisite letters, returning only when her tent was ready, her dinner awaiting her, her bed prepared.

———◦❧◦———

Christopher Scaife was, as it were, one of our inner circle; another was John Carswell, also at AUB where he taught art. He has since become a world expert on the arts of Islam—particularly ceramics—and has only recently retired from being Head of that department at Sotheby's. After fifty years, we still remain close friends. One day when John was in the Old City of Jerusalem, he passed a tattooist's parlor. Such places in those days were a good deal thinner on the ground than they are now, and some of the designs in the window immediately struck him. Clearly they were immensely old, and many were of considerable iconographical interest, so he walked in. The proprietor, Mr. Razzouk, was a Copt. He told John that his family had been in the tattooing trade for several generations, catering particularly for their coreligionists from Egypt who came on pilgrimages to Jerusalem and sought a permanent record of their visit. The designs were carved on plaques of olive wood, nobody knew how old. John, predictably, was fascinated. When he returned to Beirut he immediately made an application to the Gulbenkian Foundation for a grant; and this enabled him to publish what I believe is his first work: two beautifully produced volumes entitled *Coptic Tattoo Designs,* in which Mr. Razzouk's entire collection was faithfully reproduced.

In the spring of 1960 John and I were in Jerusalem together. I already had one tattoo, of a unicorn; it had been drawn by Anne and transferred to my right bicep by Mr. George Birchett in the Waterloo Road, whose trade card advertised "Crude Work Covered or Removed" and who claimed regularly to retint the King of Denmark. Now I felt that it was time for another, and persuaded John to take me to visit Mr. Razzouk. The result is a representation of St. George and the Dragon, symmetrically placed on the left. Nowadays it has been there so long that I seldom notice it; but it still gives me pleasure when I do.

One more of our Beirut gang deserves special mention here. Theo Larsson was a Swede; but he was a Swede with a difference. His grandfather, a sea captain, had one day had a vision in which he was told that the Second Coming was at hand. He immediately left Stockholm with his family and a number of friends and settled in Jerusalem, in order to be there when the great day came. Alas, the great day failed to come, but the Larssonites, as they were called, stayed on in the city as yet another small Christian community, and it was there that Theo was born. As a result he was totally trilingual, speaking English, Swedish, and Arabic without a trace of an accent. He was wonderful company, and he knew the Middle East like the back of his hand. It was with him as our guide that we first went to the grave of Lady Hester Stanhope and the few sad ruins of her house at Djoun; he also took us to Beaufort, to say nothing of several other glorious Crusader castles. Later when we were all back in London he married his beloved B. Sanders, who had also been with us in Lebanon. I was best man at their wedding. Theo is alas no longer with us, but B remains one of my dearest friends and their brilliant son James is my godson.

Our own dear son Jason was born at the end of October, 1959, in the American Hospital, his birth being duly registered by the British Consul. By chance his godfather, my cousin by marriage Charles Farrell, passed through Beirut two days later, so we had the christening at Anne's bedside. Artemis, now six, was enchanted with her brother from the moment she saw him, instantly adopting the role of conscientious older sister. The two, I'm delighted to say, have loved each other ever since.

January, 1960, was a particularly exciting month. The representative of Alitalia in Beirut invited a small party including the Argentine Ambassadress, our dear Lebanese friend Dolly Trad, and me on the airline's inaugural flight to Bombay. (Jason being only three months old, Anne stayed behind.) We had five memorable days in India, with trips to the caves of Ajanta and the rock temples of Ellora, followed by a quick trip to Delhi to see the Independence Day parade. We even managed to squeeze in Agra and the Taj Mahal. Nowadays it is hard to believe that half a century ago Beirut-Bombay was a two-day flight, involving a night in Tehran. I had never been to Iran either, and decided that the return journey would give me a splendid opportunity to fulfill a long-held ambition by stopping off for twenty-four hours and for a quick trip to Isfahan. Alas, when I returned to Tehran a week later I found that the local airline was on strike. It was a bitter blow; but as I was retiring disconsolately to bed in the hotel my telephone rang. It was the head—I think he may have been the owner—of the airline, whom I had met at dinner on our outward journey. "You told me," he said, "that you had made plans to go to Isfahan tomorrow. I simply can't allow this ridiculous strike to affect them. Be at the airport at eight o'clock tomorrow morning. Heaven knows what it'll be, but we'll fix up something."

I of course had even less of an idea of what he would arrange. A mail plane, perhaps, or even an army one; but certainly not what

I found waiting for me—a minuscule two-seater, to be piloted by my benefactor's sixteen-year-old grandson. Never having flown in anything other than a large airliner, I felt panic welling up inside me; but in the circumstances there was obviously nothing to be done. I clambered in behind one of the twin joysticks—taking great care not to touch it—and looked around as a tousled and rather spotty youth got in beside me. There were, I distinctly remember, no seat belts. I also remember that if I looked directly downwards I could see right through the ill-fitting floorboards to the concrete runway below.

Five minutes later we were airborne and climbing steadily. The altimeter was immediately in front of me, indicating 7,000 feet, 8,000, 9,000. . . . There was no pressurization and very little heating. At 10,000 I said to the boy "Do we have to go very much higher?" He spoke, I have to admit, quite good English. "Well," he said, "the mountains are about 12,000 feet." I shut up, till half an hour later a line of huge and extremely jagged snowcapped peaks loomed up ahead. By this time the altimeter showed 11,500 and I changed my tune. "Shouldn't we be going a little higher?" I asked. "The plane won't do it," he replied, "but don't worry, we can easily fly between them."

Somehow we did, and reached Isfahan physically—though not in my case emotionally—intact. The city when I finally saw it came up to my highest expectations, but I found it hard to give proper attention to the monuments; my thoughts were only of the return journey, which would, I knew, take place entirely in the dark. This time it was the boy who, soon after we had taken off, broke the silence.

"It's funny," he said, "Isfahan seems to have run out of fuel. I couldn't find any anywhere."

"You mean," I said, "that we haven't got enough to get back?"

"Oh no," he said—I thought rather doubtfully. "We should be able to manage all right."

I looked at the fuel gauge, which showed almost exactly half full; it was obviously going to be a close thing. A few controls away along the all-black instrument panel, I noticed a single scarlet knob, above which were written the words mixture: PULL FOR WEAK, PUSH FOR RICH. To my horror, he pulled it out, at which the engine coughed and spluttered until he pushed it most of the way back in again—a process which continued regularly every few minutes until we finally bumped down in Tehran. I grasped the lad warmly by the hand and congratulated him on his skill. He was obviously pleased. "Do you know," he said, "I've never flown as far as that before."

Shortly afterwards, rather dashingly perhaps, I took another week's leave. It meant that half my annual entitlement was used up in the first six weeks of the year, but there was another opportunity not to be missed. My mother, who had arrived once again to stay with us, had somehow wangled herself, Anne, and me on to a Nile riverboat which was taking a special group of journalists from Aswan to Wadi Halfa to see all the dozen or so ancient Egyptian temples threatened with destruction by the proposed new High Dam at Aswan. We were escorted by a faintly ridiculous official from the Ministry of Information in Cairo called Mr. Adam. On our first evening he gave us an introductory talk, less about the temples we were to see than about the behavior that was expected of us. "And," he finished up, "there must be absolutely no swimming in the river, because the water is 70% crocodiles." Poor man, he never lived it down. "What percentage crocodiles this morning, Mr. Adam?" greeted him every morning at breakfast, or "Big slump in crocodiles today, Mr. Adam, down to 40% we hear."

The high point of the whole trip was, inevitably, Abu Simbel, so important a monument that the whole thing was shortly to be jacked up 200 feet to avoid the rising flood—an astonishing feat of engineering by any standards, since the innermost small chamber is 72 yards from the entrance, hewn out of the sandstone cliff. I was in that chamber to see the monument's famous *coup de théâtre*, when the first ray of the rising sun plunges through the whole depth of the temple, to illuminate the seated figure of Rameses II, flanked by three deities from the Egyptian pantheon.

The other eleven temples were far smaller—one of them, Dendur, is now in the Metropolitan Museum of Art in New York—several with only a single chamber; but all were imbued with that strange atmosphere to be encountered nowhere else. Only in Egypt does one learn the lesson that unremitting sunlight can be every bit as mysterious as darkness and gloom.

———⊙⊦⊙———

We returned (via Luxor) to Beirut, where our delightful life continued. We loved every minute, and I felt that I could willingly have stayed there for the rest of my life. All too soon, however, I was summoned by Moore and told that I had been posted back to London. It was a sad blow, but there was nothing to be done. Anne flew back with the children and settled them in with my mother at Chantilly, then returned to supervise the packing up. Finally, at the beginning of May, 1960, we climbed into the car and set off for home. Our route was to take us through Syria, Turkey, Bulgaria, Yugoslavia, Austria, Germany, and France; the only unknown territory was Turkey, which we had never visited apart from our one short stay in Istanbul four years before. Much of it was still under military control, so we had taken the precaution of getting a special *laissez-passer* from the Turkish Embassy before our departure.

For two reasons, that drive through Turkey was unforgettable. The first was the astonishing beauty of the south coast. In those days the roads were narrow and dusty, but that was a small price to pay for the virtual absence of traffic; here, almost unbelievably, was a shore of the Mediterranean that was still utterly unspoilt. One of the best moments was when we rounded a bend to see a herd of cows standing fetlock deep in the sea, drinking. Not even Poussin, not even Claude, would have risked that one. We stopped to investigate and found that ice-cold fresh water was bubbling up from a whole series of springs in the shallows.

At Antalya we turned inland towards Istanbul, and that evening found ourselves in the little town of Kütahya, celebrated then as now for its pottery. We strolled around before dinner and bought a set of dinner plates; they might do rather well, we thought, in the London house that we should have to start looking for when we returned. The only problem was that we had no money to pay for them. We therefore asked the proprietor to pack up the plates, explaining that we would go to the bank first thing in the morning, cash some traveler's checks and be back at 9 AM to collect our purchases.

We woke at first light to sounds of considerable hubbub. There was a lot of excited shouting beneath our hotel window, with martial music being played at full volume on the loudspeakers which for some reason lined the street. Mystified, we got dressed and headed off to the bank—only to find on the doorstep two soldiers with submachine guns blocking our way. Since I spoke not a word of Turkish, I had no means of discovering what all the fuss was about; but then, by an astonishing stroke of luck, two girls who were obviously employees of the bank arrived, chatting between themselves in a language that I at once recognized as Serbian. (After a recent agreement between Turkey and Yugoslavia, a considerable number of ethnic Turks from Bosnia had returned to their original homeland a year or two before.) After three years of disuse my own Serbian was rapidly rusting, but I managed to ask them what had happened. It seemed that there had been a military *coup* against the government; the Prime Minister, Adnan Menderes, was under arrest and was at that very moment being held in the local castle, which we could see on a hilltop only a mile or two away.

Had I been the journalist my mother had wanted me to be, this would have been a scoop; but as a junior diplomat, knowing from experience the tendency of Third World countries to ascribe all unexpected reverses to the CIA or, failing that, to the British Secret Service, I knew that my job was to get out as soon as possible. There was still, however, the matter of those dinner plates. I explained the situation to the Bosnian girls, who rather to my surprise told the soldiers to let us into the bank and cashed my traveler's check without hesitation. We went to the plate shop, collected our purchases, and soon afterwards were on our way. Alas, our problems were far from over. Between Kütahya and Istanbul there must have been twenty military checkpoints. Foreign diplomats were rare on the roads of central Anatolia, and by definition suspect. True, we had our *laissez-passer* from the Turkish Ambassador in Beirut; but he was almost certain to be a Menderes appointee, and his signature in present circumstances might well do more harm than good. I produced it anyway, and though some checkpoints were more cooperative than others—on several occasions we were held for up to an hour while the soldiery made anxious telephone calls—we reached Istanbul without serious mishap.

The rest of the journey home was uneventful, and seemed something of an anticlimax. We called at Chantilly to see my mother and the children, but left them with her as we had nowhere to take them to; a day or two later we were back in London—and the house hunting began.

Chapter Nine
Watershed

IT WAS OVER more quickly than we had expected. We looked at perhaps half a dozen other houses in the week after our return to England, but none of them seemed remotely as desirable as No. 24 Blomfield Road—in which, after nearly half a century, I find myself writing these words. Little Venice—I have always considered the description distinctly optimistic—has changed a good deal in the interim, both for better and for worse. On the one hand it has undergone considerable gentrification. Despite being the property of the Church Commissioners, during the 1930s it was notorious as a red-light district: most of the premises—apart from a single house inhabited by Nancy Mitford—had been, if not frankly brothels, at least *garçonnières* or houses of assignation.[1] By 1960 it had regained much of its respectability, but was still somewhat down-at-heel—fortunately for us, since it is unlikely that we should otherwise have been able

---

1 Our house is on the corner of Randolph Road; a block away are Randolph Avenue and Randolph Crescent. I have recently read that we need to look no further for the origin of the word "randy."

to acquire a twelve-year leasehold for £7,200. Today it is sought-after as it has never been before. Our decision to move in was more fortunate than we knew.

On the debit side has been the fate of the Regent's Canal. In the sixties it was still a working waterway, with strings of up to four or five barges passing every few minutes, laden with coal, timber, or other merchandise. There were a few houseboats along the bank, but not many; on sunny days the ceilings of the rooms on the upper floors would catch the reflections of the water below, with designs of what looked like golden wire netting dancing across them. Now the houseboats form a continuous line along both banks, so the wire netting has gone; the only passing boats are pleasure craft, most of them shuttling backwards and forwards to the London Zoo. Still, Little Venice remains a highly agreeable place in which to live; and it is here—since some years ago I managed to acquire the house's freehold—that I hope (and confidently expect) to die.

In 1961 my mother also became a Little Venetian. Ever since my father's death she had longed to return to England; she had stayed on in France throughout the fifties only because she had continued to hope that I should at any moment be sent to the Paris Embassy. But my return to England in 1960, probably for three or four years at least, decided the matter. She gave up hope, left Chantilly without a pang of regret, and took the lease of a house at 10 Warwick Avenue, less than a quarter of a mile away from us across the Canal. There she was to live happily for another twenty-five years.

Since our house when we found it was in poor shape, there was quite a lot of work to be done on it and we lived for a few months in a flat in St. John's Wood before moving in early in 1961. At one moment I had toyed with the idea of going to work at the Foreign Office by boat, sailing down the Canal and up the Thames to

Westminster; but a few enquiries revealed that the journey—via the Isle of Dogs—would have taken about four hours each way, so I regretfully abandoned it in favor of the more prosaic but reliable Bakerloo Line.

My new position was that of Middle East Regional Adviser to Information Policy Department, which was a good deal less distinguished than it sounds. In essence the job was to cooperate with the Central Office of Information in the circulation of pro-British propaganda to the Arab world, by means of the press (we ran an Arabic language magazine), the radio (quite apart from the BBC Arabic Service, we distributed vast quantities of recorded tapes to radio stations all over the Middle East), and by cultivating Arab journalists in London. In this last activity I possessed one huge advantage: soon after I left Oxford my father had made me a member of Buck's Club, which was regularly patronized at lunchtime by Harold Macmillan, then Prime Minister. Every week I would telephone his private secretary Philip de Zulueta, and ask him on what days his boss would be lunching at Buck's; I would then invite an Arab journalist on the appropriate day, taking care to place him where he had a good view of the long central table, which members arriving on their own automatically joined. Around half-past one the Prime Minister would come shuffling in and silently take his place at this table, his neighbors—if they were already in conversation—hardly bothering to notice him. Suddenly my own guest would stop in mid-sentence and stare across the room. "Tell me," he would say incredulously, "is that not your Prime Minister?" I would glance around nonchalantly. "Oh yes," I would say, "he comes here quite often." For any Middle Eastern Head of Government to behave in such a way—and then to be effectively ignored—was obviously unthinkable. Reactions were invariably gratifying; the best response I ever received was the question "But where are his motorcycles?"

———◦⟡◦———

In the late autumn of 1961, when Anne's younger sister Pandora was married to Michael Astor—son of the famous Nancy—and lived at Bruern Abbey, a lovely house in Oxfordshire, we used to go there regularly for weekends. For one of these they had also invited a beautiful young American woman by whom I was enormously struck. Her name was Ricki Huston. She was the daughter of an American-Italian restaurateur called Tony Soma, whose restaurant—Tony's—had been something of a New York institution. She had started her career in the ballet, and had once had the distinction of appearing on the cover of "LIFE" magazine; but she had grown too tall, had given up dancing and had married the film director John Huston as his fourth wife. The two were now amicably separated, and she was living with their two children, Tony and Anjelica, partly in London and partly in Ireland, in a small house on her husband's estate of St. Cleran's in County Galway. It was—at least for me—love at first sight. A week or two later, when Anne happened to be accompanying her father on a trip to Egypt, I gave a little dinner party to which I invited Ricki; and I am embarrassed to confess, our affair began. It was to continue for the next five years.

Early in 1962 the Foreign Office transferred me to Disarmament Department just in time for the start of an eighteen-nation conference on the subject in Geneva, and for the next six months I shuttled backwards and forwards between there and London. No one knew how long the conference was going to continue, so I was put up in the Beau Rivage Hotel while Anne and the children stayed in London. All in all, Geneva was a pleasant enough place to be. From time to time Ricki would come out and join me clandestinely for a day or two; I had colleagues who were both intelligent and amusing; the food was delicious; and the city was a wonderful jumping-off place if one had a free weekend. My stay there also gave me the opportunity of boasting that I had lunch and dinner with Charlie Chaplin.

I had met him staying with Paul-Louis Weiller at La Reine Jeanne and he had invited me to look him up if I were ever near Lausanne, so one day I did precisely that: found his name in the telephone book—in those days the concept of "ex-directory" was unknown in Switzerland—and dialed his number. Rather to my surprise, he answered the telephone himself; still more to my surprise, he remembered me and invited me over to lunch. My greatest astonishment was when, on arrival at Lausanne station, he was there in person on the platform to meet me. Nobody seemed to recognize him; he bundled me into what seemed quite an ordinary car and drove me himself to the house. With his wife Oona and several lovely daughters we had a delicious barbecue on the lawn, he personally doing most of the cooking. This was quite fascinating to watch: there, again and again, were all the little mannerisms that one knew so well from his films—the quick shrug of the shoulders, the cocking of the head to one side, the lightning smile, gone almost before it appeared. And he had a wonderful fund of stories; one that I well remember was his chance meeting with the evangelist Aimée Semple MacPherson[2] in a Marseille hotel. Both were alone, so he invited her out to dinner; and the evening ended in his bedroom. Just as she was about to join him in the bed, she knelt down by its side and prayed for a good fifteen minutes. He did a wonderful imitation of how he reached out an arm and lethargically tousled her curly hair as she did so.

Professionally, however, those months in Geneva represented a frustrating chapter in my life. It wasn't simply because I was absent—for the most part—from both my family and from Ricki;

2 Osbert Sitwell was always said greatly to have upset his protégé William Walton, composer of *Belshazzar's Feast*, by suggesting that the writing on the wall was not, as the Bible tells us, *Mene mene tekel upharsin* but *Aimée Aimée Semple MacPherson*.

it was because I had no faith in what I was doing. Every morning the representatives of the eighteen nations would assemble in the old League of Nations chamber with its vast ceiling painting by José Maria Sert, members of their staff sitting immediately behind them; every afternoon I would settle down in my shared office (the loveliest I ever had, with a breathtaking view across the lake to Mont Blanc) and write the speech that our Minister of State, Joseph Godber MP, would make the following day. The trouble was that we were none of us infinitesimally advancing the cause of disarmament; all we were doing was scoring cheap debating points off the Russians and allowing them to score equally cheap ones against us: "Strange that Mr. Zorin should say that; in his speech of February 22 he suggested precisely the reverse" and so on. Everybody knew that we should get a breakthrough when Mr. Khrushchev wanted a breakthrough and not a moment before. We did get a minor one about halfway through my time: immediately all objections were forgotten, Lord Hailsham flew out from London and signed a paper and for a moment some of us thought we were getting somewhere. But the basic problem was that of inspection, and that was obviously insoluble. If two countries do not trust each other, country A must insist on inspection rights throughout country B to ensure that country B is not holding back weapons that it claims to have destroyed. To have allowed such rights was something the Russians would never have contemplated for a second; and even if they had, how would we have started a search? It would have meant looking under every bed in the Soviet Union.

I returned to London when the Conference was over: glad to be back from Geneva but still fairly unhappy and frustrated at my disarmament job and conscious that I wasn't even doing it particularly well. Then one day in the summer of 1963 the telephone rang. It was John Henniker-Major, Head of Personnel Department. "John Julius, tell me—how good is your Italian?"

"Well John, it's sort of holiday Italian, shopping Italian, but frankly not up to all that much. Why do you ask?"

"Oh, only that we were thinking of sending you as dogsbody to the Duke of Norfolk, who's representing the Queen at the Pope's coronation."

I backpedaled as hard as I could. "Oh well I mean, you know, it's perfectly OK for conversational purposes, I mean I can chat away all right if that's all you want. . . ."

I heard him chuckle, but I got the job; and a few days later the Duke and I found ourselves in first class seats heading for Rome, and in particular for the British Legation to the Holy See where we were to stay. I had never met him before, but loved him from the start; he was friendly, chatty, and without a grain of pomposity. "You see," he said, "I've still got the Earl Marshal's uniform that was made for my father. Wore it at the Coronation ten years ago, but afraid I've put on a bit of weight since then, so the moment I heard the old Pope had hiccups I went on a diet. Been on it ever since. Ought just about to get into that uniform if I hold my breath, but it's going to be a damn close thing." Soon afterwards he got on to the love of his life, cricket. Feeling rather differently about the game, I trod water as best I could. Then he started to speculate on the reception for the Commonwealth Cardinals, which was to be held an hour or two after our arrival. "Oh my word," he said, "I do hope old Gracious will be there. Haven't seen old Gracious for ages—wonderful to see him again."

He went on in this vein for some time; at last I had to interrupt.

"Forgive me, sir," I said, "but—who is old Gracious?"

"Oh sorry," he said, "thought you knew. Cardinal Bishop of Bombay. Gracias, I think he pronounces it, or something like that, but I always call him old Gracious. Splendid chap, used to play for Middlesex."

We arrived to find Rome in the grip of a heat wave. Safe at the Legation, we just managed to fit in a cold shower and put on our blue suits in time for the reception. In those days—and, I very much hope, still today—cardinals attending formal functions of this kind would come in full cardinalian fig—robes in those wonderful clashing shades of purple, scarlet, and orange and preceded by two men carrying long lighted candles. There were six altogether from the Commonwealth, and old Gracious arrived first: a vision of ecclesiastical splendor, well over six foot, his dark face glowing in the candlelight. The Duke immediately charged towards him and did a quick genuflection, but almost before he was upright the cardinal had grasped him by the hand. "Oh my dear Duke, what a pleasure to see you again. I say, what are Yorkshire thinking they are doing? 158 for 7, oh my God, it's a bloody disaster. . . ." The two went into a huddle at the end of the room; they were still there half an hour later.

I, meanwhile, was mixing with the other guests. They were at least 90% male, and 80% churchmen. It was a world with which I was totally unfamiliar, and I was fascinated. There could have been no more exciting moment to be in Rome. Pope John XXIII had died less than a month before, and it was less than a week since the Conclave had elected as his successor Cardinal Giovanni Battista Montini of Milan, who had chosen the title of Paul VI. There were now to be two or three days of celebration and preparation, building up to the great service of Coronation itself—which, in view of the heat, it had been rather imaginatively decided to hold not in St. Peter's itself but on the outer loggia, with the congregation filling the Bernini Piazza just below. The talk at the reception, not surprisingly, was of nothing else. Most of it, I was intrigued to find, turned on clothes. Somebody had found a little man just behind the Porta Pia who could run you up a really lovely little chasuble in a couple of days for practically nothing; somebody else expressed extreme surprise that the College of Cardinals was to be in white, not red, for the Coronation; and everybody was horrified by the brand new Triple Crown, a gift from the people of Milan and apparently made of chromium, which was to be lowered on to the papal head. "Ut lükes more like a büllet," remarked the intensely Scottish Cardinal Heard, who after some sixty years in Rome had never lost the accent of his homeland.

On the eve of the Coronation there was another much larger reception, given by the Vatican authorities for all the special representatives and delegations attending. The heat was savage. We were all encased in sweltering woollen uniforms—the Duke resplendent in scarlet and gold (one or two of the more unobtrusive buttons having been surreptitiously replaced by safety pins), myself rather more sober in diplomatic dress, black with a certain amount of gold braid but in my view nowhere near enough, a sword clanking at my side. Cars in those days had no air conditioning, and we had to queue for a good half hour in the sun until we could be deposited at the end of the waiting red carpet—only to find another queue, almost as long, winding through the vestibule and up the long flight of stairs leading to the celebrated Borgia Apartments in which the party was to be held. While we were waiting, the British Minister to the Holy See Peter Scarlett, who had been Head of Chancery in Paris under my father, murmured "Watch the drinks, they're lethal." I assumed this to be a joke about the Borgias—(plenty of people would say, "we're dining with the Borgias tonight," but nobody ever said, "we dined with the Borgias last night.")—and laughed politely; by this time I needed a drink so badly that I would hardly have cared whether it was poisoned or not. At last we arrived—and there was exactly what I had been dreaming of: a long, long line of tables, white damask cloths to the ground, bearing row upon row of huge wine glasses, all full to the brim with an almost colorless liquid, their surfaces dripping with condensation like a television commercial. "A lovely dry Soave," I thought to myself, seized the nearest glass, took a mighty swig—and choked. It was a dry martini—one of the largest and most powerful that I have ever encountered. I saw Peter smile. "I told you so," he said. "Until a few years ago people coming to the Vatican were lucky if they got an eggcupful of warm Vermouth; but then a number of young American monsignor arrived—and they've gingered the place up a lot." The party was, I can only say, a howling success.

And so to the great service itself. Since the heat showed no sign of letting up it did not begin till the late afternoon. As representative of the Queen, the Duke (and therefore I) had superb seats immediately behind the cardinals—who were in white, with enormous white mitres that made them look like chessmen in a ballet. (Some two hours into the ceremony I noticed a cardinal sitting immediately in front of me who suddenly focused on the robe of his neighbor, running a finger and thumb down the edge of it before giving him an appreciative nod.) The full service took a good three hours, during which darkness fell and was gradually replaced by floodlighting, at first so faint as to be barely perceptible but slowly increasing in strength until the great Piazza looked like a stage set. Into it the newly crowned Pope emerged, seated in his swaying Gestatorial Chair as it was carried through the cheering crowds, his arms working up and down like clockwork as he rhythmically took up with his right hand one of the thousands of white skullcaps which were being held up to him, laid it momentarily on his head, then removed it with his left and passed it down into the sea of the frenzied faithful.

The following day was given over to papal audiences. The Duke was allotted, as I remember, twenty minutes; I was to be allowed in at the very end to escort him from the audience chamber. The protocol was nowhere nearly as elaborate as it had been when my mother and I had our audience with Pius XII; still, it was impressive enough. In I went, made my carefully rehearsed reverences and received a blessing—accompanied, to my surprise, by a small leather case. The Pope explained. He had already given the Duke a commemorative medal bearing his portrait struck in gold; he wished me to have a silver one, but unfortunately the silver ones were not yet ready. Mine would be sent as soon as possible (it was) but meanwhile he would like me to have something to take with me now. "And so," he said, "I give you this silver medal of my predecessor, Pope John. And believe me, that's so much better." I could see that he meant it, and felt the tears come into my eyes. They do so again as I write these words.

I count those three or four days as one of the great experiences of my life. Of course they were fascinating, of course they were fun; but they were also immensely impressive. The Duke, as Earl Marshal of England, had been personally responsible for all the arrangements in connection with the Queen's Coronation in 1953;[3] no one understood the complications better than he. But, he pointed out, he had had over a year to organize the event. The Vatican had only a couple of weeks. Yet in that time they had invited representatives from every country in the world, found accommodation for them, laid on countless receptions, tackled a thousand problems of precedence and protocol and—as far as any of us could see—not once put a foot wrong. They had even managed to get a gold commemorative medal designed and struck. Had he not seen it himself, the Duke said, he would not have believed it possible. Neither would I.

3 He was also to be responsible for the State Funeral of Sir Winston Churchill in 1965.

———⚬∤⚬———

Already while I was still in Geneva I had begun to wonder whether I was really intended for the Foreign Service. I had been happy in Belgrade, and still happier in Beirut. I loved the travel and the adventure and the camaraderie, and the constant uncertainty of where one might be going next. But I had never enjoyed working in the vast, impersonal Foreign Office in London, and had actively disliked Disarmament Department, which had confirmed me in my long-held belief that its professed objective would never be more than a pipe dream. The Bomb was perfectly obviously here to stay. It could not be disinvented; you could no more effectively ban it than you could ban the wheel. Besides, we were at the height of the Cold War. Even if we had come to an agreement without inspection, how would either of us have known whether the other was playing the game? It was surely more than likely that the Russians would keep a few bombs back just to be on the safe side; and I strongly suspected—and devoutly hoped—that we should too.

Before long, as I was well aware, I should be transferred—most probably to another post abroad. But did I really want one? Was I—if I were to be brutally honest with myself—even interested enough in foreign affairs? I was far from sure. Over the past few years I had increasingly longed to write, and I had found a subject—the history of the Normans in Sicily—that I could hardly wait to get my teeth into. Several of my friends in the service— Philip Ziegler and Douglas Hurd, to name but two—seemed to find no difficulty in turning out a first-rate book every couple of years in their spare time; but I clearly lacked their dedication, and anyway I needed to work in a library. Diplomacy or authorship? Clearly it had to be one or the other. If I chose to continue with the first, I should be assured of a steady and fairly respectable salary, excellent prospects (ending—with any luck—with a nice little embassy of my own) and a pension. If I plumped for the second I should be my own boss, a free spirit, able to organize my life as I wished and doing what in my heart I most wanted to do; but security would go out of the window. Besides, never in my life had I written anything longer than a Foreign Office dispatch; was I capable of writing a full-length book? And even if I were, what was I going to do for money? I had hardly any of my own, Anne had less, and we had two children to support. It would be a huge risk. Was I morally justified in taking it?

In September, 1963, I went to see John Henniker-Major, told him that I was thinking of resignation and tried to explain why. He was, as I knew he would be, profoundly sympathetic, not trying to influence me either way, just wanting me to be certain that I knew what I was doing. "Look," he said, "why not go off for a year *en disponibilité*? That means you're free to do what you like, as long as you don't go on anyone else's payroll or get yourself involved in politics. Then after a year you can take your choice: leave for good, with all our best wishes for your future, or be welcomed back into the fold." The agonizing decision postponed for twelve whole months—I could hardly believe my good luck. I thanked him from the bottom of my heart and walked out of his office with a new spring in my step.

———— ❦ ————

From that day my life changed. I celebrated my newfound freedom by flying off by myself to Africa. The ultimate object of my journey was to stay with my parents'—and by now also my own—old friends Dot and Antony Head in Nigeria. (Antony had been unlucky enough to be serving as Anthony Eden's Defense Minister at the time of Suez, and was now British High Commissioner in Lagos.) But I knew nothing of West or Central

Africa, and it seemed stupid and unimaginative to fly straight there. I fully intended to finance my trip with an article or two, for which I felt I should need material rather more colorful that than that which was likely to be afforded by a British High Commission, so I decided to fly to Niamey—the capital of the Republic of Niger—and then to hire a car and drive myself south to Lomé in Togo, where I would turn eastward along the coast through Dahomey (now Benin) and finally to Lagos.

My overriding impression of that journey was how much more stylishly the French ran their overseas empire than we did. I flew from Marseille at midnight, and arrived at Niamey around four in the morning, emerging from the plane into an atmosphere indistinguishable, both in temperature and in that wonderful smell of hot, damp earth, from that of the Tropical Greenhouse at Kew. It was pitch dark as we drove to the hotel, where I fell into bed—only to wake up four hours later to a loud and regular slapping noise. Mystified, I drew open the curtains and gazed out on to a scene I shall never forget. There below me was a huge bend in the Niger, on both banks of which stood hundreds of women, all dressed in dazzlingly brilliant colors, apparently trying to smash the rocks with their laundry. "Slap, slap, slap" they went against the stone; when they had finished with a given item they spread it out on the ground behind them before taking up the next. Many of these items were equally dazzling long strips of cloth, presumably intended for wrapping round and round the body in the African fashion; the entire riverbank had been transformed into an enormous rainbow. That was surprise number one. Surprise number two followed soon after when I went down to breakfast. There, instead of an egg, I was given a superb *truite aux amandes*, as good as anything I could have got in Paris—the fish fresh as a daisy, both of us having arrived on the same plane.

The three or four days I spent in French West Africa—the countries may already have been technically independent, but all the signs were in French and there seemed to be French people, both military and civilian, everywhere—confirmed this first impression. The hotels were simple but spotless, the food invariably superb, the bars stocked with Pernod and Dubonnet, the Sancerre deliciously cold. The countryside through which I drove was that of ageless Africa, but the towns radiated *chic*: Afro-*chic* perhaps, but all the better for that. How different was the Nigerian frontier, staffed as I remember by a single giantess in uniform looking like an enormous khaki dice, her two breast pockets projecting horizontally in front of her, sitting at a rickety wooden table ringed like a coat of mail by the circular stains of a thousand outsized beer tankards, from one of which she was thoughtfully swigging as she did the British football pools.

I finally arrived in Lagos only just in time, for Dot and Antony were preparing to depart. Their time in Nigeria had been one long love affair: they had adored the Nigerians and been adored in return. Every evening there was a farewell party, one or two at the High Commission, the rest in various Nigerian houses. The most memorable of all was given by the Mayor of Lagos. He had a resident orchestra of about twenty, all women and all on various kinds of percussion, belting out rhythms such as I have never heard before or since—rhythms of such extraordinary subtlety as to defy any system of musical notation. They played in a huge garden, in the middle of which I suddenly spotted a gigantic man in a magnificent silver robe adorned with dollar signs, dancing all by himself, an expression of sheer ecstasy on his face. I watched him, fascinated, and eventually asked who he was. He turned out to be the Minister of Finance.

The High Commission was recently built, open-plan, largely glass fronted, and ablaze with light. It was also in the highest degree exotic. Thanks to Dot's passion for animals, there was a wonderfully acrobatic gibbon who had free run of the house, two crested cranes that wandered round the garden and took food from your hand and a small regiment of parrots. I stayed there for about a week, enjoying myself hugely, then at my host's suggestion drove up to Kano in the north, where the Consul—a charming man with the wonderful name of St. Elmo Nelson—and his wife kindly put me up in their fine mud house. I loved Kano. Where Lagos is theoretically Christian but also very largely pagan, the north is Muslim to a man. Architecturally, it is—or was, forty years ago—almost entirely built of mud. I was taken on a tour of the Emir's Palace, in which the mud was full of mica—natural or artificially added I was unable to discover—which made every wall sparkle, even those on the inside.

The Emir himself had recently died, and his successor was due to be formally inducted the following spring. The Nelsons told me that this was one of the most astonishingly picturesque ceremonies that even Nigeria could offer; what a pity, they said, that I couldn't come back for it. Well, I thought, if it was really that good, why shouldn't I? I was after all a free agent now; one reason why I had left the Foreign Office was in order to be able to seize opportunities like this. With any luck, moreover, the trip could be paid for by a well-placed article or two.

And so, some six months later, I took the plunge—and the experience proved more thrilling than I could ever have dared to hope. All the greatest and richest potentates of Northern Nigeria had gathered in Kano for the occasion, all accompanied by enormous retinues, all dressed in almost unbelievable splendor, some of them in robes which seemed also to be flecked with mica, glistening and glittering in the sun. Their horses and their camels were gorgeously caparisoned; and since many of them had brought their private orchestras, the assault on the ear was almost as great as that on the eye. And yet, despite the dazzling colors and the deafening drumming, the atmosphere was one of intense solemnity. There was no laughter, no suggestion of celebration, as there would certainly have been in the South. These were princes, possessed of all the dignity of Islam, sitting proud and unsmiling in their saddles, fully conscious of their own nobility and of the significance of the ceremony that was being performed. I felt that I was attending a modern Field of the Cloth of Gold, transported to Africa and translated into African.

————⚬٭⚬————

But my intended book was still waiting to be written. My first agent was not a success, but now thanks to my friend James Pope-Hennessy, I had a wonderful new one, Diana Crawfurd; and thanks to her I had a publisher—Longmans—and a contract. I knew that I could not go on gallivanting around the world; my nose belonged at the grindstone—and that meant getting into a routine. Instead of heading every morning for the Foreign Office I would now go off to the London Library. I have now worked there regularly for over half a century. For me it will always be the best library in the world, largely because it keeps all its books on open shelves, ranged alphabetically according to subject and author. Most professional librarians are horrified by so simple a system, but for the readers it is a constant joy. Moreover you can take the books home—quite a few of them at a time—and are hardly ever chivvied to return one unless some other reader wants it. This means, inevitably, that you may occasionally not find the book you want on its shelf; but you will see any number of other books on the same subject, several of which may prove a good deal more informative than the one you were looking for. If, as I did—and indeed still do—you work most of every day in the

Reading Room, you have one of the best collections of reference books in the country ranged all round you. Nowadays there are even computer sockets into which to plug your laptop.

Gradually I began to piece together the story I so longed to write: the story of a bunch of footloose young Normans, passing through South Italy in 1015 on their way back from a pilgrimage to Jerusalem, being accosted by a Lombard separatist and invited to help his compatriots kick out the Byzantines, who were occupying Lombard lands. The Normans agree, and over the next half-century increasing numbers of their friends and relations ride south from Normandy to join them. By the 1050s they are powerful enough to defeat a papal army in pitched battle, capturing the Pope in person; and in 1061 they invade Sicily. Their leaders are five of the ten sons of a rather dim Norman knight of the Cotentin peninsula named Tancred de Hauteville; and one of these sons, Roger, establishes a Sicilian state which his son, Roger II, converts in 1130 into a Kingdom.

Already we have a superb rags-to-riches story—of a few hundred young men who start as little more than brigands and produce, in just over a century, a dynasty of Kings; but there is more to it than this. Sicily, originally Greek, was invaded and partially occupied in the ninth century by Arabs from North Africa. The Normans added a third ingredient to the brew, and it was their task to weld these three radically different communities into a single nation. They achieved it triumphantly. They made no attempt to impose themselves as a sort of *Herrenvolk*; theirs was a multilingual, multiracial, multiconfessional society. Under a Norman King the Greeks, who had seamanship in their blood, ran the all-important navy; the state finances, meanwhile, were in the hands of the Arabs, whose mathematics were always better than anyone else's. Norman French, Latin, Greek, and Arabic were all official languages. To take but one example, in the Palatine Chapel in Palermo you find a western European ground plan (nave, two side aisles, chancel), walls entirely covered with Byzantine mosaics as fine as anything to be found in Constantinople, and—most astonishing of all—a painted stalactite roof in purest Arabic style, more reminiscent of Cordova or Damascus than of any Christian state. And then you remember that all this happened less than a hundred years after the Great Schism between the Eastern and the Western Churches, and actually during the period of the Crusades—while, in one island in the middle of the Mediterranean, all three peoples and religions, everywhere else at each other's throats, came together in harmony to provide an example of cooperation and toleration which has never been repeated.

There, it seemed to me, was the substance of a riveting book. Anne and I had first gone to Sicily in 1961, only because we had a Middle Eastern crisis throughout the summer—Iraq had made one of its periodic attempts to take over Kuwait—and it was late October before I got any leave. If, we thought, we were to get any warmth or sunshine we should have to go as far south as we could. I think I had dimly heard about this exotic Norman Kingdom, but I knew nothing about it; and I had been knocked sideways by the splendor of what we had seen. On our return to London I had gone straight to the London Library to find out more, and had discovered to my astonishment that there was nothing readable about it in English. It was then that the first seeds were planted of the idea that was to change my life; and now, two years later in 1963, I was finally able to get down to work. Now, too, I began to realize two things. First, that the story was even better than I had imagined. My agent Diana, to whom I confided the first draft chapter—only partially emboldened, I seem to remember, by a delicious lunch at Cunningham's—later told me that the hairs had risen on the back of her neck as she read. It was full of incident, often exciting and occasionally hilarious. Second, that my luck was greater than I had dared suspect. Monsieur Ferdinand Chalandon, a Frenchman who described himself as *archiviste-paléographe*, had produced two hefty volumes on the subject in 1907. He had done all the research, spending years in monastic and other libraries. He had unearthed all the facts, produced bibliography, references, even—all too rare in French books of that time—an index. The only thing he had not done was to see the point. He related fact after fact, without comment and, heaven knows, without humor. His book is boring to the point of unreadability. But he was my benefactor. All I had to do was to make M. Chalandon fun; and I think—I hope—I succeeded.

I worked hard at the Normans, but was always conscious that time was passing. After a year *en disponibilité* I had amassed vast quantities of notes but had still not written the first page. Personnel Department played me on a long line: my time was up at the end of September and it was almost Christmas before the dread telephone rang.

"Hello John Julius, how's it all going?"

I told them that I was hard at work, and that things were going very well; but I was summoned to Carlton House Terrace and knew that the great decision would now have to be made. A day or two later I was sitting in the tube on my way there, still wondering what I was going to say. I knew what I *wanted* to do; but did I dare do it? For the last year I hadn't earned a penny, and my book wouldn't be finished for another three years at the earliest. I was the father of a growing family; was I mad—or perhaps criminally irresponsible—to throw up a safe and enjoyable career for a pipe dream? I walked into John Henniker's office. Still I didn't know how I was going to answer the inevitable question. Then I heard my voice say—and I can hear it still—"No John, I'm afraid I'm leaving."

Already as I spoke and as he grasped me warmly by the hand and wished me luck, I regretted it; and all the way home I cursed myself for an idiot. Would I return the next day, I wondered—on all fours—and say "Take me back, take me back, I didn't mean it?" But there: I never did, and I now realize that this was one of the best decisions of my life. Indeed it was more than a decision, for it marked the watershed. Until that day, technically speaking at any rate, I had been an employee, bound to turn up at the office in the morning, obey orders, go where I was sent, ask permission if I wanted to take the afternoon off. I had never particularly minded my committed state, and was fully aware that all my colleagues and most of my friends were in the same position; but I had always envied the self-employed, and was thrilled at the thought that I had at last cut the cord and was henceforth to be one of them myself. By evening I had overcome my misgivings and was conscious of a feeling of genuine elation. Anne and I opened a bottle of champagne. I was free. From this time forth my life and my time were my own.

There remained, of course, the problem of how I was going to feed my children; but once again I struck lucky. A few weeks later I went to a dinner party and met an American lady called Dee Wells, the former wife of the Minister at the American Embassy. She was doing a regular television program five evenings a week, and she asked me if I would like to join her on it. The program was called *Three After Six*; basically it consisted of three people who watched the six o'clock news and then chatted about it for twenty minutes afterwards. Dee was the anchorwoman; the other two varied. At the time I was involved Alan Brien and Benny Green were the two most regular favorites, but Nicholas Tomalin and several others turned up from time to time. I usually did three programs a week, and as I was paid £50 for each appearance—still in those days quite a lot of money—it made a considerable difference to our domestic budget. Besides, one job led to another; by the end of the year I found myself doing a fair amount of broadcasting.

Most of my working day, nevertheless, continued to be spent in the London Library—then as now my spiritual home—scribbling away about the Normans; writing in loose-leaf notebooks, on one side of the paper only and on every other line, so as always to have enough room for corrections. At the end of the day the pages would often be almost illegible, so the next morning before breakfast I would type them out with—remembering what had happened to Thomas Carlyle and Lawrence of Arabia—as many carbon copies as I could squeeze into the typewriter. How, I ask myself nowadays, did I ever live without the laptop?

Chapter Ten

The Mountain and the Desert

HARD AS I was working on my Norman book, it was not the first thing I published. In the late summer of 1963 I went, with my friends Costa Achillopoulos and Reresby Sitwell, to Mount Athos. I had spent a few days of my leave there two years before, but that first expedition had proved a disaster. It was, I admit, largely my fault. It had never occurred to me that the sun would not be beating down; I had not even taken an anorak. As things turned out it pelted with rain uninterruptedly for as long as I was there. I had also been led to believe that mules were available on demand, so had brought not a rucksack but a suitcase. In fact there was not a mule to be found anywhere and the suitcase, being too heavy to carry any distance, had to be left at Daphne, the little port of entry—which in turn meant that I had no dry clothes. After a day or two, sodden, frozen and dispirited, I gave up and headed for home.

This time I was determined to do better, and to learn from my past mistakes. We all went properly equipped, and we had the

inestimable advantage that one of us spoke fluent Greek. Costa—
he was never called anything but that, and many of his friends did
not even know his surname—was a constant joy. He must have
been well into his sixties and looked like a cross between Nehru
and Picasso. (Since he had a little house near Grasse, he was frequently taken for the latter at restaurants and willingly gave auto-
graphs when requested.) His job, insofar as he had one, was pho-
tography; but he was never much more than competent at it and
really used it only as a way of financing his travels. There seemed
to be nowhere that he had not been, and could not describe brilliantly in any one of three or four languages. He has been dead
these twenty-five years, and I still miss him more than I can say;
he was as much fun as anyone I have ever known.

This time Athos was a joy. Day after day, the sun beat down.
We walked from monastery to monastery—there are twenty of
them, and I think we notched up seventeen—staying in a different one every night and during the day wandering through some
of the most ravishingly beautiful country in the world—the more
so because it is utterly unspoilt: no one swims in the limpid little bays, the flowers have never had children to pick them. The
views—particularly as you head south, where the Holy Mountain
rises to its 6,000-foot summit—are breathtaking. The monks,
once they were persuaded that we were not Roman Catholics,
were friendly and in their way hospitable. (I qualify this last
remark only because Athonite food is—or was in those days—in
a class by itself for horror; every meal was a gastronomic nightmare, and if we had not taken copious provisions with us from
London it is unlikely that we should have survived.) I had only
one unfortunate *contretemps*, when, one morning at dawn, I was
giving myself a much-needed strip wash in the bathhouse of the
most venerable of all the monasteries, the Grand Lavra, standing in a long trough and clad in nothing but soapsuds, when the

guest-master appeared. Never have I seen a man so angry. His outpouring of hysterical Greek was largely incomprehensible to me, but the message was plain enough: by standing stark naked under the very roof of the Lavra I was desecrating the monastery. I grabbed my clothes, struggled into one or two of them, and fled, soapsuds and all.

I have often wondered: could this incident possibly have occurred in any community in which women were not rigidly excluded? There is something disturbingly unnatural about this negation of all femininity—which extends not only to human beings but to cows, ewes, bitches, and in theory even to hens—engendering as it does an almost pathological terror of sex of which this seems to me a perfect illustration. After ten days or so on the Holy Mountain I began to find the total absence of womankind strangely oppressive—above all in the little village of Karyes which serves as the Athonite capital. Every other village in the world has women and children living in it; Karyes has none. When we finally returned to the outside world and I saw my first woman for a fortnight, I could have thrown my arms round her and kissed her—not, heaven knows, for any reasons of sexual frustration but simply for the values she represented.

But one soon learns the ways of the Mountain, and when one has done so the rewards are immense. I shall never forget the mornings walking through those forests or striding along those silent, lonely beaches; the excitement of arriving at an unknown monastery just before sunset (at which moment the gates are locked), speculating on the warmth of the welcome that awaited us; the evenings on those vertiginous balconies, ouzo in hand, gazing out over the sea and holding one old monk after another spellbound by comparing the populations of London and Paris, Tokyo, and New York; or the nights when we crossed a moonlit courtyard to the *katholikon* and listened, leaning back in our stalls, while dark and shrouded figures exchanged the droning supplications of their liturgy back and forth across the echoing church, and the frescoed saints glowed and glimmered in the candlelight.

Yet always, at the back of our minds, was anxiety about the state of the Holy Mountain itself. Time and again we would ask the same questions, and receive what were essentially the same answers:

"How many monks was this monastery built for?"

"Two hundred and fifty."

"How many does it have today?"

"Eleven."

"How old is the youngest?"

"Seventy-four."

Clearly, we thought, the end was near. Athos had been in existence for well over a thousand years, yet it seemed impossible that it should now survive our own lifetimes. Occasionally we voiced our fears—and were surprised that when we did so no monk ever showed a trace of anxiety. "God will provide," they would say with a shrug. And how right they were; for that was forty-five years ago, and I am told that today every monastery is still going strong and that there are indeed more monks on the Mountain than there have been for a century.

In those days there were very few books about Mount Athos. Before my first visit I had already read every one I could find. One of the worst was called *The Six Thousand Beards of Mount Athos*, which surely says it all; another atrocious one was *Un été chez les hommes*, by a sensationalist Frenchwoman who claimed to have had her breasts amputated in order to pass muster as a young novice. By far the best was *The Station* by Robert Byron, that hugely talented if insufferable author who wrote several brilliant books in the interwar years—including my bible *The Byzantine Achievement*—and would doubtless have written a good many more had his ship not been torpedoed in 1941 on the way to Egypt, two days before his thirty-sixth birthday. But they were all long out of print, and it seemed to us—and fortunately to Messrs. Hutchinson, the publishers—that there was room for another. Costa, sadly, preferred to speak only through his camera; Reresby and I—though we also contributed a fair number of photographs to the finished volume—were consequently responsible for the text. I kicked off with an essay covering the history of the Mountain, together with a few other aspects which I thought worth mentioning; he followed with a day-by-day account of our journey. The resulting slim volume was designed by George Rainbird and looked lovely. It sold quite well at the time, but was never reprinted.

———⊙⊺⊚———

Slowly, my book on the Normans ploughed ahead. By now I had realized that it would have to be in two volumes; and one day in February, 1966, when I had just reached the coronation of my hero Roger II in 1130, I decided that it was halftime. The next morning, as usual, I typed out the previous day's work, and within five minutes of my banging out—extremely hard, in a mixture of triumph and relief—the last full stop, the telephone rang. It was Costa. "Then," he said—he started most sentences with the word—"Then, I have some friends who are anxious to go to the Sahara, where they want to make a film. I have agreed to go with them, and if we can find one more person we shall be able to have three Land Rovers instead of two, which will be much safer. Then, can you come?"

I would probably have accepted anyway—the opportunity seemed far too good to miss—but the timing was such that I felt that my mind had somehow been made up for me. I was asked to contribute £400 up front—I think there may have been another

£100 later, but even then £500 didn't seem exorbitant for a six-week trans-Saharan expedition—and a month or so later we were on our way.

This journey too was to become the subject of a book—*Sahara*, also designed by Rainbird and published (this time by Longmans) in 1968. It too has long since disappeared, but machinery for finding secondhand or out-of-print books is nowadays so efficient that anybody remotely interested in seeing a copy could always find one. There is consequently little point in my going over the ground again in too much detail. On the other hand, the Saharan expedition was by far the greatest physical adventure of my life, so something of it must be recorded here. Apart from Costa, I knew none of my traveling companions. The leader—and maker of the intended film—was Anne Balfour-Fraser, who was bringing with her two French friends, Marie-Thérèse d'Arcangues, an experienced *saharienne*, and Micheline Holzer. There was also Johnny Hinchingbrooke (now Lord Sandwich), a Jordanian cameraman called Mustafa Hammuri, and our French professional guide and cicerone Jean Sudriez. A local driver made nine, so that we were three per Land Rover.

On March 7, 1966, Costa and I flew to Tamanrasset and the following morning to Djanet, an oasis in the far south of Algeria, where our Land Rover was waiting; the other two were being driven down from Algiers. When we were reunited, all three were packed to the roof with provisions—mostly in jerry cans, because dehydration is always a danger and on trips such as these you have to carry as much water as petrol. Then, after a couple of days preparation and acclimatization, we were off, on a route that was to take us more or less due east, right across the Republic of Niger and into that of Chad, where we would spend a week in the highly volcanic mountains of Tibesti.

The golden rule when driving in the Sahara is to avoid the great dunes. They are ravishingly beautiful, but virtually uncrossable by anything except camels, and even camels find them pretty heavy going. Fortunately the *erg*, as it is called, extends over only about one-seventh of the desert; the rest is mostly hard and flat, covered sometimes by gravel, sometimes by a thin layer of sand. There are also mountains, rocky outcrops, and the occasional emerald green oasis, often with a population of a thousand or more. Thus the scenery is seldom dull, and often stunning.

Two other things struck me about the Sahara: it is perfectly silent, and it is perfectly clean. As I wrote in my book:

> Here in the civilized, sophisticated world, the air around us is never still. We have forgotten—if indeed we ever knew—what silence is. Even when we think we have found it we are, like as not, subconsciously shutting our ears to the sounds of nature—the rustle of branches, the trickle of water, the cry of a distant animal. In the open desert, even these sounds are exceptions; silence stands no longer as a negative concept but as a positive, present thing, wrapping itself round you like a cloak. And as with sound, so with dirt. Where, outside an operating theater, does cleanliness exist around us? Nowhere, and perhaps it is just as well. It is certainly not our fault. Life means dirt, and so does death; for ours is a damp world, and where damp is there is also decay, and decay means dirt too. But in the Sahara, outside the oases, these things do not exist. An animal collapses; whatever the reason, the immediate cause of its death is nearly always thirst. It is desiccated even before it dies; and long before it decomposes its bones will have been pecked dry by vultures. Clean again, pure again, and the sand sparkles in celebration. Only in one other environment that I know of is one conscious of such peacefulness and virginity; that of the high mountains. The atmosphere

is strangely similar, and so is the state of mind it engenders. The mountain snows and the desert: both are immaculate, untouched by humanity and indifferent to it. We enter them not perhaps as trespassers, but yet on their terms—which, if we do not accept, we perish.[1]

At night we would unroll our sleeping bags, put on all the extra clothing we could find—for the desert, having no moisture to hold the heat of the day, becomes perishingly cold at night—and sleep under the stars. And what stars they were. Before I left England I had taken the precaution of going to the Madame Tussaud's Planetarium, where for a ridiculously small sum I was shown precisely the constellations that I should be seeing at given dates and latitudes; as a result, by the time I encountered them they were already old friends. Occasionally, when we were at moderately high altitudes, the cold was almost too great to stick my head out of the sleeping bag; but by the time the journey was over the night sky held few secrets.

The Land Rovers took us as far as an oasis called Bardai in the foothills of the Tibesti, where the terrain obliged us to exchange them for camels. On the Sahara shelves of the London Library there is a book dedicated

> To
> FERI N'GASHI
> Only a Camel
> But Steel-True
> And Great of Heart.

I can only say that I doubt it. In ten days spent in disagreeable proximity to a good many of them, I found camels without

---

1 On re-reading it, I realize that—grammatically speaking—there is something seriously wrong with the last sentence. But that's what I wrote then, so that's what it has to be now.

exception to be faithless, pusillanimous, and lazy. They also suffer from a halitosis unique in my experience. We rode them occasionally, but the local saddles basically consisted of a single forked branch, which even with half a dozen blankets on top of it inflicted, after a few minutes, a degree of pain that I hardly knew existed. It was infinitely more comfortable—and, incidentally, a good deal safer—to walk, which in the mornings we usually did, clambering on to the camels only for the last couple of hours of the day.

On the afternoon of the fourth day's steady climb we arrived at our final destination—Soborom. It is not a village, nor an oasis, nor yet a mountain. It is a geological phenomenon, one of the most spectacular centers of continuous volcanic activity in the world, a land of perpetual turmoil. Our descent into it had a Dante-esque quality. We and the camels had to thread our way between great natural cauldrons of seething mud; the air was thick with the fumes of brimstone; and the ground itself rang ominously hollow underfoot, a constant reminder of the nameless horrors that lurked beneath. The colors, too, were not of this world: a green which spread over the sand and rocks like a creeping mineral mold, a brilliant yellow and orange produced by other sinister subterranean exhalations, and a dirty white natron, looking like old, spilt milk on a railway platform.

As March gave way to April we turned the camels' heads back towards Bardai; and three or four days later, in the late afternoon when we were less than an hour from the oasis, disaster struck. Costa was perched high on his camel when it suddenly smelt home, greenery, and water—and broke into a gallop. Horses do much the same, but horses have stirrups and bridles; camels have neither. In the circumstances, Costa did the only possible thing. He fell off. A hundred yards or so ahead of him, I was having trouble with my own mount, but managed to keep my seat till we reached the French army fort where we had stayed on our outward journey. Then Jean came dashing up. *"Viens vite,"* he shouted, *"Costa a eu un accident."* The two of us seized a heavy mattress from one of the huts, flung it into the nearest Land Rover and drove as quickly as we dared to where poor Costa lay, conscious but in agonizing pain and quite unable to move.

There was no doctor at Bardai, far less any X-ray equipment. For all we knew he had broken his back; the slightest wrong movement might snap the spinal cord and paralyze him for life. We lifted him as gently as we could on to the mattress and into the Land Rover and at last, driving at a snail's pace, got him to a bed.

The next four days were a nightmare. Costa showed no sign of recovery; he could not even turn over in bed without help. There was clearly no question of his being able to return the thousand-odd miles back to Djanet; somehow we had to get him to hospital as soon as we could. The fort, manned by a dozen or so local soldiers, was theoretically in radio contact with the regional center at Faya-Largeau, some 200 miles over the mountains to the south, but by a cruel stroke of luck the electric generator had broken down two days before and all contact with the outside world had been lost. Costa, worn out by pain—we had some morphia with us but nowhere near enough—had made up his mind that he was dying, and we for our part were by no means sure that he was wrong.

Then, on the morning of the second or third day after the accident, I saw a line of camels approaching across the sand. Ahead of them walked a European in a khaki tunic, with a pale blue army *képi* on his head. I ran up to him, and he introduced himself as Sergeant Jean-François Renn, one of the last members of the French army still patrolling the Sahara. His presence, he explained, was purely fortuitous; after a month on patrol he was running short of supplies and was calling at Bardai for replenishment. Did he, I asked, have a radio? Of course he did. Could he send an SOS for us? Of course he could. In five minutes his aerial was set up; one of his eight-man platoon of *goumiers*[2] was sitting in the sand, cranking away at a hand generator; and our message was on its way to Faya-Largeau. It was a beginning, but we still had no clear idea of what, if anything, could be done. Two more days of suspense followed, till finally there came a message—not from Faya-Largeau this time, but from Fort Lamy, then the capital of the Republic of Chad. A flying doctor and two male nurses were on their way. An hour later they arrived, and twenty minutes later they were gone, taking Costa with them; they had a seven-hour flight ahead of them, and since Fort Lamy had no facilities for night landing they had to be back before dark.

Costa recovered. Three vertebrae had been impacted together and he had been put in a plaster cast; but nothing was broken. It was only later, when we were all home again, that we heard the full, hair-raising story of his sufferings at Fort Lamy. Not so long before, in pre-independence days, this had been one of the leading French hospitals in Africa; and even then he had nothing but praise for the one or two remaining French doctors and the treatment they gave him. It was not their fault that the supply of anesthetics was so short that they had to set his spine without any; never, he later told us, had he experienced such exquisite pain. Nor could they help it when the family of a patient in the next bed, seriously ill and unconscious, burst into the ward *en masse* with much assorted livestock, tore aside the drip feed and crammed handfuls of rice into his unresisting mouth. Without an adequate staff of trained nurses such incidents were—indeed, probably still are—unavoidable in the hospitals of Central Africa. Untrained nurses seem to have been plentiful enough, but their

---

2 Local troops.

methods tended to be unorthodox. Costa, lying paralyzed in his cast, could do nothing when his ward orderly, whose duty it was to wash him down every morning, concentrated on one particular part of his anatomy to the virtual exclusion of all the rest. "*Georgette, Georgette,*" he used to cry in rising embarrassment, "*pourquoi tu fais ça?*" "*Ça m'amuse,*" she would reply with a grin, and continue the good work.

———————— ❧ ————————

It was at half-past nine in the morning on Easter Monday, April 11, a month to the day after our departure, that we roared— two of our three silencers had given out—back into Djanet. Only then did we realize how serious was the fault in one of the Land Rovers—a fault that had caused it, over the past day or so, to consume almost as much petrol as the other two together. We finished our thousand-mile drive—apart from what remained in the tanks—with just fifteen liters to spare.

Reassured about Costa by a waiting telegram, we could concentrate on our own arrangements. The others, sadly, had to return to civilization, but I still had one more Saharan ambition to fulfill—to go up to the high plateau of the Tassili, which only ten years before had become celebrated as the world's most exciting natural gallery of prehistoric painting; suddenly I found that I had a chance to do so. I might not have chosen to see the Tassili with a party of two dozen strangers sent out in a package by the *Touring-Club de France*, but it was clearly an opportunity not to be missed.

Before setting off, I cast a glance over my new traveling companions. They were not a bit like those I had just left: most of them looked well advanced in their retirement, more suited for a week in Aix-les-Bains than a trek over the Tassili. Our journey began with a backbreaking four-hour climb, taking us through scenery of almost unbelievable splendor but leaving us limp with exhaustion. After over five weeks in the Sahara I felt myself to be more or less acclimatized and in moderately good physical condition; but several of the others were septuagenarians twice my age, who had left France only two days before, who had only twenty-four hours to adapt themselves to the heat and the altitude, and who were now being asked to climb from a starting level of 4,000 feet to a plateau another 2,000 feet above that, under a blistering Sahara sun. Nor was that all: there followed another three miles of stony, shadeless desolation.

Then, suddenly, everything changed. Instead of the usual limitless expanses, the eye was brought up short by soaring verticals—mountain walls rising perpendicular, wind-sculpted columns of rock like petrified tornados, transforming the land into the semblance of an empty city, dividing it into streets and alleys and crescents and an occasional vast piazza. The next three days were a revelation. As we walked, some twenty miles a day, the rocks grew ever wilder in color, ever more fantastic in shape, corkscrewing up from the desert floor, forming arches and viaducts and colonnades. And, most fantastic of all, the paintings: paintings in their thousands, little patches of ochre and yellow on the rock walls, the documents of a savannah people and its herds, dating from the early Neolithic times of around 6000 BCE down to that melancholy day, only a few centuries before our era, when increasing desiccation finally put an end to settled life on the plateau and the shepherds wandered off to seek richer pastures elsewhere. The art reached its peak during what was clearly the golden age of the Tassili—say around 4,000 BCE. The subjects are surprisingly varied: there are no longer the hippos and rhinos, the elephants and giraffes and ostriches that we see in the earliest paintings, but there are sheep and oxen and goats and deer and antelope, no two of them ever exactly alike, seldom even drawn from the same angle. But the artists did not confine themselves to animals: they painted themselves, their wives, and their children: hunting, eating, running, making love. One picture shows a particularly nasty murder—a man clubbing another to death—but apart from this one instance the paintings are remarkably free of violence.

Nowadays the Tassili is empty apart from a few wandering Touareg. The Tibesti had been the land of the Toubou, who are probably the last surviving remnant of a prehistoric and probably aboriginal Saharan race: noble, immensely tough, but in appearance fairly unprepossessing. The Tassili, on the other hand, has always been Touareg country, and the Touareg must be among the most picturesque people on earth: the men immensely tall, in long robes of blue or sometimes green, with that huge black veil—it is really more of a mask—which they never seem to remove, even when eating and drinking. Just about every European in the Sahara wears a *chèche*, a length of white cheesecloth wrapped round the head and face as a protection against sun and wind, and one naturally assumes that the Touareg *litham* serves a similar purpose; but this does not explain why Touareg women never veil their faces at all, despite the fact that they are out and about every bit as much as their menfolk. The Touareg woman, though, is an exception to every rule, since hers is one of the most feminist societies on earth. It is she who chooses her husband—whom, if he proves unsatisfactory, she is free to leave whenever she likes.

Wonderful as this last, unexpected stage of my desert adventure had been, I was growing tired; and as we dragged ourselves back to Djanet I found myself looking forward heartily to my return to civilization. For six long weeks my whole existence had been bound up in the Sahara. It had fascinated me and taught me much about myself; but for all its beauty and purity and grandeur it had not, thank God, ultimately ensnared me. A day or two later I took a rather enjoyable oasis-hopping flight back to Algiers, where I had the most welcome hot bath of my life; and the day after that, almost unrecognizably bronzed and bearded but to my intense relief, I was home.

Chapter Eleven

The Stone Stops Rolling

FTER MY RETURN from Geneva and my resignation from the Foreign Service, Ricki and I had continued to see each other regularly—though still secretly—in London, where she had bought a house just across the Canal in Maida Avenue; then, in January, 1964, she told me that she was pregnant. My first reaction, predictably enough, was dismay: suddenly, our relationship had acquired a new and terrifying dimension. My own two children were still very young—Artemis ten, Jason four—while Anne, I am deeply ashamed to say, still knew nothing of what was going on. I loathed the deception and on several occasions found myself on the point of confession; but the thought of the pain that the news would cause her always stopped me in my tracks.

At the end of August Ricki gave birth to a daughter, Allegra. I shared in her happiness, but was too consumed by guilt to do much rejoicing, conscious all the time that Anne would have to know, and that it was I who would have to tell her. Not until January, 1965—the night, as it happened, that Winston Churchill died—did I find the courage to do so.

The next few months were the worst of both our lives. My poor Anne, who had suspected nothing, was utterly shattered; and I, watching her condition deteriorate with every day that passed, was desperate with anxiety. I continued to love her—loved her perhaps even more, seeing what I had done to her—and would have done anything to give her back her happiness. Except to give up Ricki. That of course was the obvious answer; but anyone who has been through this particular experience knows that things are not as easy as that. Ricki loved me as I did her; she had borne and was raising my child; she was a foreigner in London; I was the only man in her life, and emotionally she was entirely dependent on me. On the other hand there could be no question of my leaving Anne: how could I? Of course I should never have got myself into this nightmare—that went without saying—but now that I had done so the problem seemed to have no solution. And so the grim weeks went on until Good Friday, when I drove my distraught wife to the Westminster Hospital and she was put under psychiatric care. Thank God, she responded—though it was well into the summer before she was completely recovered and we could once again talk freely of what had happened.

And our marriage survived. Not for years did we even discuss divorce: on the contrary, we continued to love each other and—particularly after someone else had entered her life—were to enter into a happy brother-and-sisterly relationship that continues to this day. Meanwhile—probably as a result of this crisis, and of my refusal to leave Anne, my relationship with Ricki came, slowly and rather painfully, to an end. Though she never once said so, she must have hoped that my marriage would not survive the birth of Allegra and that her baby would after all have a proper father. When she realized that this hope was in vain, I believe that she began, perhaps subconsciously, perhaps deliberately, to distance herself from me. Nor do I for a moment blame her for doing so. She was still only in her middle thirties. I had let her down; very well, she must look elsewhere. Slowly, her attitude towards me changed, and our relations reached a point where for a whole year, despite the proximity of our houses, we thought it better not to see each other. In 1968 there was a semireconciliation, largely because we were both anxious that I should see Allegra; but then, all too soon, came tragedy.

On January 30, 1969, we had organized the annual presentation party for the Duff Cooper Memorial Prize, the literary award that had been instituted and endowed by my father's friends after his death. There were usually some three hundred guests at the ceremony; my task was to introduce the prizewinner and the presenter—Professor Ivan Morris and Harold Macmillan—and have them and the judges, with their respective husbands and wives—back to dinner afterwards. It would have been a taxing day at the best of times; and it was not helped by the fact that it found me that year laid low with a vicious attack of influenza. At four o'clock that afternoon, when I was groaning in bed and wondering how I was going to get through the evening, the telephone rang. It was Leslie Waddington—an old friend of Ricki's and one of our few confidants—calling to say that on the previous day she had been involved in a hideous motor accident in France and had been killed outright. The three-year-old Allegra, who had remained in London, was left alone.

I called to Anne and told her at once; her first words, to her eternal honor, were "Of course, we must take in Allegra." We would have happily done so—perhaps indeed we should have; but when John Huston, her legal father, asked if he could take her we did not object. Fortunately she had a wonderful Irish nanny, who had been with her since she was born and whom she adored, and so the two of them flew off to Ireland. She was nine by the time I saw her again; but that is another story.

———◦⁊◦———

Some years ago the Headmaster of Eton invited me down to judge the Loder Declamation Prize, which is awarded annually for the recitation of poetry and prose. I replied that nothing would give me greater pleasure; on the other hand I felt I should point out that I had received a similar invitation only a year or two before; I wondered whether it might not be better to wait a little longer before coming down again. A few days later there arrived another letter from the Headmaster. He had been somewhat surprised, he said, by my response and had done a little research. It was in fact *nineteen* years since my previous visit. Since at that time none of this year's contestants had actually been born, he saw no reason to delay my return any longer.

The point of this story is to illustrate the difficulty which now faces me. Until my resignation from the Foreign Service, my life had fallen into a series of separate chapters—chapters so easily definable that they have set the structure for most of this book. After 1963, however, I find that this structure no longer applies. Since then I have always been based in London, living in the same house on the Regent's Canal, writing books, occasionally broadcasting or filming, traveling as often as possible, but never—apart from the Sahara expedition in 1966—for much more than a fortnight at a stretch. In such conditions the past has to be viewed through a wider lens than before. With increasing age, too, memory starts to play tricks; and as the years go by faster and faster—it's not the speed of time's passing that appals, it's the steady acceleration—I find it impossible to remember exactly when things occurred. All I do know, from bitter experience, is that they almost certainly date from longer ago than I could have thought possible. I have, alas, never kept a diary. If therefore what remains of this book is a good deal more impressionistic than what has gone before, I can only crave indulgence.

From the mid-1960s I was a fairly regular attender of the House of Lords. In my Foreign Office days I had been obliged to keep my nose out of politics altogether; we never knew what sort of government we should have to represent next. Now that I was a free spirit, there were no longer any restrictions. None, at least, except one: I had never been terribly interested. To my father—though they were to lose their attraction for him in his later years—politics had been the breath of life. At home in my youth, they had dominated lunch and dinner conversation ever since I could remember. Looking back on it, I suspect that—perhaps as a result of this early saturation—they rather frightened me. To this day, although I count a fair number of politicians among my friends, I would nearly always rather talk to them about something else.

Still, for better or worse, I was a peer. To begin with, the title had taken a certain amount of getting used to; in the 1950s it cut a good deal more ice than it does today. Usages are different too. When I wrote my first book, under the name of John Julius Norwich—I received a furious letter from Nancy Mitford. "You can't call yourself that," she protested. "You're either John Julius Cooper or you're Lord Norwich, you'll have to choose." Technically, she was perfectly right; my neighbor Patrick Kinross had—after he stopped being Patrick Balfour—written all his books as "Lord Kinross." But somehow the idea of "Lord Norwich" on the title page stuck in my gullet. I replied to Nancy that I had decided to take "John Julius Norwich" as my *nom de plume*, and that was that.

The point is, surely, that usage is really only a matter of fashion. Language has an organic life of its own, and is as subject to change as any other living thing. Half a century ago any peer writing, for example, to a newspaper would have signed with a single name—that of his title—and would have been perfectly correct to do so. Nowadays this is getting rarer day by day. I sign "Norwich" on checks, contracts and a very few formal business letters; otherwise, it's "John Julius

Norwich" every time. And I suspect that most of my fellow peers
do the same. I would argue, therefore, that almost imperceptibly
the rules have changed; and that as they have always been unwrit-
ten, there is no reason why they shouldn't. What was a vile solecism
in Nancy Mitford's day is, half a century later, perfectly OK. "The
Viscount Norwich" appears less and less frequently on envelopes,
"Mr. J.J. Norwich" more and more. Just occasionally there are other,
wilder variants. Best of all was a letter which arrived some years ago
addressed to "The Discount Norwich." It made my week.

I decided from the start that I would take my seat as a cross-
bencher. I should probably not be attending very regularly; I had
a job of my own to do, and the last thing I wanted was to be has-
sled by party whips. So one afternoon, pretty frightened and in
robes rented that morning from Moss Bros., I walked into the
Chamber, bowed to the Lord Chancellor on the woolsack, took
the oath and found myself a spare seat at the far end, facing the
Throne. It was several weeks later that I got up to speak for the
first time. Their Lordships were debating capital punishment.
Hanging has always struck me as barbarous, and I prayed that the
strength of my feelings against it would give me courage. I went
to a great deal of trouble preparing that maiden speech, which
I was determined to make without notes. My father, who was a
first-rate speaker, had always scorned them—except when dealing
with army and navy estimates, since he had no head for figures—
maintaining that they halved the impact of a speech. If you did
your homework properly, he argued, and knew exactly what you
wanted to say before you got up to say it, notes were unnecessary.
Even if without them you forgot a point here and there, that was
a small price to pay for the advantage gained. In all my lamentably
undistinguished parliamentary life, I remember only one other
piece of advice about public speaking, which was also to serve
me well. It came from one of the best speakers I have ever heard,

Lady Violet Bonham Carter. "Swim between islands," she said. In other words, have a few really good punch lines prepared, and then make your way from one to the next as best you can.

I was due to speak between half-past three and four; by two-thirty I was walking up and down by Rodin's Burghers of Calais below the Victoria Tower, going through my speech again and again. I am not normally given to stage fright: I have done a good deal of public speaking in my life and on the whole enjoy it enormously. That afternoon I was terrified. The palms of my hands, I remember, were wringing wet—a phenomenon which I have never known before or, thank God, since. But the moment came, and I think I acquitted myself reasonably well. The black-cassocked Methodist Lord Soper, who followed me and consequently had to deliver the traditional congratulations on a maiden speech, drew particular attention to my notelessness, which pleased me very much. Thereafter I would hold forth without a qualm—but I always put in a good hour's hard work in advance.

Capital punishment was duly abolished. Soon afterwards, my days as a cross-bencher came to an end. Lord Gladwyn, who as Sir Gladwyn Jebb had been my father's second successor at the Paris Embassy, had become a member of the Liberal Party on his retirement and was now working enthusiastically in the cause of Europe. I too was emotionally pro-European—though I had never properly understood the economic arguments involved— and needed little persuading to join him. Thus it was that I soon found myself, somewhat to my surprise, the Liberal spokesman not on Europe but on sex—a subject upon which our laws were still hopelessly outdated. First, I was appointed to my first (and last) Parliamentary Committee to abolish the censorship of plays by the Lord Chamberlain; over the following years we went on to legalize homosexuality and abortion, and loosened up a good deal on pornography.

The use of the first person plural is not meant to suggest that the Upper House was alone responsible; all final decisions, of course, rest with the House of Commons. But one of the many advantages of the old House of Lords before New Labour got its hands on it was that it was far easier for peers than for members of the House of Commons to initiate legislation. Despite repeated but always unsuccessful efforts by Sidney Silverman MP to get the death penalty abolished, the Bill which finally brought it to an end was initiated in the Upper House; and the credit for the Sexual Offenses Bill which decriminalized homosexuality belongs in a very large part to the late Earl of Arran—known to his countless friends as Boofy—who devoted all his considerable energies to the task. On his second attempt he achieved complete success and was accordingly free to turn his attention to the protection of wildlife. "The trouble is," he used to say, "that Their Lordships are far more interested in badgering buggers than they are in buggering badgers."

⸙

One of the things I most enjoyed about having a seat in Parliament was that it enabled one to make a fuss. One particular case seems worth mentioning here, as an example of the extraordinary attitudes that prevailed in certain quarters—notably the police—less than forty years ago. Some time in February, 1970, I was approached by Thelma Holt, an actress who ran an admirable little experimental theater on Tottenham Court Road—in New York it would have been described as off-Broadway—known as the Open Space. It had just received a grant from the Arts Council, and quite right too: a recent performance there of *Macbeth* had been the most exciting I had ever seen. It had since been invited to perform at both the Rome and the Holland Festivals.

Until January the Open Space had never shown a film. It then did so, ironically enough, only because John Trevelyan, then Chairman of the British Board of Film Censors, had been much impressed by a film called *Flesh*, produced by Andy Warhol. He had decided, understandably, that it was not entirely suitable for public release at the local Odeon; but he himself had suggested to the distributors that they should approach the Open Space. Thelma had accepted it, and the film ran for three weeks without, so far as could be seen, causing anybody any annoyance. By that time it had been seen by all the principal critics. The great Dilys Powell had written in the *Sunday Times* that it was "often funny, sometimes pathetic, and once, when the handsome naked boy plays with his baby and feeds her, warm, delicate, and pretty"; another reviewer, Charlotte Jennings, wrote that it left her "with a sense of peace."

A sense of peace was not, however, the prevailing emotion when, at 7:30 on the evening of February, 3, in an incident which, had it not been so damaging, would have been inescapably reminiscent of *The Pirates of Penzance*, the police swooped. As Thelma later testified:

> A police superintendent and thirty-two constables and plainclothesmen stormed into the Open Space . . . seized the copy of Andy Warhol's *Flesh* . . . and proceeded to confiscate our projector, screen, and sound equipment. At the time, the superintendent informed the theater's directors that the seizure was being made under the Obscene Publications Act 1959. The following day . . . we were obliquely informed that the offense was not obscenity but infringement of the licensing laws. The day after that it was implied that the real offense was violation of fire regulations.

Whatever the reason, the figure of thirty-three officers might have seemed somewhat excessive. She continued:

> Towards the end of that week... it was darkly hinted that
> we were suspected of being concerned in a "conspiracy
> to defraud"—although it was never made clear whom
> we were defrauding of what, and by what means. ....
> We are still uninformed as to the charges that may be
> brought against us. The books, letters, records, and
> accounts seized, along with the copy of the film, are
> still being kept.

These records, incidentally, included the card indexes with
the names and addresses of members, many of whom had made
advance bookings and now needed to have their money refunded.
But that was not all. The Open Space lost two weeks' income,
while having to continue to pay the expenses of extra rehearsal
space which—with its own theater dark—it no longer required.
On February 24, the day I raised the matter in the House of
Lords, no charges had yet been preferred; the directors had still
received nothing back from the police. They even remained
uncertain whether they could accept their invitations to Rome
and Holland; for all they knew, they might be in prison by then.
Meanwhile, within half a mile of the Open Space, the strip clubs,
clip joints, and pornographic bookshops of Soho were going flat
out, all apparently immune from police attention.

The year 1965 had seen the introduction of the Sexual Offenses
Bill—in fact a misnomer, since it was exclusively concerned with
homosexuality. Reading through the report of the debates again, I
am astonished at the violence of the opposition, the almost hysterical vituperation in many of the speeches, and the wildness of the
prognostications. National morale would collapse; "buggers" clubs
would spring up all over the country. Such was the degree of public
feeling that the BBC courageously announced that in the course
of its program *The World at One* it would include "an interview
with a practicing homosexual." I have already told the story of Field

Marshal Montgomery suggesting that nothing of that sort had ever occurred in any unit under his command; later he proposed that the age of consent should be raised to eighty. ("You would always have the Old Age Pension to help pay off the blackmail.")

Five years later, on April 21, 1971, Lord Longford moved a motion "to call attention to the problems and incipient menace of pornography in Great Britain," setting forth many of the more lurid details of his recent "homework." The House was, predictably, full to bursting. Any number of speakers declared—some, I thought, a little too sanctimoniously—how shocked they had been by *Oh, Calcutta!*—a shamelessly erotic stage production recently presented by the great Kenneth Tynan—and by the dirty magazines that, in almost every case, "people had shown them." It came as a breath of fresh air when Dora Gaitskell[1] remarked that she did not regard shockability as a test of virtue, and when Jennie Lee[2] cheerfully remarked of pornography: "Everybody likes a little bit of it now and then, at the right time." (I often noticed in the House of Lords how much more sense was talked by women than by men.) Gasps of surprise greeted one speech in which a noble Lord lamented that *The Times* had devoted thirty column inches to Lord Longford's "homework," but had not mentioned the fact that only the night before the House had a most interesting and important debate on Parish Records. Another enquired rather anxiously "What are we going to do about the Old Testament?" and quoted a rather alarming passage from the New English Bible:

> "Here is my daughter, a virgin; let me bring her out to you. Rape her and do to her what you please; but you shall not commit such an outrage against this man."

---

1 Baroness Gaitskell (1901–1989, widow of Hugh Gaitskell, leader of the Labour Party 1955–1963, and a considerable political figure in her own right.

2 Baroness Lee of Asheridge (1904–1988), widow of Aneurin Bevan MP, the first and finest Minister for the Arts.

But the men were not satisfied so the guest took hold
of his concubine and thrust her outside for them. They
assaulted her and abused her and finally killed her, and
her master cut up her body limb by limb into six pieces.

There was a memorable moment, too, when a third told us
about a United States Congressional Commission on obscenity
and pornography. "Subjects," read the subsequent report, "were
shown three films, and controls were monitored for heart rate,
respiration, blood volume, pulse and penile circumference." The
last named was, it turned out, "the most sensitive and discriminat-
ing measurement." Their Lordships sagely nodded their approval.

———⟡———

But my services in the cause of sexual enlightenment were not
what Lord Gladwyn had in mind when he suggested that I
join him on the Liberal benches. Once I was safely on board, he
lost no time in making me the only other Liberal delegate from
the Parliament to the Council of Europe at Strasbourg and to the
Western European Union, which usually met in Paris or Brussels.
Gladwyn was a large, formidable, indeed at times distinctly alarming figure until you got to know him, and the first time we traveled to Strasbourg together I felt woefully inadequate. In those
days the city seemed to be one of the most inaccessible in Europe:
it had no airport, so our practice was to take an evening flight to
Paris, spend the night in the hotel of the Gare de l'Est—which
had the additional advantage of a two-star restaurant—and take
the train around seven the next morning, arriving in Strasbourg
in time for lunch. Over so many hours *tête-à-tête*, I could not hope
to conceal my shameful ignorance of European politics and economics; my conversational powers were clearly to be tested to the
limit. But I needn't have worried. Gladwyn's pomposity proved

far more apparent than real, and beneath it there lay a refreshingly wicked sense of humor.

I soon discovered, too, that he rather enjoyed being teased. On one of our Strasbourg visits, soon after the colonels had seized power in Greece, the Council had a debate on whether the Greek delegation should thenceforth be barred from the Assembly, representing as it did a government that had not been freely elected. Gladwyn made a stirring speech. Greece, he thundered, had invented democracy; now she herself had betrayed it. The Greek delegation should certainly not be permitted to set foot in the building until the loathsome adventurers whom it represented had themselves been cast out, and replaced by a government freely elected by the people. He continued in this vein for several minutes; but as he sat down to polite applause I couldn't resist reminding him that he and I were the only two members of the Assembly for whom not one single vote had ever been cast, and that unless we kept very quiet indeed we might well find ourselves following our Greek brethren into the outer darkness.

One summer day in—I think—1965, we all arrived in Strasbourg to find, in each of our pigeonholes, the most enormous envelopes, of the kind that the Fish Footman gives to the Frog Footman in *Alice in Wonderland*. Within was a heavily gilt-edged card announcing that Mr. Robert Maxwell MP requested the pleasure of our company in the garden of the Palais de l'Europe on the following afternoon. Mr. Maxwell had entered Parliament only the previous year. Even in England, few people had yet heard of him; outside the country he was still almost unknown. So far as anyone was aware, no member of the Council of Europe had ever given a garden party there before. "*Mais qui est-ce, ce Maxwell?*" everyone was asking, in tones that unmistakably carried the supplementary question "And who does he think he is?" The

Council staff were particularly disgruntled, nobody having asked their permission for the party or even notified them in advance.

Few, on the other hand, were those who did not turn up the next day. There on the lawn endless serving tables groaned under kilos of caviar, with whole regiments of bottles of iced vodka and champagne, to which the assembled delegates were soon doing full justice. One thing only was lacking: any sign of our mysterious host. The party was already showing signs of breaking up in bewilderment when the sound of a helicopter was heard—a sound that grew to a deafening crescendo as the machine approached and landed virtually in our midst. Out of it stepped a beaming Robert Maxwell. He uttered a few words of welcome—as I remember, in excellent and almost unaccented French—to his guests, and wandered briefly around shaking hands. Within ten minutes he was back in the helicopter; within fifteen, there was no sign that he had ever been with us at all. It was a truly astonishing exercise in public relations. Even in those far-off days it must have cost him many thousands of pounds; but he had impressed himself and his personality on every delegate present. No one who was there would ever forget him.

———— ❧ ————

My last happy recollection of these visits was of a meeting, in 1970 or thereabouts, of the Western European Union in Brussels. It was high summer and swelteringly hot; our sessions were held in a huge, subterranean, windowless hall with neon strip lighting. The first day was of paralyzing tedium, and the prospect of the second—which was to be devoted to military affairs, of which I knew nothing—was more than I could bear. Soon after my return to London I was due to make a program for BBC television about Napoleon's Hundred Days—the period that began with his escape from Elba and ended with Waterloo—and I had never seen the great battlefield. I decided simply to take the day off, and go there. Over breakfast I found three colleagues who felt much the same way, so the four of us hired a car and set off.

I remember passing a house with an enormous sign outside it bearing the words: *DANGER DE MORT: CHIEN LUNATIQUE, BIZARRE ET MECHANT*. Then, as we entered Waterloo itself, there was another even larger sign—of the kind which was presumably erected by the Belgian Road Safety Council in every town and village in the country, announcing the number of victims of local road accidents in the previous month or year. This one read: *WATERLOO: 8 MORTS, 17 BLESSES*. If only, I thought, if only....

It was by now lunchtime. We found a delightful restaurant with a garden in which we could eat *al fresco*, sat down and opened the menus. I then made a discovery which was not only totally unexpected but which even now I have difficulty in believing: that the entire battlefield complex of Waterloo is today one vast monument to Napoleon. Apart from a single postcard with a caption on the back about how he had distinguished himself in India, we failed to find any mention anywhere of the Duke of Wellington. The menu said it all: *Hors d'oeuvres Toulon, Poulet Marengo, Suprême de veau Austerlitz, Pommes de Terre Iéna, Petits Pois Friedland....* There was a picture of the Emperor on every plate and coffee cup. The four of us drank a toast to Wellington—indeed, we may have drunk several—and then walked, perhaps a trifle unsteadily, across to the battlefield itself. On our way we passed a school. It was closed for the summer holidays, but in front of it was a playground with swings and a delightful little four-seater roundabout which you operated yourself by cranking a central lever. The four of us clambered on and span happily round for several minutes—our happiness further increased by speculation on how the Russians would have reacted if they could have seen us: four British parliamentarians playing truant from an important military conference, moderately plastered and howling with laughter on a children's roundabout. . . .

Apart from the hideous and quite unnecessary memorial mound at one end, the battlefield of Waterloo is quite astonishingly unchanged. Hougomont is still there, and *La Belle Alliance*; and thanks to admirable booklets and maps you can follow the whole course of the battle. But that idolization of Napoleon continued to rankle. That evening we returned to Brussels, infuriated by the atrocious driving by just about everyone on the road— Belgium was then I believe the only country in Western Europe that issued driving licenses to sixteen-year-olds without a test. I remember shaking my fist out of the window at one particular road hog and shouting "We won!"

———◦✦◦———

By the beginning of the seventies, I had a new love in my life. Working one day in the London Library I glimpsed, emerging from below a table opposite, a pair of the longest legs I had ever seen; above the table was a beautiful face crowned by a mass of dark hair with a silver streak running through it. We got into conversation, and I asked her out to tea at Fortnum's. Her name was Mollie Philipps; her father, Sir Roger Makins, had been our Ambassador in Washington and one of the top men in the Foreign Office while I was one of the bottom. At this time she and I were both still married, and our unofficial engagement was to last for the next fifteen years or so, during which we were able to spend increasing amounts of time together. For the past twenty years she has been my wife.

At this time, too, Anne's and my children were fast growing up. Artemis, seventeen in 1970, we had removed from the convent of the Sacred Heart at Woldingham in Surrey, not because she was unhappy—she wasn't—but because we had suddenly realized that it was an ivory tower, nothing to do with the life that was going on outside it. We sent her instead to Camden School for Girls, from which for the first couple of weeks she came back every evening almost in tears. Anne and I felt dreadful: here was a child who had always been happy and contented; what had we done to her? And then one evening she came home, smiling from ear to ear, and said "Papa, thank you so much for moving me. Suddenly I see how much I needed it." It was thanks to Camden, I am perfectly sure, that she was accepted by St. Hugh's College, Oxford. Before going to Oxford she spent a brief period in Venice restoring paintings, and after taking her degree she enlisted with Voluntary Service Overseas, which sent her off to Egypt to teach English at the University of Alexandria. The result, a few years later, was her book *Cairo in the War, 1939–1945*, which was hailed by the critics as a quite astonishing evocation of a world which had vanished ten years before she was born.

Jason, six years younger, was still at Eton. Anne and I had been far from certain that we wanted to send him there; indeed, we had looked at several other schools before making up our minds. Our eventual decision—which we never regretted—was due to the fact that in the quarter of a century since my own departure the place had changed out of all recognition. At last it had a theater and a swimming pool. The curriculum had been modernized, with less insistence on the classics. Excellence at games, though still encouraged, was no longer a requirement. Eton had another advantage, too, which I had not fully appreciated during my time there: despite being only twenty miles from central London it gave the feeling of being deep in the country, and boasted apparently limitless space.

Later, I was also enormously impressed by the way it had pounced on Jason's remarkable mechanical and designing skills; before long he had been given his own key to the School of Mechanics, which he was allowed to use at night and even in the holidays. Such a thing would have been inconceivable in my day. When he eventually followed me to New College I had vaguely expected him to read engineering and was quite surprised when he plumped for English; but after his graduation and a year or two of designing and building cars he returned to Oxford—the Polytechnic this time—to read architecture. Once qualified, he worked for Arup and for Michael Hopkins and finally set up on his own.

My other lovely daughter Allegra I had not seen since 1968, when after Ricki's death she had gone to join John Huston, first in Ireland and later in California. At first it had been agreed that she should not—at least for the moment—be told about me. She had a putative father and stepmother, and was living with a family which she had every reason to think was her own: why therefore introduce a new element which might prove distressing, perhaps even traumatic? But five or six years later the situation had changed. John had once again divorced, Allegra's domestic life—though never, I hope and pray, actively unhappy—had become a good deal more unsettled; and, rightly or wrongly, she had been told about me. In 1972 I happened to be lecturing in Los Angeles and went to see her. I was full of trepidation—but I needn't have worried. A totally self-possessed nine-year-old walked into the room, gave me a warm hug and instantly put me at my ease. "Hello," she said, "I'm Allegra. You're my father, aren't you?" I remember choking back the tears. She told me about her life, and her school—at which she was doing outstandingly well—and we agreed to write regularly to each other, which for the next few years we did.

Then in 1980, aged just seventeen, she wrote that she had decided to live in England. She was coming to London, where she would go to a crammer in order to pass the Oxford examination. I tried to explain that this might not be so easy as she seemed to think, but her confidence was complete. She declined our invitation to live at Blomfield Road; she preferred to be independent. She would find her own accommodation, look after herself, pay her own tuition. There was no argument; faced with such certainty, we had no course but to agree. Two years later she was accepted into Hertford College, Oxford. By this time we had all welcomed her into the family with open arms—not only lovingly, but with huge admiration as well. Her childhood, after her mother's tragically early death, had inevitably been often troubled—more troubled at times, perhaps, than she had ever told me. I can say only that a sweeter, saner, better balanced human being, both mentally and emotionally, would be hard to find.[3]

Shortly before I left for the Sahara, I had delivered the typescript of Volume I of my Norman book to Longmans; and at the suggestion of my agent Diana I had written a short summary of the whole story and sent it to BBC Television, which in those days ran a perfectly splendid series on history and archaeology called *Chronicle*. For quite a long time after my return I heard nothing—there was not even an acknowledgement. I felt, as I remember, fairly philosophical about it. A television program would have been fun, and good publicity for the book; but there was no suggestion that I should have been very actively involved. Besides, I was busy with proofs, indexes, illustrations, and all the other jobs that are loaded on to an author just as he thinks he

3 Her recent book, *Love Child*, in which she tells the story of her life and upbringing far more brilliantly and movingly than I could possibly have done, has proved a bestseller.

has transferred all the responsibility to the publisher. Meanwhile I was getting most agreeably involved with Volume II. Then, one evening when Anne and I were in the kitchen having dinner, the telephone rang. "Hello," said a voice, "you don't know me, but my name is Ken Shepheard and I work for *Chronicle* at the BBC. We're interested in your Norman story and we'd like to discuss it with you. Are you free for lunch tomorrow?"

I was; and in a little restaurant in Romilly Street the following day I met the man who for nearly twenty years was to be one of my dearest friends. Within minutes I realized that I was in the presence of one of the quickest and most agile minds I had ever encountered, one that sent every conversational tennis ball I served whistling back over the net. He had a wonderfully quirkish sense of humor too, and was a hilarious raconteur. He asked me a lot of questions about the Normans which I answered as well as I could, and as the coffee was laid on the table said—as by this time I very much hoped he would—"Right, we'd very much like to make a program about this, and we'd like you to write it and present it." Nothing, I told him, would give me greater pleasure. A month later Ken and I were with a three-man camera crew in Sicily.

This was in the late summer of 1966, when filming was a very different business from what it is today. Videotape was still unheard of; the fifty-minute program was shot on black and white 16-millimetre film. My microphone had never been near a radio; it was attached to a wire which ran under my shirt, down my trouser leg and along the ground to a tape recorder. Every night that it was possible, the day's rushes were flown back to the BBC and a report on them sent back by telex so that we could immediately reshoot any unsatisfactory sequences; we ourselves did not see a foot of film until we got back to the cutting room in London. Still, for me it was a hugely exciting adventure and I loved almost every minute of it. The qualification is due entirely to one man:

a certain Monsignor Pottino, who was in charge of the Palatine Chapel in Palermo. Now this chapel—already described—is one of the miracles of the world, demonstrating as it does the dazzling fusion of the three great cultures which were combined in Norman Sicily: the Latin, the Greek, and the Arab. Mgr. Pottino cannot be blamed for not wanting it damaged; but he proved more obstructive than any other authority I was to come across during any of the thirty-odd filming expeditions which were to follow. First he said that we could not use our tripod, since it would damage the marble floor. Refraining from pointing out that several hundred female tourists with stiletto heels were passing through the chapel daily, we produced our tripod stand, which prevents the three points from touching the ground; but he shook his head. "No tripods" was the order, and that was that.

If we were to be limited to a handheld camera, the only hope of stopping it wobbling was to use enough light to allow very fast exposures; but here again the Monsignor put his foot down. Our lights, he objected, would create heat, and the heat would damage the mosaics. We argued that the mosaics, being high up on the walls, would receive virtually no heat at all, and that we should need our lights anyway for not more than three minutes; once again we argued in vain. Never was there a suggestion of a smile, still less any polite expression of regret. By this time Ken, who spoke excellent Italian, was beginning to lose his temper and to resort to threats. "Our presenter," he finally shouted to my horror, "is a viscount. He will raise the matter with the Italian Embassy, perhaps even in the House of Lords, when he returns to London." Mgr. Pottino smiled for the first time. "*Io,*" he said quietly, "*sono marchese.*"[4]

Game, set and match.

---

4 "I am a Marquis."

———⊙⊱⊙———

Although that first program was in black and white, color was well on its way. In America it had already been the rule for some years, and the BBC was due to transmit its first color programs in 1967; so when the Norman film found favor and I was asked to make another historical documentary, color was taken for granted. For a subject we had agreed on the Fall of Constantinople to the Ottoman Turks in 1453, and I confess to having been momentarily unnerved when our cameraman on his arrival in Istanbul handed me a four-page memorandum on "color technique." This extraordinary document warned me *inter alia* that I should on no account touch alcohol for at least four hours before appearing before the camera, since even if the resultant facial discoloration were not apparent to the human eye it would inevitably show up on film. Knowing just how enthusiastically this information would be received by most of my fellow performers, I decided to ignore it. Within weeks, the entire memorandum was forgotten.

The fifty-five day siege of Constantinople by Sultan Mehmet II in 1453 is one of the great epics of history; and there are still a number of highly evocative Byzantine monuments in modern Istanbul—including the five mile line of fifth-century Land Walls that remain the most magnificent urban fortification in the world[5]—crying out to be filmed. Thus our program could hardly have failed; and yet for me the most exciting moment of our three week stay in the city was completely unrelated to it. Soon after my arrival I had met Ernest Hawkins. When in the 1930s the late Professor Thomas Whittemore was given permission by Kemal Atatürk to uncover the mosaics in St. Sophia,

---

5 All this was well before the disastrous restoration of the Walls some fifteen years ago, which has made certain stretches look more like a Hollywood film set.

Hawkins—beginning as a virtually untrained assistant—soon rose to be his righthand man; and thirty years later he was still living in Istanbul, advising on various restoration projects. It happened that at the time work was going on in the old Byzantine church formerly known as the Theotokos Kyriotissa, which stands almost at the foot of the Aqueduct of Valens. (Like nearly all the Byzantine churches in Istanbul, it had been converted into a mosque soon after the Turkish conquest and so had acquired the name of Kalenderhane Camii.) One morning Ernest telephoned in a high state of excitement. Could I come along? He had something very exciting to show me.

Our filming schedule naturally came first, but I got there as soon as I could and was taken into a small chapel just to the right of the apse, the floor of which was thickly covered with fragments of painted plaster. Most of these, alas, were tragically small, but several were big enough to show parts of an inscription, together with representations of little men in monks' robes feeding and apparently speaking to birds. Clearly they had been part of a series of frescoes depicting the life of St. Francis; but what made the discovery still more interesting was the fact that the inscription was not in Greek but in Latin. This firmly connected the series with the Latin occupation of Constantinople after the Fourth Crusade; in other words it had to date from between 1205 and 1261, when that occupation ended. Since St. Francis died in 1226, it follows that the whole thing must have been painted within thirty-odd years of his death—two or three decades before Giotto began his work at Assisi. What we were looking at were the remains of the earliest Franciscan cycle known anywhere in the world.[6]

---

6 Sadly, it has not proved possible to reconstitute the jigsaw; but at the time of writing the pieces are kept in the Archaeological Museum of Istanbul, where they may usually be seen on request. This Museum is an absolute must for any visitor to the city, since it also contains the so-called Alexander Sarcophagus, the greatest piece of classical sculpture in existence (see Chapter Seven).

The Fall of Constantinople had a somewhat eerie sequel. Shortly before we made the film, Sir Steven Runciman had published a book with the same title. He was at that time the *doyen* of the world's Byzantinists; but that was only the beginning. He also knew all the most scandalous inside gossip of every imperial, royal, and princely family of Europe, which he would recount with relish at the drop of a hat. It was he who told me of the occasional verses of Queen Alexandra, which were to be found only on the labels attached to wreaths sent from the Palace to her departed friends. I remember, alas, only one; it was written for Lady Feodora Gleichen, the first woman member of the Royal Society of British Sculptors:

> To dear Feo Gleichen,
> Who was always so near our heart;
> Oh how we shall miss her,
> Nor her wonderful works of art.

Finally—and, for the purpose of this story, most important of all—he prided himself on his powers of witchcraft. These were annually proved at his regular summer garden party in Elm Tree Road, St. John's Wood, when, year after year, there was never a cloud in the sky.

I had naturally drawn copiously on Steven's book while writing my script, and when I next saw him I congratulated him on it and mentioned how valuable it had been to me. He raised his eyebrows and put on his quizzical look. "But where are my royalties?" he asked. As so often with Steven, one never quite knew to what extent he was joking. Faintly embarrassed, I pointed out that I was merely a freelance employee of the BBC; but I promised to mention the matter to them. I did so and, just as I expected, they laughed me to scorn. This of course—as Steven well knew—is one of the great drawbacks of being a serious historian. You may spend months and years rootling though monastic libraries, deciphering medieval manuscripts, poring over palimpsests; but history knows no copyright. Once you have published, the result of your labors is the property of the world. The facts that you have unearthed may be repeated *ad infinitum* by others; no fees are payable.

Finally our film was ready and scheduled for transmission. It seemed to me to be rather good, and I naturally wanted as many as possible of my friends to see it. The problem was that few if any of us in those days possessed color television. The only place I knew that did was the Royal Automobile Club in Pall Mall, of which I was then a member; so I decided to give a party there, with plenty of wine and a modest buffet, after which at 9 o'clock everyone would go next door and watch the program. I naturally invited Steven, but he declined.

The great day came, about thirty guests turned up and the dinner—such as it was—was served. At 8:50 PM I went next door and turned the television on to BBC2; the picture was perfect. At 8:55 PM I clapped my hands and invited everybody to take their seats; then at 9 PM our program began—and before the title sequence was over the whole picture dissolved into a snowstorm. Frantically I fiddled with the knobs, but in vain. My recorded voice came through loud and clear, but the snowstorm continued to rage. After five minutes I admitted defeat, apologized to everybody, and told them to go back and drown their disappointment—again, such as it was—in another glass or two of wine. The evening had been a disaster.

A week or two later Nathalie Brooke happened to see Steven at a party and told him what had happened. She reported to me later that he smiled and rubbed his hands together in quiet satisfaction. "I know," he said.

Chapter Twelve
The Moss Begins to Gather

B Y THIS TIME my life as a self-employed author was beginning to develop a pattern of its own. For nine or ten
months of the year I was writing in the London Library:
the second volume of the Norman story, *The Kingdom in the Sun*,
was published in 1970. Then two or three weeks would be spent
filming—*The Conquest of Mexico* in 1968, *Napoleon's Hundred
Days* in 1969—and for most of the other absences we were on
pleasure bent. In this latter category there were two regular fix-
tures: in the summer, the annual fortnight with my cousin Liz at
Zell-am-See, in the autumn, the Wexford Opera Festival.

Liz Paget was the second daughter of my uncle Charlie Anglesey
and my mother's eldest sister Marjorie. She was startlingly beautiful; in the 1930s she had enjoyed the same sort of *réclame* that my
mother had for the previous generation, and it was my mother
who in 1937 had introduced to her one of her own dearest friends,
Raimund von Hofmannsthal, whom she had first known when
he was nineteen and had played a bit part in *The Miracle*. For both
Raimund and Liz, it was love at first sight. Her parents had been

horrified. With her extraordinary beauty and charm, their daughter could have married the greatest in the land; Raimund might have been the son of Austria's most celebrated poet—Hugo von Hofmannsthal had been the librettist of six of Richard Strauss's greatest operas, including *Der Rosenkavalier* and *Arabella*—but he was Austrian, part Jewish (which shouldn't have mattered but I fear probably did), with a failed marriage behind him, and two children, and virtually penniless. That summer, my parents were doing a Mediterranean cruise on the *Enchantress*, and Marjorie implored my mother to take Liz with them, in the hopes that she might forget him. My mother agreed—though privately she was all for the match—but it was no use. The Angleseys had underestimated their man. At every port at which the ship called, there was Raimund waiting on the quayside, his arms full of flowers. At last her parents gave in. The two of them were married in 1938, and I was a page at their wedding.

During the war Raimund—who was by now an American citizen—had served in the US army as a GI. Afterwards, when he got a well-paid job on *Time* magazine in London, he and Liz settled into a corner of Connaught Square; and by the time Anne and I married in 1952, although they were considerably older, we were seeing them all the time. Without intending to—without even being aware of it—Raimund influenced me as much as any man I have ever known, my father (and just possibly Paddy Leigh Fermor)[1] alone excepted. How he did it I shall never understand. Though possessed of extraordinary, knockout charm—which a musical-comedy Austrian accent did nothing to diminish—he was never a particularly forceful character and was totally devoid of personal ambition. What he liked—and understood—was elegance. But his elegance was inborn, never assumed; I sometimes

---

[1] See Chapter Six.

wonder whether he ever knew it was there. He was endlessly hospitable and endlessly generous; always beautifully dressed; a lover of good food and good wine and always genuinely upset if he found that someone else had paid the bill. No one was ever less sanctimonious; yet never once did I hear him say anything bitchy or unkind about anyone. Instead, he would call attention to their virtues. The things that caused him genuine distress were ugliness, coarseness, and cruelty; if any of these entered a conversation he seldom said anything—his manners were the best I have ever known—but one could see a flicker of pain cross his face. As a good Viennese, he was steeped in the culture of Central Europe; music was his passion, fully shared by his wife—Mozart above all. I shall remember him, and be grateful to him, till I die.

When Raimund himself died, in March, 1974, his friends were all determined to establish something in his memory. The best idea came from his old friend Loelia Lindsay: to commission a silver rose which would be used for the Presentation scene in all future productions of his father's *Rosenkavalier* at Covent Garden. When not in use it would occupy a glass case, perhaps in the Crush Bar, with an explanatory label. And so it came about. One evening a few months later, before the curtain went up on the opera, I clambered on to the stage and formally presented the silver rose, not in this case to Sophie but to Sir Claus Moser, then the Chairman of Covent Garden. The rose is still there, and is still regularly presented by Octavian to Sophie.

As soon as possible after the war, Raimund and Liz took back a house which had, I think, long been in his family. Prielau, just outside Zell-am-See, had been built in the sixteenth century almost entirely of wood, one imagines for some well-to-do yeoman farmer. Within its stuccoed exterior the rooms all had paneled wooden walls and wooden floors of bare, unpolished planks covered by the occasional carpet. Over the lintel of every door was scribbled—

roughly, in ordinary blackboard chalk—$K + M + B$ and the current year, the letters standing for the Three Kings—Kaspar, Melchior, and Balthasar—the year to show that the room had received its annual Christmas blessing from the local priest. Every room, too, had its huge porcelain stove—often welcome even on a summer evening. And in the sitting room behind the paneling was a special luxury, wonderfully typical of Raimund: a small, refrigerated cupboard, which opened to reveal a set of five identical engraved decanters, each containing a different variety of *schnapps*.

One thing only was less than perfect: the weather. Summer in the province of Salzburg—as any regular visitor to the Festival can testify—tends to be the rainy season. Day after day we would wake to the steady drip, drip off the eaves, and look from the window at a steel-grey ceiling of cloud about a hundred feet above our heads, the surrounding mountains invisible in the murk. I used to think of my friends on the Mediterranean, of how they would be gazing out at a cobalt sea, listening instead to little waves breaking on the shore or the slapping of water on a boat's keel. But breakfast would be waiting—the coffee was superb, Austrian bread is the best in the world—and the warm, ever-welcoming atmosphere of the house did the rest. The Mediterranean faded away. Before long I was thinking how lucky I was, after all.

———— ❧ ————

One day while I was working on the Normans in the London Library I ran into Robin Fedden, then Historic Buildings Secretary of the National Trust. He was concerned, he told me, that a forthcoming cruise which he had organized had had a distinctly disappointing response. Surprised, too, because he had planned a wonderful itinerary—first to cross the Channel to France and visit Le Bois des Moutiers, a beautiful Lutyens house in Normandy; then to sail gently up the Seine as far as Rouen; returning, round Land's End and look at one or two National Trust houses in Cornwall and Devon before putting in at Ilfracombe. From there the ship would sail to the offshore island of Skomer in Pembrokeshire—a pullulating sanctuary for puffins and other sea birds—and so on up the west coast, stopping at various other places of interest. The last of these would be Gigha, a little Hebridean island off Kintyre which enjoyed, thanks to the Gulf Stream, its own microclimate. This had enabled Sir James Horlick (of malted milk fame) to create an astonishing sub-tropical garden. Our ship would then continue to Glasgow and we would all take the sleeper back to London. Would Anne and I like to join it? If so, he could make us a very special price. I replied that in the present state of our finances we couldn't afford any price, however special. Robin first looked disappointed, then brightened up. "Tell you what," he said, "You're writing about the Normans, aren't you? Well, we shall be sailing through Normandy. Give us a lecture or two on the way and you can come for nothing."

And so I did. Anne had some engagement in London, and so yielded her place to my mother for the French half of the trip; they swapped places at Ilfracombe, my mother went home and Anne completed the journey. It was a great success, and for me it had two results that were to change my life. First, I found that I greatly enjoyed lecturing and was in fact rather good at it. Those lectures as we sailed up the Seine were, so far as I can remember, the first I had ever delivered; since then I must have chalked up several hundred. Lecturing nowadays makes an appreciable difference to my income; probably ninety percent of it takes place in England, but it has also taken me the length and breadth of the United States and on two fascinating tours of Australia; and after nearly half a century I find that I get the same kick out of it as I did when I first began.

But in the early days a lecturer's life could be hard. There were far fewer groups that wanted to listen, and few of them were prepared to pay more than a pittance. I remember one particularly dreadful morning in Boston—Lincolnshire, not Massachusetts—where I had been invited to address, I think, the local Mothers' Union. I arrived at 10:30 AM for a lecture at 11 AM, only to find that there was no projector. A panicky enquiry revealed that the Union didn't actually possess one, but that Mrs. Sedgbrook's daughter did and had kindly promised to lend it. Unfortunately Mrs. Sedgbrook had not yet arrived with the machine. When she did, it was found that there was nowhere to plug it in—its cable was about eighteen inches long—and nobody had thought to provide a table to put it on. They had also forgotten the screen. In fact none of this mattered, because the sun was streaming in and there were no curtains to the windows; the slides would have been virtually invisible, so it made little difference when eventually I gave the lecture without them. But there: such fiascos are rare indeed nowadays, and thanks to the invention of the dread PowerPoint—with which I am still unhappily wrestling—even slides themselves are a thing of the past.

The second result of that National Trust Cruise was that I discovered a genuine passion—which I never knew I possessed—for ancient buildings. This in its turn led in the following year to my being invited to join the Executive Committee of the Trust, on which I was to sit for the next quarter of a century. My admiration for this magnificent organization knows no bounds: I would hate to think what England would be like today had it never existed. Certainly, as conservation bodies go, it is in a class by itself: no other in Europe or America has had anything like the same degree of success. This success, I feel sure, is based on two fundamental principles: that it must always be a *private* charity, and that the only long-term guarantee of preservation, whether of buildings or of land, is *ownership.* Its independence means that it need not hesitate to oppose government planning when it feels the need to do so; on the other hand, it rarely takes up the cudgels on behalf of any property that it does not legally possess, since it knows that without possession there is no way of providing permanent protection. And even possession is not enough: thanks to an inspired Act of Parliament passed in 1905—ten years after its foundation—the Trust can declare any of its properties *inalienable,* which means that it could not sell it off even if it wished to do so. No landowner, after all, would make over his house or his land to a body which could dispose of it whenever it liked.

When I first became involved with the National Trust it had, as I remember, some 50,000 members and operated out of two adjoining houses in Queen Anne's Gate. Our Committee consisted of only about a dozen members; our Chairman, Ran Antrim, was one of the most delightful men I have ever known. Jokes abounded, and every few minutes he would become prostrate with mirth, mopping his eyes with an enormous handkerchief, moaning quietly as he tried to collect himself. He was universally loved, and ran the Trust superbly. But it was already growing at an alarming rate. Within a few years it was forced to move into a vast building across the road, looking out on to St. James's Park, and most recently it has established its new headquarters in—of all places—Swindon. It still does a magnificent job; but inevitably, with a membership now of three and a half million, it is no longer the Trust that I knew and loved.

Our annual weekend at Wexford we owed to Alfred and Clementine Beit. They lived at Russborough in County Wicklow, perhaps the most beautiful of all the great Georgian houses of Ireland, which Alfred—whose grandfather Otto Beit had been one of the first and most successful of the "Randlords," making an immense South African fortune at Kimberley—could afford to keep up in the style it deserved. We would fly over on a Thursday afternoon towards the end of October and be there in time for dinner, usually about eight of us, meeting for drinks in the Saloon; around us, on the crimson cut velvet walls, glowed perhaps a dozen paintings—but what paintings! The only Vermeer in private hands, a memorable Velazquez, others by Rubens, Ruysdael, Hobbema . . . every time I saw them, particularly in such a setting, they took my breath away. Alas, since those days they have been the object of three separate robberies, during the first of which Alfred and Clementine were tied up and left for the police to find. Perhaps it is just as well that the pictures are at Russborough only in the summer months; when Alfred died in 1994 he left them to the National Gallery of Ireland, where they hang for the rest of the year.

After lunch on the following day we would drive down to Wexford—two hours or so, much of it through ravishing country along the River Slaney—and settle into the Talbot Hotel to prepare for the first of the three operas that awaited us. And why, you may ask, was there a single opera, let alone three, in a small town tucked away in the southeast corner of Ireland? The Festival had started in 1951, when two young collectors of opera recordings approached Dr. Tom Walsh, the anesthetist at the local hospital, with the idea of starting a local opera study group. Fortunately Wexford could boast a tiny eighteenth-century theater, totally unmodernized but just about able to serve the purpose; and in the autumn of 1951 the group managed to put on a performance of Balfe's *Rose of Castille* [*sic*]. This led to an annual three-opera festival under the direction of Dr. Walsh, who until his retirement in 1966 traveled annually to Italy to recruit the principals and supervised the training of the local amateur chorus. He knew that with the funds available he could only audition at third-league opera companies; on the other hand he possessed a first-rate ear. Among his discoveries, all unknown young singers at the very outset of their careers, were Janet Baker, Graziella Sciutti (unattractively misspelt Scuitti in the first program), and Mirella Freni, who—long after she had become an international star—returned more than once to Wexford in gratitude.

Year by year the Festival gathered momentum. In the early sixties you might still see the singers walking to the theater in full costume, often under umbrellas. Attentive members of the audience might notice, too, that they made all their entrances and exits stage left: stage right led directly on to the street outside. The theater in those days had no bar; fortunately—as always in Wexford—there were half a dozen pubs within easy reach, several of them inscribed with the words "singing lounge." This meant that you drank your Guinness or your Jameson's to rousing choruses of "Sure I love the dear silver that shoines in her hair. . . ." before returning to the mad scene of *Lucia di Lammermoor*. But the opera itself was only the beginning. It would be followed by dinner, after which we would stroll along to White's Hotel where there was always a party going on, lasting until well into the small hours. One evening during our first visit—it must have been 1962 or thereabouts—I remember queuing up at a buffet supper around 2 AM when Alfred, who was standing just in front of me, was suddenly approached by a giant—a good six foot six, and majestically drunk.

"Humphrey, Humphrey," he said, clapping Alfred on the shoulder with a hand the size of anybody else's foot, "Whoy d'ye pass me boy so peremptory?"

Alfred replied politely that he was very sorry if he had given offense, but that his name was not actually Humphrey. Could this by any chance be a case of mistaken identity?

"Whoy," the giant interrupted, "Whoy d'ye use such long words at me, Humphrey—words like *Marmalade* and *Corrugated bloody Iron*?" Whereupon his eyes glazed over and he fell like a pine tree to the floor.

That turned out to be typical of Wexford parties. Another late-night characteristic was the impromptu singsong. In the early days these were superb, since several of the professionals would be there to join in, and with so many musicians around there would always be at least one brilliant pianist. The only trouble was that the singers would yell themselves hoarse and be completely unable to perform the following evening; after a year or two they were banned from participating, and the quality of the singsong deteriorated sharply as a result. But still the festivities went on. I have a clear recollection of falling into bed one night just as dawn was breaking, and hearing a deafening chorus coming up from the street below, to the tune of "She'll be Coming Round the Mountain":

> She's got a foine and lovely bottom,
> She's got a foine and lovely bottom,
> She's got a foine and lovely bottom set o' teeth. . . .

The productions themselves—like those of any opera house—varied in quality; the best were very good indeed. Another major advantage for me was the fact that at least two out of the three annual offerings were operas that I had never seen before. Many of them were French. Apart from *Carmen* and perhaps *Faust*, French opera is relatively seldom performed in England; one reason, I have always suspected, is that the language is impossibly difficult for singers who are not French born. There are of course exceptions—the late Dame Maggie Teyte built her reputation on French opera and *chanson*, and of today's artists the name of Felicity Lott springs instantly to mind—but on the whole foreign singers tend to be baffled by the nasal vowels and in particular by the feminine endings in–*e*, which they nearly always approximate to–*er*. Wexford French may not have been invariably impeccable; but I can safely say that of the eighty-odd operas I have seen there over the years, well over fifty were new to me.

I remember only one near disaster; indeed I could never possibly forget it. The year is 1979 and we are attending the last performance of *La Vestale*, by Gaspare Spontini.[2] The curtain rises on an almost bare set of which the only feature, apart from a small altar downstage center, is a floor made apparently of glass and raked extremely steeply, at perhaps 20–30 degrees. Enter two principals, tenor and baritone, for the opening duet. All is progressing satisfactorily when suddenly the tenor's legs shoot from under him. He manages to catch hold of the altar just in time but, having difficulty in regaining his balance, continues to clutch it as the duet goes on. A minute later the baritone, who has till now managed to keep a moderately straight face, finds the same thing happening to him, and the duet ends with the two participants both clinging to the altar for dear life, before clinging to each other to make their way gingerly offstage. Enter now the chorus of Vestal Virgins. They have seen from the wings what has happened, and have all most sensibly removed their sandals; bare feet, they rightly believe, can get more of a purchase than leather soles. But even then a few of them start slithering, and gradually they form a sort of conga line, each clutching tightly at the next. By this time most of them are laughing so much that they can hardly sing. So the drama continues, and by the end of Act I the audience is in paroxysms.

After the interval, though the stage floor is unchanged, it is clear that all is now well; the cast keeps its footing throughout. Only

---

2 This incident has been described, far better than I could ever hope to describe it, by the late and sadly lamented Bernard Levin in his book *Conducted Tour*.

after the final curtain, however, do we learn what has occurred. The raked stage has been a problem from the outset, but well before the first night a solution has been found: if a gallon or two of fizzy lemonade is poured over it half an hour before curtain-up, the resulting tackiness will provide a firm foothold. This technique has worked admirably at previous performances; on this last evening, however, the lemonade has been forgotten until the last minute and is applied only as the overture is beginning. It has therefore had no time to dry and has made the stage far more slippery than it would have been without any treatment at all. Perhaps fortunately, this is the last night not only of *La Vestale* but of the whole Festival; and before we leave the Director makes his closing speech. "I think you'll all agree," he says, "that we have had a most successful festival—apart, that is, from a few slips. . . ."

The year 1967 was the year I did not go to the Seychelles. My failure to do so is one of the great regrets of my life.

In those days the islands were principally known for having been the place of exile of Archbishop Makarios of Cyprus during the island's long struggle for *Enosis*. Access to them was by ships of the British India line, which sailed every fortnight from Mombasa and took about a week. One weekend when we were staying with my millionaire brother-in-law Michael Astor, I chanced to read in a newspaper of a proposal to build an airport there, and at that moment there came to me the only good business idea that I have ever had. The airport, I realized, would obviously change the Seychelles for ever, opening them up to mass tourism; to acquire land there would be much the same as acquiring land on the French Riviera in the 1880s. I put it to Michael. How would it be, I asked him, if I went there on his behalf? He would pay my fare, in return for which I would buy a lovely length of seashore for him and a little one for me. If we acted quickly the price would still be negligible, and in ten years time we should either be enjoying our lovely tropical hideaways or be selling them at huge profits to Mr. Hilton. To my delight he agreed, and I settled down to make my plans.

There was no cheap excursion fare to Mombasa, and therefore no reason not to stop off on the way. I therefore decided to leave England ten days before my ship was due to sail, spending a few nostalgic days in Beirut and another day or two in Ethiopia—which I had always longed to visit—en route. And so, one day in early July, off I flew to the Lebanon. Or so, at least, I imagined; but it was not to be. Soon after we reached the Mediterranean, the captain's voice came over the loudspeaker. War, he said, had broken out in the Middle East. He could take us no further than Rome. It was a sad blow, but there was nothing to be done. And if I had had any sense at all I should have flown straight from Rome to Nairobi; but that would have meant arriving there much too early, and I saw no reason to give up my Ethiopian plans as well as my Lebanese ones. Was there, I asked at Rome airport, a flight to Addis Ababa in the relatively near future? There was, they told me, and it was leaving in just two hours time. It would be going via Khartoum, for which I should theoretically need a Sudanese visa, but this requirement was normally waived for passengers in transit. I hesitated for a moment; Khartoum was, after all, still part of the Arab world. On the other hand it was a good thousand miles away from Israel and there seemed relatively little chance that it would be affected, so I decided to go ahead.

We arrived there in the latish afternoon. There was a particularly unpleasant form of Sudanese sandstorm raging, called a *haboob*: the sky was thickly overcast, the very air seemed to have been dyed a pale and unattractive brown. The temperature was about 110. The airport was not air conditioned.

"You have no visa," they said.

"I know," I said, "but I was told I didn't need one. I'm only in transit. I'm going on to Addis Ababa at six."

"Oh no you're not," they said, "Don't you know there's a war on? Yours was the last flight in or out of here till further notice."

My heart sank. I asked if I could telephone the British Embassy, and to my surprise got straight through to the Ambassador himself. He turned out to be a charming man called Sir Robert Fowler, whom I remembered from when he had been number two to Antony Head in Lagos a few years before.

"Well," he said, "I can't promise you anything. All the Arab countries, including this one, have just broken off diplomatic relations, so I've no idea what's going to happen to any of us. Still, I can send a car to pick you up and bring you here—at least you'll be more comfortable than you would be at the airport."

So there I was: a guest, but also a prisoner—and there was no telling for how long. Nor was there any practicable way out of the country except by air. The British were universally suspected by every Arab to be hand in glove with Israel—memories of Suez had naturally come flooding back—and to have tried to make my way to the coast by road or rail, without a visa and with the Embassy powerless to help me if I ran into trouble, would have been insane. (Apart from anything else the Ambassador would have forbidden it, and quite rightly too.) My chances of getting to Mombasa in time for my ship suddenly seemed slim, and I went to bed that night full of forebodings.

I slept with the window open and awoke to find my pillow coated with a light layer of brownish dust, with a white patch where my head had been. The *haboob*, clearly, was not yet over. I looked out over the garden to the grass tennis court, which was being assiduously watered by two men with hoses. (Khartoum, standing as it does at the confluence of the White and Blue Niles, is untroubled by water shortages.) After breakfast with my host and hostess—who had no further news of our joint future to report—I went downtown and called in at all the airline offices to confirm that there were no outward flights. "Where do you wish to go?" they would ask; I would reply that my destination was immaterial; all I wished to do was to get out of Khartoum. They would sadly shake their heads; they could offer no hope for the immediate future. I returned, by now feeling somewhat desperate, for lunch—after which the Ambassador breezily suggested a game of tennis. I could hardly believe my ears. It was about 2 o'clock in the afternoon in the month of July. The sun, though invisible, was almost directly overhead, the temperature well over 100. But I was his guest; what could I do but accept?

We played three sets. The heat was appalling, and the Ambassador—who was bald as an egg—wore no hat; changing ends, I could almost hear his brain sizzling as we passed each other. Fortunately the court was extremely slow. The grass was rather long, he explained, because the lawn mower had broken; the necessary spare part had arrived, but there was no way of getting it out of the airport. It hardly mattered. I played abominably and he beat me hollow.

This then became our daily routine. The awakening to the sound of those hoses on the tennis court; the morning tour of the airline offices; lunch; then tennis. Every time we played, the grass after its daily watering was appreciably higher than it had been the day before, the three sets appreciably slower. How long, I wondered, could we go on? Was this to be my fate for the rest of my life, playing tennis with a mad, bald ambassador on a court which would soon be dense undergrowth and probably, in a few years, jungle? It was pure Evelyn Waugh: I remembered the hero of *A Handful of*

Dust, condemned to read Dickens aloud to his demented captor Mr. Todd, in the depths of the Amazon rain forest.

We went on like this for a fortnight. I was still there when my steamer left Mombasa for the Seychelles—perhaps even when it arrived. But then one morning I heard that a flight was leaving— as it happened, for Addis Ababa. By this time I hardly cared; all I could think of was deliverance. I thanked the Fowlers profusely. They had gone well beyond the call of duty in looking after me for so long—they could easily have shifted me to a hotel—and had done everything they could to make my stay interesting, taking me to the battlefield of Omdurman and such other few *Sehenswürdigkeiten* as were within easy range. I dread to think what I should have done without them, and I still feel a good deal more grateful than might be thought from the somewhat catty little anecdote I have just related. But I cannot pretend that I was sorry to go, and they for their part were, I am sure, every bit as relieved to wave me goodbye.

Ethiopia was not much of a success. My arrival coincided precisely with that of the rainy season; and I was unwise enough to attempt to drown my sorrows with several large gulps of the local hooch, a hideously toxic substance called *tej*. This, combined with the altitude, produced a migraine which kept me in bed all my first afternoon, longing for death and confidently expecting it. On the following day the worst was over and I hired a car to make some recommended excursion. The countryside proved spectacular, but after about four hours I saw that my petrol tank was half empty and realized that I had not passed a single filling station since I left the capital. By now there was no fight left in me. I turned the car and headed back into town. A day or two later I caught a plane home via Athens, which I was assured would be the only stop. It wasn't. Quite unexpectedly, we landed at Khartoum.

For a moment I wondered whether I could bear it. All I knew was that whatever happened I was not going to call the British Embassy. Fortunately, however, there was no need to—an hour later we were on our way once more. But I still had to live with my shame. Entirely through my own pigheadedness I had failed to get to the Seychelles, failed to buy those precious plots of land, failed to make my fortune and increase Michael's. Nor, in the circumstances, could I possibly ask him to pay my expenses. My only inspired business venture had turned out to be a catastrophe. Forty years later, I am still kicking myself.

Chapter Thirteen
The Pattern Fixed

BY THE BEGINNING of the 1970s that pattern of life which had begun to take shape after my leaving the Foreign Service was more or less crystallized. (In the first decade of the twenty-first century I find, somewhat to my surprise, that it still remains much the same.) I was no longer a rolling stone; I went on traveling as much as I could, first because I loved it and second because there were so many places in the world that I longed to see; but there was always Blomfield Road to come back to. Once my midlife crisis was over I never again changed my basic occupation; I found that I loved writing books, and was lucky enough—thanks to two of the best agents anybody ever had, Diana Crawfurd and her successor Felicity Bryan—never to have any trouble in finding a publisher for them.

Never, on the other hand, was I remotely disciplined as a writer. I had no regular working hours—there were too many other things to do. Besides, I now had a new and passionate preoccupation: Venice. It was, I think, late in 1969 or early in 1970 that I was telephoned by Ashley Clarke—he who, nearly two decades before, had mercifully scotched his colleagues' suspicions that I might be a harpist. He had recently retired after eight years as Ambassador in Rome and he wanted, he said, to talk to me about Venice. As I well knew, in November, 1966, Venice and Florence had simultaneously experienced the worst floods in their history. At first it had appeared that Florence had been the principal sufferer; largely because the city was not used to flooding and had taken virtually no precautions against it, many of its greatest treasures had been accommodated at ground-floor level.

Ashley, with his wife Frances and his old friends Carla Thorneycroft and Nathalie Brooke, had consequently founded the Italian Art and Archives Rescue Fund, which had done splendid work to rescue and conserve as much as possible. But now, three years later, it had become clear that the Florence flood had been an isolated phenomenon which would probably never recur. Venice, on the other hand, remained in mortal peril—attacked simultaneously by land, sea, and air: an alarming increase in the rate of subsidence of the city itself, an equally dramatic rise in the level of the Adriatic, and atmospheric pollution from the huge and hideous industrial zones of Mestre and Marghera, only a mile or two away on the mainland. A recent investigation by UNESCO had revealed a situation far more serious than had been suspected and had led to an international appeal for help. If action were not taken quickly, Venice might quite easily cease to exist. The time had therefore come to abolish the IAARF and to establish in its place a new fund which would be directed exclusively towards the salvation of the city. They were thinking of calling it "Venice in Peril," and hoped very much that I would agree to be its Chairman.

I told Ashley that I would obviously support him to the hilt, but that it seemed to me that he, not I, should take on the chairmanship. He, after all, had the clout. He was the ex-Ambassador; he knew all the Italian leaders personally, often by their

Christian names; he spoke their language perfectly; he could go and thump their tables in a way that I never could. "Ah," he said, "but Frances and I shall be living in Venice, since we've got to oversee all the work that we shall be doing. The Chairman must obviously be in London, where the money's going to have to come from." I could think of no other good reason to say no, so rather hesitantly agreed.

And so, in 1970, during a Post Office strike when no letters were collected or delivered, the Venice in Peril Fund was born. At much the same time, in answer to the UNESCO call, other organizations with similar aims sprang up all over the western world, to form what was by far the greatest and most ambitious conservation project ever launched—committed to saving not just a building but an entire city, and that city the most beautiful on earth. Of these organizations, Venice in Peril is neither the biggest nor the richest; but over the past thirty-five years—thanks in very large measure to Ashley and Frances, to Carla and Nathalie, and, more recently, to my successor Anna Somers Cocks—it has done a remarkable job. In the early days we concentrated on monuments; we have since been responsible for the restoration, in whole or in part, of some two dozen of the loveliest buildings of Venice. The first was the Madonna dell' Orto, Tintoretto's parish church, in which we also cleaned his pictures—eleven of them altogether. Among our biggest successes were Sansovino's little *loggetta* at the base of the Campanile of St. Mark's; the ravishing little S. Nicolò dei Mendicoli, tucked away at Venice's far western end; the immense fifteenth-century stained glass window (a rare thing in this city of glass) in SS. Giovanni e Paolo; the Oratory of the Crociferi, which was opened by the Queen Mother; and the *Sala della musica* at the Ospedaletto. We have recently finished work on the Cappella Emiliani on the cemetery island of S. Michele.

Among the most satisfying of our undertakings was the restoration of the ornamental fifteenth-century entrance to the Doge's Palace, known as the Porta della Carta. Although it stands next to St. Mark's and is one of the most striking examples of flamboyant Gothic in all Venice, this superb construction tends—perhaps because of the damage it sustained during the French conquest of the Republic in 1797—to pass relatively unnoticed. Apart from Gentile Bellini, who included just a glimpse of it in his great *Procession in St. Mark's Square* (now in the Accademia) none of the great painters of Venice—Canaletto, Guardi, Turner, Whistler, Sargent—ever painted it. Even Ruskin did only one small drawing, but fails to describe it in *The Stones of Venice*. By the middle of the twentieth century, the hideous corrosion of the four fine statues in the side niches provided a perfect example of the damage caused by atmospheric pollution in the city. Some work had been done in 1966–1967, but it was clear that far more thorough technical treatment was now necessary. When, therefore, in April, 1975, Tim and Susie Sainsbury offered us a generous donation from their charitable trust, they readily agreed that there could be no worthier cause.

The building contains no fewer than eight different materials, mostly Istrian stone and Carrara marble; and we were lucky indeed to obtain the services of Kenneth Hempel, then chief stone and marble restorer at the Victoria & Albert Museum. When he first saw the scale of the task ahead of him, he shuddered. The damage was not only the result of air pollution; there was also rainwater, frost, humidity, the deposit and crystallization of salts, and a number of other factors—including, of course, the innumerable pigeons. To all these, each constituent material had reacted differently; each needed individual treatment. The statues were cleaned with something unpleasantly called an "airbrasive" machine, which uses a mixture of air and a very fine powder—the force of which can be calibrated to infinitely low levels—in a sort of miniature sandblasting. Heavy encrustations were removed by covering them with what looked to me like toffee, and leaving them for several weeks; the toffee was then removed, and the encrustations came off with it.

To carry out the whole operation, Dr. Hempel trained up a team of six young Italian restorers—one of whom he later married, so the work was further enlivened with a touch of romance. It took four years altogether; and on Saturday, May 12, 1979, this glorious gateway was formally declared open by Princess Alexandra. No one has ever ignored it since.

———————⟨⊙⟩———————

And yet, as time goes on, Venice in Peril finds itself more and more concerned, not so much with Venice's past as with her future. How, for example, are we to prevent the city from being literally engulfed by the waves? The catastrophic flood of November 4, 1966—which had awoken the world to the danger—has not (thank God) since been equaled, though several others have run it close. What gets worse, however, year by year is the frequency of the inundations: it is nowadays hardly exceptional to have ninety or a hundred separate floods in a single year. The only long-term solution seems to be mobile barriers at each of the three entrances to the lagoon—barriers which will normally lie flat on the sea bed but will rise up when the high waters threaten. After over thirty years of argument and shilly-shallying, this vital work is at last in progress; but now a further threat is presented by global warming: this is melting the polar ice caps and will, we are told, result in a further dramatic rise in sea levels; will our barriers be high enough to cope with them?

Flooding, in any case, is not the only problem. One of the most intractable is the steady decline in the city's population—a fall of well over fifty per cent since 1945. The reasons are not far to seek. Much of the working-class housing in Venice, acceptable half a century ago, is simply not up to modern standards. Apartments on the ground floor are at best hideously damp, at worst flooded several times a year. Rich foreigners—a category which, to any good Venetian, is taken to include Italians from other cities—are buying up more and more of the better, higher, and lighter ones, thus driving up the prices. It follows that a young married couple simply cannot find anything bearable that they can afford. They prefer—and who can blame them?—to go over to Mestre, soulless as it is, where at least they can find four or five bright warm rooms in which to bring up their children in relative comfort. They can also have a car—in Italy, even more than elsewhere, the most important status symbol to be had. One of the essentials, therefore, if this downward trend is ever to be reversed, is the provision of cheap and adequate housing. Nobody wants monstrous blocks of flats in the historic city, but Venice in Peril is now working with the Venetian authorities on a program designed to show that a vast number of ancient houses can in fact be sensitively restored and modernized at relatively little cost.

Ashley, alas, is no longer with us; he died in January, 1994. I shall never forget his funeral, when his ashes were carried in a sixteen-oared gondola up a Grand Canal shrouded in morning mist, and across the almost impenetrably foggy lagoon to S. Michele. But his widow Frances is our extremely active and superbly well-informed President; as for our other two founders, Carla until her last illness in her ninetieth year never missed a meeting, nor does Nathalie to this day. I continued as Chairman until 1999, when I turned the job over to Anna Somers Cocks. She—with her professional art-historical background, her bilingual Italian, and her position with *The Art Newspaper*—does it infinitely better than I ever did. She looks better too.

———◦†◦———

This long disquisition on Venice has brought me ahead of my story. We return now to 1970, when my two books about the Normans were complete and when my friend and publisher Peter Carson, who had copy-edited them and seen them through the press, suggested that I turn my attention to a history of the Medici. Not for the first time or the last, I was forced to confess that Florence and I had never been buddies. I had somehow taken against it on my very first visit, and despite several determined attempts I had always failed to see its charm. I was not proud of this—I did not for a moment suppose that everyone was out of step but me—and I saw Peter's suggestion as the perfect opportunity to give the place one more try. I would go off there for a few weeks, do some serious research, and for the first time really get to know the city. Then, surely, the scales would fall from my eyes.

And so I did—and they didn't. The better I knew Florence, the less I liked it; the Medici too failed to endear themselves. Despairing, I returned to Peter and admitted defeat. I could not write, I told him, about that ghastly family; even if I did, the result would be a disaster—my heart simply wasn't in it. But by this time I had another idea: a history of Venice. My father had often lamented the lack of a good one; nearly all of them, he complained, portrayed the Venetian Republic as a police state, the *pozzi* and the *piombi*[1] of the state prison bursting full of political prisoners like something out of *Fidelio*. In fact, it was no more authoritarian than England or France or any other nation of the time; they all had their spies and their secret police. The real reason for Venice's

---

1 "The wells" and "the leads" respectively. "The wells" referred to cells below ground level, always damp and sometimes flooded, "the leads" to those immediately under the roof, which became ovens during the days of high summer.

reputation was simply that her intelligence services were a good deal more efficient than anyone else's.

Towards the end of his life he had decided to write a history himself, and had actually put a few notes together; but he had died before he could get any further. I liked the idea of doing the job on his behalf; more important still, I liked the idea of writing about Venice. I had long ago discovered the eternal truth that writing about a subject teaches you infinitely more than reading about it. Reading is a passive occupation: even if you are taking notes, your attention—mine at any rate—is apt to wander. Writing, on the other hand, involves active thought. Again and again you find yourself asking why and how something happened, more often than not having to work out the answer for yourself. Here, then, was a marvelous opportunity to learn more about this unique city that had also been an incredibly rich and powerful republic for over a thousand years, a period comfortably longer than that which separates us from William the Conqueror. Here too was a subject that I knew I should really enjoy, and to which I felt—at least I hoped—I could do some justice.

I set to with a will. I wish I could remember which came first, the idea for the history or Venice in Peril; all I know is that one followed close on the heels of the other, and that suddenly I found myself spending half my time writing about the city's past and the other half trying to preserve and protect its future. The two tasks, moreover, were surprisingly complementary: each taught me things that proved invaluable to the other. Venice, I realized, had taken me over—and I was very, very glad that she had.

I wrote the book, as always, in longhand in the London Library. Largely because there was no M. Chalandon to help me this time—but also because my Italian was nowhere near as good as my French—I found the research a good deal harder than that for the Normans had been, but every bit as much fun. There was only one major problem: the absence of great men. Venice simply did not go in for them. Throughout her history she cherished a deep mistrust of what we would nowadays call the cult of personality, which she was to see carried to extreme degrees all over the mainland. Her Doges—elected heads of state—tended to be septuagenarians (if not older) and enjoyed rather less personal power than the Queen of England does today. Government was quite extraordinarily impersonal, the work of faceless committees often known simply by the number of their members. How often, faced with more and more decisions by the Ten, the Three, or the Forty, did I long for the wicked old *terra firma*, with the Sforza, the Visconti, the Gonzaga—even, I regret to say, the Medici.

Again and again the Library proved its worth, and confirmed the opinion I had formed when I was working on the Normans: that, quite apart from the advantage of having all the books immediately accessible on open shelves, it was far more useful to me than the British Library could ever have been. The latter may well possess just about every work ever published in English; but there are terrible gaps where foreign publications are concerned. This, I suspect, is because hardly anyone ever presents or leaves his own personal library to it, whereas quite a number do to St. James's Square. Thus if I wanted to track down some obscure monograph published in, say, Bari in 1887, the British Library would be extremely unlikely to have it; again and again, the London Library turned up trumps.

There were occasions, inevitably, when I drew a blank, and others when I was faced with a problem—often topographical— which could be settled only on the spot. All I had to do was to keep a list of such questions; within a month or two I should very probably be in Venice wearing my Venice in Peril hat, and should return a day or two later with all the answers I needed. It was on those short but frequent visits that I developed the habit of walking for up to two hours every night after dinner. Venice is the pleasantest city in the world to walk in. The absence of motor traffic allows her to limit her municipal lighting to the occasional hundred watt bulb, so that the streets look more than ever like a stage set; after about eleven you have the whole place to yourself, with not a sound but that of your own footsteps and the occasional slap of water against an unseen gondola's keel. Nor is there any danger: never once in all those nights did I feel even a twinge of apprehension.

My ambition was to know every stone, and Venice is just small enough for this to be theoretically quite possible, even though I never achieved it myself. It is also just large enough for there always to be the chance of new discoveries: a curiously decorated doorway or window, a strange relief carving set into a wall, a faded but still legible inscription. It was those long, solitary walks—in which I would simply head off in the hopes of getting lost as quickly as possible—that taught me the city. I enjoyed them to the point where I gave as my recreation in *Who's Who* "walking at night through Venice." The words were so widely and willfully misinterpreted that I briefly removed them, but a year or two later, ashamed at my pusillanimity, I put them back in.

Already by the time I had started work on Venice I had changed agents—or, to be more accurate, agents had changed me. Diana, who had worked indefatigably for me, telephoned me one day and said that she was getting married and closing down her office. "But don't worry," she said, "I've found my successor and she's perfect—can I bring her round for a drink and introduce you both?" A day or two later I opened the front door and there was Diana with a little blonde girl whom I at first took to be about twelve but who turned out to have worked for the *Economist* in Washington. Her name was Felicity Bryan. That was some thirty-five years ago; she is still my agent—she now looks about fourteen—and I hope she always will be. Where agents are concerned, no author has ever been luckier.

But even agents are not omnipotent; and looking back on my life as a writer, I find that I have to accept one uncomfortable truth: that the popularity of my books increases inversely with the quantity of my own writing that they contain. My *Christmas Crackers*, for example, which are almost entirely the work of others, sell like hot cakes. To the most successful book with which I was ever associated I contributed—apart from a brief introduction—just four pages. It was published by Mitchell Beazley in 1975 under the only fairly inspiring title *Great Architecture of the World;* little did we know then that it would be translated into some fifteen languages and sell in every continent except Antarctica. The first pundit whom we invited to write the foreword was the great Buckminster Fuller, inventor of the geodesic dome; but his typescript—which arrived by return of post and had clearly been going the rounds for years—proved so utterly incomprehensible that we had to think again. It was lucky indeed that we did, because our second choice, Dr. Nikolaus Pevsner, provided just what we wanted—and a name to conjure with into the bargain. We had some other big names too: Anthony Blunt (well, well), James Lees-Milne, Hugh Casson, and the ninety-five-year-old Nirad C. Chaudhuri for a start. I was the so-called General Editor, which meant little more than choosing possible authors and signing commissioning letters; the hard work was all done by a brilliant young editor, Elisabeth Brayne. She it was who somehow managed to weld the whole thing together, who dealt with the isometric drawings and perspective cutaways that struck terror into my heart, and who gave me encouragement when I wondered—as I did fairly frequently—whether we were ever going to get the project off the ground. We became firm friends, and I am proud indeed to be godfather to William, her perfectly splendid son.

When from time to time I needed a change, television was an enjoyable and mildly profitable sideline. Ken Shepheard and I continued to make a fifty-minute historical documentary every year: *The Hundred Days* was a huge success, but then it couldn't have gone wrong. Elba still has two houses in which the Emperor lived, one of them—S. Martino—being quite ridiculously pretty. When he escaped from the island he landed at Golfe Juan, one of the most enchanting spots on the French Riviera. To avoid the royalist army which was advancing south down the Rhône valley to meet him, he took the *Route des Alpes*, which is scenically the most stunning road in all France. Every house in which he stayed on his journey to Paris is still standing, marked by a plaque. There are hundreds of superb portraits of him. The story is thrilling, and tragic; the weather throughout our filming was perfect; Beethoven wrote the score. Would that all our programs had been so easy.

In the seventies we kept up our average of one program a year, including ones on The Knights of Malta, the Emperor Maximilian of Mexico, and the story of Toussaint l'Ouverture, leader of the slave revolt in Haiti. That on the Knights—which we made I think in 1976—was my introduction to Malta, where I had never been. I was captivated by the beauty of Valletta, which shares with the Old City of Jerusalem that quality, all too rare in urban architecture, of being homogeneous, built as it is almost entirely of a single material: a rich, mellow, honey-colored stone that seems to absorb and then to radiate back the almost constant sunshine. Moreover, although there may be no really great buildings, I would rate a vast number of them at the very top of the second league—and of how many other cities can that be said? We were lucky, too, to discover the perfect hotel. It was called, quite simply, the British. It was far from luxurious and quite ridiculously cheap,[2] but its rooms looked straight out over Grand Harbor—and those who have never seen the most spectacular harbor anywhere in the world can have no conception of how much that means. Try sitting on your private balcony, reading an account of the Great Siege by Süleyman the Magnificent in 1565; as you look down at the scene below you, the centuries roll away and you can trace every step of one of the most exciting dramas of history.

The principal drawback to Malta—and I emphasize that I am speaking of over thirty years ago—was the food. Since the island—being little more than a great rock sticking out of the sea—boasts little vegetation at the best of times, I suspect that it has never been a gastronomic paradise; but for some two hundred years the Royal Navy had done its worst and in the seventies a decent meal was hard indeed to find. With every almost uneatable lunch and dinner Ken Shepheard and I became increasingly depressed, pursuing every recommendation and occasionally traveling for miles across the island in the hopes of finding some small oasis in the culinary desert. On one evening, I remember, we had driven even further than usual and found ourselves in a cavernous hotel, with a huge, echoing dining room in which we were alone in a sea of empty tables. The single waiter, alarmingly reminiscent of Manuel in *Fawlty Towers*, produced an outsize menu, suggesting—among a hundred others—a dish described as "Turkey Valletta." I didn't have much hope, but there seemed just a chance that this was some old Maltese recipe which might at least be something different.

"What's the turkey like?" I asked. Manuel looked completely blank as only Manuel can, so I repeated the question.

---

2 A quick check on the Internet suggests that it may have got rather grander in the past thirty years.

"I go find out," he said. He was gone a good five minutes, but finally returned, beaming.

"It is like," he said, and thought for a moment. "It is like—very big chicken."

———— ❧ ————

Particularly enjoyable to make was our film on the death of the Prince Imperial—the son of Napoleon III and the Empress Eugénie—who, despite strict instructions from Queen Victoria that he was not to be allowed anywhere near the front line, was the very first casualty of the Second Zulu War. We also made two programs about the problems facing Venice. The first of these we shot soon after the birth of Venice in Peril in an attempt to explain the gravity of the situation facing the city; the second, made ten years later, assessed the degree to which things had improved. It was while we were making the second that, one day as we were getting off the *vaporetto* at St. Mark's, I chanced to point out Harry's Bar to the crew. I was surprised by the reaction: they had all heard about it and seemed fascinated. "All right," I said, "the night we finish shooting, I'll take you all there for dinner." (The prices were a modest fraction of what they are today.) And so it was agreed. A table for five was duly booked, and on our last evening we foregathered in our hotel. The cameraman and his assistant had, like Ken and me, smartened up as best they could; our sound recordist, however—let's call him Les—was a nasty shock. He was wearing what remained of the hideous and extremely threadbare purple sweater that he had worn every day of the shoot, his hair stuck straight up on end, and his face looked even dirtier than it was under a good three days' growth of beard. Was I really going to have to introduce this human scarecrow into the rich, cosmopolitan sophistication and chic of Harry's Bar?

Yes I was. There was no alternative, so in we went. The establishment behaved, it must be said, splendidly. "Yes sir," they said, "your table is all ready"—with a quick glance at Les—"upstairs." Upstairs is fortunately a good deal less exclusive than downstairs, and I was still more relieved when we were led to a table at the far end, behind an enormous pillar. We sat down, the waiter brought the menu, I did my best to explain it in English and we all made our choice from it—all, that is, except Les, who asked for egg and chips.

Older readers may remember that delectable cartoonist HM Bateman, whose specialty was the depiction of appalling social solecisms and the shock and horror with which they were greeted: "The Dirt Track Rider who appeared in Rotten Row," "The Umpire who Confessed he wasn't Looking," "The Etonian whose Parents came by Char-a-banc" are three captions that spring to mind. Here, it seemed, was ideal grist to the Bateman mill: "The Man who Ordered Egg and Chips in Harry's Bar." He would have illustrated it to perfection. Only the waiter's reaction would have disappointed him. He did not bat an eyelid, merely noted the order and withdrew, returning a few minutes later with two exquisitely fried eggs, their whites cut into perfect circles, lying on a bed of tiny, deliciously crisp *pommes allumettes*. Les took one look—and sent them back. Only the Greasy Spoon would do. Another cartoon appeared before my eyes: "The man who *sent back* the egg and chips in Harry's Bar. . . ."

It was years before I dared to show my face there again.

———◦✝◦———

Just occasionally, too, there were special television commissions when I worked with other directors than Ken and for programs other than *Chronicle*. By far the most enjoyable of these was a series of six films about the antiquities of Turkey, which we called *The*

Gates of Asia. The idea came from John Drummond—in those days, with Humphrey Burton, running Music and Arts for BBC2—who argued that archaeologically speaking Asia Minor was the most rewarding territory in the world, since it had been inhabited by just about all the civilizations of the Eastern Mediterranean in the past three thousand years, each one having left its mark. We discussed it one day over a Soho lunch, in company with a highly intelligent young man called David Cheshire whom John had chosen as director; and a few weeks later—it was the autumn of 1972—David and I went off to Turkey on a six-week reconnaissance. That winter we planned the series and wrote the scripts, and the following summer set off again, this time with a film crew. We decided that our first offering should cover ancient civilizations like Troy and the Hittites. Subsequent programs would tackle the Greeks, the Romans, Byzantium, the Seljuk Turks, and Armenians—which reasons of space compelled us to lump together, uneasy bedfellows though they might be—and finally the Ottomans.

It was hard work; Turkish roads thirty-five years ago were by no means what they are now, and the distances to be covered were enormous. There was no way in which we could film the sites in chronological order; our only hope was to construct an itinerary which would cover all our locations from Istanbul in the west to the ancient Armenian capital of Ani in the east—nearly a thousand miles, even as the crow flies—as economically as possible, seeing the entire series as one vast program. We took a fortnight's break in England halfway through, and there was little left of the summer by the time we had finished. David could hardly have been less like Ken, but he was every bit as much fun to be with. Alas, they both died at least a quarter of a century before they should have. I have lost few friends whom I miss more.

The other great spin-off from *The Gates of Asia* was that Turkey became part of my life. I suddenly discovered that I now knew it better than any country in the world—far better than my own. Alas, the projected book of our series never materialized, I never quite knew why; it could have looked wonderful, and I certainly had the enthusiasm—if nothing else—to have done the subject justice. But to this day I often find myself lecturing about Turkey, and often take groups there; once I even made a CD ROM about it. Istanbul may not be so instantly seductive as Venice—what city is? On the other hand, what other city has been an imperial capital for over 1,500 years? The beauties of Istanbul have to be sought out, but the effort required is repaid a thousandfold.

Outside Istanbul, the place in Turkey in which I am happiest is Aphrodisias. There is no site, to my knowledge, anywhere in the classical world, which is more consistently rewarding—or which yields more every year to the archaeologist's spade. Aphrodisias was a city of ancient Greece, sacred—as its name implies—to the goddess Aphrodite; and it stood, as its ruins still stand, at the foot of a mountain of the finest marble. So superb is this marble, and so plentiful, that Aphrodisias was the center for a school of sculpture that lasted for six centuries until the city was finally destroyed by an earthquake. Sculptures from its workshops have been found as far afield as Hadrian's villa at Tivoli.

David Cheshire and I had filmed there briefly in 1973, when—although it was still largely unexcavated—I had been enraptured by the site and its setting; but I began to understand its full magic only when I returned in 1984, at the invitation of the director Christopher Miles, to make a full-length program. It was Christopher who introduced me to the great Professor Kenan Erim, a balding man in his middle fifties, dressed invariably in a tattered blue sweater and the most heavily patched pair of jeans I have ever seen, who spent every winter raising funds by lecturing on classical archaeology at New York University and every summer spending them on his annual dig. He was a strange, cosmopolitan figure who seemed every bit as happy in English and French as he was in his native Turkish. A confirmed bachelor, he loved only Aphrodisias, to which he devoted almost every moment of his waking existence. His death in 1990—in the British Embassy at Ankara, of a sudden heart attack after dinner and at the age of only sixty—was a cruel loss to archaeology.

Christopher, his wife Suzy, and I stayed with Kenan in his lovely old house amid the excavations for the best part of a week. The filming itself was relatively easy: whenever and wherever you pointed a camera in Aphrodisias, the whole place burst into song. We did, however, have something of a diplomatic problem, in the shape of an elderly Englishman called Bill Burnside. Although he seemed to have spent much of his life in Hollywood, his only real achievement as far as anyone knew—and even then we had only his word for it—was to have enjoyed a brief affair with Marilyn Monroe. He was now seriously smitten by the exquisitely beautiful wife of Asil Nadir, the Turkish owner of Polly Peck who was shortly afterwards obliged to leave England in something of a hurry. Her name was Aisha. Bill's idea was that her husband should put up the money for the film, in return for which she would appear in it as the spirit of Aphrodisias—perhaps Aphrodite herself—wafting in diaphanous Greek drapery between the columns, in and out of the shadows, visible yet unseen, intangible, elusive, tantalizing. It was a charming idea, on the strength of which a delighted Aisha instantly bought several diaphanous dresses in Paris at enormous expense; but it didn't work. Christopher was at last reduced to filming her against the ruins in a single sequence which, I suspected, was more of a tease than anything else. She certainly had no part in the final film. So furious was her husband when he saw it that he immediately bought up all the rights; as a result it has never to this day had a public showing.

———⬧———

More ill-starred yet was my program about the antiquities of Persia. Everything that could have gone wrong did so, and most of it was my fault. To begin with it wasn't meant to be about Persia at all, but about Ethiopia, where UNESCO was engaged in major restoration work on the country's ancient monuments and had commissioned a television film on the subject from the BBC. They in turn commissioned me, pointing out that the coming rainy season made it imperative for shooting to begin within a month. Having in my life spent only two extremely unsuccessful days in the country and knowing less than nothing about it, I headed as usual to the London Library for a fortnight's crash course. It was only when I was coming to the end of this that I received an embarrassed telephone call from my employers. UNESCO, it appeared, had failed to understand that a film of the kind they had proposed depended entirely on the goodwill of the Emperor. Now at last they had asked his permission—and he had refused. The money, however, had already been paid and the BBC was understandably reluctant to return it. As it happened, UNESCO were also engaged on similar restoration work in Iran; would I please go and make a film there instead? This time there would be no problem with imperial permissions: the Shah, who was about to celebrate the two thousandth anniversary of the Persian monarchy, would be only too pleased. But there was bad news too: they much regretted that Kenneth Shepheard—for whom I had particularly asked—would not be free to direct the program; nor would David Cheshire. Instead, they had assigned to me a talented young man whose only drawback was that he was totally devoid of foreign experience.

The unavailability of both Ken and David was a bitter blow: it was already plain that this would be my toughest assignment to date, and I knew that I should need all the help and support I could get. Why therefore I now took a decision which was to lead to near disaster I shall never understand. Most BBC camera crews are pleasant enough; some are actually delightful companions and great fun to be with. A few, however—I suspect a very few, and remember that I am talking of some forty years ago—can be bloodyminded from the start, ever-conscious of their rights and unwilling to put in even those vital extra five minutes when the light is dropping and the sun just about to set; and to spend two or three weeks with such people in the back of beyond, passing every waking hour and eating every meal with them, can make filming a misery. It chanced that Ken and I on our previous program had just such an experience; and without him to support me I was determined not to have another.

A few days later I was lunching with Jim Mossman, a superb television journalist who was at that time working for the BBC's *Panorama*, and asked his advice. "Why," he said, "don't you try to get Erik Durschmied? He's a superb cameraman, a freelance who needs no assistant or sound engineer and who's prepared to work all night if necessary. Absolutely no chips on the shoulder, but never stops talking. He may drive you up the wall, but you won't have a dull moment." The same, I soon realized, could not be said of the talented young director; and so, having squared the BBC without too much trouble, I telephoned Erik and hired him on the spot. It was arranged that the t.y.d. and I would leave in a fortnight for Tehran and do a ten-day reconnaissance by ourselves, after which Erik would join us.

The reconnaissance went well enough. The t.y.d. spoke no word of any foreign language, so I had to do all the talking—mostly in French—in the government offices and police stations from whom permissions had to be extracted, schedules drawn up and arrangements made, tasks which in the past I had always left to Ken; but this was no serious hardship, and the week-long whirlwind tour on which we now embarked made up for everything. Tehran and Isfahan I had already seen, but Persepolis and Shiraz, Kermanshah and Qum and Sultaniye and half a dozen other dazzling sites lifted my spirits and convinced me that this job was after all going to be enthralling. Then, two days before he was due to join us, there arrived a long telegram from Erik. He had just come down with meningitis and could not be with us for another week. But we were not to worry: he was sending out a friend of his, a brilliant young Frenchman of nineteen who had recently returned from Vietnam and to whom he had passed his flight booking.

The Frenchman duly turned up, and filming began. Within ten minutes, disaster was staring us in the face. First of all, he spoke not a word of English, which meant that there was no communication at all between director and cameraman—who, ideally, should have an almost telepathic understanding between them. Secondly, he had no equipment with him except his camera and recording machine: no lenses, no filters, not even a proper tripod. Such things would doubtless have been encumbrances in Vietnam, where much of his filming had apparently been done from a parachute; but here, when he was asked for a slow and sensitive zoom into a piece of polychrome glazed tilework, he would not even understand—and could not begin to do what was required. From the start, he and the t.y.d. loathed each other. I spent my time trying vainly to suggest compromises and somehow to keep the peace between them.

Then, suddenly, after only two or three days, Erik turned up—displaying not a trace of meningitis—and the Frenchman was packed off home. Things improved to some extent—at least we no longer had a language problem—but I now understood even more clearly the immense difference between a documentary cameraman and a war reporter. Erik, older and more experienced, had perhaps a little more equipment than his protégé, but still not a quarter as much as a BBC professional would carry as a matter of course. On the other hand he had an overpowering personality which he combined with immense self-confidence, and made little effort to conceal the contempt he felt for the t.y.d. with all his careful BBC training: within days, relations between the two were worse than they had ever been with the Frenchman. One day in Persepolis the t.y.d. asked him to illustrate the great fire with which Alexander the Great had destroyed most of the imperial palace. Erik charged around in all directions, firing indiscriminately from the hip and never once putting his eye to the viewfinder, finally as a climax—and perhaps also to irritate the t.y.d.—swinging the camera several times round his head before flinging it high in the air, whirring all the time as it spun. No BBC man would have dreamt of doing such a thing, if only because the camera would have been company property; Erik, of course, could take what risks he liked with his own. None the less, I was impressed at his readiness to take that one—and at his skill in catching a fairly heavy piece of delicate machinery. The t.y.d., it need hardly be said, was shocked and horrified.

Back in Tehran, just a day or two before we were due to leave, a telegram came from the BBC. The Shah, it appeared, had just decreed as part of his bimillennial celebrations that foreigners should be allowed free entrance into all the mosques in the country. This meant that it would after all be worth our while to go to the holy city of Meshed in the extreme northeast, whose magnificent gold domed mosque had always been closed to foreigners (though Robert Byron had once penetrated it in disguise). It looked indeed as if we might be the first western television team ever to film there. To Meshed, therefore, we flew in the next available plane, going straight from the airport to the police station to arrange our visit—preferably, we suggested, to coincide with Friday prayers the following morning. We were met, to our astonishment, with a firm refusal. But surely, we objected, His Imperial Majesty had personally authorized the opening of all mosques to foreigners. The policeman shrugged. "His Imperial Majesty can authorize what he likes," he replied. "All I can tell you is that if you go in there tomorrow morning you will be torn limb from limb, and there won't be anything we can do about it."

At this point I felt my enthusiasm rapidly waning—as, clearly, was that of the t.y.d. But I didn't want to seem wimpish, particularly since Erik had brightened up considerably and was clearly looking forward to the challenge. Besides, we had come a long way at considerable expense and I didn't want to give up at once. If, I suggested, we paid for a police or military escort, was there no discreet corner from which we could manage a few minutes filming? The prospect of remuneration gave him pause, and after long confabulation with his colleagues he came up with a proposal. The interior of the mosque was out of the question; if however we were prepared to get there a long time before prayer was due to start and if we promised to maintain the lowest possible profile, he would have us escorted to the top of the wall surrounding the inner courtyard, in which there would be a good deal of activity. It would, he warned us, be fairly expensive; the escort would after all be taking a considerable risk.

The next morning we rose soon after dawn, met our four-man escort outside the mosque, followed them one at a time up a narrow spiral staircase in a corner of the courtyard and settled down to wait. After a time we saw that the place was slowly filling with distinctly villainous-looking black-shirted men, each carrying in his hand a short flail. Then a drum began to beat, and there followed what seemed to be an orgy of self-flagellation. They started on their shirted backs, but gradually the shirts were removed and the beating continued on the bare flesh. Some were plainly sparing themselves with little more than token blows, but others were soon showing heavy welts and occasionally streaming with blood. All, it seemed, were gradually lashing themselves into a frenzy. That policeman, I realized, had been absolutely right. Had we been down there with them, we should not have got out alive.

The rest of us—escort included—were keeping well below the parapet. Erik, on the other hand, was leaning further and further over the wall, almost as excited as the flagellants below. It was inevitable that we were going to be spotted, and spotted we suddenly were. Angry cries rose from below, and furious fists were shaken. For a moment I was terrified; I was too young, I felt, to be eviscerated by religious fanatics. Even our escort began to look seriously concerned. But the bass drum continued to beat, and gradually we were forgotten as the grim work resumed. At last the ceremony was over; but it was, I remember, a long time before we crept back down the stairs.

Our Meshed adventure had certainly done something to beef up our program; but when we returned to England and I saw the rushes for the first time I felt despair. Erik had done his best; he was doubtless a superb television journalist but he had neither the training, the equipment nor, I suspect, the inclination for the sort of program that we were trying to make. Had I only accepted an ordinary BBC crew, we should have returned with the raw materials for a wonderful film; thanks entirely to my own pigheadedness, it looked as though we had barely enough to fill the required fifty minutes. Fortunately, I had underestimated the t.y.d. His milieu was a London studio. He had none of the fiery imagination, and certainly none of the fun, of Ken or David; but back on home ground, in his own element—the cutting room—he was able to show just what he could do. Somehow, he patched the pieces together and our program went out as scheduled. But it remains the only one I ever made which was never given a repeat—a fact which I nowadays contemplate with nothing but relief.

———◦⫯◦———

There was sound radio too. For years I was a regular contestant on what was believed to be the oldest BBC program still on the air, *Round Britain Quiz*. Every week during the series, a two-man team theoretically representing a different region of England competed with a similar team representing London. I, a Londoner born and bred, represented the Midlands, for no good reason that I remember apart from the fact that my name was Norwich. (East Anglia, for some reason, had been allowed no team of its own.) Each team had its own question setter—ours was Tony Quinton, one of the funniest men in London—a fact which actually made nonsense of the idea of a fair contest, since each team had a different set of questions to answer. But none of this mattered a jot. The fun of the program was in the questions themselves, which were long, involved and cryptic, often with three or more parts to them. Here are a couple of examples:

Question: What is the connection between (a) a Ben Jonson comedy that has something in common with an apostle and with Eric Morecambe; (b) a piece by Delius set in Lincolnshire; (c) John Updike's first novel which took place at a home for the destitute?

Answer: They are all fairs. (a) *Bartholomew Fair* (Eric Morecambe's real surname was Bartholomew); (b) *Brigg Fair*; (c) *The Poorhouse Fair*.

Question: Who are these three characters in search of trouble: (a) an antique firearm; (b) someone whose visage was, metaphorically speaking, covered with marine gastropods; (c) a man, two rungs up, whose very name should warn you that he was a thief? Where would you find them and how did at least two of them die? What rank would you ascribe to each of them?

Answer: They are characters from Shakespeare's *King Henry V*: (a) Ancient Pistol; (b) Bardolph—his face was covered with "whelks and bubukles"; (c) Nym (to "nim" is to take or steal). Bardolph and Nym were hanged for looting, Pistol's fate is not recorded. Pistol was an ensign ("auncient"), Bardolph a lieutenant, and Nym a corporal.

We the contestants had one immense advantage over our listeners: at the beginning of the recording our producer, Trevor Hill, would give us all the questions—though not of course the answers—written on separate pieces of paper, and we were allowed to decide in which order we wanted to answer them. This meant that we had all the various parts of the question clearly laid out before us; the unfortunate listeners had to remember them as best they could. I alone had a further secret weapon: Irene Thomas. She was a tiny Welsh lady, already I suppose in her late sixties when I first knew her, who looked rather like a miniature edition of Margaret Thatcher, always exquisitely turned out, never a hair out of place, little white gloves tidily laid beside the microphone; and she knew everything. She was in no sense a university type, or an intellectual; she had begun her adult life as a chorus girl and was almost entirely self-educated. But what an education it had been: there seemed to be not a book she hadn't read, not a poem she didn't know by heart, not a song (operatic or popular) she couldn't sing, not a period of history with which she wasn't intimately acquainted. And everything she read or learnt or sang she remembered. Finally, she possessed a flawless retrieval system; the facts came up with all the promptness and accuracy that we should nowadays expect of computers—of which in those days we had hardly heard. It sometimes happened that, to one or the other of us, one part of a question rang a bell; discussion was encouraged, and that would give us a point of departure. More often, neither of us had a clue what it was about, and we would then simply go into free association, saying the first things that came into our heads and simply hoping that something that one of us said might spark off an idea in the other. Sometimes it worked, sometimes it didn't; but we had a lovely time trying. Dear Irene—all this was thirty years ago; but until she died in 2001 she never forgot my birthday.

It was a few years after I had started doing *Round Britain Quiz*—which spawned two offshoots, in the shape of *Round Europe Quiz* (against various European countries one after the other) and *Transatlantic Quiz* (against the USA, always represented by Brendan Grill of the *New Yorker*)—that I was asked to be chairman of another old BBC faithful, *My Word!* As its name implied, this was essentially a quiz about the English language, but its real strength lay in its two permanent contestants, Frank Muir and Denis Norden, who would always end the program with a shaggy dog story, told by each in turn, inspired by a quotation or proverb and always reaching its climax with some outrageous pun. It was generally believed by the listeners (*My Word!*—unlike *Round Britain Quiz*—though subsequently broadcast around the world, was always recorded before an invited audience) that these quotations were announced only at the start of the program, and that the subsequent stories were improvised on the spur of the moment. We never bothered to reveal in so many words that they had been selected by Frank and Denis themselves, who would pass them to me just before the recording began; neither on the other hand did we ever suggest the contrary, so our consciences remained clear.

I chaired *My Word!* for three or four years and then, I suspect, signed my own death warrant. The trouble with being chairman was that every word that one was meant to say had been scripted in advance; there was, at any rate, absolutely no scope for improvisation, and I became increasingly bored. One evening I decided to amuse myself by taking wild liberties with the scoring. As anyone who ever heard the program knows, this was utterly unimportant: the number of marks allotted to the two concluding stories, for example, was decided by the length of the applause that greeted them. Anyway, I suddenly—and, as it turned out, mistakenly—thought it would be fun to allot points right and left for especially witty replies, occasionally withdrawing them just as arbitrarily when this seemed desirable. The experiment was not a success. "John Julius, just what do you think you were doing?" said the producer afterwards, without the ghost of a smile. I first tried to explain, then apologized; but when I left the studio that evening I knew that my copybook was irredeemably blotted. The next series was already in preparation; I was not invited to preside.

Chapter Fourteen
Varied Pursuits

THE 1970S WERE the decade of Serenissima. Soon after my two books on the Normans had been published, the telephone rang and a voice said "My name is Serena Fass. I work for a firm called Heritage Travel and we should very much like you to take a small group of intelligent, cultivated people round Sicily." I had often thought it might be fun to do something of the kind, so I agreed; and in May 1972 off we went, with Serena herself acting as tour manager. I have always loved showing people wonderful things and trying to inspire them with my own enthusiasm—in a way that is what the television programs were all about too—and I enjoyed the trip a lot. One evening after dinner, in the garden of the Villa Igeia in Palermo, Serena revealed that she and two of her friends, Richenda Gurney and Judy Cohen, were planning to set up a firm of their own, to be financed by Tim Sainsbury. Would I, she asked, agree to be its chairman? Of course I would; and Serenissima was born. I was rather pleased with the name: it was a neat compliment to Serena herself; it evoked my beloved Venice, known for centuries as the

Most Serene Republic; and it also allowed us to use as a subtitle "The Most Serene Way to Travel." (Later, after one or two somewhat overeventful journeys in Eastern Turkey and Central Asia, we had cause to regret this addition.)

I did not personally participate in our first three tours. The first was to Egypt, the second—which my mother enthusiastically joined—to Ethiopia, the third to Mexico. This last produced more than its share of problems. To begin with, only nine people had signed up. This meant that we should be running it at a loss, but we didn't want to disappoint our clients so decided to let it go as planned. Alas, only eight returned. One of our number, an elderly gentleman with a passion for physical fitness, decided to jog up to the top of the Great Pyramid at Uxmal in Yucatan—about a seventy-degree incline—in the intense tropical heat. Not surprisingly, he suffered a heart attack. It seemed at first to be not too serious: he was taken to Merida hospital and the tour was able to continue without him. It was only after everyone else's return to London that word came of a second attack, which had indeed proved fatal.

It was not an auspicious beginning. Before long, however, we got into our stride and were sending off twenty or thirty tours a year to every corner of the globe. The most ambitious enterprise of all—some would have called it foolhardy—was our Marco Polo tour, which lasted five weeks and went from Venice all the way across Central Asia to Karakorum, site of the palace of Kublai Khan. There were many problems with this, the first being that nobody had any idea of Marco Polo's route. The man wrote an interminable account of his travels, but brilliantly avoided ever telling his readers anything they wanted to know. Much of our itinerary was therefore guesswork, and was also largely governed by the conditions prevailing in what was then the Soviet Union.

Nevertheless, the tour filled up. I led the first—and by far the easier—half, across Asia Minor as far as Tehran. Being largely ignorant of points east of Iran, I then returned to London, handing over—with unspeakable relief—to Dr. Yolande Crowe, who knew everything about them, besides possessing a combination of toughness and charm which was to prove vitally necessary over the grueling stretches that lay ahead. These included long delays in small Siberian airports, extremely primitive accommodation, and crippling cold. After a final journey of several hours over appalling roads, the exhausted and frozen travelers were at last deposited at the site of Kublai Khan's palace, only to find that there was nothing left on the site but a very small stone tortoise—which was perhaps just as well, since the cold was such that several people refused to get out of the bus at all.

Disasters are always a lot more fun to describe in retrospect than successes, and I must beware of suggesting that Serenissima was in any way a failure. On the contrary, over the years that it remained in our hands it provided wonderful holidays for several thousand people, many of whom traveled with us annually and wrote us glowing thank you letters. I myself must have taken about a dozen tours altogether, several to Venice (including one by the newly opened Venice-Simplon-Orient Express) and to various regions of Turkey, one to Mexico—which I knew quite well after two BBC films—and one to Washington. (There may have been one or two others as well, which I have forgotten.) For nearly all of them the tour manager was Mollie, who—with Anne's full knowledge and approval—was now playing an increasingly important part in my life.

In 1987 the firm was taken over by a competitor, and its whole character changed. From the start we had prided ourselves on never doing a tour (the Marco Polo was an exception) which had not been thoroughly researched by one of our directors—inspecting hotels, timing distances, and checking on comfort stops, with particular reference to the number of loos in restaurants. (It can take a surprisingly long time to get a couple of dozen people back on the bus after lunch.) Of course things could still go wrong, particularly in remote areas, but when they did we at least had the satisfaction of knowing that it was not our fault. Our successors were in no sense lackadaisical; on the contrary, they were highly professional with an excellent track record. It was just that they had a different philosophy. For them, each trip was an adventure, and if there were no rooms at the inn and people had to sleep on the mantelpiece or the billiard table—well, that was all part of the fun. The problem was that for the first year or two after the takeover many of our clients—a fair number of whom were in their seventies—signed up innocently and then, when the going got tough, blamed us.

———— ⟡ ————

Mollie and I led two further tours after the takeover, each in its own way memorable. The first was to Albania. When I was asked to accompany it I at first protested that I knew nothing about the place. Nor, they pointed out, did anyone else; Albania had been virtually forbidden to westerners for the better part of half a century and there *were* no experts. As so often in my life, I was saved by the London Library, where half a dozen books off the Albanian shelf gave me a quick smattering of knowledge; even so, I think we all had a strong sense of the blind leading the blind. Albanian Airlines, we were informed, wisely confined themselves to the carriage of freight; so we flew not directly to Tirana, but by a Yugoslav evening flight to Titograd, the capital of still-Communist Montenegro. It was dark before we piled into the bus that was to take us to the Albanian border, and about ten o'clock before we arrived there.

A light rain was falling as we left the bus—which was now to be replaced by an Albanian one—and queued up with our suitcases in front of the barrier. As in a school roll call, Mollie read out our names from our single joint passport; and each of us went up in turn to the sentry, who by the light of a torch (hers) compared faces with photographs before nodding us on to the customs house a hundred yards further away through the rain. There—attempts to sell us 30-volume leather-bound sets of the combined speeches of Enver Hoxha in Albanian having failed—it was explained to us that there were three categories of goods that could not be imported into Albania. The first was any book or paper about the country, or that mentioned its name in the title. This included our guidebooks, all of which had to be surrendered in return for a receipt, to be reclaimed on our departure. The second was anything that smacked or savored of religion—any religion. One of our ladies had a copy of *The Oxford Book of Christian Verse*; this went the way of the guidebooks.

The third was pornography. Here, given the average age of our group, I thought we might be on fairly safe ground, but I was wrong. Somebody was found to have a copy of the color section of the *Sunday Times*, which included a long and thoughtful article on the future of Hong Kong after it ceased to be a British colony in a few years' time. At the foot of one column was a color photograph the size of a commemorative postage stamp, depicting two Hong Kong bar girls, one of whom was most regrettably topless. On the Albanian customs officer, this picture had the most extraordinary effect. Purple in the face, he tore the magazine to shreds in front of us, hurled the pieces to the floor, and then—in an action which I did not believe occurred outside the pages of children's comics—jumped up and down on them, bellowing the words *"Nicht gut!"* over and over again. It was nearly two o'clock in the morning when we reached our hotel in Shköder, only to find half a dozen waiters and waitresses, all smiling from ear to ear, ready to serve us a four-course dinner. We would all of us have preferred to go straight to bed, but that wasn't the point. As a gesture of welcome it was hard to beat. You would not get that sort of treatment, I remember thinking, at Dover.

The rest of our Albanian tour was relatively uneventful. The scenery was nearly always beautiful and occasionally breathtaking, the architecture hideous in the towns but lovely in the many unspoilt Turkish style villages. In the capital, Tirana, I was struck by the fact that none of the shops seemed to have names: they were called simply "Book Shop" or "Clothes Shop." I went into a "Book Shop" and found all the shelves fenced off, so that it was not possible to get close enough to the books to read the titles. There was no browsing; you first had to know what you wanted, then you had to ask the assistant for it. Only then would you receive a copy into your hands.

Our last tour for Serenissima after the takeover was to Egypt for a performance of *Aida* with Placido Domingo, to be staged in the Great Temple of Luxor. The major problem on our arrival was that the organizers had omitted to announce the time that the opera was due to begin; persistent enquiries produced no firm reply except that it would be some time after eight o'clock. It was generally agreed that half-past was the most probable, so shortly before that time we all took our seats and waited for something to happen. For well over an hour, nothing did; then, soon after 9:30, the orchestra arrived and we settled down for the overture. Alas, we were disappointed. There followed five speeches—each having to be translated into or out of Arabic—after which the orchestra went away again. Twenty minutes later it returned, but only to accompany six national anthems performed by the Luxor Girls' Choir. *Aida* actually began shortly before eleven.

Apart from a little difficulty with the loudspeaker system— *Celeste Aida* was seen but not heard—it proved worth waiting for, especially the Triumphal March, which brought down the curtain—or would have, had there been one—on the first half. The producers had pulled out all the stops. There were no camels, merely because in Luxor camels represent the lowest depths of banality and are of no conceivable interest to anyone; but there were lions and tigers and zebras and a huge company of superbly accoutered elephants. The fact remained that we had by now been sitting for some four hours, and when the great procession was over and the huge area it had occupied—there was no stage—was plunged in darkness for the interval, the audience rose as one man from its plastic chairs and attempted to rub some of the numbness out of its sorely tried collective bottom. By now the question uppermost in most people's minds was whether there was a) a bar and b) a loo, and if so where to find them; so a moment later some two thousand people were jostling their way across the acting space. Then the fun began. Somehow everyone had forgotten all those elephants—and what they had left behind them. In such a crowd there was no way we could see where we were stepping, and the air became loud with little yelps—and occasionally full-blooded screams—as exquisitely dressed ladies in their Guccis and Puccis (some of whom had actually flown in for the evening from Milan, on a specially chartered Concorde) went in up to the knee. Looking back on the evening, I cannot pretend that it was one of the great musical experiences of my life; but I have seldom enjoyed an opera more.

———⊙╲⊙———

My association with the BBC, meanwhile, was still going strong. By this time it had taught me a lesson that has proved invaluable in later life: that to make a television documentary—or indeed to deliver a lecture—the last thing you need to be is an expert. A couple of weeks at the London Library

is more than enough. A fifty-minute program gives little opportunity to go far beyond the bare outlines of a story—particularly in television, where you can't even go on talking all the time.
Never must the program sound like a lecture: you must allow
the pictures a chance to speak for themselves. There must also be
breaks for music, and even occasionally for silence. The truth of
this was brought home to me in the middle seventies, when John
Drummond overcame a good deal of official BBC opposition
("my dear John, you must understand, architecture just doesn't
work on the small screen") to initiate a series of eight programs
on the development of English architecture, to be called *Spirit of
the Age*. Each program was entrusted to a different presenter, all
of them—Roy Strong, Mark Girouard, John Summerson, and
Hugh Casson, to name but four—were well outside my league;
owing to a last minute cancellation, however, I was asked to
take over the program on Palladianism. "But I don't know anything about it," I protested. "Then you'll have to mug it up," John
replied, and that was that.

It proved an extremely successful series, and was subsequently
turned into a book; and for me it had an extraordinary and quite
unexpected consequence—I acquired a totally spurious reputation as an architecture buff. And so it was that some time in the
late 1970s I was approached out of the blue by Macmillans, a publisher with whom I had no dealings up to that time. Would I, they
asked, be interested in producing a volume about all the best of
English architecture?

"What about Pevsner?" I said. "He's done it already—and he
knows a thousand times more about the subject than I do."

"Ah," they said, "but haven't you noticed? Pevsner tells you
everything about every building of England except the one thing
you want to know: *is it any good*? He hardly ever gives a value
judgment. What we want is a book about the buildings you like,

and why you like them. On top of your advance, we'll pay all your hotel accommodation and petrol. What do you say?"

I said yes. Mollie agreed to tackle the vast amount of research necessary: this, we had agreed, was going to be a joint exercise from the start. A month or two later she had compiled a mighty card index which included just about every building that might conceivably qualify, and our tours of exploration began. We traveled about one weekend in four, leaving at cockcrow on Friday and returning usually quite late on Sunday night. During those three days we would visit between forty and fifty buildings, mostly country houses and parish churches. To the owners of the houses I would normally write in advance, explaining what I was trying to do and suggesting a date and approximate time of arrival. This worked extremely well on the whole; the vast majority gave us a warm welcome— sometimes rather too warm, since our schedule was always pretty tight and there were no mobile phones in those days to enable us to make last minute adjustments to the program. The only trouble was when a letter remained unanswered, and we consequently had no idea whether we were expected or not. Sometimes we would find the house deserted and had to be content with peering through the ground-floor windows; once—but only once—we were refused admittance by a clearly unbalanced occupant waving a shotgun.

Parish churches presented a different set of problems. All too many, even in those days, were locked. In many areas the very real dangers of vandalism and theft made this necessary; we asked only that there should be some indication in the porch of where the key might be found. Alas, all too often there was none, and we were condemned to waste valuable time—sometimes an hour or more—ringing doorbells, stopping passersby, enquiring at shops. We normally succeeded in the end. On only one occasion—and this was far more infuriating than the mildly ridiculous incident with the shotgun—did we come up against sheer, bloody-minded obstruction. It was at Ockham in Surrey, possessor of one of the only two seven-lancet east windows in the country.[1] We ran the vicar to earth, showed him our official letter from Macmillans and asked if we could borrow the key. He refused. Never, he said, did he let it out of his own hands. Any visitor to the church had to be escorted personally by himself. In that case, I said, much as I hated to trouble him, would he please very kindly come with us? No, he said, he would not. And that was that. The same night I wrote what I hoped was a rather biting letter to the Bishop of Guildford, pointing out that parish churches were among the greatest glories of England, that they belonged to us all, and that I felt that a basic right had been denied me. In the fullness of time I received a brief reply to the effect that my letter had been passed to the Archdeacon of Dorking. I heard nothing more.

Even when we got into a church without difficulty, problems would still remain. In the late winter afternoons the building might easily be pitch-dark—where were the lights? Gradually we got to know the most probable places: at the base of the tower, behind the vestry curtain, tucked in beside the organ. But why make it all so difficult? Why not install slot machines, like they do to illuminate pictures in Italian churches? A pound coin would light the whole church for five minutes, and the church would take the profits. Another problem in those distant days was the cold. Nowadays most of our churches seem to have heating systems of one kind or another; thirty years ago it was a very different story, and my fingers were often too numb to hold a pen. One thing only saved me: the recently invented pocket dictating machine, without whose tiny cassettes my task would have been almost impossible. As it was, my admiration for Dr. Pevsner steadily increased. Admittedly, he had a whole

---

[1] The other is at Blakeney in Norfolk.

team of helpers; but he still insisted on a table in his hotel room, at which he would spend much of the night writing up what he had seen in the day. There is evidence, too, that during his labors he suffered from the heat as well as the cold; I remember my delight in finding, in one of his volumes, the irresistible dedication "To the Inventor of the ICED LOLLY."

On and on we worked, but England is fantastically rich in ancient monuments and when in 1984, after several years on the job, I realized that we had barely started on the northern half of the country, I wrote desperately to the publishers. At this rate, I told them, it would be another five or six years before I was finished; fun as it had been so far, I wasn't sure whether I could face such a future. Anyway, they must be wanting some return on their money. Couldn't we therefore call the book *The Architecture of Southern England*, and leave the North to somebody else? To my delight they agreed, and John Martin Robinson took over. Even then, it seemed to me that what I had written was far too much for a single volume, and I implored Macmillans to distribute it over three or four smaller ones. Who, I put it to them, wanted to cart the pages and pages about Kent when they were looking at Cornwall? But I lost the battle, and the resulting tome proved almost too heavy to lift. It sold out, but (not surprisingly) was never reprinted. I still consult my copy a good deal—and, if I may say so, am constantly astonished at how good it is. But rather than carry it about with me I now simply copy the relevant pages before I leave the house. Even then the photocopier takes a long time to recover.

———— ❧ ————

Ever since my preparatory school days I had always kept a soft spot for Canada; but it was to be nearly thirty years before I returned. I eventually did so at the invitation of the Macmillan

Company of Canada, who for a number of years organized an annual get-together of British and Canadian authors for three or four days of lectures, discussions and debates. I duly arrived one evening in Toronto and, strolling out of the hotel to find myself some dinner, was not altogether surprised to find the city a good deal sparkier than I had remembered it as a schoolboy. Just how sparky it had become, however, I was not to discover until the following day, when I had been invited out to lunch with the Macmillan director, who had asked me to meet him at noon in a restaurant called, as I remember, *The Brush and Palette*. The hour struck me as being a little early, but I turned up punctually and was shown into a rather dark basement with a number of tables, all unoccupied. Of my host there was no sign. I was offered a drink, which I accepted, and sat down to wait. Two minutes later a curtain at the end of the room was drawn aside and there entered a stark naked lady of a certain age carrying a palette and a paintbrush, which she handed to me with the invitation "Paint me!" making it clear that she was to be not so much my model as my canvas.

I felt totally at a loss. Late at night, perhaps in Paris and after a good dinner, I might have dealt with the situation with more aplomb; but noon and Toronto seemed neither the time nor the place. I have already lamented my utter inadequacy as a painter or draughtsman; how happy I should have been to achieve, with a carefree laugh, some brilliant, lightning sketch on breast or buttock. Alas, a few abstract strokes were all I could manage through my blushes. The lady took back the equipment, thanked me with rather overdone politeness, and disappeared behind the curtain. A few minutes later my host arrived, grinning broadly. "Surprised?" he asked. Yes, I replied, I was, rather. "Oh well," he said, "I just thought you ought to see how this city has changed since you were last here."

That visit was the first of several that I was to make to Canada over the next ten years. The immensely rich Macdonald Stewart Foundation, established only in 1973, had decided to sponsor a biennial program of visits by British lecturers and art historians to various Canadian universities. Why I was invited on the first one I cannot imagine; but I went, greatly enjoyed it, and soon found myself a sort of nonplaying captain, selecting the team— a different period of art and architecture was chosen for each occasion—bringing them over and introducing them to their hosts and their audiences. I was to do this three or four times, of which the last was the most enjoyable of all. The period chosen was the High Victorian. The rewards were considerable—a fattish fee, first-class flights on Air Canada, slap-up accommodation at McMaster University and, when the three-day seminar was over, a week anywhere we liked in the country as guests of the Foundation. In such conditions acceptances were almost certain. I brought in Asa and Susan Briggs, Hugh and Reta Casson, and John Betjeman, who in turn brought his friend Elizabeth Cavendish.

The outward flight was marked by one unfortunate occurrence: somehow, in the course of it, the Poet Laureate lost his suspenders. We hunted high and low, insofar as this is possible in an airplane—on the floor, behind the seats, in the loo—but there was no sign of them, and his trousers simply didn't stay up without. All the way through immigration and customs he was clutching them in his hand; it was only when we passed the last barrier that the delightful representative of McMaster who had come to meet us ripped off his own belt and handed it over. The University is a Baptist foundation, so the belt—a magnificent object of thick leather with a huge pewter buckle, the sort of thing that might have been worn by Oliver Cromwell—became known as the Baptist Belt and saved the situation until the end of our trip.

We all enjoyed ourselves enormously: John in particular was a huge success, mobbed by all the students—many of whom seemed to know his poems by heart—and besieged with requests to sign copies of his books. (*Le Maple Leaf Pour Toujours* was a favorite postscript.) When our work was done we all seven of us flew off to Calgary, whence the following morning we took the spectacular drive through Banff to Lake Louise. There we lunched in the magnificent old Canadian Pacific Hotel and caught the afternoon train that, some sixteen hours later, was to deposit us in Vancouver. Much amusement was afforded on the platform of Lake Louise station by a large party of Japanese businessmen, filling in time by practicing their golf swings with imaginary clubs. Hugh—who could produce an exquisite little drawing in less time than anyone else needed to take a photograph—filled up a dozen pages of his sketchbook. John collapsed into helpless laughter. The rest of us kept straight faces as best we could.

Things got even better on the train. The Macdonald Stewart people had arranged de luxe accommodation at the back, giving straight out on to the observation platform. Here we settled ourselves with a large bottle of rye whisky, gazing out on the scenery as it grew increasingly spectacular in the setting sun. We were none of us feeling, perhaps, our absolute best when the train drew up the following morning in Vancouver, but our brilliant guide somehow instinctively divined where our tastes lay. The particular Betjeman favorite, as I remember, was an ornate 1930s banking hall. The approach to it was up an escalator, which permitted a gradual revelation of the interior as one reached its floor level. John went up the escalator about half a dozen times, raising his hat every time as he reached the top. "Oh I say, nothing Baptist about this one, eh? Episcopalian through and through. . . ."

It was thanks to the National Trust—of which I was still on the Executive Committee—that, early in 1976, I had my first and last direct experience of *Son et Lumière*. Would I, they asked, be interested in writing a script for such a program, to be performed throughout the coming summer at Chartwell, Sir Winston Churchill's house near Westerham in Kent? Having all my life found it almost impossible to say no to an invitation, I accepted. It was only over the next week or two that I began to see the difficulties. The first was architectural. The building, despite its Tudor origins, has been radically altered and is far from beautiful; the more light you throw at it, the worse it looks. The second—a good deal more serious—was the fact that although Chartwell obviously meant Churchill, and Churchill equally obviously meant the Second World War, in fact during the five years of hostilities he was hardly there at all. The house was directly on the flight path of the German bombers flying towards London, and was immediately identifiable from the air by reason of its three lakes, dug in the interwar years by Churchill himself. (It was said that he had insisted on three because Lloyd George had two.) The Prime Minister tended instead to spend his wartime weekends at Ditchley in Oxfordshire, while Chartwell was left uninhabited; there was moreover a blackout, which suggested that we might have something of a problem with the *lumière*. How therefore was this all-important chapter to be covered?

I was rather pleased with my solution. The only lights visible in a wartime blackout were searchlights, so searchlights were what we should have. Two mighty beams would rake the sky and then suddenly converge, together tracing a path in which one might easily imagine a German squadron on its way to London. As for the *son*, it would have two separate elements: extracts from Churchill's recorded speeches, and the popular marching songs of the Second World War. I made a list of the extracts I needed ("*We shall fight on the beaches,*" "*Never in the field of human conflict has so much been owed by so many to so few,*" and several other stirring examples) and of the obvious song titles (*Run Rabbit Run, The Quartermaster's Stores, Roll Out the Barrel, We're Going to Hang out the Washing on the Siegfried Line*) and handed it to the producer, who I was assured had long experience of the medium and was far and away the best in the business. Then I thought no more about it until we got to Chartwell on the opening night.

The beginning and end of the program proved to be not too bad; but the coverage of the war was a disaster. I had not realized when I asked for the searchlights that the wartime ones were mounted on huge lorries with their own deafening generators; these, moreover, were obtainable only from the Army, which hired them out only at prohibitive cost. We had to make do with pathetic affairs hardly more powerful than ordinary floodlights, and though these could be focused to make beams they were barely visible if you didn't know where to look. As it happened, I was comforted by an old RAF man who told me that even the lorry-mounted ones would have made little impact at that time, because a searchlight beam is actually the illumination of millions of tiny droplets of moisture in the atmosphere. This was the year of the great drought, and the air was as dry as a bone. The light would have been visible only on the clouds, and clouds in that astonishing summer were few indeed.

The *son* was even more of a catastrophe than the *lumière*. One or two extracts from the speeches worked well; but most of them were taken from a subsequent set of recordings, made by the Prime Minister some years after the war was over. He was by then an old man, and the later versions had none of the energy and drama of the originals. As for the songs, I should of course have stipulated that they should be sung the way they were meant to be sung—by rough, untrained soldiers voices, to an accompaniment (if any) of marching feet. Even so, I could hardly have expected to hear them rendered to a piano accompaniment by the boys of Sevenoaks School; you could almost see the choirmaster conducting them. I buried my face in my hands.

The only good thing to come out of this mildly humiliating adventure was a number of splendid Churchill stories. In 1976 the old man had been dead for only a decade, and there were still plenty of people around who had known him well—few, outside his own family, better than Antony Head, with whom I had stayed in Lagos a dozen or so years before. Many of Antony's reminiscences—alas, untranslatable into *son et lumière* terms—were inspired by one of Churchill's most endearing characteristics—his childishness. One Sunday, Antony told me, he and Dot had been invited down to Chartwell for lunch. They arrived shortly before one o'clock, and Lady Churchill's first words to him were "Antony, for heaven's sake go upstairs and get Winston out of the bath. He's been there for nearly an hour; Mr. Canellopoulos[2] will be arriving any moment— he's terribly touchy and he won't like it a bit if his host isn't there to receive him. So go up and see what you can do."

Antony knew perfectly well that he could do nothing: that the great man would get out of the bath when he felt like getting out of the bath, and not a moment before. But he could hardly disobey, so upstairs he went. There at the end of the passage was the bathroom door, wide open and with clouds of steam belching forth; and there in the bath was the Prime Minister, wielding an enormous sponge. He was lying back, throwing the sponge down to his feet, kicking it back to his hands again and, as the sponge flew back and forth, singing to himself: "*Can*ellopoulos, *Can't*ellopoulos, *Can*ellopoulos, *Can't*ellopoulos...."

2 Panayotis Canellopoulos, Greek conservative statesman, twice—very briefly—Prime Minister.

On another occasion Antony was at Chartwell for dinner. Among the guests as always was Churchill's scientific adviser Lord Cherwell, the former Professor Lindemann, always known as "the Prof." Dinner was over, and the Prime Minister was expatiating on the virtues of brandy, a large glass of which stood on the table before him. "I think I can safely claim," he was saying, "that, with very few exceptions, since the age of eighteen I have always drunk at least two good glasses of brandy after dinner, and they have done me nothing but good. Now that, you will agree, is a very great quantity of brandy. Tell me, Prof, if all the brandy I have ever drunk were poured into this room, how high up the wall would it rise?" It was a question that no one else could conceivably have asked, but Cherwell was ready. He looked quickly round the room to size it up, then whipped out his slide rule. "About five-eighths of an inch, Prime Minister" he said. Churchill said nothing, but his face took on that characteristic scowl that his friends knew only too well. Furious, he left the table and went to bed.

———— ❦ ————

When we had first arrived in Beirut in 1957, it was still an eight-hour flight from London; anyone bound for the further east was almost certain to come down there and possibly spend a night or two. Consequently we had a lot of guests in search of dinner or, occasionally, a bed, and when my mother came to stay she decided to give us a visitors' book. In due course it arrived: a magnificent volume of 150-odd blank pages, bound in beautiful blue Nigerian goatskin. Unfortunately, its arrival coincided with *les événements*[3] and the consequent introduction of a curfew; the airport was closed and for months we had not a single visitor from abroad.

---

3 See Chapter Eight, page 216.

Now a sunset curfew may have its disadvantages, but it affords a marvelous opportunity for catching up with one's reading; and I had recently got into the habit of copying out into a little notebook various passages of prose or poetry that had for one reason or another caught my fancy and that I wanted to remember. The notebook was fast filling up and becoming increasingly dog-eared; I decided that the blue goatskin would be an infinitely worthier repository; and the next few evenings were spent in happy transcription, in my very best and most careful handwriting.

Then a strange thing happened. In the splendor of their new environment the extracts I had copied out seemed to take on a new, corporate character. What had been heretofore simply a jumble of literary odds and ends suddenly became a single entity, something to be cultivated and cared for. And the volume itself, with its tooled and gilded decoration around the edges and the spine—that too I found myself contemplating with new pleasure and pride. No longer was it just a fine piece of bookbinding; it was my commonplace collection.

As the years went by, the blue volume filled up and was succeeded by a similar one in red; and I came to realize that I had stumbled, more than half accidentally, on one of the most wholly satisfying subjects for collection that the world has to offer. First of all, it costs literally nothing: nicely bound volumes may be useful for providing the initial impetus and for helping to create the sense of pride that every collector must develop to keep him going, but they are by no means essential. Secondly, being totally divorced from monetary wealth, it knows no restriction of size or scope, only those limitations which the collector himself decides to impose; it follows that no other form of collection can so fully reflect his taste and personality. Thirdly, he is on his own, far from the world of experts and dealers, catalogs and salerooms. Indeed, one of the first lessons he learns is never to go out looking for items. He is very unlikely to find any if he does, and the very act of searching seems somehow to blunt his antennae. If he can only keep these sharp, there is no telling when and where he will make his next *trouvaille*. He may not even need to wait till he next picks up a book; a chance remark, a letter from a friend, an opera program, an advertisement, the instructions for the new washing machine, a visit to a country church, a notice in a hotel room or a railway station, any of these things or a thousand others can reveal the occasional nugget of pure gold.

In one respect, however, the commonplace collector shows himself to be no different from the rest of his kind. Like them he feels, sooner or later, an irrepressible urge to share his collection with others; and it was in response to that urge—the-come-up-and-see-my-etchings syndrome—that in 1970 I hit upon the idea of having a little booklet printed containing a couple of dozen of my favorite items, and of distributing it to my friends as a sort of glorified Christmas card. Production costs in those days were not excessive and might, I thought, be largely offset if I were to order a few more copies than I needed and persuade one or two well-disposed booksellers to dispose of them as best they could. The title, as always, posed a bit of a problem. The first one I thought of, *A Christmas Cracker*, seemed something less than inspired; but nobody seemed able to think of a better one so I settled for it, adding the year just in case the outcome of the experiment made it seem worth repeating at any time in the future.

Rather to my surprise it worked—and better than I had dared to hope. A fortnight before Christmas my two commercial outlets, Heywood Hill and Vanessa Williams-Ellis (who had a lovely bookshop just around the corner from our house in Little Venice), had both sold out and I was down to my last copy. Then an American lady, Alison Henning, whom I had never met—though she, her husband, and her daughter subsequently became dear friends—telephoned to ask if she could have fifty more printed at her own expense. I replied that nothing would give me greater pleasure, asking only that she should run off an extra dozen for me. This was encouragement indeed; and in the following year I not only prepared a new *Cracker* but upped the print order, in a reckless burst of optimism, from two to three hundred.

And so the uncertain seedling became a moderately hardy annual, and soon after writing these words I shall be preparing my thirty-ninth. I shall send off about 600 and sell about 4,000, so I now even make a modest annual profit. Every ten years the harvest of the decade is published in a bound volume, first between stiff covers and then in paperback. *Christmas Crackers, More Christmas Crackers,* and *Still More Christmas Crackers* have already appeared; the title for the fourth volume to be published in 2010—should I get that far—may present something of a problem. Meanwhile the collecting continues: I am now well into my eleventh goatskin volume. They are all bound in different colors but otherwise identical, and they represent my only financial outlay. My mother probably paid about £50 for the first; they now cost about £600 each, but as I need a new one only every four or five years I stump up willingly when the moment comes. It is worth it for the sheer pleasure I get out of the whole operation—far more, I am perfectly certain, than anyone else.

Finally, the *Crackers* provide ideal material for public readings. I hate reading from my own work but hugely enjoy doing so from other people's, and I now have enough material to change the program time and time again. It makes a change from lecturing, and the resulting laughter is music to my ears. Recently I have even taken to livening up the program still further by injecting a few songs to the piano. With the exception of an occasional one-off evening at Wilton's Music Hall, however, I restrict myself—I'm sure wisely—to only the very smallest theaters, like the Jermyn

Street and the Gate, Notting Hill. There is no point in risking rows of empty seats, with the unsettling feeling that one is entertaining an audience of several.

Chapter Fifteen
Work and Play

THE STRESSES AND strains of *The Architecture of Southern England* could easily have destroyed Mollie's and my relationship; in fact it had the opposite effect, and by the time it was over we found that we had grown into each others' lives. Anne had been aware of everything almost from the start, and—being herself happily involved elsewhere—had shown us constant sympathy and understanding. The eventual divorce was consequently as friendly as it could possibly have been—to the point where we both employed the same lawyer, whom we used to visit together to work out the details. To this day she and I have a happy sibling relationship and see each other every three or four weeks for lunch. Mollie very reasonably felt that she should delay any action on her part till her children were grown-up; but in 1983 she moved into Blomfield Road and six years later the knot was tied. Soon afterwards her former husband Hugo also remarried. Divorces are always sad, and she had a far more difficult situation to deal with than I did; but I like to think that with ours, at least, no hearts were broken.

My own children had already left the nest. They were fully aware that their parents were only regularizing what had for many years been a *fait accompli* and were not, I hope and believe, unduly upset. Besides, they were now primarily occupied with their own lives. From time to time Artemis and I used to talk about her future, and occasionally—since this is a subject on which parents should always tread warily—on her eventual marriage. "My darling," I used to say to her, "when the moment comes to choose a husband, the important thing is to get your priorities right. It doesn't matter whether he's good-looking, or intelligent, or sexy; all those things are fine, but they're not really important. Ask yourself one question only: is he going to be a good son-in-law to *me*?" As always, she delivered the goods. Antony Beevor, whom she married in 1986, is the best anyone could have: not just our finest living military historian—who has proved that works of serious military history can also be international bestsellers—but wonderful company, full of wisdom, and superlatively good at all the things I am hopeless at—like the law, and finance, and jobs around the house. Their first coproduction was a riveting and superbly researched book, *Paris after the Liberation;* they have since provided me with two glorious and beloved grandchildren, Nella and Adam; I love them all dearly and owe them more than I can ever repay.

Nella, however, we very nearly lost. She was born in January, 1990, and nobody had ever seen a happier, healthier baby. Eight months later, on the first Monday in September, she was on the point of death. She was vomiting violently, her body was limp, her skin yellowish-grey, her eyes huge and hooded; it seemed, as Artemis wrote later, as if her life was draining away in front of us all. She was rushed to the Charing Cross Hospital, where they quickly realized just how ill she was and, since they had no pediatric surgery unit of their own, transferred her by ambulance to the Westminster Children's Hospital, in those days in Vincent Square.

There she was to remain until the last day of October. None of us will ever forget those first two nightmare weeks. One of the most frightening aspects was that for a long time no one could find out what was wrong. She underwent three major operations in five days; after the second, the surgeon looked her mother in the eye and murmured "I am afraid there is very little hope." Such was her internal bleeding that in the course of twenty-four hours she was given the equivalent of six complete blood transfusions, and matters reached the point where Antony had to beg the doctors, if the situation was truly hopeless, not to keep her alive artificially. A day or two later one of them said to him, "You do realize that even if she lives she may never be able to eat solids again."

The following Sunday, when she had been in hospital nearly a week, she began to recover consciousness. This of course meant becoming aware of the acute discomfort she was in and the terrifying treatments she was having to suffer; that second week was almost more wearing for Artemis than the first and was made worse by the knowledge that her little daughter was still desperately ill. She would have to be fed intravenously for a very long time, and her gut was so badly damaged that it might never heal. It was then that we were told about EGF. Epidermal Growth Factor is a synthetic hormone which mirrors, molecule for molecule, the hormone used by the body to regenerate damaged tissue. It was still in the experimental stage, but there was apparently a batch of it in a laboratory in Cambridge; ICI, to whom it belonged, kindly agreed to provide a little. The treatment that was contemplated had never been attempted before in a case like Nella's; there seemed to be a chance, however, that it might be just what she needed.

And it was. Despite the fact that the quantity used was measured in nanograms—millionths of a gram—the effects were immediate and startling. Within twenty-four hours the inflammation was noticeably less, and on Monday, September 17, Nella was wheeled out of intensive care, her life no longer in immediate danger. Artemis, who had scarcely left her side for a fortnight, accompanied her to her new room, where she slept on a camp bed. Another two weeks passed, and then came the news we had all been praying for. The EGF had done its work. The villi[1] were growing again. There was still a long and painful way to go, but at last Nella was on the mend. On Wednesday, October 31, she left the hospital. The ordeal was over. Now, sixteen years later, she is—among many other things—a licensed scuba diver. Looking at her or talking to her, you would never suspect that she had had a day's illness in her life.

In 1992 Artemis told her story in a book, which she called *Watching in the Dark* and which she dedicated "To the doctors and nurses of the Westminster Children's Hospital, who brought Nella back to life." It is wonderfully done, written without a trace of mawkishness or sentimentality and one of the most moving accounts I have ever read. Going through it again to write this short and most inadequate account, I have felt the tears pouring down my cheeks; I would challenge anyone to read it dry-eyed.

———— ❧ ————

Jason, as I have already recorded, is an architect; and I need hardly add that today Jason Cooper, Architects, is—by a very long way—the most distinguished architectural firm in the country. He may not yet be quite as well known as Messrs. Foster, Rogers, or Grimshaw, but they are the older generation; his time will come. Any firm wishing to be at the cutting edge of British architecture in the years ahead should contact him without delay. If he were not an architect, he might easily have been a professional

---

1 The tiny soft hairs that line the inside of the gut.

entertainer: he is an inspired mimic and raconteur. I know of no one who can so quickly reduce me to helpless paroxysms of laughter—an unusual compliment, I suspect, for a man to pay to his own son. We have another great bond too: we both love to sing. The late but incomparable Mrs. Florence Foster Jenkins[2]—who had absolutely no voice and even less technique, but used nevertheless to hire Carnegie Hall for concerts in which she sang the Queen of the Night's arias from *The Magic Flute* and the Jewel Song from *Faust*—once summed up her vocal career with the words: "Well, they may say I couldn't sing, but no one will ever say I *didn't* sing"; Jason and I can make much the same claim. He shares my passion for the old songs of the twenties and thirties, and we render them—separately or together—at the top of our voices whenever we get the chance.

Allegra, when she left Oxford, went into publishing, working for ten years or so for George Weidenfeld. Since she came to England at sixteen she has been an integral part of our family, and indeed is Nella's godmother; but her Hollywood background eventually proved too strong and she decided to be a scriptwriter like her half brother Tony Huston, who had settled in Taos, New Mexico. Eventually she went to join him there to collaborate on a joint project, and there she too has now settled with her partner Cisco Guevara—who runs the white water rafting on the Rio Grande—and their little son Rafael.

Rafa's christening took place on Sunday, June 8, 2003. Artemis, Jason and I flew out for the occasion to Taos, where some hundred and twenty of Allegra's and Cisco's friends had gathered. At five o'clock in the evening two busloads of us drove off to a remote bend in the river—still at this point quite narrow—

---

2 At least one of her records is, I think, still obtainable at good record shops and is enthusiastically recommended. I know of none funnier.

and assembled on the bank. Presently a flower-bedecked boat rounded the bend, in which sat the eight-month-old Rafa and his parents. Allegra's half sister Anjelica had just been making a film about King Arthur, and had consequently been able to bring with her from California some wonderful Arthurian dresses of vaguely pre-Raphaelite design, which she, Allegra, and the godmothers were all wearing.

The ceremony began with a poem read by Anjelica. This was followed by not one but two christenings, both performed knee-deep in the fast flowing river, first by an elderly gentleman wearing khaki shorts, a wreath of flowers around his head in the manner of Ophelia, and a white walrus moustache—I presumed him to be a Christian clergyman, though his denomination was not clear—and then by an immensely distinguished local Indian. He too scooped up a handful of water and poured it over Rafa's uncomplaining head, talking to him quietly in his native language—Allegra has since informed me that it was Tewa—and then briefly translating what he had said for our benefit. The whole service, including the singing before and afterwards, must have lasted the best part of an hour. We know all too well how sooner or later in most christenings—which last ten or fifteen minutes at most—the baby starts to bellow; Rafa spent most of the time sitting high on his godmother's shoulders, beaming delightedly at the crowd, acknowledging their acclamations with a gracious wave of the hand. The Queen Mother couldn't have done it better.

As night was beginning to fall we drove back to a country restaurant for the serious celebrations. The party, I am told, continued long into the night; I, alas, had to take a car back the three hours to Albuquerque, there to catch a seven o'clock plane the following morning. But I didn't really mind: I had after all been there when it mattered, and it was something that I would not have missed for the world.

———— ◦†◦ ————

Back now to the 1980s. My beloved mother was getting old; having been married for thirty-five years, she was to be a widow for thirty-three. The weeks she spent at her house in Warwick Avenue, only three or four hundred yards from our own, the weekends in Buckinghamshire with her niece Kitty Farrell and Kitty's husband Charles, who allowed her to feel their house to be her own, and for whose unfailing goodness to her during her declining years I can never be sufficiently grateful. And so she lived contentedly for the next quarter of a century, giving frequent luncheon parties—much enlivened by her own blockbuster cocktails—driving her little mini at terrifying speeds through London, and bringing up her grandchildren as only she could.

Her driving style, too, was peculiarly her own. She had a passion for illegality for its own sake: every "No Entry" sign was to her a personal challenge. No wonder that she was the model for Evelyn Waugh's Mrs. Stitch; and if she never went quite so far as taking her mini down the steps into the Underground, I have no doubt that she would enormously have enjoyed doing so. She certainly thought nothing of driving considerable distances along the pavement when the need arose. Parking restrictions were another of her bugbears. For most of her driving life they had not existed, and when they were finally introduced she flouted them wherever possible—frequently leaving little notes for the wardens tucked under the windscreen wiper. "Dear Warden," she would write, "Taken sad child to cinemar [sic]—please forgive"; or "Dearest Warden—Front tooth broken off: look like 81-year-old pirate, so at dentist 19a. Very old, very lame, no metres [sic]. Have mercy!" The extraordinary thing about this technique was how often it worked; again and again she would return to find an addition to the note: "Forgiven—Warden." Unanswered notes, successful or not, she put under the dashboard for future use. I used to look there whenever I borrowed the car, and eventually made quite a collection; the best I even included in a Christmas Cracker.

Already by the early seventies, however, I was receiving telephone calls from people whom she had driven home from some dinner party the night before. "You *must* stop her driving," they would say, "before she kills herself." "Just try it," I would reply. I had of course tried it myself, many times; she would always protest "but darling, I'm perfectly safe. I've been driving over sixty years and I've never had an accident." There was a perfectly good answer to this, which was that it depended on what you meant by "accident." She had indeed never had a serious one in which anyone had been hurt; but the number of dented mudguards that she had left behind her was beyond computation. These (including her own) she saw as necessary facts of life, to be accepted philosophically as part and parcel of the driving experience. It was, she considered, extremely bad form to mind. There was only one word for the sort of people who got out of the car, noted license numbers, and swapped the names of insurers—common. "What," she would ask, "are bumpers for?"

But at last even she had to accept that her driving days were over. One day she was driving alone down Wigmore Street and hit a bollard. She backed off it, did one of her celebrated U-turns and returned instantly to Warwick Avenue, where she locked the car—something that she normally never dreamt of doing—and went straight up to bed. She never drove again. "I didn't see it," she told me afterwards. "It might have been a child." She was eighty-nine years old, and from that moment—as I knew it would—her decline began. Driving had meant everything to her. It was not only a means of getting from place to place; it spelt freedom, and independence, and doing what she liked when she liked. Without it she was lost. Never would she have dreamt of taking a taxi; they were far too expensive. Once, as a Christmas present, I gave her an account with the local firm of minicabs. "Send me the bill every month," I told them, "but on no account let any of your drivers tell my mother the fare." The very first time she used them, she asked—and was told. She rang me up the next morning and insisted that I cancel the arrangement; she preferred to stay at home.

She went to bed, and remained there. For a year or two her life was tolerable enough: she could still read, and watch her hero David Attenborough's programs on television. But gradually the eyes went, and then the hearing. I would call in every day for half an hour, and *tête-à-tête* conversations went quite well—her mind remained clear. If a third person were present, on the other hand, she couldn't keep up, and this depressed her terribly. Even worse was when a doctor—she hated doctors and would only see National Health ones—told her that she had the constitution of a woman of fifty, for by now she was longing to die. "You can't imagine what it's like," she said to me one day, "lying here staring at the same bit of wallpaper all day, with nothing to look forward to." The words haunted me; they still do.

On June 17, 1986, I went to see her in the evening as usual and found her in moderately good spirits. At eight the next morning her beloved maid Wanda went into her room with a cup of hot chocolate. She was dead. There was nothing organically wrong; she had died, as much as anything else, of boredom. We buried her at Belvoir, next to my father. I walk or drive past her house almost every day—never without a pang.

———— ❧ ————

My mother's death had one unexpected result: the recovery of her correspondence with Evelyn Waugh. The two had met in the early summer of 1932, when Waugh was twenty-eight and my mother nearly forty—"faded," she would describe herself, "but not, thank God, overblown." They continued to write to each other: he sent her some three hundred letters, postcards, telegrams—until his death on Easter Sunday, 1966. Their relationship can best be described as an *amitié amoureuse*; Waugh's strict Catholicism would not have allowed him anything more, and it was certainly the last thing my mother would have wanted. His religion also caused him at first to take great exception to *The Miracle*, which he saw shortly before their first meeting. In April, 1932, he wrote to his friend Dorothy Lygon:

> So I went to see a disgusting thing called *The Mira-cle*. . . . And I sat next to the Duke of Norfolk. He didn't know me but I knew him and I thought here is a man I respect as the natural leader of English Catholics and why is he at this blasphemous play because it is full of blasphemy as an egg is full of meat.

Just eleven months later he wrote to my mother from British Guiana:

> I think of this week with tears in my eyes as being the last week of *The Miracle*—but perhaps it will be given another few months. What fun if it was still on when I got back.

It wasn't—indeed, it had already ended. But by this time he was well up-country:

> I have stayed—among others—with a black man who in a vision saw the Love of God and pronounced it to be spherical in shape and slightly larger than a football, and a lady who had a son by her brother. Now I am with a priest who has never had a visitor before and couldn't sleep for the first 3 nights of my visit on account of excitement.

Nearly a quarter of a century later, on March 12, 1956:

> Coote Lygon is setting off to be governess to a Greek
> family in Constantinople. Her charge, aged 4, speaks 4
> languages and her father thinks she needs someone to
> retard her development; hence Coote's appointment.

One day in 1976 my mother was visited by Mark Amory, who
was then preparing the collected edition of Waugh's letters. She
was as usual in bed, and directed him to the basement in which
she kept virtually every letter she had ever received; but Mark
found only a handful. My mother then remembered that she had
lent the letters some years before to her old friend Christopher
Sykes who was at that time writing Waugh's biography, and realized that she had never seen them since. She immediately telephoned Christopher—I was in the room when she did so—to
ask if he still had them. No, he replied, he had returned them long
ago. So there it was: the letters were gone, their fate unknown. It
seemed unlikely that we should ever see them again.

Christopher died in December, 1986, just six months after my
mother. Then, towards the end of September, 1987, I was telephoned by Anthony Rota, a distinguished London dealer in
antiquarian books and manuscripts. We had never met, so I was
mildly surprised when he invited me to lunch at the Garrick.
Soon after we sat down, surprise gave way to astonishment. "Did
you know," he asked me, "that the correspondence between your
mother and Evelyn Waugh is being offered for sale by an obscure
book dealer in Marlborough?"

How odd, I thought, that the letters had vanished some fifteen
years before, and had reappeared only a few months after both
Christopher and my mother were dead. It was clear that some
dirty work was afoot, so after lunch I telephoned Lord Goodman,
probably London's leading solicitor and a pillar of its legal and

social life. Arnold Goodman was a huge, heavy giant of a man, from whose almost grotesquely ugly face a strange light seemed always to shine—a light of kindness and humor and compassion. ("He looks," my mother once remarked, "as if he is just about to turn into a fairy prince.") Artemis was with me, and we sat, fascinated, while he made a few telephone calls and without much difficulty traced the correspondence back to the Marlborough dealer, a man called Christopher Gange. Gange informed him that he had bought the letters for £3,000 from the man who had acquired them from Christopher Sykes: his near neighbor, another dealer who traded under the name of Rupert Collens but was better known to the public and the police as Sir Rupert Mackeson.

Sir Rupert had first hit the headlines in January, 1979, when he had been jailed in Rhodesia (as it then was) pending deportation on charges of fraud after the collapse of his travel company. This deportation, however, proved to be rather less simple than might have been expected, a struggling Sir Rupert having to be carried bodily on to the aircraft. Even then the commotion he created when the plane landed at Johannesburg airport persuaded the captain, alarmed for the safety of his other passengers, to refuse to carry him any further. This posed something of a problem to Scotland Yard, and it was agreed that he should be imprisoned in South Africa until the local authorities had decided what to do with him. On August 2, the *Daily Telegraph* reported that they were at their wits' end, and that Sir Rupert was most likely to be sent back to Rhodesia in the back of a lorry.

Although Sir Rupert's deportation from Rhodesia was subsequently ruled illegal, I remembered the story well, and was not reassured. I remained mystified, however, as to how Sir Rupert had acquired the letters from Christopher Sykes—who was honest as the day and would not have dreamt of selling them to anyone— until I discovered that one of his greatest friends was Christopher's son Mark. Had Mark been asked by his father to return the letters but mistakenly taken them to Sir Rupert instead? I could see no other explanation. Still, my only object was to get the letters back—Artemis was longing to edit them—and it was a great relief when, after strong opposition from Gange's solicitors, we got an injunction preventing the letters from being sold or otherwise disposed of until the question of ownership had been settled.

An additional complication was that Sir Rupert now claimed that he had sold the letters to Gange not in Marlborough but in the Portobello Road, where he had a stall at the time. Now Portobello Market enjoyed the status of *marché ouvert*, which essentially means that anything bought there is considered to belong to the purchaser, whether or not the vendor had legal title to it. The sale, however, did not prevent Sir Rupert from acting as if the letters were still his property, since it was he—not Gange—who now took full charge of the negotiations. And what negotiations they were. We were contacted by a mysterious informer whom we knew as "Deep Throat," who regaled us with much fascinating— if largely irrelevant—information; Mark Sykes offered to act as mediator and took Artemis and me out to lunch to discuss it; Sir Rupert was meanwhile demanding £50,000 for the letters and at one point threatened that if we did not drop our claim he would publish all he knew about the Cooper family and, in particular, reveal what had really happened to his friend Lord Lucan— darkly implying that I had been involved in his disappearance.

I for my part was prepared to risk prosecution for the murder of a fellow peer and was determined to sue. It was Arnold Goodman who finally persuaded me not to. There was no doubt, he told me, that I should win; but if, as seemed more than likely, Sir Rupert were unable to pay the costs I should have to pay them myself—a sum comfortably within the five-figure bracket. By this time Sir Rupert had brought his price down to £5,000; if I really wanted the letters, this represented by far the cheapest way of getting them. Seething, I wrote the check. Never in my life have I signed my name with more reluctance.

The story, however, has a happy ending. The collected letters, under the title of *Mr. Wu and Mrs. Stitch*[3] were beautifully edited by Artemis and sold gratifyingly well; I recovered my £5,000, and rather more beside. My only regret is that there are far more of Waugh's letters than my mother's. The reason is simply that she kept all of his, while he lost most of hers—a pity, because hers are every bit as good.

The Republic of Iceland, it may be remembered, has already come in for a passing mention. The idea of it had always fascinated me, and in August, 1974, Anne and I and the fifteen-year-old Jason had gone there on a camping holiday. In the space of two weeks we drove in an enormous figure-of-eight from one end of the country to the other and back again, sometimes passing through savage lunar landscapes (in one of which the first American astronauts had practiced their moon walks), sometimes gazing out over mountains, glaciers, geysers, volcanoes, crystal clear rivers, or vast meadows of an almost unbelievable green. Nothing was spoilt, nothing sullied or corrupted. It never got dark and, since the sun never rose more than a few degrees above the horizon, the whole land was continuously bathed in that glorious golden light, casting long, long shadows, that most of us associate with evening. The almost total absence of trees seemed to make the ever-changing landscapes more, rather than less, impressive. And then there

---

3 "Wu," or "Mr. Wu" was my mother's nickname for Waugh. "Mrs. Stitch" is a fictitious character based on her, who features in several of his novels.

were the waterfalls. Never had I seen waterfalls to touch them—
waterfalls of a size, speed, and ear-splitting fury that made Niagara
look like a dripping tap. Several produced a continuous thunder
that could easily be heard from ten miles or more away.

There were no hotels; we usually spent the night in our sleeping bags, on the floors of village schools, all empty for the summer holidays. We queued—though never for very long—for
meals, and made frequent stops to walk, to admire a waterfall or,
quite often, to swim in one of Iceland's innumerable hot lakes. We
would pull up by the lake side, there would be a frantic pulling-
off of clothes and everyone would plunge, stark naked, into water
the temperature of the perfect hot bath. The only anguish was
getting out afterwards; even on an August afternoon, the Icelandic wind cuts like a knife.

Why do I remember that distant holiday with such clarity, long
after more recent—and a good deal more comfortable—ones
have been forgotten? Perhaps because it was so unlike any other:
the wildness and intense strangeness of the country, the feeling
that there was nothing between you and Nature at her most for-
bidding, the quality of the light, the remoteness, the utter lack
of any communication with the outside world. It was not till we
returned to England that we learnt that Gerald Ford had already
been President of the United States for ten whole days.

At any rate, I was hooked; and when in the early eighties Mollie
and I met a perfectly delightful American couple on holiday and
discovered that he was the Ambassador to Iceland, we more or
less invited ourselves to stay. Marshall and Pamela Brement gave
us a terrific welcome—they didn't have too many house guests—
and though my second visit to the country could hardly have been
more different from the first it was to prove even more enjoyable.
The first thing we realized was that our hosts were probably the
most popular diplomats that Iceland had ever seen. They were

both in love with the country. Marshall, a remarkable linguist, had quickly mastered the fiendishly difficult language in a way that few foreigners had ever done and was busy translating all the young Icelandic poets; Pamela had made herself an expert on the Sagas, and would take us on fascinating drives to the sites where battles had been fought, revenges exacted, or ladies seduced. These extraordinary epics were written in the twelfth and thirteenth centuries—well before Chaucer—but the language has changed little and the landscape not at all in the interim, so that again and again a setting described nearly a thousand years ago can be instantly recognized.

And this time, of course, we met the Icelanders. My word, they know how to enjoy themselves. At a dinner party the night of our arrival, the singing started before the end of the main course and did not stop for several hours. But they are also enviably cultivated—voracious readers in several languages, poets, painters, singers, composers. The Brements seemed to know them all. On our second weekend the four of us went on a long drive up the west coast and then took a ferry to the tiny island of Flatey, where we stayed the night with a young composer who was writing settings for a cycle of a friend's poems. I remember sitting late after dinner while, by candlelight in the not quite dark, he read the poems in Icelandic, Marshall following with his English translations. Never, I thought, have I been anywhere as remote as this, or anywhere more magical.

At about the time of this second Icelandic trip I signed a contract to write a history of Byzantium; but before I did so I received another proposal, which intrigued me strangely. It came from Naim Atallah, at that time running Quartet Books, and it proposed a long essay on hashish, to accompany a series of photographs on the same subject by an Italian named Suomi la Valle. Of all the books I have written this was to have the least impact—something which seems to me now mildly surprising since although the text may have been of limited interest to most readers, the photographs—which traced the process of hashish manufacture from the harvesting of the plant (in the Bekaa Valley of Lebanon) to its final consumption—were astonishing. A good many of my earlier works have sunk without trace, but none I think as completely as this. Until a few months ago I myself had virtually forgotten it, and was quite surprised to see a copy on my bookshelf.

Unlike hashish—which, incidentally, I had tried only once, with absolutely no effect, when it was offered me in Beirut by a high court judge—the subject of Byzantium had fascinated me ever since I read Robert Byron's *The Byzantine Achievement* while I was in Belgrade; when I had finished my two volumes on Venice, to write its history seemed the logical thing to do. I had certain initial misgivings, the most serious of which was my shameful ignorance of Greek; I had studied it for some three years at Eton, but had abandoned it at the earliest possible moment—a decision I have regretted all my life—and had by now forgotten almost every word. But I soon realized that this would not be a major disadvantage, since my work would as usual have no pretensions as to scholarship: if it was to cover—even in three volumes—all the 1,123 years of Byzantine history from the founding of Constantinople by Constantine the Great in 330 to the conquest of the city by the Turks in 1453, it could only hope to be a superficial survey, the mere telling of a long story as interestingly, amusingly, and accurately as I could. Besides, all the principal primary sources existed in English or French translation. The hell with it, I thought—and went ahead.

In some ways it proved a harder job than Venice, in others a good deal easier. I mentioned in the previous chapter the extraordinary lack of outsize personalities in Venetian history; no one could ever say that about Byzantium. Emperors—and Empresses as well—were a lot more fun than Doges. True, many of them were monsters, but they were none the less fascinating for that. When the work was done, several reviewers remarked on the violence of Byzantine life, the mutilations, the blindings, the slitting of noses. At times, I admitted, I had been a little shocked myself; but, frankly, was western Europe any better? After all, was beheading not a mutilation? We did plenty of that. And if I were given the choice between losing my head or my ears, I know which I should choose. And what about the Massacre of St. Bartholomew, or the Holocaust? Or the knights of the First Crusade who, when they captured Jerusalem in 1099, slaughtered every Muslim in the city and burnt all the Jews alive in the main synagogue? Was the Emperor Basil II the Bulgar-Slayer[4] any worse than they?

And the end of Byzantium, when I finally got there, was a good deal more inspiring than the end of Venice. The Venetians, hypnotized with terror by the advance of the young Napoleon, simply caved in. On Friday, May 12, 1797, the Great Council of the Republic was in session to approve a motion of surrender when there came the sound of firing. It was almost immediately traced to a troop of Dalmatian soldiers, discharging their muskets as a parting salute to the city; but the debate was abandoned and the legislators

---

4 After the battle of Cimbalongus in 1014, Edward Gibbon informs us that "[Basil's] cruelty inflicted a cool and exquisite vengeance on the fifteen thousand captives who had been guilty of the defense of their country. They were deprived of sight, but to one of each hundred a single eye was left, that he might conduct his blind century to the presence of their king. Their king is said to have expired of grief and horror; the nation was awed by this terrible example; the Bulgarians were swept away from their settlements, and circumscribed within a narrow province; the surviving chiefs bequeathed to their children the advice of patience and the duty of revenge." (Gibbon).

of Venice rushed to the ballot boxes. The result was approval of the motion by 512 to 20; even before it was announced, most of them had fled. The fall of Constantinople was very different. There, in one of the greatest sieges of history, some fifteen thousand defenders somehow held the walls against an Ottoman army estimated at a quarter of a million for no less than fifty-five days. When those walls finally collapsed under Turkish cannon, the Emperor himself plunged into the hand-to-hand fighting and died in the *mêlée*. Neither he nor his subjects ever surrendered. The Byzantine bang was infinitely preferable to the Venetian whimper.

The last part of the trilogy was published in 1995, and all three volumes sold quite well. Then in 1997 the greatest ever Byzantine exhibition was put on at the Metropolitan Museum of Art in New York and my American publishers came up with a proposal. Here, they pointed out, was a superb marketing opportunity. Trilogies were notoriously difficult to shift; a one-volume abridgement, on the other hand, should sell thousands in the Museum alone. The idea had little appeal for me, but I would have been mad to refuse. For a fortnight in the winter of 1996–1997 we rented Anthony Blond's house in Sri Lanka; and there I sat for hour after hour in a deckchair in the garden, heavy red pencil in hand, cutting and cutting, utterly miserable. At times the task seemed to savor less of pruning than of infanticide; many of my favorite brainchildren—anecdotes, digressions, and pen portraits, to say nothing of any number of rather good jokes—found their quietus on the cutting room floor. Where in the complete version I had described myself as only skating over the surface of my subject, in the condensed one I often felt that I had exchanged my skates for a hovercraft. The job was soon done and proved, financially at least, well worth doing; I cried all the way to the bank. But *A Short History of Byzantium* remains the only one of my books for which I have absolutely no affection.

When people tell me that they have read it I find it hard to suppress a wince; the trilogy may be longer, I tell them, but it is ever so much more fun.

———— ⟡ ————

W ork on Byzantium was rather dramatically interrupted in 1985 by a major commission from American television. For some years my friend Carter Brown, Director of the National Gallery of Art in Washington, had been planning a vast exhibition called *Treasure Houses of Britain*, in which he proposed to gather all the best pictures, sculptures, furniture, and *objets d'art* from English country house collections. He certainly managed to assemble most of them, and the result was a triumph. He was lucky enough to recruit, as the show's Curator, the young Architectural Adviser to the National Trust, Gervase Jackson-Stops. In his introduction to the catalog, Carter referred to Gervase's "extraordinary knowledge, energy, persuasive charm, literary gifts, and passionate dedication to the cause of the British country house," but that was only the beginning. In every sphere in which he was involved, Gervase possessed a flair that was something akin to genius. He seemed to keep in his head a complete inventory of the contents of all the great houses of England, and that "persuasive charm" which—despite (or perhaps because of) a stammer that could suspend conversation for up to half a minute at a time—did the rest: no one was able to refuse him.

One of his most astonishing *trouvailles* was the early eighteenth-century state bed from Calke Abbey in Derbyshire, originally a gift from Queen Caroline of Ansbach, wife of King George II. On its arrival at Calke it had never been erected, but had remained untouched in its packing cases from 1734 until the house was given to the National Trust, in the same year as the

Exhibition. Its condition was thus immaculate, the colors of its hangings as brilliant as if they had only just been dyed. Henry Harpur-Crewe, the last of his family to live at Calke, had like all the lenders been invited to Washington for the opening of the Exhibition. He had never seen the bed until that evening. Soon after the doors were opened I saw him standing in front of it, open mouthed in wonder; two hours later when I was leaving, he was still there.

There was only one drawback to this glorious show: although it included plenty of treasures, the country houses themselves were (not surprisingly) missing. That was where I came in. I was asked by Public Broadcasting Television to make a series of three hour-long programs featuring as many country houses, of as many different styles and periods, as I possibly could. The job took about three months, and I loved every moment of it. The research for my book on the architecture of Southern England had already given me plenty of ideas for what houses to include—though I naturally added Haddon, Chatsworth, and a number of other houses in the North—and the sun seemed to shine almost every day. The finished programs were not only widely broadcast; they were also shown daily at the National Gallery in Washington, throughout the duration of the Exhibition and for quite some time afterwards.

The 1990s brought two further excitements. The first was Classic FM. The country's first—and still, so far as I know, only—commercial radio station broadcasting exclusively classical music had recently come into being, and I was invited to present, on six nights a week, the two-hour evening concert. The company at first suggested that I might like to choose all the music myself, but I declined. I knew quite a lot of classical music, but nowhere near enough to allow me to plan so many concerts of such a length. Timing was another problem: if a program I had devised turned out to be, say, eleven minutes too short, how would I ever find a suitable piece of precisely the right length to fill the gap? The company computer, it need hardly be said, could instantly flash up dozens. And so our agreement was reached. The in-house staff would plan the programs, which they would send to me together with all the relevant record covers; with the help of these, and a complete hardback set of the twenty-volume *New Grove's Dictionary of Music and Musicians* which I was given as a necessary tool of my trade, I would write the commentary. This—if only for the sake of my social life—would be recorded in advance. And so the routine began. One morning a week I would go into the studio in Oval Road, Primrose Hill, where I would record all the links for the week—a process which took perhaps two hours. After this, all I had to do was pray that the producer would drop in the right records when the moment came. Only once was there a mistake. I introduced Schubert's *Erlkönig*, making great play with the dramatic element: the father galloping through the night and wind, his sick and terrified child in his arms, the Erl King pursuing them, first wheedling, then threatening, the action steadily building up to that rarest and most effective of climaxes, the dying fall—*In seinen Armen das Kind war tot*. All would have been well had they not played *Heidenröslein*—the little boy with the rosebud—by mistake.

I loved Classic FM. Never had I been paid so much to do so little; and that was only the beginning. Above all I loved the atmosphere, the youthfulness of everyone—my producer, Lisa Kerr, was a wonderful Scots girl young enough to be my granddaughter—and the all-round enthusiasm. I was grateful, too, for all it taught me—about composers ranging from Hildegarde of Bingen to George Benjamin: at one time or another we played them all. Each of them had to be introduced, and his or her work explained, clearly and at the same time chattily, as best I could.

I learnt more about music during my three-year stint than I had since my Oxford days.

I learnt about it in other ways too; for it was at about this time that we adopted the habit of an annual visit to another music festival: the *Schubertiade* at Hohenems. We did so at the insistence of our dear friend Bernard Levin. Bernard had a passion for music festivals, to which indeed he was to devote a whole book, *Conducted Tour*. In his black cloak and collapsible opera hat, he had for years been a fixture at Wexford. Among composers he cherished two passionate loves, Wagner and Schubert. Even he was unable to get tickets every year for Wagner at Bayreuth, but Schubert at Hohenems he never missed. As composers go, Franz Schubert must have been one of the most prolific that ever lived: he produced nine symphonies, five operas (alas, hardly ever performed), vast quantities of some of the loveliest piano and chamber music ever written, and over six hundred songs before dying at the age of thirty-one. And yet, we read, he enjoyed nothing more than parties, or picnics with his friends in the Vienna Woods, or those marvelous musical evenings known as *Schubertiads*, where all the guests took their turns to perform, the master presiding at the piano.

Hohenems—just in Austria but only a few kilometers from Germany, Switzerland and Liechtenstein—managed in its early days to preserve that same Schubertian lightness of touch. The concerts were given in what was known as the *Rittersaal*—the Knights' Hall—of the little castle, with the Count and Countess sitting in the front row and countless stags' heads staring down from the walls. The quality of the music was never less than first-rate, with singers like Dietrich Fischer-Dieskau and Peter Schreier, pianists like Alfred Brendel and Andras Schiff, and chamber music groups like the Beaux Arts Trio and the Hagen Quartet. At least twice a day Bernard would do his best to cajole us into eating enormous slices of *Apfelstrudel* or *Sachertorte* smothered in whipped cream, vast quantities of which he himself would consume with no apparent effect; we usually managed to resist, but Mollie and I and any friends who might be with us would get together with him of an evening and rejoice in the company of one of the most scintillating minds of his generation. It was a tragedy indeed when he was struck down by Alzheimer's well before he was seventy. I have had few friends in my life whom I miss more.

The second excitement was the World Monuments Fund. I had known of its existence for some thirty years. In its early days it was called the International Fund for Monuments, and when UNESCO launched its world appeal for Venice in 1967 it had been one of the first organizations to respond. It had since done magnificent work on the church of the Pietà, the Scuola di S. Giovanni Evangelista and several other buildings, it had collaborated closely with Venice in Peril, and I had got to know several of its staff extremely well during our regular Venice meetings.

WMF, as we now call it, was founded in 1965 in New York by a remarkable retired army colonel by the name of James A. Gray.

It was from the beginning a private charity, the only one to be dedicated to the preservation of all ancient monuments, wherever in the world they might be. It has done, for example, much valuable work on the giant carved heads of Easter Island, and it has been a continuous presence at Angkor since very shortly after the departure of the Khmer Rouge. Since its foundation it has been responsible for some two hundred and fifty major operations in some hundred different countries, and it is still working flat out. But the real miracle of WMF is how much it is able to achieve with the relatively limited funds at its disposal. It may inject a little seed money to start a project; after that it acts primarily as a catalyst, securing matching funds whenever possible and in various ways casting the spotlight on the building concerned, giving it global and local publicity and generally persuading the world of its beauty, value, and importance. In recent years, thanks to a generous donation from American Express, it has instituted a program known as World Monuments Watch, which publishes a biennial list of the hundred most endangered buildings on the planet. Some seventy-five of the hundred have usually been taken in hand, to a greater or lesser degree, by the end of the year. In 2008 we are engaged on twenty-seven key projects in twenty-three countries; they include the Qianlong Garden in the Forbidden City of Beijing, the Temple of Phnom Bakheng at Angkor, two Buddhist temples in Japan, Diocletian's Palace in Split, Croatia, and the Temple to the God Quetzalcoatl in Teotihuacan, Mexico.

We established the British affiliate, World Monuments Fund in Britain, in 1998, and were almost immediately joined by Colin Amery. He was our Director for our first decade, and we could not have hoped for anyone more dedicated or more effective. Those first ten years have been pretty busy. Our first major project was St. George's Hall in Liverpool, one of the great neoclassical buildings of the world and certainly one of the largest. Recently, too, we have completed work on the only remaining commemorative monument of its kind in Ireland, an extraordinary hundred-foot column a few miles outside Wexford. It was built in 1839 by General Robert Browne-Clayton, in memory of the 1801 Egyptian campaign against Napoleon and in particular of Browne-Clayton's commanding officer, General Sir Ralph Abercromby; and it stood undamaged for over a century and a half until December 29, 1995, when a bolt of lightning split it apart down a third of its height. After two years work, thanks to donations from the Irish Government, the Irish National Trust, the Kress Foundation, and a number of private benefactors, it now stands as proudly as ever it did.

More exciting still has been our complete restoration, with the help of a magnificent bequest from the late Paul Mellon, of St. George's Bloomsbury, one of the greatest of Nicholas Hawksmoor's six London churches. Two features of this work have given us particular satisfaction, both of them marking returns to the architect's original design. The first has been an effective rotation of the whole church through ninety degrees. As his ground plan makes clear, Hawksmoor had intended the altar to be placed, as might have been expected, at the east end; unfortunately, the shape of the site demanded that the main entrance with its impressive classical portico should be to the south, giving on to what is today Bloomsbury Way. At an early stage, therefore, the altar and the magnificent wooden reredos were shifted round to the north side, so that they would be facing members of the congregation as they entered the church. We have now moved them back to the east where they belong. Hawksmoor would recognize his church again.

The second has been the tower. This is the most eccentric feature of the building. Not quite a steeple, not quite a spire, it was inspired by the Mausoleum of Halicarnassus—one of the Seven Wonders of the Ancient World—the few surviving remains of which can be seen in the British Museum only a few hundred yards away. In Hawksmoor's original design the tower was crowned by a statue of George I, while the four corners at the base were adorned by two lions and two unicorns, both ten or twelve feet high, the unicorns facing upwards, the lions down; in 1870, however, while George I was allowed to remain, these splendid beasts were removed on safety grounds. At an early stage in the restoration planning we decided to replace them, and this we have now done. As we had no accurate information about the originals—though the tower can be seen in the distance in Hogarth's engraving of *Gin Lane*—we organized a competition. It was won by a genius sculptor named Tim Crawley, who produced four superb animals, each twelve feet high, which are not just decorations but each in its own right a major work of art. All passersby along Bloomsbury Way are strongly advised to look up at that astonishing tower; they will, I think, be surprised.

———— ⚬⟊⚬ ————

Byzantium was behind me: what was I to do next? It was my publisher Peter Carson who came up with a suggestion for a book about Shakespeare's history plays, showing how far they diverged from historical truth. Surely, I thought, there must have been any number of such books; but Peter assured me that he knew of none. It was, I remembered, a question that had occurred to me on my first introduction to the plays in 1944, when my parents took me, aged fifteen, to see the two parts of *King Henry IV*, in consecutive matinée and evening performances. Laurence Olivier was a blazing Hotspur, Ralph Richardson an unforgettable Falstaff, and I felt for the first time that I was being transported in a time capsule back to the middle ages. These, I kept reminding myself, were real people—people of flesh and blood, people who had really lived, who were something more than figments of an author's imagination. But—the question was inescapable—just how real were they? Where did history stop and drama begin?

I decided at the outset that I would ignore mythical monarchs like Lear, pseudo-historical ones like Cymbeline, and all the others outside the Plantagenet canon like *King John* or *Henry VIII*, the major part of which is probably by John Fletcher anyway. On the other hand, I had the luck to start work just after the fairly definitive authentication of *Edward III*[5] as a genuine work of Shakespeare.

---

5 This is not the place to discuss *Edward III* in detail. Interested readers will find a text and excellent commentary in the New Cambridge edition, easily available.

This proved a godsend. Edward was the royal patriarch, from whose loins all the subsequent Plantagenet rulers directly or indirectly sprang. Virtually nothing in the whole mighty epic—not the Hundred Years War nor the Wars of the Roses, not the deposition of Edward's grandson Richard II nor the murderous ambition of his great-great-grandson Richard III—can be properly understood without going back to him. His story had somehow to be told, and had it not been for the play I should have had to write at least a hundred introductory pages without a mention of Shakespeare. Now I could tell it through him.

And so I worked through the nine plays—trying, as it were, to hold each in turn up to the light to see where and how far the author had departed from the truth. The conclusion to which I came was that, nearly every time he did so, his motive was the same: to make a better play. He was, after all, a playwright, not a historian. To him the cause of the drama was of infinitely greater importance than slavish historical accuracy. He was young and inexperienced—the three parts of *Henry VI* and *Richard III* are among the first plays he ever wrote, while the entire canon was finished before his thirty-sixth birthday—and the challenge of molding one of the most turbulent periods of English history into a coherent series was a formidable one indeed. No wonder he took liberties; no wonder he frequently combined two or three different events, which in fact occurred months or even years apart, into a single scene. The miracle is that he was able to stick as close to the truth as he did, weaving together all the various strands to create a single epic masterpiece which, for all its minor inaccuracies, is almost always right when it really matters. A would-be student of the period with only the plays to inform him might draw a number of false conclusions; but the overall picture he received—including that of the reign of Richard III— would not, I believe, be very far wrong.

For *Shakespeare's Kings* the London Library was less of a neces-
sity than it had been for my previous books; all I needed was a
good scholarly edition of the plays—I found the little Arden
paperbacks by far the best—and a few works of fourteenth-
and fifteenth-century English history. This as it happened was
extremely lucky: by this time I had become wedded to my laptop, and the Library was only just beginning to develop facilities
to accommodate personal computers. I therefore wrote a good
deal of the book at home, or in the weekend cottage that Mollie
and I had recently acquired a mile or so outside Castle Combe in
Wiltshire and that had now become an integral part of our lives.
Though it has only six rooms, one of which (my study) we built
on ourselves, it seems to be an amalgamation of two even smaller
cottages probably dating from around 1700—a period when the
hidden and still roadless valley in which it stands boasted a whole
series of fulling mills along its banks. The old millstream, after
running through the village itself, passes within a few yards of us,
and when the water levels are right—and there is no danger of
flooding—produces a waterfall which gives me intense pleasure.
Half a mile from the nearest house, it is as quiet and peaceful as
anywhere in England. Virtually every word of this book—including those that I am writing now—have been written in this idyllic place, looking out at the stream and at the birds that flutter
round our feeder: tits mostly, but with the occasional nuthatch
(the only English bird, I am told, that regularly feeds head downwards) and woodpecker. The nearby village is a celebrated beauty
spot; some thirty years ago it was used as a location for *Dr. Dolittle* and is consequently much frequented by coach tours—which
on weekends bring in inordinate quantities of Japanese, all pho-
tographing each other like mad. But we are far enough away, our
approach track—it can hardly be described as a drive—is long
and extremely muddy, so we seldom see a soul.

W hen at last the London Library could accommodate lap-
tops without difficulty, the way was clear for me to work
on a book that I had long had in mind—a book about Venice
in the nineteenth century. The Republic had come to an end in
1797; what, many people enquired, happened then? Politically,
the story was a sad one. Venice, having fallen to Napoleon, was
almost immediately handed over by him to the Austrians; he
took it back, however, after Austerlitz in 1805, and in January,
1806, the French returned in strength. This time they stayed nine
years, subjecting the city to appalling depredations; then, thank
God, came Waterloo; and the Congress of Vienna returned Vene-
tia-Lombardy once more to the Habsburgs. The revolutionary
year of 1848 saw a brief, heroic, but ultimately doomed attempt
to revive the old Republic, but the Austrians soon bombarded the
city into submission and held it until 1866, when at last it became
part of a united Italy.

I had no wish to dwell more than was absolutely necessary
on such a chapter of disasters, so hit upon the idea of concen-
trating on a number of distinguished foreigners who, for longer
or shorter periods of time, came to live in Venice. I began with
Napoleon himself, who in November–December, 1807, spent ten
days of pouring rain in the city on his only visit and hated every
moment of it. His chapter was followed by ones on—among others—Byron, Ruskin, Wagner, Henry James, Browning, Whistler, and Sargent. I ended with the unspeakable Frederick Rolfe,
"Baron Corvo": a cheat, since he actually died in 1913, but his
sheer awfulness was more than I could resist.

The book was called *Paradise of Cities*—a quotation from one
of Ruskin's early letters to his parents. I enjoyed writing it enormously, and in the course of my research came upon a mystery

which has intrigued me ever since. Perhaps thirty years ago, in a Venetian second-hand bookshop, I had come upon a slim volume entitled *I dieci giorni di Napoleone I a Venezia*—"Napoleon I's Ten Days in Venice." It showed every sign of meticulous homework, detailing the Emperor's program for each day of his visit—which makes it even stranger that the author should have introduced a strange thread of romance. He speaks of a certain Countess Nahir de Lusignan, with whom he claims that Napoleon was having a passionate affair. She had come to Venice on purpose to be with him; unfortunately they were able to spend only a single afternoon together (in the church of S. Giobbe) as she was laid low with severe bronchitis for the rest of his stay.

The author of the book died long ago. Maddeningly, he has left us no source references or bibliography. I have scoured the London Library and two libraries in Paris for references to this lady but have found not a single reference to her, and all the experts I have consulted are agreed that she must be a figment of the author's imagination. Perhaps she is; but in the back of my mind there remains a lingering shadow of doubt. Why, in an account that is otherwise entirely factual and clearly based on painstaking research, should he introduce a purely imaginary character, giving us not only her intriguing name but quite a lot of other circumstantial detail as well? Was it simply to inject a little spice into his story? If so, why should he spoil it all with the bronchitis? I told this story—at slightly greater length—at the end of my chapter on Napoleon, appealing to my readers for any information or suggestions that they might have; but none, alas, have responded.

In the summer of 2005 I handed in to my publishers the typescript of a history of the Mediterranean. I had started at the beginning—or as near the beginning as I could—with Ancient Egypt. To decide on the cutoff date proved a good deal harder: history doesn't end, it simply catches up with one and then becomes current events. Eventually I decided on the year 1919 and the Treaty of Versailles. But 1919 is now nearly a century ago; was I, I asked myself, being just a little bit wimpish in not pursuing the story at least until the end of the Second World War? Well, perhaps I was; had I done so, however, a book that was already long would have been a great deal longer; I should have become inextricably enmeshed in the problem of Palestine; and the reader, for whom I had hoped to ensure a smooth and happy voyage, might well have found himself shipwrecked.

Writing the book was a good deal more fun than I had expected. With Sicily, Venice, and Byzantium behind me, for a lot of it I was on home ground; my one area of almost total ignorance was Spain. I had been there many times over the years, but I knew little of its history and I had never learnt Spanish—not, heaven knows, for lack of interest but simply because I was terrified of ruining my all-too-shaky Italian which, for a good many years, I was using almost every day. One evening I confessed this to the Spanish Ambassador, Santiago de Tamaròn. "Oh well," he said, "I think we may be able to help you there." A few weeks later Mollie and I received an invitation from the Fondaciòn Carolina— the Spanish answer, perhaps, to the British Council—to spend ten days in the country, escorted by a full-time guide/interpreter, visiting anywhere we liked. That tour taught me much—and, I hope, stopped me disgracing myself.

Spain in fact was to prove a good deal less of a problem than Italy. It was, at least from the days of Ferdinand and Isabella, effectively a single country, whereas Italy remained for several more centuries a *minestrone*. City against city, Pope against Emperor, Guelph against Ghibelline—the fighting never seemed to stop, the alliances endlessly shifting and realigning themselves until one could scream. Even when writing about Venice—one of the few constants in this dizzy kaleidoscope—thirty-odd years before, I had occasionally thrown up my hands in despair; now, with the entire peninsula to deal with, my confusion was a thousand times worse. It was a great moment when I at last reached the *Risorgimento*; no one—not Mazzini, not Cavour, not the great Garibaldi himself—ever longed for Italian unity more than I did.

In the autumn of 2005 Mollie and I edited and published my father's diaries. We did so with some trepidation. He wrote for his eyes only, and with quite brutal honesty. The politics, the social life, the diplomacy are all there; but so also are his endless sexual adventures, recounted with a frankness which shocked his nephew and publisher Rupert Hart-Davis—to whom he left them—to the point where he decided that they were better destroyed. Fortunately he told me before he took action; after long pleading I persuaded him to give them to me instead. They remained in our attic for another twenty years; then Mollie put the whole lot on a computer and we had a good look at them for the first time.

A few pages from the end my father writes: "I hope John Julius never reads this." Well, John Julius has not only read it; he has published it. Is this not a deplorable betrayal by a son? Well, perhaps it is; but somehow I don't think so. He has now been dead for well over half a century, and the ladies concerned—together with most of their children—have long since gone to their graves. The diary from which all the sex life had been excised would have been a sad, truncated, emasculated affair; my father in his lifetime never pretended to be a plaster saint, and I would frankly prefer to depict him as he was, rather than as some people might have wished him to be.

What gave me rather more cause for worry was the thought that some readers of his diary might be seriously shocked, and consequently take a dislike to him. I tried to explain in the Introduction that diaries are dangerously one-sided things. Any diary—if it is written with such unwavering honesty as this one— is bound to contain a lot that the writer would not want his family or his friends to see. By definition it will also be introspective, and will confess to a number of unworthy thoughts; it will not, on the other hand, begin to reflect the good side to his nature. At his memorial service—which was filled to overflowing with those who loved him—Bob Boothby mentioned in his address that my father was "absolute for friendship"; and so he was. He was also absolute for courage, for loyalty, for generosity, for wit, and for countless other qualities to which the diary does scant justice.

As it turned out, my fears were unjustified. One critic only adopted a high moral tone in his review. ("Look who's talking," I murmured to myself as I read it.) And one paper—predictably enough, the *Daily Mail*—concentrated exclusively on the sex life. The rest were far more interested in the First World War, the abdication of Edward VIII—"Hard as nails and doesn't love him," was my father's verdict after his first meeting with Wallis Simpson— his resignation from Neville Chamberlain's government in protest over the Munich agreement and of course his years at the Paris Embassy.

As for the sales, they surpassed all our expectations.

———— ❧ ————

And so, if I were asked how I would wish to spend the rest of my life, I should suggest no major changes. Looking back over the past three-quarters of a century, I am staggered to think how lucky I have been. I might have been born a paraplegic beggar in the slums of Calcutta; instead, I was the only child of devoted parents, who loved me and gave me an upbringing that was comfortable and secure. For nearly four-score years I have had a wonderful life, and have enjoyed it to the full. Of course there have been moments of unhappiness—what life has been without them?—but they have been in a mercifully small minority, easily outweighed by times of deep content. At the time of writing I have had hardly a day's illness in my life, and have never broken a bone. I have known great love, little jealousy, and no hatred. For how much longer I shall get away with it heaven only knows; for as long as possible I hope—or at least for as long as I remain *compos mentis* and continent. When, however, independence goes, my children have strict instructions to pull the plug of the life support machine at the earliest possible moment. Of one thing I am certain: whatever Fate may have in store, I shall die with endless gratitude—and not a little astonishment—in my heart.

Index